REINVENTING ANARCHY, AGAIN

REINVENTING ANARCHY, AGAIN

edited by
Howard J. Ehrlich

"Everything that needs to be said has already been said. But since no one was listening, everything must be said again."
— Andre Gide

AK
PRESS

Library of Congress Cataloguing-in-Publication Data

Re-inventing anarchy, again / edited by Howard J. Ehrlich
     p.   cm.
  Rev. ed. of : Reinventing anarchy, 1978
  ISBN 1-873176-88-0 (paper)
   1. Anarchism. I. Ehrlich, Howard J. II. Reinventing
anarchy.
HX833.R43 1995
320-5'7--dc20   95-41020
                                                  CIP

British Library Cataloguing in Publication Data

A catalogue record for this title is available from the
British Library.

First published in 1996 by

AK Press   AK Press
P.O. Box 12766   P.O. Box 40682
Edinburgh, Scotland San Francisco, CA
EH8 9YE   94140-0682

Typesetting and design donated by Freddie Baer.

*The production of this book is dedicated to the memory of Ishmael
Torres Jr. by his friend Tom A.*

TABLE OF CONTENTS

PREFACE

Reinventing Anarchy — The first anthology

With David DeLeon, Carol Ehrlich, and Glenda Morris, I began talking about the need for a good collection of anarchist materials in early 1973. Not only did we feel that we personally weren't ready for the undertaking, we also felt that there simply weren't enough good contemporary materials. We were not satisfied with earlier anthologies that excerpted long-dead anarchist writers or mixed together liberals and libertarians, socialists and capitalists. And we certainly didn't want detached discourses on the nature of authority or political events that the writer studied at a safe distance. We wanted to bring together the works of living, working anarchists.

By the spring of 1976, we not only felt more secure in our knowledge, but we had now accumulated an extraordinary collection of anarchist materials. We also came to the realization that some topics we would have to write about ourselves, and that some other important topics would have to go uncovered since contemporary anarchists weren't writing about them, or weren't writing very carefully about them.

In selecting articles we had several explicit criteria. First of all, the articles had to be available in English. Second, the materials had to be current. Third, we included only articles that were reasonably well written and that offered new ideas or a new synthesis of old ideas. Fourth, fifth, sixth, and seventh: we wanted mainly new materials, by practicing anarchists, by anarchists whose orientation was social (as opposed to individualist), and by anarchists who addressed themselves to the political and social questions that people are asking today. We had no interest, for example, in a new discussion of the Paris Commune or the Kronstadt uprising.

The anthology was quite successful. We put together 37 pieces, most of which were simply not accessible in the average public or even college library, and one-third of our selections had not been published before. In 1979 Routledge and Kegan Paul published the book. By the end of 1982, it had sold out. By then, the editors had dispersed and all were engaged in other projects.

The initial success of the anthology led us, in 1980, to start the magazine, *Social Anarchism: A journal of practice and theory*. Most of the original editors and writers had been contributors to the anthology, and five selections from the magazine are included in this edition.

REINVENTING ANARCHY, AGAIN — THIS ANTHOLOGY

Twelve years passed from the original publication to the time I began assembling this collection. For this edition, I reviewed the archives of *Social Anarchism* (1980-1991), which has a substantial collection of anarchist periodicals and ephemera, and solicited articles and suggestions from all of its contributors. Notices were sent to writers and publications in the United States, Canada, England, and Australia. I tried to conform to the seven criteria of selection we laid down in compiling the earlier edition. I believe they represented the correct decisions.

The editing process was filled by periods of nostalgia and the reviewing of old memories. I reread the first edition with some wonder. It had really weathered well. Many of the selections which I decided to drop were still noteworthy. Some, like the discussion of SDS and the Clamshell Alliance, were now historical examples that I thought would have less meaning to a new generation of readers. Some of the manifestoes and leaflets were now ready for the archives, and some articles were dropped because I found other writers who (building on those earlier pieces) had been able to extend our perspective.

It is my observation that there has been a substantial change in the anarchist literature over the past 20 years. It has become much more serious, much more willing to address fundamental philosophical and practical political questions. I have tried to reflect that change in this edition. Anarchists also seemed less concerned with marxism and marxist movements. At the same time, while we may not be adrift intellectually, we are certainly more of a drift than a social movement. My feeling is that the intellectual work we are doing now will provide an underpinning for a new anarchist movement. As J. P. Sartre reminded us, "There may be other times, but this one is ours."

My work on the book was facilitated by a fellowship at the Berkshire Forum's Radical Writer's Retreat. This enabled me to make the final selections and write all of the section introductions. My work was also facilitated by my colleague and friend, Chris Stadler, the managing editor of *Social Anarchism*. And, of course, this book is built on the work of my former coeditors, David DeLeon, Carol Ehrlich, and Glenda Morris.

To the members of the Great Atlantic Radio Conspiracy collectives (1972–1992), I owe a great debt. In many ways they made this book possible. Finally I want to acknowledge my dear friend, JZG, whose support and deep friendship kept a roof over my head and enabled me to complete this book.

1
WHAT IS
ANARCHISM

Johann Humyn Being

an·arch \\'an-,ärk\\ *n* [back-formation fr. *anarchy*] : a leader or advocate of revolt or anarchy
an·ar·chic \\a-'när-kik, ə-\\ *adj* **1 a** : of, relating to, or advocating anarchy **b** : likely to bring about anarchy ⟨∼ violence⟩ **2** : lacking order, regularity, or definiteness ⟨∼ art forms⟩
an·ar·chism \\'an-ər-,kiz-əm, -,är-\\ *n* **1** : a political theory holding all forms of governmental authority to be unnecessary and undesirable and advocating a society based on voluntary cooperation and free association of individuals and groups **2** : the advocacy or practice of anarchistic principles
an·ar·chist \\'an-ər-kəst, -,är-\\ *n* **1** : one who rebels against any authority, established order, or ruling power **2** : one who believes in, advocates, or promotes anarchism or anarchy; *esp* : one who uses violent means to overthrow the established order — **anar·chist** *or* **an·ar·chis·tic** \\,an-ər-'kis-tik, -(,)är-\\ *adj*
an·ar·chy \\'an-ər-kē, -,är-\\ *n* [ML *anarchia,* fr. Gk. fr. *anarchos* having no ruler, fr. *an-* + *archos* ruler — more at ARCH·] **1 a** : absence of government **b** : a state of lawlessness or political disorder due to the absence of governmental authority **c** : a utopian society made up of individuals who have no government and who enjoy complete freedom **2** : absence of order : DISORDER **3** : ANARCHISM

Freddie Baer

Warning Label

Phylis Campbell Dryden

Caution: The Federal
Fooled and Drugged
Administration
has found that
the active ingredients
in this publication
may cause undue change
of attitude,
itching, swelling,
burning of the brain.
If symptoms desist,
consult a physician
immediately.
For internal use only.
Keep this and all other
indoctrinations
out of the mouths
of babes.

QUESTIONS AND ANSWERS ABOUT ANARCHISM

HOWARD J. EHRLICH, CAROL EHRLICH, DAVID DeLEON, AND GLENDA MORRIS

1. How would an anarchist revolution come about?

For social anarchists revolution is a process, a process leading to the total deflation of state authority. That process entails self and collective education and the building of alternative institutions as mechanisms of survival, of training and as models of a new society. Continuing parts of that process are repeated symbolic protests and direct assaults on ruling class institutions.

As more and more people regard the anarchist alternatives as preferable to the status quo, state power begins to be deflated. When the state can no longer maintain the confidence of substantial segments of the population, its agents will have to rely increasingly on the mobilization of the police and the military. Of course, that increase in force has multiple possible outcomes, ranging from the total repression of the Left to the further leftward mobilization of the population that regards this increased use of force illegitimate.

Our scenario does not rule out guerrilla warfare and armed struggle. But in the United States, for example, with its mammoth police apparatus, extensive files and surveillance of radicals, and its over 3,600 underground 'emergency operating centers' for ruling class and military retreats, the idea of a primarily military revolution is an atavistic Marxist fantasy.

So where do we go from here? The next act in the revolutionary drama remains to be written. Drawing a battle plan today seems pointless. The overthrow of the state — the building of anarchist societies — will be an overwhelming majoritarian act. It cannot be otherwise. When, say, 5-10 percent of the population identify themselves as anarchists, it is our guess that there would be a range of contingencies available that we could not possibly anticipate today.

2. Who will make the anarchist revolution?

Everyone. Every day in their daily lives.

3. How can an anarchist society prevent the development of informal elites, new bureaucracies and a reconcentration of power?

There is nothing integral to the nature of human social organization that makes hierarchy, centralization and elitism inescapable. These organizational forms persist, in part, because they serve the interests of those at the top. They persist, too, because we have learned to accept roles of leadership and followership; we have come to define hierarchy as necessary, and centralization as efficient. All of this is to say that we learned the ideological justifications for elite organizational forms quite well.

We could dismiss the question by pointing out that social motivations to power, elites and elitism and bureaucracy would not exist in an anarchist society. The question should not be dismissed, however, when we talk about building an anarchist society in the shell of another. In such a context we will inevitably be struggling against the life-denying values of our socialization. Hierarchy, dominance and submission, repression and power — these are facts of everyday life. Revolution is a process, and even the eradication of coercive institutions will not automatically create a liberatory society. We create that society by building new institutions, by changing the character of our social relationships, by changing ourselves — and throughout that process by changing the distribution of power in society. It is by the constant building of new forms of organization, by the continual critical evaluation of our successes and failures, that we prevent old ideas and old forms of organization from re-emerging.

If we cannot begin this revolutionary project here and now, then we cannot make a revolution.

4. How will decisions be made? by consensus? by majority?

Groups will make decisions by consensus because majority rule is unacceptable for people who think that everyone should run his or her own life. Decision making by majority rule means that the minority voluntarily gives up control over the policies that affect them.

To operate by consensus, groups will discuss an issue until it is resolved to the satisfaction of everyone. This doesn't mean that there's only one way of doing things. People must accept that many ways can coexist. They also must realize that there can be multiple policies on most issues with people free to choose which policy they want.

The principle of consensus can be effective because membership in a community is voluntary and because that membership entails agreements on its basic goals and values.

The workings of consensual decisions have many advantages. It is the only way to prevent a permanent minority from developing. It takes into consideration the strength of feelings. It is more efficient for group action because people are genuinely involved in achieving consensus and are therefore more likely to act on their decisions.

One of the things people have difficulty understanding about group consensus is that it does take into account the strength of feelings and differences in perspectives of all of the people involved. In a social anarchist meeting the process of decisionmaking is as important as the outcome itself.

Of course, people will have to learn to recognize what they want and to express their desires in a constructive way. If they do not know what they want, a false consensus develops because people are just trying to go along with the group so as not to make trouble. If decisions are reached this way people remain unhappy about the outcome; their participation may drop to a low level and they may ultimately feel that they have to leave the group.

5. How can people be motivated to participate in decisions that affect them if they don't want to participate?

In the kinds of societies in which we live now, this is a pseudo-question. People are managed; they are rarely asked to participate. The unmotivated citizen of the capitalist/socialist state has sized up the situation correctly, and has concluded that nonparticipation is the only realistic choice.

What about an anarchist community, where everyone would have genuine control over his or her life? We would assume that nonparticipants would be few — but if they existed, we would have to ask why. This is no idle question: if it wished to survive, an anarchist community would have to solve this problem. If it failed to do so, the community would be on the road back to social inequality. And it would no longer be anarchist.

There are two reasons why a person might not participate in making decisions. The first would be lack of time. But if a person is too busy, then either s/he has voluntarily taken on too much work, or the others are shirking. In neither case is the community functioning on genuine social anarchist principles.

The second reason is quite different. Nonparticipation would be due not to working too much out of a misplaced sense of priorities, but to failure to see the linkage between personal autonomy and community functioning. Some people may feel that community decisionmaking is beneath them; this 'star' mentality needs to be effectively challenged every time it occurs. Others may genuinely believe that the community affords them everything they need for their physical and psychological well-being, so they are perfectly happy letting others make the decisions. Still others may feel alienated, or lack confidence in their ability to make competent decisions.

All of these people are handicapped by 'old ideas.' These are well suited to a stratified society in which a few run the lives of everyone, but they are severely damaging to an anarchist community. People who think in these ways need loving support from others, a feeling of being an essential part of the community, and gentle (but firm) pressure to participate. This may take time, but it can be done.

6. When does a community become too large to operate with direct participation by everyone? Is a system of representation ever justified?

We do not really know the maximum or optimum size of a community that would still allow effective participation, but there are numerous examples of communities, some as large as 8,000 people, where all the people actively participated in self-government. For example, during the Spanish Revolution self-governed villages all over Spain formed into federations to coordinate decisions affecting all of them. In Denmark in 1971, about 600 people occupied an army camp and set up a viable functioning community that not only lasted for years but was able to defend itself nonviolently from attacks by the government.

In these examples everyone made decisions about the goals of the community and how to achieve them. Then the people who were actually doing the particular tasks were able to work in their own way.

In a decentralized society that is composed of many communities, the lines of communication go in multiple directions. Two-way television and other technological improvements make direct democracy possible in larger groups, but there will probably still be times when representatives will be necessary. Selection procedures for these representatives would no doubt vary. Sometimes representatives could be drawn by lot and other times on the basis of task-specific skills or abilities.

The system of representation, however, must meet certain criteria. Representatives must come from the group of people whom they represent and they must be accountable to that group. To make them accountable, representatives should be assigned for a brief period of time or to do a specific task. In an anarchist society no one could make a career of 'politics.' The role of representative could be rotated among members of the community. All important decisions would be made by the group as a whole; the representatives would just communicate the decisions of their group to the larger group. Representatives must also be subject to immediate recall.

The decisions about what functions best for one community or one group will have to be made by that group at the time depending upon the circumstances. But there is every reason to believe that people can effectively participate in managing their own lives.

7. Will there still be experts and specialization? If so, how will experts be trained? How will we know they are competent? Can we have experts in a nonhierarchical society?

Differences in skill and knowledge will continue to exist. Such differences are compatible with a free and egalitarian society. People may also want to develop their abilities in their own way. And this too is compatible with social anarchism.

Much of the work that is now done by specialists can be learned in a relatively short time so that it could be done by nearly everyone. One problem with specialists in our society is that they restrain the number of people who are trained. Obviously there is some work, such as surgery or architecture, that requires a high degree of skill acquired through lengthy training. No one wants to be operated on by someone who has only two weeks of training, and few people would feel comfortable in a five-story building assembled without blueprints. The real problem becomes training specialists who will be accountable to the people they serve. We want cooperation between specialist and 'client,' not solidarity among specialists. To ensure this there could be no positions of privilege for specialists, and they must be committed to sharing their knowledge with everyone.

In a decentralized or small society, judging the competence of someone whose labor is highly visible, such as a carpenter, is not difficult. In somewhat more complex cases, say in judging the competence of a surgeon, one possibility is to have the people who work with the surgeon along with those from the community be the judge of the quality of work.

Expertise and nonhierarchy can co-exist only if specialization does not convey special privileges; only if people who are experts do not monopolize or control resources or information; and only if people are committed to cooperative and collective work rather than destructive competition.

8. Who will do the dirty work?

We all will. In an anarchist community, people wouldn't categorize work as 'dirty' or 'clean,' as 'white-collar' or 'blue-collar.' That way of thinking can exist only in a class-stratified society — one that teaches its members that maintenance tasks are undignified, demeaning, and to be avoided if possible. For anarchists, all socially useful work has dignity, and everyone would cooperate to sustain the community at a mutually agreed-upon level of health, comfort and beauty. Those who refuse to collect the garbage, clean streets and buildings, trim the grass, provide a clean water supply and so on would be acting in a most irresponsible fashion. It they continued to refuse, they would be asked to leave.

Does this seem coercive? A successfully self-governed community must be comprised of people who voluntarily live and work together, who agree on the necessary tasks, and who have the self-discipline to carry out their share of these tasks (no more and no less). Those who refuse are coercing others; they are implicitly saying that *their* time is to be spent doing more important things; that *they* are above such menial tasks. In an anarchist community no one is 'above' anyone else; no one is more important than anyone else. To think so will destroy both equality and freedom.

One of the things that makes 'dirty' work so onerous is that only some people do it, and they work at it full-time. Very few maintenance tasks would seem totally awful if they were rotated, and each person knew s/he would be doing it for a short period of time. Short work periods on the garbage truck, or cleaning public bathrooms, or fertilizing fields would seem — well, not *fun* of course (anarchists aren't stupid) but would be tolerable if each person knew they would end soon.

9. Will any people have more money and property than others? Who will control the means of production and how will profits be distributed?

In an anarchist society everyone will have an equal right to the basic liberties and material goods, which is consistent with a similar right for others. People would, of course, maintain personal possessions, but we would expect that the matter of the accumulation of property and property rights would be very different. Certainly the meaning of money and property would be quite different in an egalitarian and nonhierarchical society.

It is hard to conceive of a serious alternative to a market economy. However, unlike the capitalist market place, the anarchist economy would not be based on the maximization of control and profit. Therefore, there would be no need to monopolize resources, expand markets or create useless products and/or consumer demands. Worker and community control of the workplace would be the organizational form for regulating productivity and profits in keeping with the needs of the community.

While an anarchist economic theory remains to be written, its theorems will all have to be derived from principles of social justice, from principles that claim the maximum values of freedom and equality for all people.

10. Aren't anarchists ignoring the complexity of urban life? Aren't they rejecting technology and industrial development? Don't they really want to go back to a simpler society?

Any anarchists who ignore the complexities of modern urban-industrial societies are wrong. A return to a 'simpler' society is a fantasy of escapists, not of persons seriously committed to building a new society.

The underlying issue for us as social anarchists is the determination of the optimum size for urban settlements. The equation for an optimum size would doubtless have to balance factors of self-sufficiency, self-governance and the minimizing of damage to the ecosystem.

The related technological problems must be taken seriously by all anarchists. Can we satisfy our energy requirements with technologies that do minimal environmental damage? Can we develop a technology that can be comprehended by most people? Can we develop a technology that is a genuine substitute for human labor? The answer to these questions is yes. The technology and knowledge are already here: the issue is their implementation.

The result of implementing such technological changes and building self-governing and relatively self-sufficient communities would probably bring about substantial differences in urban settlements. We suspect that these differences would yield even more 'complex' urban arrangements than we now have. We suspect, too, that they would result in more genuinely humane cities.

11. How will an anarchist society meet the threat of foreign invasion?

Paradoxically, the more successfully it meets the threat of armed force, the more likely it is to move away from anarchist principles. War always seems to turn relatively free and open societies into repressive ones. Why? Because war is irrational: it fosters fear and hopelessness in the gentle; it brings out aggression, hatred and brutality in the truculent; it destroys the balance between people and nature; it shrinks the sense of community down to one's immediately endangered group; and under conditions of starvation and deprivation it pits neighbor against neighbor in the fight for survival. If a besieged anarchist community did successfully resist foreign invasion, then it should immediately work to reestablish the interrelationships of trust, mutual aid, equality and freedom that have probably been damaged. "War is the health of the state"; but it can be a fatal disease for an anarchist community.

If war came, however, how would the society organize to defend itself? Let us assume that the anarchist federation of North America is invaded by troops of the Chinese, Swedish, Saudi Arabian or Brazilian government. What would happen? There would be no state apparatus to seize; instead, the invaders would have to conquer a network of small communities, one by one. There would be no single army to defeat, but an entire, armed population. The people would challenge the invasion with resistance — strikes, psychological warfare, and non-cooperation as well as with guerrilla tactics and larger armed actions. Under these circumstances, it is unlikely that the invaders would conquer the federation.

12. What about crime?

Much of what is now defined as crime would no longer exist. The communalization of property and an ethic of mutual aid would reduce both the necessity and the motivation for property crimes.

Crimes against people seem more complex, but we reject the idea that they are rooted in 'original sin' or 'human nature.' To the degree that such crimes stem from societally-based disorders of personality, we can only anticipate that their incidence — as well as their actual form — would be radically altered.

In a social anarchist society, crime would be defined solely as an act harmful to the liberties of others. It would not be a crime to be different from other people, but it would be a crime to harm someone. Such hostile acts against the community could be prevented, above all, by inculcating a respect for the dignity of each person. Anarchist values would be reinforced with the strongest of human bonds, those of affection and self-respect.

Remaining crimes would not be administered by masses of lawyers, police and judges; and criminals would not be tossed into prisons, which Kropotkin once labeled 'universities of crime.' Common law and regularly rotated juries could decide whether a particular act was a crime, and could criticize, censure, ostracize or even banish the criminal. However, in most cases we anticipate that criminals would be placed in the care and guidance of members of the community.

13. How shall public health issues be handled?

Public health issues would be handled like all other issues. This means that decisions about inoculations and other health issues would be made at the local level by the people who would be affected by the decision. This would result in a very different type of health care. Health care workers would be members of the community where they worked. Their function would be to provide day-to-day care and advice to people on how to remain healthy. People would have a chance to talk frequently with these workers and would know that they were really concerned about health and not about making money or gaining status in the community.

If there were a threatened epidemic of some deadly flu and a vaccine were developed, the people in the community would be able to get together to discuss the risks and benefits of the inoculations. Once the group decided that inoculations would benefit the community they would try to persuade everyone to be inoculated because the more people who were protected the less likelihood there would be of an epidemic. If there were a clear case of people being a danger to the health of the entire community then they would be asked to make a choice between being vaccinated and remaining in the community, or leaving to find another group that was more compatible.

14. There are times when the state takes care of the sick and elderly, or protects individuals against coercion (for example, children brutalized by parents; blacks attacked by whites). If the state disappears, who will take over these functions?

People who look at the world this way believe that there are only two possibilities: either there is state regulation and an orderly society, or there is a stateless chaos in which life is nasty, brutish and short. In fact, even when the state functions in a benevolent or protective manner, it is capricious: sometimes it helps the helpless; other times it doesn't. Sometimes social welfare workers remove a child from a vicious environment — and other times the child is left at home, perhaps to be further brutalized, even killed. Sometimes the state protects the civil rights of oppressed minorities; other times it ignores these rights or even joins in the persecution. We cannot count on the state to do anything to protect us. It is, after all, the major task of the agents of the state to protect the distribution of power. Social justice is a secondary concern.

In fact, we can only count on ourselves, or on those with whom we are freely associated in community. This means that helping functions will be performed by those groups that have always done them, with or without the state: voluntary associations. However, in an anarchist community, the need for such services will be less frequent. For example, if there is no longer systematic poisoning of the environment, diseases caused by this pollution (pesticide poisoning, asbestosis, Minimata disease) won't happen; if there are no longer extremes of wealth and poverty, diseases caused by lack of adequate food, shelter, and medical care will not exist; if children and adults can freely choose whether or not to live together, much violence against 'loved ones' will disappear; if racism is systematically attacked, then the majority ethnic group won't harass minorities. There will, of course, still be a need for mutual aid and protection — but this will be provided by the community, for *all* its members.

15. Would an anarchist society be more likely to be sexist? racist?

Anarchists usually talk about the illegitimacy of authority, basing their arguments on the premise that no person should have power over another. A logical extension of this argument is to attack the power relationships in which men dominate women and some racial and ethnic groups dominate others. Thus anarchism creates the preconditions for abolishing sexism and racism.

Anarchism is philosophically opposed to all manifestations of racism and sexism. Equally important as its philosophical commitments is the fact that with anarchism there would be no economic basis to support racist or sexist ideas or practices. Work and income would be divided equitably, so there would be no need to subordinate a class of people to do the dirty work or to work at low pay to support the dominant class.

Sexism and racism would not automatically disappear in the process of building an anarchist society. A conscious effort would have to be made to change old behavior and attitudes.

16. What do anarchists think about sex, monogamy, and family?

Anarchists believe that how you live your daily life is an important political statement. Most people in industrialized societies spend a significant portion of their lives in what may be the last bulwark of capitalism and state socialism — the monogamous nuclear family. The family serves as the primary agent for reproducing the dominant values of the society, both through the socialization of children and the social control of its members. Within the family all of the pathologies of the larger society are reproduced: privatized social relations, escapism, patriarchal dominance, economic dependency (in capitalist society), consumerism, and the treatment of people as property.

In an anarchist society, social relations will be based on trust, mutual aid, friendship and love. These may occur in the context of the family (if people choose to live in a family setting), but they certainly do not have to. Indeed, these conditions may be more easily achieved outside the family.

Will there be monogamous relations in an anarchist society? Clearly, people will have the option to choose how they want to live, with whom, and how long they want to live in these relationships. This will of course include the option of monogamy. However, without a system based on patriarchy, economic insecurity and religious or state authority, we doubt that monogamy would be anything more than an anachronism. If and when people did elect to live monogamously, it presumably would be seen as a choice made by both persons. Today, of course, monogamy is considered far more important for women than for men. This is called the double standard; and it has no place in a society of free and equal women and men.

The family? The nuclear family is not universal, but social systems for the rearing of the young, the care of the elderly, and companionate relations are. We think that whole new forms of communal and collective living arrangements will grow to replace the traditional family system.

Sex? Of course. But this does not mean that all kinds of sexual behavior would be condoned. We cannot imagine a truly anarchist society condoning rape, sexual exploitation of children, or sex that inflicts pain or humiliation, or involves dominance and submission. In sexual behavior, as in all other forms of behavior, social anarchism is based on freedom, trust and respect for the dignity of others. In fact, in an anarchist society sexuality would lose all the inegalitarian and oppressive meanings it now has.

17. Is it coercive to require education for children? What should its content and structure be?

When people today worry about the coercive character of mandatory public education, we think that their concern really stems from the authoritarian character of schooling. Schools are an extension of the state; they reproduce the class, sex, race and other divisions on which the state is built. In an anarchist society, the social function of schools and the potential of education would be quite different.

Even today, we think that the implications of withholding basic education from young children are far more coercive than the requirement that they be educated. Without at least a minimal level of literacy, people would be much worse off than they already are. In an anarchist society education would, of course, provide far more. Education would be fundamentally liberating because it would help people learn how to learn; and it would teach them much more than they could ever acquire on their own about the physical world and the world of ideas. It would also help them learn to be free and self-directed.

Such education is so important for young children that neither they nor their parents should be able to decide that the child doesn't need it. Bakunin stated the reason well:

> Children do not constitute anyone's property . . . they belong only to their own future freedom. But in children this freedom is not yet real; it is only potential. For real freedom . . . based upon a feeling of one's dignity and upon the genuine respect for someone else's freedom and dignity, i.e., upon justice — such freedom can develop in children only through the rational development of their minds, character, and will.

What would anarchist education teach the young? Intellectual and physical skills that help to develop literate, healthy and competent people should be taught. Essential intellectual materials would include some that children now learn, and some that they don't: reading and writing, self-care (emotional and physical), farming and carpentry, cooking, and physical education. Children in the upper elementary grades would be introduced to literature and the other arts, cross-cultural materials, and the principles of anarchist community organization and economics. However, the content of these materials should reflect anarchist values: it would be senseless to teach the principles of capitalist politics and economics (except perhaps as a horrible example), an acceptance of stratification, or materials that advocate racist, sexist or other inegalitarian ideas.

Not only the content, but also the structure of anarchist education is vitally important. It is difficult to develop liberatory modes of thought and action in an atmosphere of intimidation, regimentation, boredom and respect for authority. We do not mean to imply that children should devalue teachers; but genuine respect must be based upon what someone knows and how effectively s/he teaches it, not upon position, age or credentials. It will be difficult to create an atmosphere of mutual respect and orderly process without imposing discipline. But liberatory education cannot take place in an authoritarian setting.

What else? Well, schools should be small, so that each child can get the attention and stimulation s/he needs. Activities should be varied, and distinctions between work and play narrowed as far as possible. Grading and competition with each other would be eliminated. Students would learn to set standards for themselves, and to try to meet them. (If they did not, the child should not evaluate him/herself negatively. Guilt and self-deprecation are enemies of autonomy and healthy functioning.) Teachers would be selected on the basis of knowledge and interpersonal competence, not upon the possession of formal credentials. Probably few people would make a career of teaching, but many members of the community (including some older children) would spend time doing it. Schools would be integrated into the community, and everyone would participate in the direction of the schools.

When would education end? Ideally, never. Instead of being a prison, which inmates flee as soon as the guard's back is turned (which is what many public schools are like today), the anarchist school would encourage people to see education as a lifelong process. As the child becomes an adult, education would increasingly become an informal, self-directed activity which would take place outside the school. But people would return for further formal study as often, and as long, as they wish.

18. What is the relation of children to authority?

The line between nurturance and the authoritarian control of children is difficult to draw. Perhaps in an anarchist society that boundary line will be more clearly sketched.

Infants and young children are unquestionably dependent on others for their survival. Perhaps the difference between nurturance and authoritarianism arises when a child has acquired the skills for her or his own survival. If we accept that boundary, then we will have to work at determining what those skills minimally are. The skills themselves — once we go beyond the acquisition of language — are not absolute. They are relative to the social conditions under which people live. For example, under capitalism, where income and work are tied together and where both are prerequisites for food, housing, medical care and the like, survival training must last longer. Partly because of this long period of dependency, there has been a strong tradition in such settings to view the child (and young adult) as property, hence at the disposal of the family or state. Certainly, the political economy is one condition that fosters dependence on authority.

Fostering authoritarian dependence is, in fact, a major mechanism of social control in capitalist and state socialist societies. Today it is easier to catalog examples of dependence and authoritarian social conditions than it is to provide examples of social conditions that encourage self-management and autonomous behavior.

The quintessence of nurturant childrearing in an anarchist community would be the teaching of children to like themselves, to learn how to learn, and how to set standards for self-evaluation.

19. Has there ever been a successful anarchist organization? If so, why don't they last longer?

Yes, there has been. In fact, there have been many groups that have been organized without centralized government, hierarchy, privilege and formal authority. Some have been explicitly anarchist: perhaps the best-known examples are the Spanish industrial and agricultural collectives, which functioned quite successfully for several years until destroyed by the combined forces of the authoritarian Left and the Right.

Most anarchist organizations are not called that — even by their members. Anthropological literature is full of descriptions of human societies that have existed without centralized government or institutionalized authority. (However, as contemporary feminist anthropologists point out, many so-called 'egalitarian' cultures are sexist.)

Industrialized societies also contain many groups that are anarchist in practice. As the British anarchist Colin Ward says, "an anarchist society, a society which organizes itself without authority, is always in existence, like a seed beneath the snow." Examples include the leaderless small groups developed by radical feminists, coops, clinics, learning networks, media collectives, direct action organizations; the spontaneous groupings that occur in response to disasters, strikes, revolutions and emergencies; community-controlled day-care centers; neighborhood groups; tenant and workplace organizing; and so on. Not all such groups are anarchist, of course, but a surprising number function without leadership and authority to provide mutual aid, resist the government, and develop better ways of doing things.

Why don't they last longer? People who ask this question expect anarchist organizations to meet standards of permanence that most anarchists, who value flexibility and change, do not hold; and that most non-anarchist groups cannot meet. There is, of course, another reason why many anarchist organizations do not last longer than they do. Anarchists are enemies of the state — and the state managers do not react kindly to enemies. Anarchist organizations are blocked, harassed, and sometimes (as in the case of Spain, and more recently Portugal) deliberately smashed. Under such circumstances, it is a tribute to the persistence and capabilities of many anarchists that their organizations last as long as they often do.

Anarchism: Past and Present

Murray Bookchin

There is a grave danger of dealing with anarchism simplistically, the way we deal with most radical "isms" today — as a fixed body of theory and practice — such as so often reduces socialism to the textual works of Marx and Engels and their expositors. I do not mean to ignore the generic meaning of the term *socialism*, but there have been many socialisms, ranging from the utopian to the Leninist, from the ethical to the "scientific." I simply wish to stake out a similar claim for anarchism: There have been many forms of anarchism, notably anarchosyndicalism, anarcho-individualism, anarcho-collectivism, anarchocommunism, and amusingly enough, anarcho-Bolshevism, if I read certain tendencies in the history of the Spanish anarchist movement correctly. Indeed, anarchist theories and movements have been burdened by all the intramural conflicts we encounter among socialists.

Not only does anarchism encompass a wide variety of theories and movements, but as I cannot stress strongly enough, it has a very rich *historical* genesis, and the various anarchisms are rooted in distinct historical as well as social settings. Indeed, more than any radical movement with which we are familiar, anarchism has usually taken the form of a popular movement, as distinguished from the party-type organizations that we associate with the Left these days. Not only the vitality of anarchism but its theoretical forms, indeed its very *raison d'être* stems from its capacity to express the aspirations of peoples to create their own egalitarian or at least self-administered social structures, their own forms of human consociation by which they can exercise control over their lives. Anarchism has often been a folk or people's social outlook and practice in the fullest sense, just as the folk song constitutes the emotional, aesthetic, and spiritual expression of a people.

Historically, anarchism has found expression in varying degrees in nonauthoritarian clans, tribes, and tribal federations; in the democratic institutions of the Athenian *polis*; in early medieval communes; in the radical Puritan congregations of the English Revolution; in the democratic town meetings that spread from Boston to Charleston after 1760; in the Parisian sectional assemblies of 1793 and the Paris Commune of 1871; in the soviets of 1905 and 1917; and in the anarchist *pueblos*, *barrios*, and worker-controlled shops of the Spanish Revolution of 1936 — in short, in the self-directed social forms of humanity, both early and contemporary, that have institutionally involved people in face-to-face relations based on direct democracy, self-management, active citizenship, and personal participation.[1]

It is within this electric public sphere that the anarchist credo of direct action found its actualization. Indeed, direct action can mean not only occupying a nuclear power plant site or blocking a weapons production plant, but also the less dramatic, often prosaic, even tedious but most important forms of self-management that required patience, commitment to democratic procedures, lengthy debates, and a decent respect for the opinions of others within one's community.

This public institutional framework and sensibility is the authentic milieu of anarchism, indeed its very protoplasm. The phenomena that hopefully emerge from the activity of this protoplasm include forms of self-reflexive rationality that impart to action its coherence and direction. To my thinking, the Digger Winstanley, the *enragé* Varlet, the artisan Proudhon, the worker Pelloutier, and the Russian intellectuals Bakunin and Kropotkin voiced at various levels of consciousness different but clearly delineable phases of humanity's evolution toward ever-broader conceptions of freedom. One can closely associate these individuals and the ideas they advanced with the actual popular social forms to which they gave ideological coherence. Thus one can justifiably associate Winstanley's ideas with the agrarian anarchism of yeomen communities in seventeenth-century England; Varlet's with the urban neighborhood anarchism of the revolutionary sections or local assemblies fostered by the *enragé* movement of Paris in 1793; Proudhon's with the artisan anarchism of craftspeople in preindustrial France; Bakunin's with the collectivistic movement of peasant villages in Russia and Spain; Pelloutier's with the syndicalist proclivities of the turn-of-the-century French industrial proletariat; and perhaps most prophetically, Kropotkin's with communistic notions of distribution in our own era, notions that deal with the ecological, decentralist, technological, and urban issues that are in the foreground of social life today.

The antistatist and antiparliamentary views of these anarchist thinkers should not obscure the *positive* content of their views. They rejected the Marxian notion that human "socialization" reaches its most advanced historical form over all previous ones with bourgeois society — "advanced" in that it presumably strips humanity of the "biosocial" trappings it has retained from its evolution as an animal.[2] As I have argued elsewhere (in "On Neo-Marxism, Bureaucracy, and the Body Politic" in *Toward an Ecological Society*), society can never free itself of its natural matrix, least of all in relations among individuals. The actual issue here, if one is to learn from the ecological problems of our time, concerns the *nature* of the natural world in which society conceives itself as rooted — be it organic (as was the case in many precapitalist communities) or inorganic (as is the case in market society today). The clan, the tribe, the *polis*, the medieval commune, the Parisian sections of 1793, the Paris Commune of 1871, and certainly the villages and decentralized towns of the past were rooted in qualitative biosocial forms of relations. Market society, with its atomization, its competition, its objectification of the individual and his or her labor power, and in recent times its economization of almost every facet of human life; not to speak of the bureaucratic sinews that hold this lifeless structure together, such as the concrete, steel, and glass cities and suburbs that pervade its environments; and the quantification that permeates every aspect of its activity — all these not only deny life in the biological and organic sense but reduce it to its molecular components in the physical and inorganic senses. Although bourgeois society cannot achieve its claim to "dominate" nature, it renders both society and the natural world increasingly inorganic and mineralized, spiritually as well as materially, literally *desocializing* society. Bureaucracy colonizes the social institutions of humanity; the concrete city colonizes the organic relations of nature; the mass media colonizes the individual's personality. Market "society," in short, seeks to colonize every aspect of personal, social, and natural life.

I cannot emphasize too strongly that anarchist ideas and desires largely give expression to organic societies, allowing for the qualifications I have made. Nor can I desist from emphasizing that Marxism, by contrast, is linked to that most inorganic of all human structures, the state; with that most inorganic of all oppressed classes, the proletariat; and with such inorganic forms of centralized power as the factory, the party, and the bureaucracy. Marx's celebration of the "universality" of the proletariat as a result of its dehumanization by capital, and his association of the proletariat with technological centralization, domination, and economic rationalization such as to render it a presumably revolutionary force, tragically reveals the roots of Marx's own theoretical corpus in the least self-reflexive forms of bourgeois ideology. Celebrating this "universality," as we can now see, celebrates the "hollowing out" of society itself, and its increasing vulnerability to bureaucratic manipulation in industry and politics by capital and trade unions. "Schooled" by the nuclear family, by vocational supervisors, by the hierarchical factory structure, and by the division of labor, the proletariat as a "universal" agent for change turns out to be, in fact, a faceless proletariat that expresses not the general interests of humanity but its own particularistic class interests, indeed, of *interest as such* as the expression of bourgeois egoism. The factory does not *unite* the proletariat; it *defines* it. And no tendency more clearly expresses proletarians' real *human* desires than their attempt to escape from the factory and recover their human face as members of a creative community — as free *citizens*.

II

The far-reaching distinction between anarchism as a social movement and Marxism as a statist one requires further emendation. With the great wealth of Marx's writings, particularly his work on alienation and his analyses of the commodity relationship and the accumulation of capital, I have no quarrel. His historical theories require correction by the best work of Max Weber and Karl Polanyi. But our concern is not that Marx's writings must be updated; their limits are defined by their fundamentally bourgeois origins and their susceptibility to state-oriented ideologies — all products of the early industrial revolution and the rise of the nation-state. Historically, it is not accidental that agrarian anarchism in Spain and in the Ukraine, and in its Zapatista form in Mexico, could be crushed only by the nearly genocidal destruction of its social roots, notably the village. Marxian movements, where they suffered defeat, were crushed merely by demolishing the party — indeed, often little more than their leaders. Anarchism's respect for artisanship, its commitment to the mutual aid, its high regard for the natural world, and its emphasis on an ethical socialism are its virtues insofar as they seek to retain those richly articulated, cooperative, and self-expressive forms of human consociation scaled to human dimensions. The seeming "effectiveness" of Marxism — in replicating the state in the form of the party, in its appeal to state controls, and in its economism at the expense of new social and personal values — is its shortcoming. Marxist parties did not *demolish* the nation-state but rather incorporated the very substance of protest and revolution into itself, and in the process effacing libertarian traditions as "archaisms" that were mere "precursors" to a "socialist science."

Not accidentally, Marxism has been most sharply alienated from itself. Attempts to "update" Marxian theory, to give it contemporary relevance, have added an obfuscating, eclectic dimension to its ideological corpus. As early as 1905, in response to the general strike movement that was then shaking tsarism to its foundations, Rosa Luxemburg was cynically obliged to make the "mass strike" — a typically anarchist "strategy" — palatable to the Second International by grossly distorting Engels's view on the subject and the anarchist view as well.[3] Lenin performed much the same sort of acrobatics in *State and Revolution* in 1917, when events favored the Paris Commune of 1871 as a "paradigm," assailing the anarchists while concealing Marx's own harsh denigration of the Commune in the last years of his life. Similar acrobatics were performed by Ernest Mandel, Andre Gorz, et al. in May-June 1968, when it seemed that all of France was being swept into a near-revolutionary situation.

What is significant here is the agility with which Marxian theory *follows* events that are essentially alien to its analysis. Marxist theorists initially dismissed the ecological and feminist movements that emerged in the late 1960s and the neighborhood movements of later years as "petty bourgeois" phenomena. Only the sheer force of events obliged Marxists — and socialists generally — to acknowledge the importance of these developments, try to interpret them according to economistic Marxist criteria, then make every effort to absorb them, even claiming priority in evoking them under the rubric of "new social movements." At this point it was not anarchism, to which these issues are literally *indigenous*, that was acknowledged as the arena to which these developments legitimately belonged, but a bouquet of "neo," "democratic," and even "ecological" Marxisms and socialisms. These obfuscating developments have impeded the evolution of revolutionary consciousness at its very roots and gravely obstructed the development of a truly self-reflexive revolutionary movement.

By the same token, anarchism acquired some bad habits of its own, notably an ahistorical and entrenched commitment to its own past. The decline of the New Left and the transformation of the sixties counterculture into more institutionalized cultural forms compatible with the status quo created among many committed anarchists a longing for the ideological security and pedigree that also afflicts the dwindling Marxist sects of our day. This yearning to return to a past that was less inglorious, coinciding with a short-lived resurgence of Spanish anarchosyndicalism after Franco's death, fostered an anarchism whose lack of creativity was chillingly similar to that of libertarian forms of proletarian socialism that existed in a prior era. What was lacking in both cases was the "hegemonic" proletariat and the constellation of historical circumstances that marked "proletarian socialism" in all its forms between 1848 and 1938. Anarchist commitments to the factory and to the struggle of wage labor against capital shared much of the crude economism of sectarian Marxism. What redeemed the anarchosyndicalists from outright congruence with authoritarian Marxists was the form that their libertarian variant of "proletarian socialism" acquired. Their emphasis on an ethical socialism, on direct action, and on control from below, as well as their antistatist stance, served to keep them afloat in this respect. But what vitiated anarchosyndicalist efforts — quite aside from the historical decline of the workers' movement as a revolutionary force — was the authoritarian nature of the factory itself, the corresponding pyramidal structure adopted by syndicalist theory, and the reliance that anarchosyndicalists placed on the unique role of the proletariat and effects of the social nature of its conflict with capital.

Despite their many insights, anarchosyndicalism, Proudhonianism, and Bakuninism belong to an irrecoverable past. They do not lack ideological coherence and meaning — indeed, Proudhon's emphasis on federalism still enjoys considerable validity — but they speak to epochs that have faded into history. There is much they can teach us, but their significance has long been transcended by historically new issues — issues that, in my view, are more fundamental in their libertarian implications — to which the entire Left must address itself. This does not mean the "death" of anarchism, once we view the word in its changing historical contexts. Quite to the contrary: the issues that confront us today are more distinctly communal and ethical than they have been at any time in the past. They literally involve the recreation of a new public sphere as a civic, confederal counterpower to the state, structured around an institutionally new *politics* (to use the term in its Hellenic rather than its parliamentary sense) based on directly democratic institutions and full public participation. The fact that these issues and solutions are meaningless in a Marxian context reveals the extent to which Marxian ideas have become an "ideology" in a socially accommodating sense and their perpetuation a typically academic exercise whose products feed university presses and professional journals.

III

We are no longer living in a world where revolutionary consciousness can be developed primarily or even significantly around the issue of wage labor versus capital. I do not wish to denigrate the significance of this century-old conflict. That a class struggle exists between the proletariat and the bourgeoisie (however broadly we choose to define the term *proletariat*) hardly requires discussion, any more than the fact that we live in a capitalist society that is ruled by a capitalist class (again, however broadly we choose to define the term *capitalist*) or that evolutionary changes can be made without the full support and participation of the working class. But we must recognize that a class *struggle* does not mean a class *war* in the revolutionary sense of the term. If the past century has demonstrated anything, I submit, it is that the conflict between the proletariat and the bourgeoisie has been neither more nor less revolutionary than was the conflict between plebeians and patricians in the ancient world and between serfs and the nobility in the feudal world. These conflicts did not simply end in an impasse; rather, they never contained the authentic possibilities for transcending the social, economic, and cultural forms within which they occurred. Indeed, the notion of history as a history of class struggle is not exhausted by conflicting economic interests, or by class consciousness and identity, or by the rootedness of socialist and syndicalist ideologies in reductionist economic theories, or what is blithely called a class analysis.

What lies on the horizon of the remaining portion of this century is not class struggle as we have known it in the metaphors of "proletarian socialism" — socialist *or* anarchist. The monumental crisis that bourgeois society has created in the form of a disequilibrium between humanity and the natural world has telescoped entire geological epochs into a single century or two; an expansive notion of human freedom has given rise to women's liberation movements; a hollowing out of the human community and citizenship threatens the very claims of individuality, subjectivity, and democratic consciousness — ironically, the greatest claim that Marx made for the bourgeois epoch as a force for progress; a paralyzing sense of powerlessness in the face of evergreater urban, corporate, and political gigantism; and a sense of political involvement that has been steadily replaced by a retreat into privatism. All of these major regressions have rendered economistic interpretations of social phenomena, traditional "class analyses," and parliamentary strategies in the form of traditional statist "politics" and party structures woefully inadequate. One must truly torture these issues and grossly warp and distort them to fit them into Marxian categories. Perhaps no less significantly, the far-reaching economization of society — the reduction of social life to a huge shopping mall — and the emergence of ever-growing, indeed cancerous bureaucracies have given to the state sweeping historical functions that go far beyond its early role as a so-called "executive committee of the ruling class."

One must realize the entirely new conditions that this constellation of circumstances had produced for radicalism, and the extent to which they redefine the revolutionary project, both theoretically and practically. The technical progress that socialism once regarded as decisive for humanity's "domination of nature" and as a precondition for human freedom has been used with chilling effect to achieve the very real domination of human by human. Technology now reinforces class and hierarchical rule by adding powerful instrumentalities of control and destruction to institutional forces of domination. The wedding of the economy to the state, far from simplifying the revolutionary project as Engels had so naïvely believed it would in *Anti-Dühring*, has enhanced the powers of the state with material resources that even the most despotic regimes of the past never had at their command. The growing recognition that the proletariat has become — and probably has always been — an integral part of capitalism, not a revolutionary agent gestating within the womb of the capitalist system, has raised anew the problem of the "revolutionary agent" in an entirely new and non-Marxian form.

Finally, the need for the revolutionary project to view itself as a cultural, ethical, and democratic one that encompasses the needs of human subjectivity, the empowerment of the individual, the "ecologization" of the revolutionary ideal has led in turn to a need to explore the structural nature, internal relations, and institutional forms of any revolutionary movement that hopes to compensate, if only in part, for the cultural, subjective, and social negation of the public sphere. Indeed, we must redefine the very meaning of the word *Left* today. We must ask if radicalism should be reduced to a form of social democracy that patently operates within the established order with a view toward acquiring mindless mass constituencies, as Laclau, Mouffe, Walzer, and so many self-proclaimed socialists would have it do, or if it must create a far-reaching revolutionary challenge to desocialization, disempowerment, and every aspect of domination, be it in everyday life or in the broader social arena of the coming historic epoch.

IV

Whatever else anarchism has meant in the past — be it the millennarian movements of Christianity, the peasant movements of the Anabaptists, the Makhnovite and Zapatista militias, the Parisian *enragés* and Communards, the Proudhonian artisans, or the early industrial workers who entered the syndicalist CGT in France and the CNT in Spain — it is my view that contemporary anarchism must address itself in the most knowledgeable and radical terms to capitalist society, indeed to *hierarchical* society as such. To relegate anarchism to an ahistorical moral movement based on the virtues of "natural man" and on "instincts" for mutual aid or for revolution; to define it merely in terms of its *opposition* to the state as the source of all evil; or worse, to describe it entirely in terms of only one of its variants — be it the anarchism of Stirner, Proudhon, Bakunin, or Kropotkin — is to grossly misread anarchism as a historical movement, to ignore its existence as a social movement in specific social contexts. Anarchism should not be burdened by the textual exclusivity of Marxism's body of authoritative writings, with its commentators and academicians. Conceived as a social movement rather than as a statist one, anarchism is deeply woven into the development of humanity and requires historical understanding, not simply textual exegesis.

Do I mean to assert, then, that anarchism should be *dissolved* into history and do without theoretical identity? Emphatically not. But what should unite anarchist theories and movements today is not only their defense of society against the state but a commitment to participation in municipalist politics in its classical civic sense, and additionally, I would contend, an attempt to create a popular confederal counterpower to the nation-state. Anarchism by definition reaches beyond class exploitation (whose significance it never denies) to demand the abolition of *hierarchical relations*, whose historical significance it carefully analyzes as the source of domination as such. The domination of the young by the old in tribal gerontocracies and of women by men in patriarchal families, and the notion that humanity is destined to dominate the natural world — these *preceded* class society and economic exploitation, and they would continue to exist even if classes and economic exploitation were eliminated. In fact, they remain the crucial residual spheres of authority that Marxism and socialism retain all too comfortably in their notions of a classless society. Anarchism, in effect, advances an analysis of the nature of freedom and domination that looks beyond the conventional economistic nexus of capitalist society into the very structure, sensibilities, and nature of human consociation *as such*. Hierarchy, which Marx saw as an inevitable extension of biology into society and which Engels considered indispensable to industrial activities in all circumstances, is seen by anarchism as a social and cultural phenomenon that can be eliminated in a free and rational society. For anarchism, hierarchy and domination inevitably lead to the objectification of the natural world as mere natural resources, of human beings as mere human resources, of community as mere urban resources — in short, to the reduction of the world itself to inorganic material and to the rise of a technocratic sensibility that sees humankind as a mere instrument of production.

As I have indicated in my essay "Marxism as Bourgeois Sociology" (in *Toward an Ecological Society*) Marx unwittingly sophisticated this trend and extended it into socialism. What concerns me for the present is that anarchism, often intuitively, has assembled the materials for a deeper, richer, and most significantly, *broader* insight into and grasp of the dialectic of domination and freedom by looking beyond the factory and even the marketplace into hierarchical relations that prevail in the family, the educational system, the community, and the relationship of humanity to the natural world, not to speak of the state, the bureaucracy, and the party. Accordingly, issues of ecological dislocation, sexism, ethnic oppression, and community breakdown are indigenous concerns of anarchism, issues that it has often raised even before they acquired social immediacy — not problems that must be tacked onto its theoretical corpus and altered to accommodate an economistic, class-oriented viewpoint. Hence anarchism, by making these problems central to its social analysis and practice, can acquire a relevance that by far overshadows most trends in present-day socialism. Indeed, to a great extent anarchism has become the trough from which socialism eclectically nourishes itself on a libertarian diet that it initially rejected, notably feminism, ecology, and urban communitarian issues. Insofar as socialists have been taking up these issues in recent years, they have done so without trying to cohere them into a unified body of social ideas or rooting them in a theory of hierarchy and domination. As a result, they tend to deal with these issues in a fragmentary manner, or they artificially wed them to economistic revisions of traditional Marxist theories, such as Andre Gorz's attempts to explain the ecology crisis as a result of a dubious "declining rate of profit" or to highly abstract, often fallacious interpretations of what constitutes a "working class," to cite the most conspicuous of such "neo-Marxist" quirks.

Secondly, anarchism has tried to deal with the urgent problem of structuring itself as a revolutionary movement in the form of the very society it seeks to create. It should hardly be necessary to demolish the preposterous notion that hierarchical forms of organization are synonymous with organization as such, any more than it should be necessary to demolish the notion that the state has always been synonymous with a civic, confederal politics based on direct democracy. What could uniquely distinguish anarchism from socialism today is a commitment to a community movement and a civic political culture based on the coordination of human-scaled municipalities along confederal lines. At a time when consociation is faced with the corrosive phenomenon of dissociation, anarchism can advance municipal confederations in opposition to the nation-state, and individual empowerment through direct democracy in opposition to representative republics structured around bureaucratic and statist institutions. Thus anarchism would not only be the practice of citizenship within a new public sphere, or as I have emphasized, a new politics, but the self-administration of the revolutionary movement itself. The very process of building an anarchist movement from below would be viewed as a process of consociation, self-activity, and self-management that would hopefully yield that revolutionary "self" or citizen that can act upon, change, and manage an authentic society.

V

The basic tenets of a new anarchist theoretical corpus and critique upon which I have focused here would require volumes to develop in detail.[4] Let me emphasize that the most advanced anarchist theories today do not involve a mystical return to a "natural man," a simple antistatism, a denial of the need for organization, a conception of direct action as violence and terrorism, a mindless rejection of sophisticated theory, or a refusal to see what is living in the work of *all* socialist theorists. Nor would I regard as viable a reliance by traditionalist anarchists on any supposed revolutionary or mutualistic "instincts," or on classical anarchistic notions of *contractual* "agreements" as distinguished from the *ethical* communistic maxim "From each according to his or her ability, to each according to his or her needs."

Limitations of space makes it impossible for me to deal with such important questions as the nature of the "revolutionary agent" today, the relationship of anarchist theory and practice to the political sphere, the details of anarchist organizational structures, and the relationship of anarchism to the ecology and feminist movements. But allow me to conclude with this very important consideration. At a time when the proletariat is historically quiescent, I believe, as a *revolutionary* class and the traditional factory faces technological extinction, anarchism in its present form has raised to the foreground those ecological, sexist, and community issues that socialism began to cope with only much later. Anarchism has also explored at all times and from the outset the problems of self-empowerment, the forms of decentralization, and the concepts of self-administration that are now at the foreground of a new leftist politics generally. And it has raised these issues from within its very *substance* as a theory and practice directed against hierarchy and domination, not belatedly acknowledged them as problems that had to be "coped with" or "integrated" into class analysis and interpretations of economic exploitation.

These features of anarchism, particularly in its present-day form, are much too important to ignore. They raise the profound question of whether socialists — particularly Marxists — will exercise a degree of self-reflexivity that will make revolution and human freedom the real goal of their project rather than incorporate them into a reified theoretics that seems to have become an end in itself, subject to academic peer pressures that demand ideological conformity and are largely confined to the haven of the academy.

This lecture was delivered to the Critical Theory seminar of the Conference on Marxism and anarchism, held at the University of California at Los Angeles on May 29, 1980. It was revised in August 1992.

FOOTNOTES

[1] It would be well at this point to stress that I am discussing the institutional *structure* of the social forms cited above. That they variously excluded women, strangers, and often nonconformists of various religious and ethnic backgrounds, not to speak of slaves and people lacking property, does not diminish humanity's capacity to recreate anarchic institutions on more egalitarian levels. Rather, it indicates that *despite* their historical limitations of time and place, such institutions were both possible and functional, often with remarkable success.

[2] The term *biosocial*, as I use it here, should not be confused with *sociobiological*, with its excessive emphasis on the genetic sources of behavior. The term *biosocial* more clearly approximates the sense of Marx's term *natural societies*, which were structured around biological facts like kinship and gender differences and the use of fairly simple implements.

[3] A distortion all the more disquieting because the Social Democratic rank and file had been deeply moved, ideologically as well as emotionally, by the 1905 events in Russia. "The anarchists and syndicalists who had previously been driven underground by orthodox Social Democracy now rose to the surface like mushrooms on the periphery of the SPD," Peter Nettl observes snidely in his biography of Luxemburg; "when it came to something resembling 'their' general strike they felt they were close to legitimacy once more." And indeed, for good reason: "For the first time for years anarchist speakers appeared on provincial socialist platforms by invitation. The orthodox party press led by *Vorwärts* was much more cautious; but it, too, gave pride of place [albeit not of doctrine — M.B.] to Russian events and for the first few months abstained from wagging blunt and cautious fingers over the difference between Russian chaos and German order." (Peter Nettl, *Rosa Luxemburg*, abridged ed. [Oxford University Press, 1969], pp. 203-204.)

[4] See in particular my *Remaking Society* and *Urbanization Without Cities* (formerly titled *The Rise of Urbanization and the Decline of Citizenship*), among other works I have written in the past decade.

WHY THE BLACK FLAG ?

The black flag is the symbol of anarchy. It evokes reactions ranging from horror to delight among those who recognize it. Find out
what it means and prepare to see it at more and more public gatherings. . . . Anarchists are against all government because they believe
that the free and informed will of the individual is the ultimate strength
of groups and of society itself. Anarchists believe in individual responsibility and initiative and in the whole-hearted cooperation of
groups composed of free individuals. Government is the opposite of
this ideal, relying as it does on brute force and deliberate fraud to
expedite control of the many by the few. Whether this cruel and fraudulent process is validated by such mythical concepts as the divine right
of kings, democratic elections, or a people's revolutionary government
makes little difference to anarchists. We reject the whole concept of
government itself and postulate a radical reliance on the problem-solving capacity of free human beings.

Why is our flag black? Black is a shade of negation. The black
flag is the negation of all flags. It is a negation of nationhood which
puts the human race against itself and denies the unity of all humankind. Black is a mood of anger and outrage at all the hideous crimes
against humanity perpetrated in the name of allegiance to one state or
another. It is anger and outrage at the insult to human intelligence
implied in the pretenses, hypocrisies, and cheap chicaneries of governments. . . . Black is also a color of mourning; the black flag which
cancels out the nation also mourns its victims — the countless millions murdered in wars, external and internal, to the greater glory and
stability of some bloody state. It mourns for those whose labor is robbed
(taxed) to pay for the slaughter and oppression of other human beings. It mourns not only the death of the body but the crippling of the
spirit under **authoritarian** and hierarchic systems; it mourns the mil-

lions of brain cells blacked out with never a chance to light up the world. It is a color of inconsolable grief.

But black is also beautiful. It is a color of determination, of resolve, of strength, a color by which all others are clarified and defined. Black is the mysterious surrounding of germination, of fertility, the breeding ground of new life which always evolves, renews, refreshes, and reproduces itself in darkness. The seed hidden in the earth, the strange journey of the sperm, the secret growth of the embryo in the womb all these the blackness surrounds and protects.

So black is negation, is anger, is outrage, is mourning, is beauty, is hope, is the fostering and sheltering of new forms of human life and relationship on and with this earth. The black flag means all these things. We are proud to carry it, sorry we have to, and look forward to the day when such a symbol will no longer be necessary.

THE STATE &
SOCIAL ORGANIZATION

graphic from **Stealworks: The Graphic Details of John Yates**

Johann Humyn Being

INTRODUCTION TO
THE STATE AND SOCIAL ORGANIZATION

For oppressive social structures to persist, a number of conditions must prevail. More important than political ideology, more important than the control of the military or the police, the ruling elites need to maintain control over the symbols of their legitimation. The ruling elites already have control over the apparatus of the state. What they need is to maintain control over the *idea* of the state. When the Sandinistas ousted the Somocistas, they retained the state structure and the structure of organizations that supported it. When the Eastern bloc countries declared their independence from the Soviet Union, they did not declare their intent to modify the prevailing structure by which government power is maintained. Time after time, we observe a changing of elites with little change in people's lives.

Anarchist theory has always been regarded as dangerous by people in power. Its stereotype as a form of disorder or chaos reflects its element of danger. Anarchists challenge what no political elite ever has, namely the idea of the state as a necessary form of social organization.

There are analogous myths in Western culture: slavery and monogamy are two which have been central to social control. Both are typically described as near universal occurrences in human history. In fact, anthropological evidence makes it clear that both are not universal forms of organization. The majority of societies in human history did not practice either forms of slavery or monogamous marriage. The anarchist anthropologist Harold Barclay in his book, *People without the state* (London: Kahn and Averill, 1982), and **Kirkpatrick Sale** in his book *Human Scale* (New York: Coward, McCann & Geoghegan, 1980) have amassed voluminous evidence to show that alternative forms of societal organization have been present throughout history. Sale observes:

Examples of societies that have lived, and lived long and well without the trappings of the state are surprisingly common, once one begins combing through the scientific literature. In fact they are so common, occurring right throughout the Indian societies of both North and South America, through much of North Africa and almost all of the great region from the Sudan to the Kalahari, and throughout the islands of the South Pacific from Sumatra all the way to Polynesia, occurring among patrilineal as well as matrilineal societies, settled and pastoral as well as hunting and nomadic, large and scattered as well as small and cohesive, isolated and ingrown as well as confederative and cooperative, occurring in such variety and profusion that it comes to seem from the anthropological evidence that this is indeed the basic natural organization of human societies (p.456).

In the selection included here, Sale examines the arguments for the necessity of the state and large governments. He looks at the four major lines of argument: that the state provides defense and guarantees peace, provides economic regulation, provides vital public services, and assures social justice. He concludes that the nation state is no longer a necessary form of social organization.

What Sale did for the nation state, **Howard J. Ehrlich** does for the idea of large-scale organization and bureaucracy. Ehrlich directly tackles the problem of developing a theory of anarchist organization. He selected the strategy of attacking sociological theories of organization. His rationale was twofold. First, he believes that we need to develop a social science that is not based on authoritarian and capitalist premises. Second, he argues that the major societal consequence of sociology (of all of the social sciences) is that they create ways of looking at the world that typically provide a scientific justification for the existing distribution of power in society. Today's justifications for organizational models are generally stated in the language of social science, and make their way from professional journals to college texts to matters of common knowledge and popular culture.

Ehrlich argues that accepted criteria of organizational effectiveness, coordination and control, leadership, role segregation, as well as the essential components of bureaucracy and the separation of work and play are all based on an authoritarian metasociology. Our challenge is to build liberatory organizational forms. (See Part Eight,

"Reinventing anarchist tactics.") And that task will require a comprehension of what is true and what is false in the handbook of sociological principles. It will also require that we write an anarchist metasociolgy.

Robert Graham's "The Anarchist Contract" confronts another dilemma on the cusp of theory and practice. While anarchists recognize the need for making rules and agreements, the question is when *do* such agreements deprive the consenting parties of their autonomy.

graphic from **Stealworks: The Graphic Details of John Yates**

The "Necessity" of the State

Kirkpatrick Sale

But "let us put away our infantile fantasies, the yearning to return to an infancy of the species that never was, where mankind existed in small and totally autonomous units like tribes or villages and practiced primary democracy and knew peace and harmony. It may be that if most inhabitants and the technical know-how already existing on humanity's fragile and crowded spaceship are consumed in a thermonuclear Judgment Day, the survivors might be able to exist, for a time, in tiny, fully sovereign, widely separated units. Only a madman would think that a solution. No, because the species is interdependent, giant political systems are a necessity."

So scolds Robert Dahl, and he is such an eminent political scientist that it behooves us, I suppose, to listen. Of course, it's not true that a small village of peace and harmony "never was," nor is there any reason to believe that the world's population would have to be reduced to a handful to accommodate separate sovereign units: remember, the entire population of the world could fit into the United States with a population density less than that of England (and onto our prime agricultural land with a density less than that of Malta). And it is not easy to see in what way this "interdependence" works — the Manchurian peasant and the Chilean barber? the Ghanaian professor and the Alaskan fisherman? — or why it should necessitate "giant systems" even if it did pertain.

Still, let us put these quibbles aside, for Dahl is a learned man and he may indeed be expressing those resistant feelings any American might experience on being told that it is possible to live without a state:

As for making all large political systems vanish into thin air, when the silk scarf is pulled away there in full sight are matters that cannot be handled by completely autonomous communes, neighborhoods, or villages: matters of trade, tariffs, unemployment, health, pollution, nuclear energy, discrimination, civil liberties, freedom of movement, not to say the whole tragic range of historically given problems like the threat of war and aggression, the presence of great military establishments around the world, the danger of annihilation. These problems inexorably impel us to larger and more inclusive units of government, not to small and totally autonomous units.

Again, we must take the man seriously, though again I do sense some confusion. Aren't the problems of war and aggression and nuclear energy and tariff barriers *caused* rather than solved by big governments? (They certainly *haven't* solved them, in any case, have they?) Surely if there were no giant governments there would be no "great military establishments" around the world and a good deal less "danger of annihilation." And if we have in fact been impelled to "larger and more inclusive units of government" because in that way we would solve the problems of unemployment, pollution, and discrimination, it does not take any special genius to show that it seems to have been rather futile, or at the very best inadequate; if to provide us with high levels of health care and a profitable balance of trade, it does seem to have failed, or at the best proven highly erratic.

I would be readier to see the end of those "infantile fantasies," as Dahl calls them, if he did not put up against them so many adult ones of his own.

BUT WE SHOULD confront the philosophy that stands behind the Dahlian attack, because in truth the line of criticism is common enough and deserves examination. Historically there have been four general arguments for the necessity of the state (and, in modern terms, for the necessity of large governments):

1. To provide defense in case of attack and to guarantee peace and security.
2. To provide economic regulation and development.
3. To provide public services beyond the competence of the community and the individual.
4. To assure social justice and protect the rights of the individual.

These arguments have a persuasive feel to them — they should, they've been drummed into us for centuries — but it is fair to ask: do they stand up? are they sufficient justifications for the existence of the state? and do they refute the desirability of small-scale politics?

DEFENSE

TRADITIONALLY THE STATE's initial claim to necessity was that it prevented warfare by erecting firm barriers of defense. As we have seen, this is tommyrot: the Law of Government Size shows that the duration and severity of war has always increased with an increase in state power. Larger states, far from providing peace, merely provide larger wars, having more human and material resources to pour into them. War is the health of the state, as Randolph Bourne has said, precisely because it provides the excuse for increased state power and the means by which to achieve it. (Victory, by the same token, is incidental: many losing nations emerge from wars with more powerful governments.) In fact what goes by the name of the defense of the citizens by the state may really be better thought of as the other way around.

Insofar as "defense" implies security, the state is the instrument least capable of providing this. Indeed, in the contemporary world of massed nuclear weapons, there simply *is* no defense of the citizens from a hostile aggressor — if Russia, for example, should unleash all of its missiles against this country, the only "defense" we would have would be to launch ours back again, guaranteeing the population nothing but nuclear holocaust. The very presence of the state and its huge pile of threatening weapons endangers rather than protects the populace, by inviting pre-emptive strikes; the fact that the U.S. is now sitting on something like 8,900 hydrogen bombs, the equivalent of 600,000 Hiroshimas, cannot be said to provide the ordinary person with the sense of security and safety implied by the word "defense." (Particularly since, according to a 1977 Brookings Institution report, between 1945 and 1976 Russia and America threatened military action not just once or twice, not just every other year or so, but 330 times, an average of nearly once a month.)

Moreover, in the course of attempting to provide its defense the state exercises its own forms of coercion and violence. It conscripts young people at will and takes to itself the right to jail or kill those who resist conscription or desert after induction; it forces the wider population to pay for warfare and its preparation through increased taxation, which has never in history been paid voluntarily; it amasses an army that denies individual rights and freedoms through accepted methods of authoritarian control. And such a state, preoccupied with defense, begins to justify all acts, however dangerous, in its name (as presidents justify all crimes with "national security", — when all you own is a hammer, as Mark Twain once said, all problems begin to look like nails.

I am not positing a pollyannalysis of human nature that argues all warfare will disappear and all defense becomes unnecessary in a world of small societies. I am only suggesting there are a number of reasons to believe that the occurrence and severity of warfare would be diminished.

To begin with, it is likely that a small society, particularly if concerned with a steady-state equilibrium, would not amass the kinds of glittering riches that would attract some predatory outsider; the riches of the stable community are likely to be in its air, its range of foods, its quiet streets, its heightened participation, not the sorts of things inspiring envy and conquest. By the same token, a small society already enjoying stability and some prosperity might well be reluctant to sacrifice that for a war whose economic benefits would be so unclear; as the University of Chicago's famed economist Henry Simons once put it, "No large group anywhere can possibly gain enough from redistributing wealth to compensate for its predictable income losses from the consequent disorganization of production." Nor would such a society particularly want to divert from its economy the kind of human and material resources that would be necessary for it to amass a strong fighting force capable of successful aggression.

Yet all that supposes rationality, and since the history of warfare is marked just as much by madness as by calculation, we would have to expect that somewhere war is bound to erupt even when it seems most illogical. Still, the very nature of that warfare depends on the size of the society waging it: with limited populations and limited resources for weaponry, wars cannot have the sweep and severity they do when waged by powerful nation-states. Nuclear warfare would certainly be almost impossible, not only because of the expense of such weaponry would be beyond any stable economy but, at bottom, because no small society could think of sacrificing millions of people and still surviving in the way current superpowers can.

Historical evidence is abundant to show that even the wars that do take place in small societies tend to be — well, if not pacific, at least constrained. A typical account in the anthropological literature is the one by Australian scientists C. W. M. Hart and A. R. Pilling, in *The Tiwi of North Australia*, describing how two bands declared war, amassed their armies, met around a clearing at dawn, and then began throwing spears at each other — but with the *oldest* men throwing the spears, none too accurately, the oldest women careening around trading insults, and as a result "not infrequently the person hit was some innocent noncombatant or one of the screaming old women who weaved through the fighting men, yelling obscenities at everybody, and whose reflexes for dodging spears were not as fast as those of the men." Stateless or not, such small bands and tribes rarely engaged in warfare for plunder or conquest, and territorial aggression and enslavement is practically unknown. Similarly, we have evidence from early Greece that at least some towns and cities worked out ways to make wars more like athletic events than battles-to-the-death, fighting to "maintain honor" or display manliness with games and contests; as early as the seventh century a "war" between Khalkhis and Eretria was fought out as a kind of wrestling contest, apparently quite vicious and serious but managed without spears, arrows, or slings and with the only stakes being honor, pride, and boasting rights.

And even the small regimes of the late medieval period, though undeniably and elaborately "stated," fought their wars at scales much smaller than our Hollywood conceptions would have led us to believe. Three or four knights and several dozen crossbowmen would make up a standing army, battles would commonly rage for no more than an hour or two before everyone was exhausted, and whole wars would be over in a month, the casualties rarely more than one or two percent of the fighting force. The Duke of Tyrol, it is said, declared war on the Margrave of Bavaria over some real or pretended slight, their war went on for two weeks, one man was killed, one village overrun, one tavern emptied of its wine, and in the end the Margrave paid a hundred thalers in reparations. And however many minor feuds and wars there may have been in a Middle Europe of duchies and principalities and republics and palatinates, that was as nothing compared to the wars wrought when they were all united into the *reichs* of Germany.

In a world of small societies, in fact, size itself would likely act as some kind of deterrent to aggression. Who could picture an American continent composed of even fifty different nations deciding to pool its resources to fight a little nation around the world in the jungles of Southeast Asia? Would Texas, say, or Ohio, be sufficiently rapacious — or, let's say, heroic — to want to mobilize its forces and send them across the Pacific to save Saigon from Communism? It is hard to see how the citizens of, for example, Bavaria, no matter how bellicose they might be, could have such a grievance against the citizens of Brittany that they would want to travel half a continent away to fight about it — though as we know when those citizens are combined into the larger states of Germany and France they have no trouble going at each other's throats with some regularity. There is something in the very size of the modern nation-state that leads it not into tranquillity but into temptation and even when it builds up power that is supposed to be purely defensive it always seems to have a way of turning it offensive without much trouble. The Germans have a saying that fits: *Gelegenheit macht Diebe* — opportunity makes thieves.

Yet suppose that somehow a single large superpower should appear (or remain) in a world of smaller communities. What is to be done with the legitimate fear that, in Robert Dahl's words, "in a world of microstates, let there arise only one large and aggressive state and the microrepublics are doomed"?

Historically the response of small states to the threat of such large-scale aggression has been temporary confederation and mutual defense, and indeed the simple threat of such unity, in the form of defense treaties and leagues and alliances, has sometimes been a sufficient deterrent. The record of medieval Europe, in fact, during a period of small territories confronted by rising states, is absolutely teeming with leagues and federations and compacts and associations among towns and cities that joined together to establish peace and to resist the martial incursions from the outside. The Lombardian and Tuscan Leagues in Italy, the Westphalian, Rhenish, Swabian, and Hanseatic in Germany, the Lyonnais and the Marseillaise in France, the Flemish, the Swiss, the Dutch, everywhere small towns came together with independent cities, the cities united with each other throughout a region, and though experiences naturally differed, the rule was of long periods, several generations, of unperturbed calm that were broken seldom, if ever, by the federated small communities themselves.

Moreover, the difficulties for any large power trying to subdue a host of smaller societies are truly formidable and would be additionally so if those societies, in a human-scale world, were efficiently governed, harmonious and homogeneous, and concertedly self-protective. The problems that Nazi Germany had controlling a Europe of large nation-states were bad enough, but they would have been infinitely greater if each little community had been independent, without connections to centralized systems of administration and control, with effective traditions of local autonomy and defense. The material game of conquering — and controlling — a small society that offered a great deal in the way of resistance and very little in the way of exploitable riches would hardly seem worth the military candle.

As recent history, indeed, suggests. Despite the existence of a number of enormous states, the events of the contemporary world give little support to the idea that Gargantuas are out there dying to subdue all the Lilliputs. Lithuania, Tibet, Goa — yes, there are some such instances, though in each of those cases the usurper had some legitimate prior claims to the territory. But in general the pattern has been one of the division and independence of states, an increasing number of smaller states, not of conquest and subjugation by the superpowers. Scores of quite tiny states exist, most under the economic pull of one large state or another but politically autonomous and without much fear of being taken over. And some of the smallest states in the world — Andorra, San Marino, Liechtenstein, Switzerland — have existed for many centuries quite untouched and unthreatened.

In sum, the long human record suggests that the problem of defense and warfare is exacerbated, not solved, by the large state, and that smaller societies, especially those without governmental apparatus, tend to engage in fighting less and with less violent consequences. Indicating that a world of human-scale polities would not be a world without its conflicts and disputations, but would likely be a world of comparative stability.

ECONOMIC DEVELOPMENT

THE JUSTIFICATION for the state in classical economic theory is that it is supposed to stabilize economies over wide geographic areas, standardize currencies and measurements, establish protective tariff barriers and regulate international trade, prime the productive pumps for sustained growth and steady employment, and ultimately promote economic development and stability. To which we may add a contemporary responsibility, the regulation of businesses on behalf of the public so that it is not recklessly overcharged and endangered, fleeced and pummeled.

Of course the easy response is that if *this* is what the state is so vital for, it does not seem to have proved its worth. What has characterized all large national governments, particularly in the twentieth century, is their clear *inability* to provide economic stability, security, or employment, to secure people against the dangers of depression and inflation, in either capitalist or "socialist" worlds. A nation like the United States, assumed to be the most powerful of all, though it has a truly mighty GNP and has recently enjoyed a period of high imperial prosperity, has not been able to forestall regular depressions, prevent inflation, maintain the dollar, regulate tariffs to the benefit of national industries, provide either jobs or income security, create a stable retirement system, or manage any but the most meager protections against the corporate contaminations of food, air, water, waste, or soil.

Still, it is perfectly true that national governments do issue and protect a standard currency — the only trouble is that this is of itself one of the major causes of inflation, and always has been, and the advantages of it could be as equally well enjoyed by a congeries of cooperating communities accepting certain common tokens — much as the cities of Europe agreed to accept the coins of Florence (hence the florentine) in the thirteenth and fourteenth centuries. Nor do these governments ever manage to keep their currencies stable for very long, as theory would dictate — as the worth of the dollar would testify. Moreover, as long as there is mutuality it is possible to have a great variety of currencies in one very small area: nothing collapses in northern Europe in spite of the fact that there are *nine* major currencies (plus such international currencies as the dollar and drawing notes) operating within a 400-mile radius of Copenhagen, an area about the size of the state of Texas.

Well, then, what about tariffs — are not nations necessary to maintain them? Right enough — only the reason that tariffs exist in the first place is to protect the state, enable it to develop while new industries grow within its boundaries, for its own aggrandizement; the advantages to the consumer are negligible, if existent. Like armies, tariffs are there to safeguard the state, not vice versa.

International trade? Nothing that *couldn't* be done without the state, as is amply demonstrated by the history of Europe between 1000 and 1500, a period of the most extensive and elaborate sort of trade relations, fundamental to the development of capitalism, quite separate from any national machineries. In fact, is being done — for the operations of the current multinational corporations, as any number of studies have shown, are essentially beyond the control of any serious governmental regulation of any kind.

Pump-priming? Governments have become better at this since the advent of Keynes, but there is not one of them, including those that Keynes advised, that has succeeded in creating unabating growth without regular severe downturns, not one of them, indeed, that has succeeded in directing the flow of those pumps out of the front yards of the rich and toward the backyards of the poor. And might a process efficient at sustaining growth — even if the nation-state could achieve it — be outmoded in a world where it is not growth but stability we wish to sustain, where growth has in fact become a threat?

Shortages? The idea that big governments are good for monitoring and allocating precious resources — as with gasoline shortages, for example — so as to distribute them fairly to all has a nice socialist ring about it and is John Kenneth Galbraith's favorite idea for the 1980s ("more big government"). But those who remember the government's skill at monitoring and planning Vietnam and swine-flu shots and public housing, and — need I go on? — may not relish the prospect of its handling irreplaceable resources.

Regulation? Aside from added costs to consumer and taxpayer, the trouble with governmental regulation is that it is always a catch-up operation, fighting the problem at the wrong end *after* the damage has been done. If the only criteria in the economy are those that capitalism dictates, as they are, then of course there will be those problems that no amount of government law or supervision can correct; if the primary purpose of the government is to protect the smooth workings of the corporate system, as it is, then of course its duodena attempt to restrain its excesses by patchwork edicts is always doomed to failure. Thus the famous actions against cartels and monopolies have proved insignificant, as the existence and growth of conglomerates and oligopolies makes clear; the regulation of public utilities has been almost useless, as the existence of telephone gougers and electricity polluters, the awful failure of nuclear plants, makes obvious. But wouldn't the consumer be in ever more trouble *without* government regulation, however expensive and inept? Perhaps so. But probably not if at the same time the myriad government supports favoring large (and therefore largely unresponsive) businesses were withdrawn and the small firms in the market had to offer — as they did in an earlier age — "good goods at a fair price" in order to compete successfully. (It is not competition but the *lack* of it that fosters abuses, not the neighborhood butchers but the large meatpackers that produced the fetid *Jungle.*) Certainly not if in each office and shop the full range of workers made self-managed policies, in each community the full range of citizens set democratic decisions, as to what products and services would be sold.

One needn't claim that economic relations among small and self-rewarding communities are going to be untrammeled bliss to reject the notion that state supervision will solve more difficulties than it manufactures. Yes, the kinds of cooperation within a community, the kinds of federations among communities, would, in the absence of a state, take skill and savvy. Yes, careful balances would have to be wrought between upriver towns and downriver cities (the word "rivalry," after all, comes from the Latin *rivus*, for river); between the community that had surplus steel and the community with surplus grain; between the city with all the copper and the other with all the zinc. But it need not be all that complicated, nor need it entail some *deus ex civitas.* After all, the stamps of all 152 independent nations of the world are recognized by all the others and the mail goes around the world without any state to guarantee it; the railroad cars of thirty-one sovereign nations travel the same rails for 4 million square miles throughout Europe without any state, not even any central agency, to oversee them. International telephone and telegraph systems, worldwide maritime regulations, international airline agreements, global currency exchanges, and dozens of other forms of cooperative arrangements all prove to be successful without any universal state, or anything near it, to supervise them. Would the cooperation of a half-a-dozen small communities in a single limited bioregion be all that hard to effect?

PUBLIC SERVICES

As ROBERT DAHL puts it, the state is ultimately necessary on grounds of the "criterion of competence": "Only the nation-state has the capacity to respond fully to collective preferences," only the state can supply public goods in the common interest, which individuals and communities won't do by themselves. Who but the state can control population growth, say, or feed the starving, secure public health, build highway systems, provide welfare, offer disaster relief, distribute scarce supplies? Who but the state — to pick the most commonly cited example — can control pollution?

This is the way Dahl poses the problem, given a polluted Lake Michigan:

> Let us assume, without arguing the matter, that the capacity to reduce pollution in Lake Michigan is, up to some threshold, a function of size. A citizen who wants the lake cleaned up might well reason as follows: If the authority to deal with pollution is left to local governments, the job is unlikely to be accomplished even if a majority of people around the lake — not to say in the whole country — would like it cleaned up. For those favoring vigorous pollution control may be in a minority in some towns. Consequently that town will probably continue to pollute the lake. Thus only a regional or perhaps even a federal agency, responsible to regional or national opinion, can be effective. Of course I am bound to have only negligible influence on the decisions of such an agency, whereas I might be highly influential in my own town. Nonetheless, on balance I prefer the agency to the present system of decentralized and uncoordinated units.

The hidden assumption here, of course, is that the Federal government is in fact a solution. In real life it doesn't quite work out that way. The first problem is to get the government to take any action at all, to rouse the politicians or the bureaucrats somehow, to force the courts to intervene, and that may be an expensive and time-consuming task for any individual, especially since the object of the appeal is probably 600 miles away in Washington, D.C. The next problem is to see to it that the action will be appropriate, that the decisions of all these people will be wise.[1] Immediately following comes the problem of making sure that the wise decision can actually be carried out, that the competence to do the job is in human, or at least bureaucratic, hands in the first place; the inability of any government to keep the various oil spills from polluting Texas beaches in 1979 suggests that there are some matters as yet beyond our skills to solve. And making sure that it *is* carried out, and carried out properly, by government officials whose interest in the task may be minimal and whose budgets may be small, without any unintended side effects. And the final problem is keeping the government always around to make sure that the elegant solutions stay in place and the errant polluters don't backslide when no one is looking — since the solutions have been imposed on them by a higher authority rather than drawn from them by cooperation and negotiation. Oh — and paying for it all.

Still, even if we concede that the federal government *is* a solution, and a benevolent one, wouldn't it be more rational for Dahl's citizen to figure out why that pollution exists in the first place and trace the problem to its source? The cause may be an accident, or ignorance, in which case the polluter doesn't need the heavy hand of federal regulation but a little help, or information, or some money, any of which can be supplied far more easily and cheaply by the concerned majority around the lake than by federal intervention. If the pollution is found to be deliberate, it is most likely to come from some anti-social corporation — the battery company, the detergent manufacturer — passing its "external" costs on to the public, which it has been allowed to do by provisions of governmental law for a hundred years or more, and ignoring any but its own sheer profit considerations, which it is explicitly *protected* in doing by the same long line of laws. Or if the pollution is from a municipal agency, it is probably because of federal provisions that defy ecological balance — for example, Washington's funding complex sewage systems instead of septic tanks and composting toilets, or giving tax credits to utilities for expansion but not for conservation, or spending billions to develop nuclear rather than solar power. In other words, Dahl's citizen would find that the state may be the underlying *cause* of the pollution Dahl would ask it to *cure*.

To find the government as the root cause of such problems, of course, should not surprise us by now: it is in the nature of the state, we have repeatedly seen, to create the problems that it then steps in to correct and uses to justify its existence. But there is a further point to that process that is pertinent here; in the words of British philosopher Michael Taylor:

> The state . . . in order to expand domestic markets, facilitate common defense, and so on, encourages the weakening of local communities in favor of the national community. In doing so, it relieves individuals of the necessity to cooperate voluntarily amongst themselves on a local basis, making them more dependent upon the state. The result is that altruism and cooperative behavior gradually decay. The state is thereby strengthened and made more effective in its work of weakening the local community.

This is important: it is exactly this that accounts for the inability of the Lake Michigan communities to regulate their pollution problems in the first place. Communities that were in control of their own affairs, whose citizens had an effective voice in the matters that touched their lives, would almost certainly choose not to pollute their own waters or to permit local industries to do so, out of sheer self-interest if not out of good sense — particularly if they were small, ecology-minded, economically stable, and democratically governed. (And if by some chance a community or two did go on polluting, resistant to all appeals, their toxic effects would likely not overstrain the lake's ability to absorb them.) It is this process, moreover, that accounts for the failure of the concerned majority to have cleaned up the pollution once it existed. Individuals and communities conditioned to cooperative and federative behavior, particularly those whose interests are greatest (in this case fishing villages, towns with bathing beaches, beach clubs, marinas, lakefront hotels, boardwalk businesses), would almost certainly work out, and pay for, a way to restore the lake — especially if there were no federal or state governments to siphon off the locally generated money through taxation.

As with pollution, so with the other public services of the state. There is not a one of them, not one, that has not in the past been the province of the community or some agency within the community (family, church, guild) and that has been taken on by the state only because it first destroyed that province. There is not a one of them that could not be reabsorbed by a community in control of its own destiny and able to see what its natural humanitarian obligations, its humanitarian *opportunities*, would be. Invariably when the state has taken over the job of supplying blood for hospitals, there is a shortage, even when it offers money — the U.S. now gets much of its blood from overseas; invariably when a community is asked to do it voluntarily, and when the community perceives that the blood is to be used for its own needs, there is a surplus. This is not magic altruism, the by-product of utopia — this is perceived *self-interest,* community-interest, made possible (capable of being perceived by the individual) only at the human scale.

Indeed, there is not one public service, not one, that could not be *better* supplied at the local level, where the problem is understood best and quickest, the solutions are most accessible, the refinements and adjustments are easiest to make, the monitoring is most convenient. If it be said that there is not sufficient expertise in a small community to tackle some of the complicated problems that come along, the answer is surely not a standing pool of federal talent but an appeal throughout neighboring communities and regions for a person or group who can come in to do the job. (This is in fact what the federal government itself most often does today, hence the great reliance on contract firms and $500-a-day consultants.) If it be said that some problems are too big for a small community to handle alone (an epidemic, a forest fire, or some widespread disaster), the answer is clearly not the intervention of some outside force but the ready cooperation of the communities and regions involved, whose own self-interest, even survival, is after all at stake. And if it be said that there is not enough money in a small community to handle such problems — well, where do you suppose the government got its money in the first place, and how much more might there be in local pockets if $500 billion of it weren't spent by Washington, $200 billion by state capitals, every year?

I cannot imagine a world without problems and crises, without social and economic dislocations demanding some public response. I see no difficulty, however, in imagining a world where those are responded to at the immediate human level by those who perceive the immediate human effects and control their own immediate human destinies.

SOCIAL JUSTICE

THE FINAL ARGUMENT for the necessity of the state is that it alone can provide social justice for all its citizens and guarantee civil rights and liberties to every individual.

To be sure, it *doesn't*, not anywhere in the world. Even in this country, so concerned with these matters, the areas of social injustice and individual repression are wide, and certain people — American Indians, poor blacks, prisoners, Chicanos, homosexuals among them — are particularly ill-served by the state. Indeed the case could easily be made that over the years as many inequities and injustices have been *caused* or fostered by the government with its left hand — let's mention only slavery, Indian genocide, union suppression, the Palmer Raids, Japanese prison camps, FBI and CIA illegalities, and Watergate — as are *prevented* by its right. Not that the U.S. should be singled out in this regard: over the world, states have been claiming to offer social justice and equality for five hundred years now without ever having achieved it, or an approximation of it, not even the most benevolent of them. And even the well-meaning attempts to do so, which have proved extremely costly and in many instances socially rebarbative, have very often been accompanied by iniquitous or punitive or violent ends, the state taking more power to itself in order to make its interference more successful — perhaps the long British campaign against slave-trading and the American Civil War and its aftermath may stand as sufficient examples of this.

But still, the state presumably *means* to protect its individuals, and presumably they would be worse off without state intervention. Didn't the American government abolish slavery, establish civil rights for blacks, outlaw segregated schools, and work to end racial discrimination in housing, hotelling, hiring? Hasn't it treated minorities — the Inuit in Alaska, the Chicanos in Texas — better than they would have been treated in racist local communities?

Perhaps. The record is by no means perfect even here on its more positive (right-hand) side, and many would say that alacrity was not among its notable features — but yes, the American government has effected certain reforms and has maintained certain freedoms. But who exactly would want to say that this is *because* of the state, that the government accomplished these goals by sighting a problem on its own, tackling it boldly, wresting a solution? I cannot think of a single victory in this area that has not been extracted by force from the government, has not been achieved by the affected parties themselves, pushing, cajoling, petitioning, suing, marching, demonstrating, usually quite on their own; and as often as not — as with the abolitionists of the 1840s, the labor organizers of the 1890s, the strikers of the 1930s, the McCarthy victims of the 1950s, the initial civil-rights demonstrators of the 1960s — they did so *against* the agents and stated policies of the national government. When we look at the great accomplishments here, what we find is the state against the victims of injustice — against Zenger, Thoreau, John Brown, Nat Turner, Susan B. Anthony, Eugene Debs, Margaret Sanger,

W.E.B. DuBois, Norman Thomas, Martin Luther King, the NAACP, the ACLU, the Communist Party, SDS, the *New York Times,* the *Progressive.*

What we generally have, in other words, is another example of the state, having taken power into its own hands, sitting on those hands until somebody shoves it off — at which point one of the hands goes to congratulate the shover and the other points grandly in a gesture of "Look-what-I've-done!" That minorities are protected as much as they are is due mostly to minorities; that individuals have the opportunities they have is due mostly to individuals; that the press has its freedoms is due mostly to the press. The Bill of Rights, we must not forget, was put there not as an instrument of the state for the citizens but as a means of protecting the citizens *from* the state.

It is also worth noting that even after all of these gains, it is fairly said that the freedom of the press is enjoyed only by the person who is rich enough to own one. Individuals still as a rule have very limited use of freedom of the press, very circumscribed access to free speech beyond their own shouting range, very restrained possibilities of free assembly that the police do not sanction; they still have very fragile real-world protection against searches, seizures, brutality, and cruel and unusual punishment by police agents of the state; and they still have only the most tenuous guarantees in practical terms of truly due processes of law, speedy trials, impartial (or any) juries, or freedom from cruel punishment in prison. And what is true for the ordinary, God-fearing, white, well-dressed, comfortable, and respectable individual is, sadly, even more true for the tinted, tattered, timid, tasteless, or tipsy one.

But is there an alternative: is it possible to think of a community achieving justice for individuals and minorities it did not find congenial?

Historically the community is noted for its failure in this regard: small towns, neighborhoods, even homogeneous cities, can be extraordinarily narrow-minded and cruel, inhospitable and downright vicious to people and opinions and customs they don't happen to like. But it is also true that they can be very receptive to minorities that they do not think of as threatening or that they regard as enriching, and they have a well-known capacity to tolerate a great variety of eccentric individuals — the town drunks, the Elwood P. Dowds, the Tom Edisons — who accept them in return. Should we posit communities in true harmony with their surroundings, with some democratic and cooperative operation of their economy, and some form of participatory governance, then it would be reasonable to suppose that much in the community would already operate to soften personal animosities, to accommodate differing minorities, to harmonize a wide range of opinions and beliefs. Without outside pressures, either legal or coercive, such a town could no doubt mute if not solve the essential problems of injustice and intolerance.

But even should this not be possible, there are the recourses known to centuries, indeed millennia, of human history: migration and division.

For the individual, the most successful relief from injustice, should the community be unresponsive, is not the appeal to the state, whose workings are always lengthy and uncertain, but migration and relocation. This is not easy, especially for people burdened with families and homes and investments, but it is obviously the most immediate and effective solution; and in a nation where one out of five families changes residences every year anyway, it cannot be all that difficult. If the individual cannot get along with the community, and the community cannot tolerate the individual, what real good will state intervention produce — wouldn't separation be, in any world, the rational, noncoercive, nonviolent solution? Yes, it might be possible to contrive a state process that would force a Jewish Community to accept the Nazi Individual, or a White Community the despised Black, or a Fundamentalist Community the threatening Atheist. But it needs only for the principle of free travel to be observed — to the advantage of both the leavers and the stayers — and the Nazi, the Black, the Atheist can all find congenial communities of their own. The virtue of a multi-communitied world would be precisely that there would be within its multitude of varieties a home for everyone.

And for the aggrieved minority, the obvious way to win relief is not to use the state to demand rights (which only inspires hostility in the majority) or to interpose restrictions (which insures implacability in the majority), but to divide and resettle. As was true in the Dinka village and the New England town, the eternal human solution to dissension has been division, the separation and sometimes relocation of the disgruntled minority. It is possible for a minority to use the machinery of the state over many years and, at the cost of considerable anguish and enmity, secure minority rights, but it is also possible for it to relocate with peace and good will and to create its own society on its own terms somewhere else. The commodious solution is not minority *rights*, but minority *settlements*.

Clearly I am not supposing a communitarian world without problems, even its instances of inadequacy and injustice. No one could expect that. I am only positing a world in which the community is empowered to seek the solutions right where the problems erupt, to deal within its bosom with the people it knows, and to seek migration and division when all else fails. Compared to the record of what the state in all its glory, all its centuries, has accomplished, this, for all its difficulties, seems simpler, safer, cheaper, surer. [2]

IN A HIERARCHY of necessities, the things provided by the family, the neighborhood, the community, the small city, would certainly come first: love, fraternity, security, cooperation, sex, comfort, order, esteem, above all *rootedness*. ("To be rooted," as Simone Weil has shrewdly noted, "is perhaps the most important and least recognized need of the human soul.") Those provided by the state — taxation, standing armies, police, regulations, bureaucracies, courts, politicians, nuclear power, corporate subsidies, moonshots, especially when taken in balance with its deficiencies, would no doubt come last. Looked at that way, they just may not even be necessities at all.

"Giant political systems are a necessity" in the mind of someone like Robert Dahl, and who is really to blame him? But in the light of what would seem to be the irresistible decentralist tenor of our times, particularly in the United States, of the documented and apparently unavoidable failures of the encrusted state, "a system incapable of action," it is not irrational to disagree. Even such an arch-conservative as Herman Kahn has been forced to acknowledge that the institution of the state may be — though of course he probably would never use the term — "withering away." The nation-state, in his view, historically has two essential reasons-for-being: to wage war and to foster economies; it will shortly find, particularly in the developed world, that in a nuclear age the dangers of doing the first are too great to risk, and in a multinational age the second is unnecessary, so its role and importance will decline in the decades to come.

That does not seem so fantastic. If humans lived for the first million years without a state, and most of them for the next 8,000 years without one, and the experiments with the nation-state as we know it are only a few hundred years old, there is clearly nothing eternal about it. It may have been a serviceable device for one small period of human history, but as we move out of that period it may begin to lose its value and its meaning in the daily life of the planet, even eventually disintegrating from disuse, to be remembered as we now remember the wooden plow or the sundial — a quaint tool, useful no doubt for its time, but of course no longer important, no longer . . . necessary.

Notes

1. The experience of San Francisco, during its 1976-78 water crisis — to pick just one example at the large city level from a bulging file — is not encouraging. To conserve water, the city government asked people to cut consumption by 25 percent, in return for which the public utilities commission granted the water department a 43 percent rate increase so its revenues wouldn't fall. But the residents actually went and cut consumption by 40 percent, confounding the experts as usual, so the department asked for an additional 22 percent rate *hike* — and then publicly suggested that people ought to find a way, in the middle of this drought, to use *more* water so the rates wouldn't have to go so high.

2. It used to be argued that only national governments could achieve justice because they were free of the corruption of small towns — though anyone familiar with pre-Mao China or modern Africa or Asia might have doubted. Since Watergate, we hear that less often.

ANARCHISM AND FORMAL ORGANIZATIONS

HOWARD J. EHRLICH

A PREFATORY NOTE

THE STUDY OF human social organization is central to both academic sociology and anarchist theory. American sociology, however, is explicitly a capitalist enterprise; and it has never recognized anarchism or anarchist theory. Critical analyses of sociology conducted by its Marxist critics have also ignored anarchist principles, but at the same time these critiques have also ignored the sociology of organizations.

Why bother to develop a formal critique? What political purposes are served by it? Let me answer in two ways. First, we should examine what the consequences of the sociology of organization can be. To begin with, it presents a view of human organizations that is less than what organizations could be. In the process, sociologists legitimate what is and, I think, contribute to people's alienation and cynicism about the character of organization. It suppresses people's thinking about alternatives, and it promotes individualistic solutions and escape.

It is important to understand that sociology and the other social sciences are socially recognized as legitimate — in fact, preferred — modes of social inquiry. Quite obviously my claims based on my being a sociological theorist will arouse far more positive response in most circles than my claims to being an anarchist theorist. Anarchism is a political ideology and is therefore to be distrusted. Sociology, however, is a scientific discipline and warrants your trust.

In actual practice, social scientists regularly introduce ideological statements under the guise of presenting an objective analysis. Since most of the time this happens without scientists knowing they have done so, it is understandable that most people without formal analytic training are also misled. And so political assertions clothed as scientific claims come to be accepted, while naked political claims confront an often embarrassed or indignant audience.

Second, the social sciences do differ from other sciences. Social science is reflexive. That is to say, people can and do read social science materials — and they can and do act upon what they read. The social sciences do not just discover laws or organize knowledge, they also create it.

Organizational Sociology: The Paradigm

Those familiar with the state of the social sciences would not be surprised to learn that there is no singular definition of 'organizations' or any consensual scheme for their classification. Just the same, social scientists know what an organization is, and a mass of data on their structure and operation has been accumulated. The arrangement of these data is, of course, dependent on the formal or implicit theory of the scientist. There is, however, a paradigm for organizational sociology that is consensual. For example, almost all organizational theorists accept 'control' as a core concept in their theory. They see organizational authority as legitimate, non-coercive, and fundamentally rational. They view leadership and hierarchy as inescapable, if not actually desirable. There are more such paradigmatic statements, to be sure, and we will discuss them as we go along.

The character of this paradigm is essentially authoritarian. Theorists do range across a narrow spectrum. On the right are those who explicitly advocate maximizing control as the means of increasing organizational effectiveness; and just a step over the center are those who see bureaucracy as the superior mode of organization and the best designed to protect the rights of individuals.

American sociologists of organization are also capitalists. That is, they accept the idea of profit and the accumulation of capital, of the private ownership of organizations, and of mass production and mass consumption. Certainly, statements about the political economy almost never directly enter organizational theories. Nevertheless, as I shall try to show, these theories are built upon, and in turn buttress, the ideology of capitalism. It would be almost totally unprecedented for an anarchist analysis to omit 'the state', however defined. Similarly, it is almost totally unprecedented for an organizational theorist to include 'the state.'

Theodore Caplow's *Principles of Organization* presents one of those rare statements by an academic sociologist (Caplow, 1964, p. 23):

> In modern society, almost all official organizations turn out, on close inspection, to be ultimately authorized by the state, which licenses marriages, charters corporations, and registers voluntary associations. There appear to be two reasons for this phenomenon. First, property cannot be securely held without the sanction of the state. Since official organizations of any consequence have collective property, it is evident why they require authorization. Second, any organization that wields substantial power must occasionally resort to violence. In modern society, in which the state's monopoly of violence is nearly unquestioned, the state must usually provide the means of coercion for private organizations, although there are exceptions, such as criminal syndicates.
>
> The phenomenon of authorization is often overlooked. It may seem implausible that the memorandum establishing a new janitor crew in a branch factory of a manufacturing corporation is authorized ultimately by the state, but the state does confer the corporate charter from which the company's board of directors derives its right to appoint the executives who are entitled to do such things as hiring a new janitor crew.

Despite that solid beginning, the state never again appears in his 'principles of organization.'

ANARCHIST PRINCIPLES

There is no concrete theory of anarchist organization, nor is there an anarchist sociology. What there is, rather, are numerous stipulations of how organizations ought to be structured. Anarchists have indicated a clear preference for small organizations where social relationships may be personalized and spontaneity in behavior maximized.

The preference for small size should not be mistaken for a rigid organizational principle. It is, rather, an expression of beliefs that (1) the size of an organization should not exceed the comprehension of the persons who make it up, and (2) the size should not exceed the point at which social relationships become impersonalized. Since that critical size will vary as people gain experience in anarchist collectives, it is premature to talk about the optimum size of anarchist organizations. For now, I think the simple preference for smallness is sound.

The fulcrum of anarchist organizational thought is the principle of the diffusion of power. Derived from the fundamental belief in human equality, this principle has been expressed in a variety of ways when applied to social organizations. Primary has been a model of equal participation in decision-making, that is, collective decision-making.

More radical, I think, is the conception that organizations be designed as impermanent, that is, actually be abolished at intervals. This idea of organizational impermanence is exploratory. It originates from many considerations: 1) the idea that an organization be socially useful and that its members disband when it is no longer of utility; 2) the idea that organizations are often formed to solve particular problems and that they are no longer necessary when the problems have been resolved; 3) the idea that the rigidification of behavior in an organization may be inescapable; and 4) the idea that over time people tend to identify organizational interests with their personal needs. In short, the principle of a temporary organization represents an attempt to prevent or to avoid the pathologies of organizations as we know them today. As we proceed in this essay, other anarchist principles should become more apparent.

EFFECTIVENESS

A standard definition of the 'effectiveness' of an organization has been defined by many sociologists as the degree of goal achievement' (Price, 1968; Etzioni, 1964). An organization's goals are presumably what the organization through its policymakers is trying to do. To study effectiveness, sociologists will generally examine the written goals of organizations as well as interview or observe those in leadership positions. All of this is very straightforward, and certainly sounds reasonable.

One inventory of research on organizational effectiveness provides us with a reasonable illustration. 'For example, a prison which has a custodial goal, and which has a low escape rate among its inmates, would be considered an effective organization.' And another: 'The successful strike indicates low degrees of morale, conformity, and effectiveness'. Now you may want to argue that you are opposed to prisons and certainly to custodial goals. As an anarchist you certainly would take that position, but the logical correctness of this sociologist's illustration is unimpeached. Similarly, you may view a worker's strike as representing the high morale and cooperative effort of an effective union. But the definition is written from the perspective of the bosses and not from that of the workers.

As a supposedly neutral sociologist, he could have said that judgments of organizational effectiveness depend on one's social position. (Having said that, he could have even written the same book by adding the qualification that he was only writing from a management perspective.) He didn't do this — not that it really would have made him neutral — and in not qualifying his inventory, he leaves us with an elitist and distorted view of organizational behavior.

The anarchist conceptualization of organizational effectiveness requires additional considerations: Who set the goals and what are their social consequences? And so an organization would be defined as effective to the degree to which all of its participants were involved in formulating its goals, to the degree to which its goals did not contribute to human discomfort, and to the degree that it achieved those goals.

Control

Organizations work because management has power. Its power is stable because it is accepted by everyone as legitimate (moral, right, correct, true, all of the above). Although sociologists seldom state it openly, they assume that persons who own or manage an organization have the right to dispose of their property as they choose. Those who control the organization contract with workers for their labor. The major conditions of that contract are dictated by the owners in the context of the scarcity of jobs and some regulation by the state. Unions are scarcely 100 years old; and minimum wage, fair employment practices, and health and safety regulations all represent fairly modern innovations in which the liberal state has restricted the nature of the contract.

The intervention of the state has added to the legitimacy of the capitalist's power. And this is partly because the state is presumed to be an entity independent of those who control the workplace. Organizational authority is exercised in the workplace through the legitimacy of ownership and under the protection of government.

Co-ordination and control are the recurrent themes of all organizational theory. Certainly no anarchist would object to a call for coordination. What about control? Control, in this context, refers to the control of the decision-making processes — who decides what to do?

For the anarchist, there is no simple solution. What I will call the *minimalist* solution is the position that control can never be held by an elite. That is, it would be unacceptable for some set of people to be able always, or almost always, to control the outcome of decisions.

Now the organizational theorist might reply that the essence of legal-rational authority is that the power to control decisions resides in positions and roles, not people. What that means to the social scientist is something like this: people are recruited to positions because they have satisfied some qualifying criteria and they can remain only as long as they perform their roles competently. Of course it is unlikely that organizations ever worked that way, and it probably represents nothing less than the social scientist's shaping of reality for the convenience of a neat theoretical package.

But the appeal to a 'role theory' could be countered on its own. That is, a proper anarchist response is that it makes no difference to have power invested in positions. And there are three quite different reasons why this is so.

First, in so far as we are talking about a work organization within a capitalist society, the decisions controlled by persons in positions of authority must be constrained by the objective of maximizing profit. This is, after all, *the* criterion of effectiveness in a capitalist organization. Thus all decisions must rationally be biased against the workers.

Elitist decision-making in a work organization within a state socialist society must also be constrained by objectives that do not necessarily correspond with those of the workers in a given organization. To be sure, the likelihood of correspondence is greater under socialism and, in some states, worker involvement in determining objectives is greater. Nevertheless, state interests are generally non-negotiable and, to that degree, will also be biased against the workers. (In the classic Marxist-Leninist formulation, only when the dictatorship of the proletariat is established will the interests of the state be identical with those of the workers. Needless to say, no anarchist expects that to happen; nor for that matter do many sociologists. But that of course is another can of theoretical worms.)

There is a second objection to the idea of power and authority being appropriate to certain positions within an organization. In modern capitalist and socialist societies, work is organized into occupational careers. A career is typically defined as some progression of jobs in the same domain, with the implication that each new job or position entails increases in responsibility and usually authority as well as increases in wages or other compensation. Now most workers are tracked. They don't have careers, or they have careers that are highly limited in the span of increased income or responsibility. In fact, the conception of careers is popularly reserved for professionals and managers.

Few persons ever get to occupy positions of power. Partly this is a consequence of the differential life chances associated with class, position, sex, and ethnicity in modern society; and partly it is a consequence of the limited number of positions of power in society. (Neither of these consequences is invariant, even in a capitalist society.) While social scientists are divided in their attitudes about the necessities of class, they do seem to be in accord that positions of power are scarce and that this is the way things ought to be.

So it is that a small set of the total population holds careers that permit them to move across positions of power. So acceptable is the idea of such a career that colleges and organizations provide some people with the option to train in administration, that is, to acquire certain resources of power and knowledge of their use. Careerists in power inevitably acquire further resources of organizational knowledge as well as administrative skills that only come with actual role performance. Thus access to organizational power resources typically has a cumulative effect.

That people can make a career of managing the lives of others is patently unacceptable within an anarchist framework. However, still within the framework of a minimalist solution, the anarchist could accept the idea of the scarcity of positions of power. There would be an obvious set of qualifications to that acceptance, namely that this scarcity is neither desirable nor inevitable, nor would it be allowed to persist. In keeping with those qualifications, the minimalist program would require that no one be permitted to make a career of positions of power. Put positively, people would rotate through such positions, and tenure would be highly limited. The consequence of this program would diffuse organizational and administrative knowledge.

There is, finally, a third objection to allocating power to positions that are held in limited number. Freedom is not just a matter of social structure; it is also a habit. The concentration of power makes followers of us all. We not only do not have the opportunities to learn how to act autonomously; we are constantly rehearsing our repertory of compliance, passivity and subordination. Having removed the constraints of oppressive institutions doesn't automatically free people. That comes only with a practice now denied to most people.

There is a basic premise in organizational sociology that the centralization of decision-making is a requisite of good organizations. This premise sustains the intellectual's distrust of the intentions and capabilities of most people.

There are the long-term decisions, mainly concerned with goals and policymaking. These are the *strategic* decisions. *Tactical* decisions are those that are mainly administrative, and these are the routine, day-to-day operational decisions. With regard to both types, many sociologists conclude that centralization — the concentration of decisionmaking power — is the key to effectiveness. Organizations that have a greater concentration of power in both strategic and tactical decision-making, most sociologists conclude, will be more effective than those that have a lower concentration of power. Within the confines of this capitalist criterion of effectiveness, it is likely that this conclusion is true as empirical generalization. Without accepting that criterion, we could pose the question of whether the rotation of persons through positions of power in highly centralized organizations would modify organizational effectiveness. And the answer is that there is normal turnover in managerial positions without long-term consequences. Such rotation does not have any inescapably negative impact on organizational effectiveness.

BUREAUCRACY

Since Max Weber wrote the first, now classical, sociological defense of bureaucracy as the form of organization most suited to capitalism, there have been few serious challenges to the belief in the necessity of bureaucratic forms. And the rationalizations for it seem never to end.

There are four essential components of a bureaucratic organization that concern us here: 1) there is a hierarchy of positions; 2) there is a specialized division of labor; 3) salaries and other rewards are distributed according to rank in the hierarchy; and 4) there are formal rules and procedures regulating organizational behavior.

It is my belief that bureaucracies are defended more because of the societal effects that social scientists *do not talk about* than because of their supposed efficiency as an organizational form. These four components may be necessary for a bureaucracy, but they are also necessary to maintain class stratification, to promote ideas of social mobility and competition, to preclude self-management and foster separatism and isolation. Bureaucratic forms — worst of all — deny people opportunities for growth and self-development; and they perpetuate a political economic standard of self-assessment — 'if you're so smart, how come you're not rich?'

Bureaucratic forms in state socialist societies have the same social consequences; that is, they are also supportive of the political economy. While collective goals, co-operation and comradeship are emphasized, hierarchy and specialization persist. In some state socialist settings, there has been a serious attempt to minimize income differences and involve workers in larger organizational decisions. And one should not overlook the guarantees of employment, housing and health care —guarantees that certainly make the life circumstances of people more secure. Just the same, the secure worker in the socialist organization is no more autonomous, no more independent, and no more free than workers in capitalist organizations.

Subordination to authority, indoctrination in the ideological justifications for hierarchy and differences in knowledge and access to information, and the lack of freedom to make basic decisions about one's life — all of these can foster in both the capitalist and socialist worker their dependence on others and a lack of self-respect.

We learn to identify authority and power early. The nuclear family with its age- and sex-based division of labor and power is the initial training ground. The school with its demands for regimentation, for discipline, and for the acceptance of the teacher as authority becomes the second level of indoctrination. Autonomy — being in charge of one's self — is not in the teacher syllabus of most public schools.

Matriculating to the workplace, most young people have already adapted to authoritarian institutions. While people are well socialized to follow orders, they are seldom engaged in the learning of modes of autonomous behavior. More likely, they have learned neither to trust nor to like themselves. Psychologically, the two go together; authoritarian acceptance and self-rejection are reciprocating characteristics of personality. Sociologically, they are necessary conditions for conforming behavior.

Everyday life in most work organizations is stultifying. Rarely is there an opportunity to conceptualize anything better. So one does what one has to do. And by going about one's work, people reaffirm their negative self-conceptions and revalidate the organizational form as something positive.

PARTICIPATION

By itself, no system of decision-making can guarantee social justice. It is a tenet of anarchist theory that social justice is more likely to be obtained through optimizing the participation of the members of an organization or community.

Even an optimum level of participation will not in and of itself mean that: 1) the right decision will be made; 2) the decision will be less arbitrary than one made by a single person; 3) that no one will necessarily suffer as a result.

LEADERSHIP

Anarchy is not without leadership. It is without followership. Anarchists do not deny that a person may be an authority about some technical or practical or intellectual matter. Anarchists do deny that a person may be in authority. An authority may extend leadership in the matter in which s/he is authoritative. But such leadership can never be coercive.

Leadership under anarchism has two other characteristics that leadership in authoritarian organizations does not have. First, it is exercised within an egalitarian framework; that is, it is based not on the presumption that the leader is a superior person but on the presumption that the leader knows more about the subject for which s/he is providing leadership. Second, leadership is exercised within an educative framework. Anarchist leaders attempt to influence outcomes through education, not through issuing directives.

VOLUNTARY ASSOCIATIONS

Sociologists have never been able to fathom 'voluntary associations.' As someone who reviewed the literature and proposed a new classificatory scheme a number of years ago, I think — in retrospect — that social scientists have been intellectually fascinated but confused by the subject. 'Voluntary associations' in the sociologist's special language are those everyday groupings such as garden clubs and civic associations, tenants' unions and softball teams, self-help groups and that ever-present display of animal clubs like the Lions, Elks, Eagles, etc. Organizational theorists typically treat these voluntary associations as something different from the other organizations they study. Why is that? I think it is because they don't correspond with a strictly capitalist model of work or an organizational theorist's model of control.

Sociologists ask with no embarrassment, 'Since member participation isn't based on wage and salary payment how is it that participation exists at all?" How can they explain such puzzling behavior? *Boredom.* Membership helps 'avoid boredom' by providing 'activities' and 'symbolic rewards.' Voluntary association membership is a phe-nomenon stemming from the fickleness of bored people and the ab-sence of a 'high degree of boundary control.' What that means is that people may enter and exit with relative ease.

Now I know of no evidence indicating that membership in volun-tary associations is any more or less transitory than residence or place of employment. I also know of no evidence that would permit a sociolo-gist to assert what the average lifespan of such associations is or was in a given time or place. But should associations live for ever? Should any organization be permanent? Or is longevity a built-in value premise of organizational theorists?

We do know, for example, in the United States alone between 30,000 and 40,000 formal business organizations fail each year, if we take bankruptcy as a criterion. And thousands more simply close down for a variety of other reasons. Organizational theorists seem to be rather unconcerned about these. This is, presumably, the natural outcome of a market economy. And what sociologists study are the survivors of organizational competition. Thus, permanence appears to be an issue only with regard to voluntary associations.

Voluntary associations are viewed also as relatively more in-effective than formal organizations: The nature of most voluntary organizations means that the notion of command and control by top management is unusual in these organizations.

In case the premises underlying the sociological analysis are not clear, let me state them directly. First, the primary incentive for organ-izational participation is money. Second, in addition, effective partici-pation requires some form of entrance exam and some obstacles to leaving that are built into the organizational structure. Finally, effec-tive organizations have a central command and control unit that can require sustained action on the part of their membership.

Another general critique of voluntary associations, and one that appears in most texts, is that they become more formal over time. That is, they become larger, develop a division of labor, a hier-archy, a paid staff, routine procedures and so on. This ostensibly simple, noncontroversial generalization, in fact, masks a complex of ideological presuppositions.

To begin with, the statement is probably neither entirely true nor entirely false. Some associations have grown and become formal-ized, and some have not. Why make a point about those that have? I think that there is a good reason why sociologists do so. If voluntary associations become formal organizations, and if this is construed as a natural tendency, then they no longer constitute an intellectual prob-

Reinventing Anarchy, Again

lem. That is, they either die or become formalized. Now this may not be good theory or rigorous science, but it is a way of writing off a social phenomenon that does not easily fit the political economics of organizational thought.

Organizations that expand and move to paid positions are surely by conventional criteria a 'success.' On the other hand, the anarchist critic would argue that becoming larger, expanding specialization of the membership, and even hiring a paid staff may well be erroneous decisions; and that these are indicators of failure. For the anarchist organizer, one criterion of success might be that the membership help other people organize their own voluntary associations. For example, instead of becoming larger, the membership would limit itself but assist others in building their own autonomous associations.

BECOMING FULLY HUMAN

People who work 'together' in large formal organizations sometimes have difficulty in recognizing their co-workers in other contexts. They are frequently surprised at discovering that people they have worked with for years have 'hidden' interests and talents; that they are real people. The regulation of behavior in the workplace is designed to suppress genuine personal relations. For the manager, this ostensibly increases people's work time and productivity. It also decreases the likelihood of worker solidarity.

People have to learn how not to be sociable, starting with the extraordinary efforts of many parents in teaching children to avoid strangers. At the adult level, privacy becomes the symbolic reward for achievement. At higher levels of achievement, it may mean one's own toilet in one's own lavatory in one's own office; eventually a stove, refrigerator, bar and bed — and the top executive need never have an accidentally non-private moment in her or his corporate life.

The reward of privacy serves a vital political function: it insulates the manager from personal contact with workers. Thus the workers can be treated as objects.

The discipline of a workforce has its roots in personal self-denial. Play is subversive to formal organizations.

Organizational sociologists don't like to talk about it. It has defied social theorists, and its occurrences are not predictable. There is no room for play in the theories of formal organization.

As a revolutionary tactic, the anarchist advocates the introduction of play into all formal organizations. As a component of anarchist theory, the relation of work and play is an unresolved equation. As the meaning of work becomes transformed in the process of building anarchist organizations, so the relation of work and play will be changed. These initial theoretical principles would probably be contained in an anarchist theory. Work becomes play to the extent that:

- it is not a matter of survival, or otherwise coercive;
- it is not producing commodities primarily to be exchanged for something else;
- the conditions and process of work are controllable by the worker;
- it is intrinsically satisfying.

(the beginning)

THE ANARCHIST CONTRACT

ROBERT GRAHAM

> The state is not something which can be destroyed by a revolution, but is a condition, a certain relationship between human beings, a mode of human behavior; we destroy it by contracting other relationships, by behaving differently.
>
> — Gustav Landauer

Freedom of contract has long been the rallying cry of proponents of "free enterprise" opposed to all manner of government regulation. Some have even translated their opposition to government interference with the economy into opposition to government as such, placing their faith in the "free market" as the solution to all social ills.

Yet some have gone even further, arguing that freedom of contract is not only incompatible with all forms of government, but with all forms of domination and exploitation, including "free market" systems based on the private ownership and control of the economy. These are the anarchist advocates of contract.

They argue that underlying the notion of contract are two fundamentally subversive ideas, freedom and equality. Any contract which fails to maintain the freedom and equality of the contracting parties is, from their point of view, inherently illegitimate. It is only to the extent that contract secures freedom and equality that it receives its justification.

The anarchist notion of contract can be seen as the natural extension of the liberal conception of society as a voluntary association of free and equal individuals. The abolition of all involuntary, coercive and unequal relationships by means of contract is just the final step in the movement from status to contract which began in Europe during the revolutionary struggles against royal absolutism, a step which liberals themselves are no longer willing to take.

As liberalism has become the official doctrine of the capitalist state, its commitment to its original ideals has become weaker and weaker, to the point of almost complete abandonment. Liberals are no longer so much concerned with determining which institutions and practices are compatible with individual freedom and equality as they are concerned to justify existing power relationships. In the process, their notion of contract has been reduced to a largely rhetorical device, the primary purpose of which is to legitimate unequal and coercive relationships, all in the name of a specious individual liberty.

Where the liberal seeks to justify subordination and inequality by making them appear the result of contracts entered voluntarily by free and equal individuals, the anarchist decries as a fraud both the process and the result.

To portray the parties to an employment contract, for example, as free and equal to each other is to ignore the serious inequality of bargaining power which exists between the worker and the employer. To then go on to portray the relationship of subordination and exploitation which naturally results as the epitome of freedom is to make a mockery of both individual liberty and social justice.

The anarchist advocates of contract argue that contract will become a genuine expression of individual freedom and equality only where people are sufficiently equal to each other that none will ever be in the position of having to sell him or herself to another. Freedom and equality must be the basis of contract, not merely the largely fictitious result. Only then will contract really serve as a means of creating and maintaining a society in which people freely associate together in accordance with their individual desires and the principles of justice.

Contract then, from an anarchist perspective, should perform a dual function. Its primary purpose is to ensure individual liberty by substituting voluntary contractual relationships for all relationships based upon any form of coercion, whether it is the economic coercion exercised by the capitalist over the worker or the political and legal coercion imposed on individuals by the state. Its secondary purpose is to eliminate economic exploitation and to ensure economic justice through the equivalent exchange of products between free and equal producers.

In a "free market" system based on private ownership, massive disparities in wealth develop because the workers are forced by economic necessity to sell their labor to the capitalist at a price which does not reflect its real value. Associated together, the workers create a "collective force" greater than the sum of their individual capacities, but it is the capitalist who reaps the benefit.

Only when the workers become entitled to the full product of their labor will economic freedom and justice be achieved. Workers will then be able to exchange their products directly between themselves for products of equivalent value. No longer will anyone be in a position to exploit the needs of others for his or her own superior advantage. Instead, contract will become a means of exchange between free and equal individuals which imposes reciprocal obligations on the parties to their mutual benefit.

The purposes of such contracts need not be limited to economic matters. They may include social or political objectives as well. The important thing is that whatever the specific nature or purpose of the contract, the parties must be of roughly equal bargaining power, and what they exchange must be of equal value, so that everyone benefits equally from the exchange and no one becomes so powerful as to dominate the others.

Only then can it be said that the terms of the contract have been freely accepted by all the parties to the agreement, and only then is it likely that the effect of the contract will be to maintain everyone's freedom and equality. For when everyone is roughly equal to each other, no one will any longer be in a position where he or she will have no choice but to accept the terms of a contract which results in his or her own exploitation or domination.

In political terms, this notion of contract as a free agreement based on equivalent exchange necessarily excludes the idea of government. Government, despite the claims of the social contract theorists, is not based on free agreement. Rather, the anarchists claim, it is a coercive imposition.

According to social contract theorists, society and the state should be conceived as having been created by a voluntary agreement between free and equal individuals. In the "state of nature" which exists prior to this agreement, each person's freedom is under constant threat, so they claim, because there is no authority to prevent anyone from violating the rights and liberties of each other.

To escape this wretched condition, people agree to submit themselves to a state authority which will then secure and protect their individual rights and liberties. The state ensures that people will abide by their commitments and refrain from violating the rights and liberties of others. Because the benefits of creating a state are allegedly so obvious, social contract theorists assume that the agreement to create the state must have been unanimous. Everyone has a positive obligation to obey the commands of the state because everyone has, in one way or another, agreed to do so.

Social contract theorists have shown great imagination in detailing the ways in which one can bind oneself to state authority, from voting to accepting social benefits. Some have even gone so far as to argue that the agreement to obey the laws of the state can be inferred from the mere fact of living in society, on the pretext that this indicates acceptance of state authority in exchange for the benefits which purportedly result from the creation of the state.

Anarchists have never been much impressed by these sorts of arguments. In the first place, even if it could be plausibly argued that everyone has agreed to the "social contract," what it really amounts to is the sacrificing of individual liberty, not the securing of it, in exchange for state protection. Once that fateful exchange is made the individual must obey whatever the state commands, a condition which can hardly be described as one of freedom. That people may have a right to vote does not alter the fact that they may be required to submit to laws to which they have never expressly agreed and which they may actively oppose.

Where the parties to the contract are unequal to each other, what is in fact secured by the social contract is that very inequality, which is now protected by force of law. The rich need no longer fear being deprived of their possessions by the poor because the state will protect everyone's property rights. For those who lack property, it is difficult to see the attraction of this bargain.

It is absurd to claim that by virtue of their passive acceptance of this institutionalized inequality the disadvantaged have assumed an obligation to obey the laws which serve to maintain their unequal status. Acquiescence to state authority may be based on any number of factors, from fear and intimidation to the lack of any viable alternatives, none of which may indicate support for the state or the social order which it upholds.

Not only is the social contract an historical fiction, it is a conceptual impossibility. If prior to the creation of the state people really had lived in a "state of nature" in which they were constantly at each other's throats, the very notion of a social contract would have been inconceivable. In conditions of such great uncertainty and conflict, the social practice of contracting with others would never arise because no one would have any reason to expect that anyone else would ever fulfill the terms of a contract which he or she may have entered.

The idea of making commitments to others and abiding by them would only occur to people involved in on-going social relationships based on at least a minimal degree of trust. Before one can enter a contract with others, one must share a common language or means of communication. Only people who share a common conception of what it means to contract will understand what is expected of themselves and of others when they enter into one. Society is the basis, not the result, of contract.

Moreover, the ability to enter contractual relations with others presupposes a level of individual development and self-awareness which can only be achieved within society. For a contract to be a genuine agreement, it must be the result of critical, informed and uncorked choice. Such a level of individual autonomy is only possible in certain social conditions. Autonomous contracting agents do not appear out of nowhere. The free and equal individual of the social contract is the product, not the author, of society.

In place of the fiction of the social contract, anarchists propose that all associations are based on contracts which have actually been negotiated and agreed to by all of the members of the association. Such contracts of association must expressly reserve the rights and liberties of the parties, including the right to vary the terms of the contract of association and the freedom to withdraw from the association itself.

However, that individual autonomy is a social artifact points to a potential problem with the anarchist ideal of society as a voluntary association of free and equal individuals. Contractual relationships presuppose a sphere of noncontractual relationships, such as the family, in which the individual develops the moral and social capacities necessary to engage in the social practice of contracting. Anarchists must be careful to ensure that this noncontractual sphere does not replicate the relations of inequality and subordination which they oppose in other spheres of society. This requires a genuine commitment to nonsexist and nonhierarchical personal relationships.

Central to the anarchist notion of contract is the concept of equivalent exchange. Yet many anarchists have come to reject this notion, while remaining committed to the idea of free agreement, the other aspect of the anarchist contract. They argue that the notion of equivalent exchange is confused and unworkable when applied in the economic sphere, while it is inappropriate and inapplicable to noneconomic relationships.

One of the central problems confronting advocates of equivalent exchange is to arrive at a common standard by which to determine something's true value. Without such a standard, it is impossible to determine whether the parties to a contract have agreed to exchange something of equivalent value and thereby stand to benefit equally from the exchange.

That this whole manner of evaluation is inapplicable to agreements which do not involve an exchange of goods should be readily apparent. People can and do freely assume obligations the fulfillment of which is not dependent on the receipt of some equivalent benefit, as when someone promises to help another person with no expectation of reward.

To require the receipt of some benefit for an agreement to be binding would be to reduce all voluntary social relationships to a series of self-interested bargains. People would only keep their agreements when it was to their advantage, and break them whenever it was not. Social life would be robbed of its spontaneity as people would engage in an endless series of calculations of their individual benefit in which there would be no place for love, generosity or genuine concern for others.

Even if the notion of equivalent exchange were held applicable only to economic contracts involving an exchange of goods, similar problems would arise. Those who were unable, for whatever reason, to produce goods with an appreciable exchange value would have to rely on the charity of others who would have no obligation and no reason to assist them. Although, strictly speaking, this would involve no exploitation of the economically disabled, in terms of individual autonomy and well-being they would clearly be in a far worse position than the economic producers, and completely dependent on the latter's goodwill.

Those anarchists who endorse the notion of equivalent exchange are primarily concerned with eliminating economic exploitation. They have searched for a standard for measuring economic value which accurately reflects the moral worth of the individual producer's labor so as to ensure that the producers receive what they truly deserve. That search has been in vain.

When labor itself is treated as the basis for exchange, as some anarchists advocate, its market value, even if uniform, will not necessarily reflect either the moral worth of the individual worker's labor or the social utility of the product itself. An individual worker may spend considerable time and effort producing something with little or no exchange value. Other workers, in suitably favorable circumstances, may be able to produce highly valued goods with ease.

The disparity in value may very well be due to factors which are beyond individual control and for which the workers are not personally responsible, such as better access to markets and resources and more advanced technology. Because these economic advantages can never be evenly distributed, it is impossible to devise a system in which economic reward matches individual desert.

The concept of individual desert is itself highly problematic. If the instruments of labor, the means of distribution and exchange and the capacity to labor itself are the collective products of society, as most anarchists agree, then it is impossible to determine the actual moral worth of any particular person's contribution to the economy. So even if individual desert provided a fair basis for distributing wealth, a claim which itself is open to question, in a society of any degree of complexity such a scheme is simply unworkable.

This is but one of the reasons why many anarchists now advocate distribution according to need and advocate the complete abolition of wage labor. Another reason is to ensure that the agreements people do make are freely entered into. Where people are guaranteed the satisfaction of their needs, it will no longer be necessary for them to agree to certain courses of action simply to ensure their own survival. Instead, they will be free to choose whatever suits them best.

More importantly, they will no longer have to seek to maximize their own advantage through competition with others. They can freely give themselves unto others with no expectation of reward, giving free reign to spontaneity and their most generous feelings. Any contracts or agreements which they may wish to enter will become the public expression of free choice between persons whose relationships are characterized by cooperation and mutual aid instead of the maneuvering for competitive advantage found in capitalist society.

Some individualist anarchists go a step further and argue that the very notion of contract as free agreement should also be done away with. The problem with contract, from their point of view, is that it requires someone to act according to prior commitments rather than his or her present understanding or choice. The notion of a "free agreement" is a contradiction in terms, they claim, because the obligations which result from an agreement constrain future liberty of action and initiative just as much as economic necessity may constrain one's present choice.

Anarchists who endorse free agreement reply that far from conflicting with individual autonomy, the obligations which arise from truly free agreements presuppose it. To enter an agreement and to assume an obligation to perform a certain act requires making reasoned choices and critically evaluating the various courses of action which are open to one. The terms of the agreement, and therefore the content of any resulting obligation, are defined by the person making it.

It is always open to a person who has assumed an obligation by means of free agreement to re-evaluate his or her commitments and, if necessary, to change them. It is a mistake to think that the self-assumed obligations which arise from various forms of free agreement, whether contracts or promises, are binding in the same sense that laws are. Laws are binding in the sense that they are enforced by some sort of political authority. Yet one can freely assume an obligation by agreeing to perform a certain action without this entailing any form of coercion.

Whether the failure to abide by an agreement results in the application of a coercive sanction depends on the existence of some sort of enforcement agency, not on the nature of the obligations which may result from entering the agreement. Absent such coercive institutions, nothing prevents people from continuing to exercise their critical judgment after assuming an obligation by means of free agreement, or from later deciding that, all things considered, it ought not to be performed.

Those anarchists who oppose any kind of obligation as an infringement of individual liberty would perhaps respond that this is to confuse the process with the result. Although the act of making an agreement may presuppose a certain level of individual autonomy, the resulting obligations may nevertheless be completely incompatible with it, as when someone agrees to obey the commands of another. That people may freely agree to forfeit their autonomy is sufficient, in their view, to justify completely dispensing with any notion of obligation itself. After all, is it not by appeal to some notion of obligation that the social contract theorists attempt to justify the authority of the state?

Anarchists who endorse free agreement look at things differently. They conceive of obligation, freely assumed, more as an extension of individual autonomy than as a limitation to it. Through cooperation with others on the basis of free agreement and association, individuals expand their scope of action and initiative. Free association is seen as a form of collective self-empowerment, as a way of uniting various individuals on a strictly voluntary basis for the mutually beneficial satisfaction of their many needs and interests. Through the creation of social relationships of reciprocal obligation, free association gives expression to and reaffirms human solidarity and community.

Underlying this disagreement are differing conceptions of individuality and community. For individualist anarchists, association and cooperation of any sort threaten individual autonomy, because they require individuals to conform their actions to the needs and expectations of others, so that they may work in concert. Yet by opposing association and cooperation, the individualist anarchists deprive people of any means of transcending their individual circumstances through solidarity with others.

There can be no prospect of genuine community in a society composed of isolated individuals concerned only with their own interests. It is doubtful that there would be any society at all. In the absence of any on-going social relationships, the "autonomous individual" would cease to exist, as there would be no human society from which such an individual would be able to emerge. It is a mistake to conceive of freedom and autonomy as merely the absence of coercion or constraint; they are kinds of social relationships. This fundamental error effectively relegates the individualist anarchist ideal to the realm of intellectual fantasy.

However, anarchists who favor free agreement do not go to the other extreme and argue that one must always fulfill one's obligations. They argue that in so far as the process by which an agreement is reached, or the content of the agreement itself, is incompatible with the anarchist ideals of freedom and community, no binding obligation can arise from it. Between worker and capitalist there can be no free agreement because of the inequalities of power existing between them. Particular social preconditions must exist before it can be said that agreements genuinely have been freely entered into, namely equal well-being for all and the abolition of all hierarchical social relationships.

Promises to obey, contracts of (wage) slavery, agreements requiring the acceptance of a subordinate status, are all illegitimate because they do constrict and restrain individual autonomy. But far from justifying the complete rejection of the notion of self-assured obligation, this merely emphasizes the continuing need for people to exercise their critical judgment and choice when deciding whether an obligation ought to be assumed or performed.

Individualist anarchists originally isolated obligation as the underlying concept which gave social contract theory its particular force as a justification of political authority. They would argue that by accepting the notion of obligation, the anarchist advocates of free agreement leave open the possibility that some forms of political authority are legitimate, thereby fatally compromising their anarchism. In fact, in *The Problem of Political Obligation*, the feminist political theorist, Carole Pateman, has argued that the notion of self-assumed obligation provides a conceptual basis for a theory of direct, or self-managing, democracy.

Direct democratic voting can be seen as the political counterpart of promising or free agreement. By directly voting in favor of a particular law or proposal, the individual citizen assumes an obligation to abide by it. The citizen, in concert with others, defines the content of his or her political obligations, and in so doing must exercise critical judgment and choice. Political obligation in this context is not owed to a separate entity above society, such as the state, but to one's fellow citizens.

Although the assembled citizens collectively legislate the rules governing their association, and are bound by them as individuals, they are also superior to them in the sense that these rules can always be modified or repealed. Collectively the associated citizens can be said to constitute a kind of political authority, but their authority is based on horizontal relationships of obligation between themselves, rather than on the vertical relationship existing between the individual and the state.

The citizens do not exchange their obedience for the protection of the state, as in the social contract, but create reciprocal relationships of obligation in their collective undertakings and social life, from the workplace to the community, on the basis of their own voluntary choice. Each vote constitutes an express renewal of the social compact, which may be dissolved at the will of the parties, who remain free to dissociate from each other.

Society is conceived as a complex web of directly democratic voluntary associations. This scheme remains anarchist in the sense that there is no central authority, or state, claiming sovereignty over the various associations. Rather there is an association of associations, each having a directly democratic structure, freely federated with one another.

If this scheme looks familiar, it should, for it closely resembles the anarchist theory of federation. The relationship between anarchism and democratic theory has always been ambiguous. Many anarchists have advocated the application of democratic principles in the voluntary groups which they see as the base units of a future free society. Yet anarchists have claimed to reject all political authority, denouncing the tyranny of the majority and the fraud of universal suffrage.

Critics of anarchism would claim that this merely demonstrates the conceptual incoherence of anarchism. But if one conceives of direct democratic voting as an expression and extension of self-assumed obligation, as Pateman does, then this supposed incoherence disappears. It is perfectly consistent for the anarchist proponents of free agreement to support direct democracy when it is conceived as giving political expression to the ideals of self-assumed obligation and individual autonomy which they support. While this may commit the anarchists to some sort of political authority, it is not the same kind of authority as that claimed by the state.

The political authority claimed by the state is hierarchical, coercive, and monopolistic. The state is necessarily authoritarian. It is not a voluntary association created by free agreement, but a compulsory body exercising authority over everyone whom it asserts falls within its jurisdiction, regardless of their individual consent. The most it offers its subjects is the opportunity to elect their rulers during periodic elections. The content of the law, and hence of the citizen's political obligations, is decided by someone else. The political obligation owed by the citizen to the state is not and cannot be self-assumed.

When anarchists denounce universal suffrage as the counter-revolution they do not necessarily denounce democracy as a whole. Universal suffrage, by itself, is counterrevolutionary because it gives the people the illusion of self-government when in fact they remain subject to the authority of the state. Parliamentary forms of democracy score no great advance beyond aristocratic forms of government because the essentially hierarchical structure of political authority remains intact.

It is for this reason that anarchists have also denounced the socialist "people's state" as a dangerous illusion, because it still retains the distinction between the ruler and the ruled, a distinction which can only lead to the domination of the governed masses. Charges that anarchism is anti-democratic betray a confusion between parliamentary and direct democracy, between obligations which are imposed and those which are self-assumed.

Some confusion regarding the anarchist attitude to democracy results from the anarchists' own concern that democracy, no matter how direct, may constitute a new form of domination by the majority over the minority, and is therefore unacceptable. The question which then arises is whether the idea of direct democracy is necessarily tied to the concept of majority rule. If direct democracy is conceived as a form of self-assumed obligation, as in Pateman's scheme, then clearly it is not.

People who find themselves in a minority on a particular vote, or who abstain completely, are confronted with the choice either of consenting to the majority decision or of refusing to recognize it as binding on them. To deny the minority the opportunity to exercise its independent judgment and choice is to infringe its autonomy and to impose obligations upon it which it has not freely accepted. The coercive imposition of the majority will is completely contrary to the ideal of self-assumed obligation itself.

We can begin to see then how the notion of self-assumed obligation and the political implications of that notion help to clarify a number of issues confronting anarchist theory and practice. Self-assumed obligation is one of the ideas underlying notions of contract and free agreement which gives them their peculiar attraction and force. By recognizing the implicit role of self-assumed obligation in anarchist theory it is possible to make sense of the anarchists' ambivalent response to democracy.

As anarchists have abandoned the notion of contract as equivalent exchange, the notion of contract as free agreement has come to the fore, pointing the way to a new conception of direct democracy which is both radical and anti-authoritarian, helping to show us the way in which we may, in Landauer's words, destroy the state by contracting other relationships.

Sources

Robert Graham, "The Role of Contract in Anarchist Ideology," in *For Anarchism: History, Theory and Practice*, ed. David Goodway (Routledge: London, 1989).

Carole Pateman, *The Problem of Political Obligation: A Critique of Liberal Theory* (Cambridge : Polity Press, 1985).

3

MOVING TOWARD
ANARCHIST SOCIETY

graphic from **Stealworks: The Graphic Details of John Yates**

RESERVED FOR DOCTORS	THOU SHALT NOT PARK HERE	DON'T EVEN THINK OF PARKING HERE	NO PARKING ANY TIME	NO PARKING DRIVE WAY
NO PARKING OR STOPPING	NO STOPPING OR STANDING	NO PARKING PRIVATE DRIVE	NO PARKING THIS SIDE	NO PARKING

NO PARKING HERE TO CORNER	 NO PARKING ⟷	ANY TIME	 NO PARKING	FIRE LANE

ONE HOUR PARKING	AUTHORIZED VEHICLES ONLY	COMPANY VEHICLES ONLY	RESERVED FOR CAR	PRIVATE PARKING
COMPACT CARS ONLY	UNAUTHORIZED VEHICLES WILL BE TOWED AWAY AT OWNER'S EXPENSE	ADDITIONAL PARKING IN REAR		NOT LOCK DELIVERY

Introduction To
Moving Toward Anarchist Society

In the final section of the book, we examine the specific tactics that may be required to move toward anarchist societies. In this section our objectives are more philosophical and strategic. Here our focus is on the kinds of questions that anarchists have to consider.

John Clark's essay begins with a consideration of questions of global import. He addresses how anarchists can cope with problems of population size and growth, the scarcity of material goods, and the complexities in the distribution of natural and human resources.

David Bouchier's "Hard questions for social anarchists" is a signal example of the dilemmas faced by all political analysts. The questions Bouchier raises are those we must answer now as we go about our daily lives. These are the questions dealing with modernity and technology, equality and community, individual freedom, conflict and violence, and social change. He points to the way. The answers are ours.

In a classic model of political writing, **Brian Martin** presents a detailed critique of voting and elections and their function in maintaining the legitimacy of the state. Martin focuses on three critiques of elections: they don't work for challenging the prevailing systems of power; they divert people from direct action and as a consequence disempower people; and they depend on and reinforce the legitimacy and power of the state. He reminds us that "elections empower the politicians and not the voters."

Martin goes on to consider alternatives to elections and their problems. His discussion includes the use of referenda, consensus decision-making, reductions in group size, and federations and delegate systems.

In the final section, he introduces the concept of "demarchy," which is defined as "a random selection of individuals to serve in decision-making groups which deal with particular functions or services." These limited domain groups are seen as replacing the state and state bureaucracies.

The strength of these two essays is their ability to raise questions about issues which are so fundamental that few people are even aware that these were problematic areas. Even more significant is the fact that they present their critique while at the same time pointing to options and alternatives that can guide people to action.

Anarchism and the Present World Crisis

John Clark

WE ARE NOW AT A POINT in history at which the need for a new political vision is becoming acutely evident. In the industrialized West, we find increasing dissatisfaction with traditional political options and a loss of faith in formal democracy. This dissatisfaction has manifested itself thus far primarily through a process of depolitization in which there has been a drastic loss of confidence in political parties and non-voting on a massive scale. In the East, we find a growing movement of dissent, which challenges the Marxist orthodoxy, often silently, through withdrawal of allegiance and cooperation, sometimes dramatically, in periodical revolt. And in both West and East we find in many countries and to varying degrees a cultural opposition which vaguely, yet perhaps prophetically, points to the need for a new unifying vision.

One premise of the present discussion is that this disillusionment with both liberal capitalism and state socialism is justified. The prevailing world systems, in this view, no longer over us a hopeful prospect of resolving the vast social and ecological crises which now confront humanity. In fact, it is becoming increasingly clear that these systems, with their deep commitment to such values as industrialism, high technology, centralism, urbanization, and the state, have been instrumental in creating the social atomization and ecological imbalance which are at the core of these crises. For this reason, what is necessary is an alternative vision of society, the future, and indeed reality itself: a vision which departs from the traditional ideologies on all these fundamental questions. This vision, I will argue, is anarchism.

In discussing the anarchist approach to the present world crisis, I will focus on some of the objections which opponents of anarchism have raised to the view that it can be a viable global strategy. In particular, I will deal with the points made by Alan Wertheimer in his analysis of "the case for anarchy" in the recent *Nomos* volume on anarchism.[1] In his essay, Wertheimer contends that anarchism is unable to successfully deal with four presently existing world social conditions. These are: 1) that "the population of the earth is (perhaps) too large, but increasing at a rapid rate with no immediate prospect for a serious reduction"; 2) that "in much of the world, basic human needs are not being satisfied"; 3) that "the world's natural and human resources are not evenly distributed across the globe"; and, finally 4) that "the present level of subsistence is based on a high level of social and economic interdependence among various regions of the world and also within the regions themselves."[2] In addition, Wertheimer contends that anarchism is unable to cope with conflicts between individual self-interest and social needs, particularly as this relates to the question of defense.

In considering the anarchist response to these problems, it is important to understand the meaning of the term "anarchism." What I take here to be anarchism is a tradition of theory and practice which has developed and evolved within an actually existing historical movement (calling itself the "anarchist movement") over the past century and a half. I take this movement to have at its present stage of development such guiding principles as the rejection of all forms of domination; the acceptance of forms of human interaction based on cooperation, autonomy, and respect for the person; and insofar as its underlying ontological premises are systematically developed, an organicist, ecological view of society, nature, and reality in general. In practice (and this is the main focus of the present essay) these principles lead anarchists to propose such policies as the replacement of nation-states by federations of communal and workplace associations; replacement of corporate capitalist and state ownership by self-management of production by the producers; replacement of the patriarchal authoritarian family by libertarian family and living arrangements; replacement of the megalopolis and centralized population distribution by decentralized, ecologically balanced population patterns; and replacement of centralized, high technology by more humanly scaled alternative technologies, which are compatible with decentralized, democratic decision making, and which are not destructive of the social and natural environments. These principles have been developed considerably by the mainstream of anarchist theory, beginning with Bakunin and Kropotkin, and by the historical anarchist movement in its predominating anarcho-syndicalist and anarcho-communist forms. Yet an equally great contribution to this development has been made by a related libertarian tradition, which has been called "utopian" and "communalist," and is represented by such social theorists as Fourier, Gustav Landauer, and Martin Buber. These two lines of development have reached a synthesis and, I believe, their most advanced stage of theoretical development in contemporary communal-ecological anarchism, which is the form being defended here.[3]

POPULATION PROBLEMS: DENSITY AND GROWTH

THE POPULATION QUESTION POSES several problems for the anarchist position . One of the most basic is the issue of whether anarchistic forms of social organization are even possible in societies with either absolutely large populations or high levels or population density. According to one line of criticism, systems of law (and indeed extensive ones) are unavoidable in highly populated societies. For this reason, anarchy, which assumes the absence of a legal system, cannot be workable in these societies.[4]

It is important to emphasize that anarchists recognize the necessity for *rule-making* in all societies. The important consideration is not whether there shall be rules, but rather the level at which the rules are made, the processes used to determine them, and the nature and extent of the rules themselves. Anarchists argue that whenever feasible, voluntary rule-making, through processes like arbitration and consensus, should be used. But since this is often not possible, the next step is to develop systems of rule-making through democratic processes at the communal level (although many decisions will no doubt be left to even smaller groups and to individuals if the community is to maintain its libertarian character). This communal democracy may be interpreted as requiring formal systems of local law which can, insofar as communities are in agreement, be extended in scope through federation. There is, however, a strong tendency to favor case-by-case consideration of issues by local assemblies and popular judicial bodies, much on the model of some aspects of the Greek polis and certain tribal decision-making processes. There do not seem to be any obvious reasons why such systems of decentralist and federative rule making could not be developed in some form in highly populated societies.

But even if possible, can this decentralized decision-making be practical in such societies? In fact, there is evidence that the relative advantages may be greater in the more complex, highly populated societies. As value and interest conflicts multiply with population growth and urbanization, the centralized state apparatus becomes increasingly more inept as a means of coping with rapidly proliferating crisis situations. The typical tactic of the state is to expand bureaucratization and centralized planning, which results in further dissociation between the planning mechanism and social reality. Increasingly particularized problems are confronted in an increasingly generalized manner. Decentralized and federative decision-making, on the other hand, is inherently more capable of dealing with complexity since it is itself complex and diversified. Multiplication of loci of problems calls for a corresponding multiplication of loci of information-gathering, discussion, and decision-making.

There are, however, alternative approaches available to the centralized state. One is to incorporate more decentralized mechanisms into the overall centralized structure. Given the strong centralist economic and political tendencies of contemporary society, it is not surprising that such attempts are usually superficial and ineffective (not, for example, the degree of bureaucratization and economic concentration under supposedly "anti-bureaucratic" Republican administrations in post-war America). Another possibility is to resort to increased authoritarian and repressive controls, given the disintegration of traditional internalized controls and the failure of bureaucratic methods of problem-solving and control. This will become a more appealing option as social atomization continues its development and crisis situations become more severe. Significantly, the process of bureaucratization itself contributes neatly to the simplification and atomization of society. It could be argued that if this process were allowed to reach its perfection, then centralized bureaucratic processes would be the most appropriate structure for society. Yet this success for bureaucracy would be won at the expense of the complete dissolution of the organic fabric of society, a price that few would wish to pay. For the above reasons, anarchists argue that decentralized decision-making is a more adequate response to the size and complexity of society, and also that it is more desirable in terms of preserving what is of value in social complexity.

This should not be taken to imply, however, that the anarchist sees a high level of urbanization or high densities of population as in any way desirable. There are many kinds of social and ecological complexity. The cultural diversity of ethnically variegated urban areas may embody a social value which can be preserved during the process of deurbanization. On the other hand, the sort of complexity entailed in planning transportation systems, or protecting the environment in areas where over concentration makes these problems virtually insoluble, is a complexity which is dispensable. So the problem of overpopulation must be solved, and anarchist decentralism is an attempt at a solution. The question of the anarchist approach to the problem of the numerically high level of population in relation to ecological constraints will be investigated shortly. This is necessary since anarchist strategies would be obviously unrealistic if they demanded a much lower *global* density of population than that presently existing, or could not cope with the high rate of growth that will be inevitable for some time. It should be noted first, however, that decentralization of population does not demand an overall low density of population. It is well known that many Third World countries, in which population is primarily dispersed in villages, have a higher density of population nationally than many other countries in which the population is concentrated in urban centers. Furthermore, there is anthropological evidence that societies with economic and political systems more loosely organized than those proposed by contemporary anarchists have had rather high densities of population. [5] It can be argued that decentralist policies increase the level of population that can be maintained within a given area, in view of the decreased ecological stress which results from dispersion of population, industry, waste production, etc. (assuming the practicality of decentralist technology) .

This does not mean, of course, that anarchists look with equanimity at levels of population growth which threaten to rapidly strain the limits of our planet's capacity to support human life, or that they merely hope to increase this capacity through decentralization. So a second, and more important, question arises: can there be anarchist strategies to limit population growth so as to stabilize population at a level most conducive to human well-being and optimal ecological balance? As Wertheimer points out, "while we preach birth control, the Indian peasant continues to propagate children in order that he have help in working in the fields and in order that someone will survive to take care of him when he is too old and infirm to take care of himself."[6] Though he may understand the disastrous social consequences of his action, can we expect him to do otherwise than mitigate his own suffering? Consequently, the argument continues, a rational population policy with state powers of enforcement is necessary.

This argument is based, however, on a false dilemma. The apparent alternatives are anarchic reproduction (which is in fact not "anarchic" in the anarchist sense, but rather controlled by the prevailing hierarchical and inegalitarian socioeconomic system), and controlled reproduction (which is subject to the additional control of the coercive apparatus of the state). But these are far from the only alternatives and neither would be advocated by anarchists. They advocate instead that in societies like India the social and economic system be thoroughly transformed, although in ways which are more compatible with village population distribution and traditional methods of production than are centralist governmental policies. Furthermore, they maintain that state policies aimed at preservation of the existing economic system while instituting compulsory birth control (along with promoting urbanization and high technology, under the Indira Gandhi regime) will only perpetuate the present level of misery and exploitation, while aggravating the damaging ecological effects of overpopulation. The anarchist approach to peasant societies in which tenancy or small-holding predominates requires the replacement of these forms by cooperative cultivation of the soil by associations of producers. When such a system is instituted, the members of the associations are in a position to overcome their previously quite understandable concern for maximizing the labor supply and they can then provide for their old age and undertake other social welfare measures by the cooperative regulation of their surplus production. This is, of course, based on the assumption that the technology for adequate cooperative production is available (an assumption that will be discussed shortly) and that if the surplus now diverted to native and external ruling classes is reclaimed, then the needs of the producers can better be fulfilled. The essential point in the context of the present discussion is that the anarchist approach to problems of overpopulation implies conscious social reorganization and cannot be equated with "libertarian" inactivity or mere moralistic encouragement. [7]

THE PROBLEM OF SCARCITY

Anarchism has always concerned itself with the problem of scarcity. Much of the appeal of anarchism to the peasants of Spain, the Ukraine, and other countries lay in its vision of greater abundance based on libertarian communalism and production for real needs. Recent anarchist theory, as exemplified by Murray Bookchin's classic *Post-Scarcity Anarchism*, has taken the question of scarcity as a central one for political theory But, of course, the important question is not whether anarchists have at times convinced large numbers of people, nor whether they have been concerned with the problem, but rather whether they have evidence that their approach of decentralized production and alternative technologies is workable.

Accordingly to Colin Ward, the proposals for labor-intensive, decentralized food production made by Kropotkin over a century ago have been shown by experience to be quite practical. As he has observed, "the Japanese experience — the evolution from domestic insufficiency, through self-sufficiency, to an embarrassing 'over-produc-tion' — illustrates the technical feasibility of Kropotkin's claims for the enormous productivity of labor-intensive agriculture. The mod-ern horticultural industry in Britain and in the continental countries fully lives up to his expectations. . . ."[8] E. F. Schumacher's Intermedi-ate Technology Group has carried on the tradition of thinkers like Kropotkin and William Morris in developing so-called "appropriate technologies" which will allow developing societies to solve their prob-lems of scarcity and unemployment while avoiding the disastrous con-sequences of heavy industrialization and urbanization. In the United States, groups like the Institute for Local Self-Reliance are exploring possibilities through which impoverished local communities can es-cape from the trap of dependence and economic exploitation by the development of community industrial and agricultural production. David Morris and Karl Hess present a rather detailed picture of some of these possibilities in their book *Neighborhood Power*,[9] which is based in part on their work with such experiments in the Adams-Morgan neighborhood in Washington, D.C. Perhaps the strongest extended argument for the kind of decentralization of production advocated by anarchists since Kropotkin can be found in Lewis Mumford's half-century of work on technology and mechanization." As he writes in *Technics and Civilization:*

> In a balanced economy, regional production of commodities becomes rational production; and inter-regional exchange becomes the export of the surplus from regions of incre-ment to regions of scarcity, or the exchange of special ma-terials and skills. . . . But even here the advantages of a par-ticular place may remain temporary. . . . With the growth of economic regionalism, the advantages of modern indus-try will be spread, not chiefly by transport — as in the nine-teenth century — but by local development.[11]

These few citations do not prove the anarchist case. Yet they do show that the case must be examined, and that it is unconvincing merely to appeal to the reigning ideology of high technology, as if its validity were self-evident.[12]

In discussing the anarchist approach to questions like scarcity and the "standard of living," it is important to note that what is being called for is not mere subsistence, but rather a society of abundance. Anarchists argue that the seeming implausibility of achieving such a society through anarchist forms of production results from a failure to question the ideology of material consumption. If abundance must rely on infinitely expanding productivity and exhaustion of nature as a resource, it obviously can never be achieved. But for anarchists, abundance is to come from the development of social needs and from satisfaction of the desire for a creative and joyful existence. In this connection, they find inspiration for their vision in the richness of symbolic imagination, the depth of communal feeling and the joy of immediate experience in many traditional societies[13] Anarchists emphasize the inability of mere increases in production to raise the qualitative standard of living once the most basic material needs are provided for. To discuss this subject adequately, one would have to deal at length with such themes (common to anarchism and humanistic/libertarian Marxism) as the nature of a society based on the model of human being as consumer, the reduction of human values to commodity values in a consumerist society, and the destruction of the human and natural environments in a society obsessed with commodity production and quantitative growth.

Yet, recognition of these seemingly abstract themes should not lead to a failure to apprehend the practical concern for forms of technological development which combine levels of production sufficiently high to fulfill basic and higher needs with the requirements for a humanly scaled, non-bureaucratic, non-hierarchical social system. What anarchists reject is a simplistic, non-dialectical approach which isolates problems of production, for instance, from the totality of social relationships, or one which sees only the alternatives of continued development of present directions of technical evolution or the immediate destruction of all that has resulted from this development. This either/or approach ignores alternative lines of development of technology and also overlooks alternative strategies for abundance, such as greater sharing of social products as opposed to individualistic consumption, abolition of wasteful consumption resulting from manipulated needs and desires, and the creation of more social needs (in which the growth of needs themselves leads to abundance rather than scarcity) rather than material consumption needs.

In evaluating the relationship between the generation of needs and the nature of various modes of production, the experience of primitive societies is enlightening. Marshall Sahlins has shown that abundance is not something that humanity is just now achieving, or that it will only achieve in the future. Rather, given the prevailing relationship between the system of needs created and the level of production, primitive hunting and gathering societies were in fact the first affluent societies and had surplus production and abundant leisure by modern standards. [14] As Marx demonstrated in his analysis of the creation of needs under capitalist production, the industrial revolution under capitalism only aggravated conditions of scarcity and toil that had arisen with the development of agrarian societies. In view of such historical evidence, it is incorrect to assume that the existence of a society of abundance necessarily has a positive correlation with the existence of large quantities of the kind of consumer goods now produced.

It is true, as Wertheimer contends, that if anarchism "implies a 'polyculturism' in which individuals are free to choose their own values, it is possible that many persons will choose to value the goods which only industrialism makes possible."[15] However, people who live in an anarchist community will find that some such "goods" will only be available if the "goods" that they hold to be the highest ones (freedom, equality, humane relationships, harmony with nature, etc.) are given up. Anarchists certainly believe that people should not be forced to desire egalitarian work relationships over hierarchical structures, non-polluting transportation over powerful cars, alternative energy sources over nuclear power, decentralized ecological communities over throwaway suburbs, and so forth. But in no sense can a society in which people seek hierarchical power, maximum consumption of commodities, and fulfillment of needs produced by advertising be called an anarchist society. For this reason the anarchist analysis discards the liberal theory of wants which takes them as an unexplained given, or as the raw material for the development of social policy. Instead, it investigates the preconditions for "wanting," "desiring," or "needing" and the methods by which people can transform their wants as part of the process of creating a humanly fulfilling, cooperative society.

THE PROBLEM OF DISTRIBUTION

IF THE PRESENT LINE OF ARGUMENT has any merit, anarchist forms of production and "liberatory technology" are capable of fulfilling basic human needs and are compatible with those social forms which lead to the fulfillment of higher ones. But an additional objection arises: even if an anarchist society could reach an adequate level of production, it can be argued that such a society is incapable of achieving an equitable distribution of goods. It is argued, first, that if nation-states are unable to transcend their "narrowness of territoriality," then anarchist communities, with their local basis, can only be expected to be even more narrow; secondly, that inequalities between communities in resources or productivity would result in injustices that could not be rectified; and, finally, that anarchist reliance on "spontaneous" re-distribution is hopeless in view of the severity of the world crisis.

The argument that anarchism leads to narrowness based on lo-cal communalism relies on an exclusive direction of attention to the anarchist emphasis on community control and decentralization and a lack of acknowledgment of the principles of federalism and mutual aid. From the time of Bakunin and Kropotkin, anarchism has stressed the importance of local, national, and global federations of communi-ties and worker collectives. There are two sides to the anarchist rejec-tion of the nation-state: one is communalism and the other is inter-nationalism (if "nation" is taken in its cultural, rather than political sense). Anarchist decentralism is not a mechanistic formula for solv-ing all "social problems." Rather, it is an integral part of a social prac-tice through which humanity can recreate itself in a more personal-ized, self-conscious, and communal form. The anarchist "commune" is a community of people attempting to create relationships and insti-tutions based on an organic, ecological, cooperative view of existence. The relationship between local communalism and global communal-ism is expressed well in the work of Martin Buber, who argues that unless the inhumane, bureaucratic, objectifying relationships created by the state, capitalism, and high technology are replaced by person-alistic, cooperative relationships arising in the primary communal group, it cannot be hoped that people will have a deep concern for humanity as a whole. In Buber's view, unless we can see humanity in our neighbors it is impossible to expect us to overcome that "narrow-ness" which prevents us from acting with a concern for the entire spe-cies. But this is not a mere moral dictum; rather it is a call for communitarian praxis. As Buber states it, "an organic commonwealth — and only such commonwealth can join together to form a shapely and articulated race of men — will never build itself up out of indi-viduals but only out of small and even smaller communities: a nation is a community to the degree that it is a community of communities."[17]

Anarchists contend that to the extent that redistribution is a ne-cessity, it will be encouraged more by the practice of mutual aid through free federation than by the continuation of action by nation-states or by the creation of a world state. Wertheimer never explicitly confronts the question of class; yet a central element of the anarchist case con-cerns the development of class interests in societies based on central-ized bureaucratic forms of organization. The relevant question is whether statist or federalist forms of organization can contribute most to the development of cooperative patterns of thought and action and, to look at the other side of the same issue, whether power does indeed corrupt in proportion to the degree to which it is centralized or concentrated. Anarchist theory asserts that as long as concentrated political or economic power remains, we can expect it to be used in the interest of those who control that power. If we look at history, it might not seem an exaggeration to say that there is some evidence in favor of this view.

We might look, for instance, at the distribution of wealth in societies which have liberal democratic processes and a state to preside over the carrying out of the will of the people. (We will later consider briefly systems outside the liberal-democratic tradition.) In the United States, a nation with the greatest concentration of wealth and one of the longest traditions of liberal democracy, there appears to be virtually no redistribution taking place between economic strata and only a fraction of one percent of the GNP is devoted to aid to poorer countries. [18] It must be conceded that modern liberalism and social democracy have at times taken steps which have had a moderately redistributive effect and that the growth of these ideologies could be expected to lead to an expansion of these programs. Yet, in view of the nature of these proposals (which is hardly a speculative theoretical question, given that liberal and social democratic regimes have been in power in numerous countries), redistribution will be for the foreseeable future primarily a gradual process within nation-states and can only be expected to be achieved on the global level over a long period of time. If, then, we are indeed in a period of crisis in which drastic measures producing redistribution are necessary (as Wertheimer claims), it hardly seems likely that these are the ideologies to which we should look for guidance.

For evidence of the nature of the alternative proposed by anarchists, we can examine the federations established by the anarcho-syndicalists in Spain in 1936. We find that the redistribution which has been largely absent over generations in liberal and social democratic countries took place in a period of a few months in collectivized areas, primarily as a result of the institution of self-managed industry and agriculture. In the short time that the collectives were able to act autonomously, they began to expand this egalitarianism beyond the limits of the individual collectives. According to Gaston Leval, perhaps the most careful student of the Spanish collectives, in areas like Castile and Aragon "the libertarian communist principle was applied not only within each Collective, but between all the Collectives."[19] Leval describes such programs as disaster relief, redistribution of fertilizer and machinery from the wealthier to the poorer collectives, and cooperative seed production for distribution to areas in need. According to Leval, there was an awareness among the collectivists that "having risen above the communalist mentality, the next thing was to overcome the regionalist spirit."[20] The Spanish anarchist experiments of the 1930s were, of course, short-lived and many of the projects initiated were undermined by the Popular Front regime and then crushed, first by the Stalinists (whose "Republican" armies actually invaded the Aragon collectives), and then by the Fascists. But the question still remains whether it is the organizational principles embodied in these collectives and federations, or the organizational principles of the state which deserve most to be developed and expanded to the global level. The guiding assumption behind anarchist proposals for social organization is that unless human beings develop patterns of life and values based on mutual aid at the level of small groups and local communities, one cannot expect them to go very far in the practice of mutual aid at any other level of social organization. This social psychological premise underlies all anarchist arguments for communal federation. Not only is this premise plausible on the basis of such theoretical analyses as Reichian mass-psychology, but it also seems to have the beginnings of a more direct historical verification in Spanish collectivist experience.

Thus far, the discussion has centered around the concept of "redistribution." Yet, this conception has been based, I am afraid, on inadequately critical presuppositions which must be examined further. As Marx points out, the problem of distribution is largely a problem of production. What is a problem of distribution under one system of production is no longer a relevant problem given different relations of production, while some problems of distribution are insoluble given certain systems of production. Wertheimer's formulation of the problem as "redistribution of the world's resources" assumes that the problems of poor societies will be solved by a flow of "resources" from societies of relative abundance to societies of relative scarcity. This hope might be questioned as being unrealistic in view of the nature of international politics, but, more fundamentally, the entire problematic of "redistribution" is based on the questionable assumption of the feasibility of seeking a solution to the problem while continuing a technological system founded on dependency and disproportions in economic power. Anarchists argue that since the technology for liberation now exists, the major problem for poor societies is the carrying through of the process of social transformation in these societies. This process, it is argued, necessitates their economic and political liberation from exploitation by imperialist powers and native ruling classes and their emancipation from patterns of domination transmitted through cultural tradition. The function of an anarchist movement in such societies is seen as the creation of a praxis adequate to displace these groups and structures and to institute liberatory forms in their place. Thus, the economic problem is not

Reinventing Anarchy, Again

seen as the absence of enforced redistribution (which is unlikely to be endorsed by the classes and states which benefit from the exploitation), but rather as the destruction of the undesirable patterns of production which result in the maldistribution and of the ideologies which legitimate the process. It is true, as Wertheimer asserts, that redistribution (like production and distribution in general) will not occur "spontaneously" in the sense that they will occur without planning or strategy. But the point of the anarchist argument is that it is much more likely that more equitable distribution will occur as a result of the self-conscious cooperative efforts of the exploited to change power relationships, than as a consequence of the agreement of exploiting powers to subject themselves to the control of some higher political authority which is to enforce redistribution.

If this analysis is correct, then the real alternative to the anarchist approach appears to be, not a liberal or social democratic optimism about global democracy, but rather Marxism-Leninism, which has enough awareness of the realities of economic power to realize that such a shift in power relationships will inevitably involve a process of global class struggle. But though anarchists may agree that the Marxist-Leninist approach can succeed in significantly reducing the extremes of economic inequality, it is judged to be a failure as a praxis of liberation Among the most important arguments for this conclusion are the following: 1) that the Marxist-Leninist view of social revolution, with its strong commitment to statism and centralism, results in a new state-capitalist and bureaucratic-centralist form of class domination perpetuating political and often economic inequality; 2) that Marxism-Leninism's uncritical acceptance of high technology leads to continued alienated production and the necessary development of a technocratic class interest and to continued domination of nature and destruction of the ecosphere; and 3) that the economistic and productivistic orientation of Marxism-Leninism blinds it to many important areas of the struggle for human liberation, not the least of which are the cultural, the aesthetic, and the erotic, and weakens its analysis of many forms of domination (including political, racial, sexual, and psychological ones).[21] These arguments are also directed at other statist and centralist positions and some of the analysis applies equally to technocratic liberalism.

THE PROBLEM OF TRANSITION

ANOTHER COMMON ARGUMENT against the anarchist position is that the transition to an anarchist society would have disastrous results, given the high degree of interdependence in the present world economy and the present level of urbanization. Anarchism is seen as implying cataclysmic change, the immediate destruction of all complex organization, and a regression to communal independence.[22]

But as has already been pointed out, anarchists do not advocate complete communal independence, but rather an organic interdependence beginning with the most basic social units and building, through federation, to humanity as a whole. Neither do anarchists propose that technological change and decentralization be taken as absolute principles to be dogmatically applied no matter what human needs may dictate. They therefore do not advocate that all technology be destroyed while we wait for liberatory alternative forms to be developed and instituted. They propose instead that research now be done on alternative technology and that people begin to use these liberatory forms to whatever degree possible, even while high technology continues to predominate. For example, while anarchists reject completely conversion to nuclear energy, they do not advocate that other energy sources be eliminated but that they be replaced progressively by solar, wind, methane, geothermal, hydroelectric, cogeneration, and other alternatives.

Similarly, anarchists do not advocate decentralization through annihilation or forced relocation of city dwellers. Many anarchists do, in fact, approve of cities of traditional scale and advocate such policies as neighborhood assemblies, integration of work, play, and living spaces, community gardens and workshops, and similar approaches to transform the urban social and physical environment. There is a long anarchist tradition dealing with the humanization and democratization of city life, as illustrated by Kropotkin's observations on the Medieval cities and Bookchin's discussion of the Greek polis and the neighborhood assemblies of the French Revolution in Paris.[23] Yet anarchists do foresee the scaling down of the inhuman megalopolis to the level of the city and an ongoing process of synthesis of town and country. What is called for as an immediate necessity is not the displacement of huge masses of people but the institution of small-scale direct democracy in the form of neighborhood and workplace assemblies. Anarchists see such factors as personality structure, economic conditions, technological forms, population distributions, and political institutions as inseparably interrelated and they reject theories of change which fail to deal with all these factors as constituents of a social totality. Yet they are not so naïve as to propose that all aspects of social transformation will proceed at the same pace. Technological change and population redistribution will obviously present material obstacles which will require a long process of constructive activity. Much of this development will continue after changes in political and economic institutions have already occurred. But it is important to note that much of the development of technological forms which will make libertarian political and economic structures seem increasingly more realistic and necessary are already taking place.

A NOTE ON SELF-DEFENSE

IT IS A FUNDAMENTAL PRINCIPLE OF ANARCHISM that if the community is to be defended, this must result from the voluntary action of the people. This leads to the criticism that the anarchist community could not effectively defend itself against the highly organized, compulsory militaries that ordinarily engage in warfare. In fact, it might not defend itself at all since, while each member might wish that the community be defended, they will each, because of self-interest, voluntarily choose that others be the ones to do the defending.

Anarchists firmly believe that "war is the health of the state," and that consequently it always threatens to be crippling, if not fatal, to freedom. To militarize a society in order to fight authoritarianism means an automatic victory for authoritarianism. For this reason anarchists insist on the necessity of limiting military activity to communal self-defense through popular militias and they oppose hierarchical, centrally directed military forces. In this context, the argument that this approach will lack popular support is not a significant one. Communities do in fact defend themselves when there is a real danger to their freedom. The theoretical objection concerning non-participation overlooks the psychological elements of war and the pervasive effects of social pressure. A cohesive community (as, for example, a tribal society) does not have difficulty securing participation in defense, although the anarchist requirement of voluntarism becomes increasingly more difficult to fulfill as the threat to the group increases in magnitude. The crucial question is therefore whether the strategy of popular self-defense can be effective when utilized.

There now seems to be growing evidence that, at least under some conditions, such means can be successful. For example, the peasant anarchist Makhnovist movement in the Ukraine developed highly successful methods of guerrilla warfare against overwhelming odds in its battles against several armies from 1918-1921. The military success of the Makhnovists was only ended when their army, by then worn down by its victories against rightist forces, was attacked by its erstwhile "ally," the Bolsheviks.[25] The Spanish collectives also achieved a remarkable degree of mobilization of the population during the period of the people's militias. In fact, support and morale only declined significantly when the militias were militarized in the hands of the state.[26] Recent experiences such as the Indochinese wars and resistance to colonialism and neo-colonialism in many areas of the world (Afghanistan being the most recent instance) have brought into question the ability of powerful nation-states to successfully (or profitably) crush opposition in areas where guerrilla warfare is vigorously supported by local communities. The case for the effectiveness (as opposed to the moral necessity) of self-defense through popular militias or community-supported guerrilla warfare has not been conclusively made. However, it is not possible to dismiss it on grounds that it could not gain popular support, or that it would be immediately crushed by traditional military forces. [27]

Conclusions

In his final argument, Wertheimer notes that contrary to what he takes to be the anarchist position, "human suffering cannot always be attributed to states and their legal superstructures."[28] This comment illustrates well one of the most common popular misconceptions about the nature of anarchism, namely, that it can be reduced to mere antistatism or opposition to government. It is essential to understand that in spite of the manner in which they have been depicted by many opponents, anarchists reject such a simplistic analysis of human problems. Despite Wertheimer's denial, anarchists have always recognized that there are natural restrictions on human well-being. In fact, one of the most distinctive contributions of anarchist thought has been its movement in the direction of a decisive break with the Western rationalist and Enlightenment belief in liberation through epistemological-technological triumph over nature. In their critique of the concept of the domination of nature (which has become an increasingly prominent theme in anarchist thought), anarchists have argued that it is our tendency to deny our limitations over against nature that has led to a will to power which lies at the core of the authoritarian consciousness. In this sense anarchist theory aims at a fully developed naturalism which is much more than a fully developed humanism.[29] But this is only a part of what is overlooked in characterizations such as Wertheimer's. It is equally significant that in analyzing social limitations on human development, anarchists have not restricted their analysis to the effects of the state. Their critique deals with the entire system of domination, including not only its statist and bureaucratic aspects, but also such factors as economic exploitation, racial oppression, sexual repression, sexism, heterosexism, ageism, and technological domination.

Reinventing Anarchy, Again

Anarchism has a highly coherent and historically founded approach to the problems mentioned by Wertheimer. The case for anarchism is not discredited, and is, in fact, hardly touched by the kinds of criticism he and many other contemporary commentators offer. In their view, anarchism is an unwise strategy for social change because it presents little hope for gain but great risk of losses for humanity. Yet, anarchist theory presents considerable evidence that the reverse may well be the case. The scope of this essay has precluded any attempt to explore thoroughly the details of this evidence. Instead, this discussion has attempted to identify more carefully the nature of the anarchist position and to present some of the central arguments and empirical data which support some of its key claims. One of the most important of these claims is that reliance on the state or a global superstate for change will lead to a continuation of many of the patterns of domination that the state has done so much to develop and reinforce in the past. If this is correct, the anarchist strategy of change "from below" in people's everyday lives, in their families, in their work and community relationships, and finally, in society at large through associations rooted in these fundamental struggles, would seem much more promising.

Anarchists maintain that the roots of the present ecological crisis can be found in the prevailing systems of industrialism and centralist high technology. The anarchist program is both a strategy for human liberation and a plan for avoiding global ecological catastrophe. While this program obviously requires a great deal of further development, even in its present form it appears to be the only political practice which offers a viable synthesis between the values of human self-development and liberation, and those of ecological balance and global survival. It is for this reason that Richard Falk concludes that "the anarchist vision . . . of a fusion between a universal confederation and organic societal forms of a communal character lies at the very center of the only hopeful prospect for the future world order."[30] If this hope is ever to be realized, what is necessary is the development of a viable libertarian and communalist theory and practice. This will require the coming of a new epoch in social theory in which there is a decisive break with both liberal and Marxist ideology and a new era of global social experimentation in which the social form legitimated by these ideologies is transcended in a practice of social and ecological regeneration.

NOTES

1. Alan Wertheimer, "Disrespect for Law and the Case for Anarchy," in *Anarchism: Nomos XIX* (New York: NYU Press, 1978), pp. 167-88.

2. *Ibid.*

3. For one of the most advanced statements of the contemporary anarchist position, see Murray Bookchin, *Post-Scarcity Anarchism* (Montreal: Black Rose Books, 1977), *Towards an Ecological Society* (Montreal: Black Rose Books, 1980), and *The Ecology of Freedom* (Palo Alto: Cheshire Books, 1982).

4. Wertheimer, *op. cit.*, pp. 182-83.

5. See "Elements of Amerindian Demography" in Pierre Clastres, *Society Against the State* (New York: Urizen Books, 1977), pp. 64-82.

6. Wertheimer, *op. cit.*, p. 184.

7. For a libertarian, decentralist view of the effects of industrialization and urbanization on Third World societies, see E.K Schumacher, *Small Is Beautiful* (New York: Harper, 1973), Part III. On the Indian anarchist Sarvodaya movement, which carries on the Gandhian tradition of village cooperative production, see Geoffrey Ostergaard and Melville Currell, *The Gentle Anarchists* (New York: Oxford University Press, 1972).

8. Peter Kropotkin, *Fields, Factories and Workshops Tomorrow*, ed. by Colin Ward (London: Allen and Unwin, 1974).

9. David Morris and Karl Hess, *Neighborhood Power* (Boston: Beacon Press, 1975). See also Bookchin's "Towards a Liberatory Technology" in *Post-Scarcity Anarchism, op. cit.*, pp. 83-139.

10. See especially Lewis Mumford, *Technics and Civilization* (New York: Harcourt, Brace and World, 1934), and *The Myth of the Machine* (New York: Harcourt, Brace, Jovanovich, 1967-70).

11. *Technics and Civilization, op. cit.*, p. 388.

12. For one of the most detailed discussions of the practical feasibility of decentralized, communitarian technology see Peter Harper and Godfrey Boyle, eds., *Radical Technology* (New York: Pantheon Books, 1976) .

13. See Dorothy Lee, *Freedom and Culture* (Englewood Cliffs: PrenticeHall, 1959); Norman O. Brown, *Love's Body* (New York: Random House, 1966); Claude Levi-Strauss, *Tristes Tropiques* (New York: Pocket Books, 1977), especially Part Seven, "Nambikwara"; Ashley Montagu, ed., *Learning Non-Aggression* (Oxford: Oxford University Press, 1978), and Bernard Rudolfsky, *Architecture Without Architects* (Garden City: Doubleday, 1964).

14. See Marshall Sahlins, *Stone Age Economics* (Chicago: Aldine Publishing Co., 1972) .

15. Wertheimer, *op. cit.*, p. 183.

16. *Ibid.*

17. Martin Buber, *Paths In Utopia* (Boston: Beacon Press, 1958), p. 136.

18. See Christopher Jencks, et al., *Inequality* (New York: Harper, 1973), especially the statistical analysis of income distribution on p. 210.

19. Gaston Leval, *Collectives in the Spanish Revolution* (London: Freedom Press, 1975), pp. 184-85.

20. *Ibid.*, p. 85. For the internationalist position of the Federacion Regional Espanola, developed as early as 1870, see Temma Kaplan, *Anarchists of Andalusia* 1868-1903 (Princeton: Princeton University Press, 1977), pp. 61-91.

21. For the anarchist critique of the Russian Revolution, see Voline, *The Unknown Revolution* (Montreal: Black Rose Books, 1974); on China, see *The Revolution Is Dead* (Montreal: Black Rose Books, 1977).

22. Wertheimer, *op. cit.*, p. 184.

23. See Kropotkin's *The State* (London: Freedom Press, 1969); Bookchin's "The Forms of Freedom" in *Post-Scarcity Anarchism*, pp. 143-69; Paul and Percival Goodman, Communitas (New York: Random House, 1960); Murray Bookchin, *Limits of the City* (New York: Harper, 1974); Robert Goodman, *After the Planners* (New York: Simon and Schuster, 1971); and the continuing discussion of the "urban question" in the Canadian libertarian journal, *Our Generation*.

24. Wertheimer, *op. cit.*, p. 185.

25. See Peter Arshinov, *History of the Makhnovist Movement* (Detroit: Black and Red, 1977).

26. See Vernon Richards, *Lessons of the Spanish Revolution* (London: Freedom Press, 1972), and Jose Peirats, *Anarchists in the Spanish Revolution* (Detroit: Black and Red, 1977).

27. For one of the few theoretical treatments of the topic, see the works of the "anarcho-Marxist" Abraham Guillen. For selections from his writings, which have been influential in Latin America, see his *Philosophy of the Urban Guerrilla* (New York: William Morrow and Co., 1973).

28. Wertheimer, *op. cit.*, p. 184.

29. This is one of the points at which contemporary anarchist theory intersects most clearly with critical theory. Cf. Herbert Marcuse, *One Dimensional Man* (Boston: Beacon Press, 1964 pp. 144-69; Max Horkheimer and Theodor Adorno, *The Dialectic of Enlightenment* (New York: Seabury, 1972), pp. 81-119, and Albrecht Wellmer, *Critical Theory of Society* (New York: Seabury 1974), pp. 129-39. For an excellent discussion relating the critique of technology and domination of nature to major themes in Eastern thought, see Hwa Yol Jung, "The Paradox of Man and Nature: Reflections On Man's Ecological Predicament" in *The Centennial Review*, vol. XVIII, no. 1.

30. "Anarchism and World Order" in Pennock and Chapman, op. ctt., p. 75.

WHERE DID KARL MARX SIT?

JIM MURRAY

to get into The Reading Room
of the formerly great British Museum
known to all who speak of it
    as the BM
you have to prove to them
    that you need books only they have.
Then they take your picture
    plastic coat it with your name
five digit #, date, and nothing else
    no mention of the BM per se
so that this lumpy lumpen ruling class
    thirty-six year old
radical American white boy me
    had to travel to the greatest storehouse
of Western imperialism to be granted
    a generic all purpose I.D.
according to which
    my beaming bespectacled face
expires end of Jan 86.

Admitted at last
    I did not ask
WHERE DID KARL MARX SIT?
    because I did not want to feel
like I hadn't done the reading
    so l bought the illustrated booklet

on the architectural and celebrity
　　　history of The Reading Room
whose dome is larger than St. Paul's
　　　held up by My Fair Lady's royalties
every Eng. Lit. writer since c. Shakespeare
　　　was a Reader
foreigners come to figure out
　　　how to make revolutions in other countries
and the question most often asked
　　　by visitors from every corner
is WHERE DID KARL MARX SIT?
　　　good to know I was in the flow

The published answer says
　　　since there are not reserved seats
we can only surmise somewhere 'tween rows K and P
　　　near the catalogs he used
But you and I know
　　　any bloke who books it for decades
sits more or less in the very same seat
　　　So I sat and thought
what would Karl carve
　　　maybe even unconsciously
into the desk of time?
　　　And then it hit me:
there is **one** statement he made . . .
　　　I jumped and within ten minutes
crawling under the wooden tables
　　　flicking my bic illegally for light
fingers and eyes darting over
　　　a hundred years of hardened gum
sure enough, there it was!
　　　I am not a Marxist

HARD QUESTIONS FOR SOCIAL ANARCHISTS

DAVID BOUCHIER

A DECENTRALIZED SOCIETY of free communities and self-confident individuals is a magnetic vision. Optimists can be found in any company to agree that such societies may have existed in the past, and that some semblance of communal, democratic life may be constructed in the present by small groups of dedicated individuals who are willing to isolate themselves from the social mainstream. But what most people find incredible is the proposition that such a society could ever result from citizen action in an industrialized nation like the United States. This incredulity is not mere pessimism, but is based on powerful arguments that radicals all too often prefer to forget. In the following pages, I have collected the most difficult of them under six headings, dealing respectively with modernity, inequality, human nature, individual freedom, social order and the possibility of social change.

BUT YOU CAN'T TURN BACK THE CLOCK: THE PROBLEM OF MODERNITY

SOCIAL ANARCHISM IS A UTOPIAN ENTERPRISE, a possibility which has been conceived but not yet realized. Utopias can be forward or backward-looking, and the tendency of communitarian and decentralist movements has undoubtedly been the latter, harking back to a smaller, simpler, less modern world. This seems damningly like a lost cause. Short of nuclear catastrophe, hundreds of millions of people are not going to vanish, nor are the great metropolises they live in, nor are the technologies and productive facilities they depend on. The communal, agrarian society which Jefferson dreamed of has vanished from the realm of possibility.

Social anarchists have recognized for years that some lateral thinking is needed here. The modern world will not go away, and cannot be bypassed by making solar heaters out of old oil drums. Radicals need to take control of modernity, not lapse into a nostalgic lyricism for the world we have lost.

One tactic has been the demystification of experts and the democratization of knowledge. The authority that scientists, technologists, and other "experts" claim, and that is so readily granted, fails to stand up under even quite casual scrutiny. Scientific experts have created (for example) chemical pollution on a global scale, the nuclear power debacle, Three Mile Island, Chernobyl, the Bhopal disaster, an impressive list of cancer-causing substances in our everyday environment, and the ability at great expense to keep dead people alive, to say nothing of the nuclear bomb, the MX missile, star wars and other engines of general extinction. Highly professionalized government machines, advised by hordes of social and military experts, have given us (for example) the Vietnam war, the Central American morass, massive poverty and homelessness, a general breakdown of law and order, and education, health and welfare systems that fail the most minimal standards of reasonable performance.

Challenging this kind of fake "expertise" is something social anarchists often find themselves doing, in every area from local government to the environment. Such actions build confidence among the challengers and undermine the priestly powers of scientists and bureaucrats. In John Dewey's words, "No man and no mind was ever emancipated merely by being left alone. . . . Positive freedom is not a state but an act which involves methods and instrumentalities for the control of conditions." In the modern world, one of the key resources for control is knowledge.

Education, in the broadest sense, has to be at the heart of any democratic action program. Citizen groups cannot educate the general public, but they can nibble at the edges of the great knowledge monopolies. The expansion of higher education in America may have the unintended consequence of helping in this process. Knowledge becomes harder to monopolize the wider it is spread, and an educated citizenry does provide a larger pool of trained, skeptical, analytical minds, even as it multiplies the numbers of self-serving experts.

Alvin Gouldner, in the pivotal volume of his trilogy, *The Dark Side of the Dialectic*, has persuasively sketched the growth of a new class of intellectuals and technical intelligentsia, whose education and values are particularly apt to the task of democratizing knowledge. This new class is the product of an education system that no longer passes on the old culture and its assumptions, but encourages an open, cosmopolitan, nonauthoritative attitude toward knowledge. As employees, members of the new class are unwilling to suffer the rigid hierarchies and disciplines of an older industrial system, and see no necessity for them.

Some trends in modern technology might encourage the democratization process. The growth of knowledge-intensive rather than capital-intensive industries, and the decentralizing possibilities of the micro-electronic revolution, have been welcomed by some radicals as forces that may reverse the centripetal tendencies of industrialism. But a focus on alternative technologies alone is unlikely to produce democratic change. Such arguments have been particularly galling to radicals on the traditional left, who claim that the whole issue of scale and centralization is a red herring, and that what matters is ownership. Certainly it is true that alternative technologies that show any signs of being successful, like solar energy, are quickly absorbed by large corporations and taken out of the public domain. *Political* decentralization is both a more urgent and a more manageable project than *technological* decentralization.

Another approach to the problem of modernity has been to search for the stresses and contradictions that the system itself creates and that might, in the long run, catalyze a revaluation of values and a revival of democratic consciousness among citizens. Social anarchists have been justly wary of grand philosophical statements about the human condition, but their work is based on a deeply felt uneasiness about the modern world, and a sense of foreboding about a future which, if present tendencies are continued, might be entirely governed by the short-term imperatives of bureaucracy and technology. Nobody expects to stop progress in its track, but the *social* changes wrought by technology have been left entirely out of human control. Technology is progress, technology is fate. If we invent a chemical, a weapon, a medical technique, we must use it. Reigning in this juggernaut seems more a progressive, forward-looking enterprise than a nostalgic one.

Human needs and desires, as neoconservative sociologist Daniel Bell has remarked, often work against the logic of economic and technological progress. Higher level demands for freedom and self-fulfillment are out of sync with the disciplines of a permanent growth economy, and these cultural contradictions cannot be resolved by governments. Here, perhaps, is a crack in the monolith. The experience of modernity, for a great many people, is one of uneasiness and conflict. Just as reformers and left-wing radicals a century ago began curbing the excesses of industrial capitalism in the cause of a more humane society, citizen radicals today have the task of showing that real human progress means more democracy and more positive freedom, not just more commodities and more science.

The democratization of expertise and the discontents of modernity do not, however, dispose of the argument that, in Peter Berger's phrase, modernity is a "package that cannot be taken apart," and that the centralization of power is an *inevitable* consequence of size and complexity. Paul Goodman and others have conceded that some *administrative* centralization *is* inevitable, simply because efficiency and economies of scale demand quite high levels of coordination from the center in the delivery of some kinds of services. For example, totally decentralized health care would entail abandoning the kinds of resources only feasible in large, regional hospitals, and facilities like interstate highways, telephone systems, power systems and air traffic control could not rationally be devolved to small, local communities. To prevent such administrative machines growing into greedy monsters of bureaucratic regulation, they would have to be subject to intense local control.

Breaking the connections in people's minds between expertise and power, technology and progress, and complexity and centralization is not shown, by any of these arguments, to be a self-evidently easy, or even a possible enterprise. But at least social anarchists who are accused of utopian nostalgia can be secure in the response that their demand for higher levels of freedom and participation is not antimodern but ultra-modern, and even futuristic. The quality of life and human value issues they raise are not dreams left over from preindustrial society, but goals that will only be realized in the most advanced, self-conscious, and humane society.

BUT THE POOR WILL BE LEFT OUT: THE PROBLEM OF EQUALITY

SOCIAL ANARCHISM TENDS to be a middle-class movement. It could hardly be otherwise. Cooperative, self-governing values and skills are hard-learned in an individualistic society, and can scarcely be learned at all by people who are struggling for a basic living standard. While the available studies are not conclusive, they seem to show that certain more educated sectors of the middle class are the most significant carriers of democratic values. Saul Alinsky, one of the most pragmatic of grass-roots organizers, was entirely clear about this. "Organization for action will . . . center upon America's white middle class. That is where the power is."

So, as old-time trade unionists used to ask, what about the workers? What about the racial and ethnic minorities? Are they to be left out of the new utopia, just as non-owners of property were excluded by Locke when he drew up his social contract for the bourgeoisie? Isn't this social anarchism just another *laissez faire* movement of the white middle class which ignores, and even tramples on working-class interests?

Equality is a painful stumbling block for citizen activists and social anarchists in America. They have been more concerned with power distribution issues than with economic distribution issues, and this is their strength in a society where socialism is an alien creed. At the same time, nobody can miss the intimate connection between equality, power and freedom.

Equality *versus* liberty is the classic, unresolved conundrum of political philosophy. Conservatives who are not closet liberals simply dismiss the "equality problem" as a dream based on an illusion fostered by envy. Many Libertarians feel much the same way. Liberals believe that they have the most workable answer in the concept of equality of opportunity, or freedom to compete. Yet, however vigorously this principle is pursued, it would most certainly lead straight back to large inequalities of result — which, according to the liberal notion, would be perceived as fair because they were the outcome of a fair competition. In its strong form, as displayed in John Rawls's *A Theory of Justice*, negative freedom to compete is maximized but the resulting level of "natural" inequality would prevent any gains in positive freedom, particularly for the economic losers.

Socialists believe they have a better answer, in following Marx's prediction that society must go through a stage of state-imposed unfreedom (state socialism) to achieve economic equality, and thus finally to arrive at freedom (stateless communism). This elegant theory is somewhat at odds with historical experience, which suggests that progress toward freedom will stick somewhere near the point of maximum state power.

The social anarchist position on inequality is often harder to discern. The word "equality" is used freely in writing and rhetoric, and is generally treated as a positive value and a subversive ideal. Many social anarchists are, after all, ex-socialists and ex-liberals. There is an unstated assumption that more democracy would lead to more equality, but the sociopolitical process which would produce this result is not specified. There is an affinity between cooperative/democratic and egalitarian values, but it is not clear how *existing* inequalities could be reduced in a nonauthoritarian way. How much economic equality is needed to allow real democracy to function? How are these lines to be drawn and held? Such questions are unanswered.

Liberals and democratic socialists, and even neoconservatives, will ask not so much "What is the ultimate balance between equality and freedom?" but rather mundane and immediate questions like, "What about the welfare state?" The great achievement of the corporate-liberal system is that it has provided a safety net of services for the poorest and most helpless members of society. Inadequate as it is, this net is enormously complex and costly, and depends on the giant, tax-fed bureaucracies of central government. If a decentralized, cooperative society could not guarantee to eliminate poverty, disease and mental illness, how would it cope with the victims? Visions arise of the infamous Poor Law system in seventeenth-century England, with paupers and sick people being driven from parish to parish, no one wanting to support them.

The theory of social anarchism defines welfare as a *community* responsibility, and holds that a democratic community would aim to integrate its poorer citizens as participants with obligations as well as rights, and not as passive dependents. While this is an attractive principle and, indeed, the very idea of community makes no sense unless it includes some protective arrangements for its weaker members, the economic and social mechanisms of such support have never been stated in detail. There is an unspoken assumption that communal and democratic relationships would have a moderating effect on poverty simply by reducing selfishness and encouraging altruism, but this assumption has never been tested.

If welfare were decentralized, to state only the most obvious difficulty, the poorest communities with fewest resources would face a catastrophic future. If resources were transferred from one community to another, we would be back to the conflict between local freedom and centralized control.

The fact is that the problem of equality sits like a hard stone, undigested in the body of social anarchist theory and practice.

But People Won't Cooperate: The Problem of "Human Nature"

THE DAILY EVIDENCE that people are individualistic, selfish and combative "by nature" often seems overwhelming. Children in playgrounds, professors in universities, drivers on highways and Congresspeople in Washington routinely behave in ways that persuade us, to quote a dispirited graffiti I saw once in a New York subway, that "Hobbes Was Right!"

It is tempting to dismiss such evidence merely as a consequence of scale. The larger the organization or group, the less people tend to feel personally accountable, and the worse they behave. But even in human-scale settings where the conditions for cooperation and community are apparently perfect, competition and infighting seem to be the rule. In churches, rural villages, comfortable middle-class suburbs, elite colleges, alternative businesses, and even within cooperative and democratic movements, apparently irresistible impulses of pride and desire to dominate often make a mockery of cooperative hopes.

It is hardly convincing, therefore, when social anarchists claim (as they sometimes do) that people are *really* cooperative "by nature" — and cite evidence from a few remote and long-dead primitive tribes — when so much everyday experience seems to prove the contrary. It makes more sense to begin with the basic wisdom of Rousseau and Marx, that people become "by nature" what they need to be to live successfully in a particular society. This at least gives the argument a firm footing in a recognizably real world.

The liberal bedrock of American political culture supports an explicit, unambiguous theory of human needs and human nature, derived by the Founding Fathers out of Locke out of Hobbes. People are fundamentally selfish, and fundamentally separate. The inevitable relationship of people in a possessive, individualistic society is one of continuous conflict over material goods. The authors of the Federalist Papers firmly believed that the mass of citizens needed a superior class of elite individuals to keep their acquisitive instincts within bounds.

The end-consequences of possessive individualism have fascinated many social philosophers in the late twentieth century, and the present upsurge in serious thinking about community and cooperation owes a lot to such politically diverse authors as C. B. MacPherson, Peter Berger, Phillip Slater, Richard Sennett, and Christopher Lasch. It is clear that possessive individualism is an ideology extremely hospitable to capitalism, in that it maximizes competitive effort and competitive consumption while undermining democratic participation. Also, especially in the United States, the solitary individual has been invested with a romantic image of independence which has become deeply rooted in the culture. It is equally clear that the description of society (capitalist or not) in terms of solitary, self-possessing individuals is simply wrong. Such is not the human condition.

Anthropology and archaeology tell us that our whole evolution has been tribal and social and that the "natural human" would be found, if anywhere, in a group. Sociobiology and psychology tell us that human beings have numerous impulses — altruism, sacrifice, loyalty, gregariousness — which make no sense outside the social context. Social psychologists, studying the process of exchange between individuals and groups, tell us that their human subjects arrive at cooperative behavior by a process of rational decision making.

Everyone *in fact* depends on a network of human relationships, however abstract some of them are. In industrial society, interdependence reaches a baroque elaboration in which there is almost no end to the ways in which people's lives connect. The romantic notion of the solitary individual inhabiting some psychic frontier, enjoying heat, light, communication, food and transportation without reference to others is the merest fantasy.

Solitariness is not a fact of life; nor is it the experience of life for most people. The propensity of Americans to create groups and voluntary associations is famous. Even within the interstices of institutional life people create small cooperative communities as naturally as they breathe, and with as little thought. The office, the factory, the college or the firehouse become miniature settings for communal life. Trust and cooperation, which are inconceivable outside, come naturally here. Such mini-communities suffer the usual problems of power, competition and jealousy. But they nevertheless demonstrate that people can unself-consciously manage cooperative relationships in everyday life.

Citizens act, very often, as though the wider community meant something to them. The phenomenon of charity in America offers a striking example. Whatever the effectiveness or genuineness of particular charitable organizations, the simple fact that some 800,000 of them exist, that they can draw on 55 million volunteers and attract some $40 billion a year in gifts suggests the survival of some remnant of communal consciousness.

Robert N. Bellah and his coauthors in their study of individualism, *Habits of the Heart*, talk about the "communities of memory" which we all carry around with us, which allow us to feel a part of (for example) a local, ethnic, religious or national community, to feel that we belong somewhere and owe loyalty somewhere. Such memories and feelings are something to build on, for radicals who aim to restore the lost habit of cooperation.

Thomas Jefferson firmly believed that the skills of self-government did not come naturally, but must be deliberately taught. One immediate educational task for social anarchists therefore is to show that cooperation works by the example of the prefigurative organization, and by drawing as many citizens as possible into the cooperative experience which teaches cooperative consciousness

But Community is restrictive: The Problem of Individual Freedom

THE THEORY OF SOCIAL ANARCHISM is grounded in the elusive concept of community, which can be and often is accused of being one of those all-purpose good words that can be bent to any political purpose. Most intellectuals and politicians are city folk, happy with the anonymity and negative freedom of the crowd, and happy not to be accountable face-to-face for their actions or ideas. Community to them means conformity, narrowness and loss of freedom.

The small community has a dismal reputation. It conjures up images of a rural village of cruel gossips, or a Maoist work group tight-knit by fear of criticism, or a religious community fiercely punitive of individuality, or a hippie commune, rigidly orthodox in its nonconformity.

This is an American nightmare, and a hard one for radicals to counter. People do create miniature communities in their everyday lives, because this is how people working or living together act, quite instinctively, to make life tolerable. Given the chance, they build relationships of trust, mutual respect and mutual aid, and quite happily sacrifice little fragments of individual freedom in the process. But the condition for the existence of such mini-communities is the freedom people feel to move easily between the closeness of community and the openness of society: the freedom, in short, to choose. They shy away from the thought of being trapped in any one communal situation. Internally authoritarian communities have existed and do exist and flourish in America. But these are still communities of choice, not necessity. Is there any way out of the equation between community and diminished personal freedom?

Alan Ritter, in his book *Anarchism: A Theoretical Analysis*, has suggested that we suffer from a conceptual problem about community which causes us to label it as the enemy of freedom. Society exists only because people more or less willingly conform to social norms, and develop an awareness of themselves as objects as well as subjects. Those who do not are psychopaths at worst, loners or destructive egotists at best. Existing social habits of conformity therefore offer a basis for what Ritter calls "communal individuality," in which the anarchist device of public censure as a form of control stimulates and enhances the individual's consciousness of others. S/he becomes a more social being, and therefore more in control of self, and more positively free. This is a development from those classic anarchist theories which try to find a balance between freedom, individualism and community in which community provides a framework for self-development, and not a strait jacket. In America, where the freedom impulse is so strong, it could be argued that the authoritarian tendencies of community would be more readily controllable.

Critics always focus on the power of censure, which communities must have over the individual. Like any other form of power, it is dangerous. The movements of the sixties, much of the time, trembled on the edge of moral authoritarianism within their own ranks, and sometimes slipped over. The unstable mixture of socialism, communalism and liberationism so characteristic of the time did not evolve into a "communal individuality" of the kind Ritter describes. In the end, it produced aberrations like the Weathermen, in which censure had indeed become an intimate tyranny.

Radicals might make the cooperative ideal more attractive by stressing the voluntaristic aspect. The idea that cooperation is collectivism, and that collectivism is the forced annihilation of individual freedom from above — as in the Soviet case — runs deep in American culture. It's no use pretending that a degree of negative individual freedom does not have to be sacrificed in exchange for the positive freedoms of a democratic community. Unlimited accumulation, unlimited consumption and the unlimited exploitation of others are just three of the things which would have to be curbed.

This is an area where more intellectual work is urgently needed. The theory of community offers no clear conception of what a society of revitalized communities would look like, or what exactly would be the social costs and benefits of such an achievement. It has been claimed that real community is attainable only in groups of five hundred people or fewer. But the notion of a country like the United States divided into half a million or so tiny, autonomous political units makes no practical sense.

A workable theory of community must show how cross-cutting bonds of solidarity might be built within and between quite large human groups, certainly many thousands, which would also be viable social, political and economic units. These units would themselves have a cellular pattern in which smaller, face-to-face units of community (neighborhoods, work groups and so on) would form the building blocks for the whole. Above all, the theory would have to explain the nature of the bond, the common interest, which would be above and beyond the many particular interests. And, if the common interest were something as abstract as a sense of participation or a feeling of belonging, how it would come to be shared with the necessary passion and unanimity. The goal so easily achieved on paper seems as unreachable as ever in the real world.

BUT THE SOCIAL ORDER WILL COLLAPSE:
THE PROBLEM OF CONFLICT AND VIOLENCE

LOOKING ON A SOCIETY and a world besieged by violence and the apparent breakdown of social order, many Americans have only a hollow laugh for the idea of citizen self-government. Any effective government at all would seem good to them. Their belief in a competitive and individualistic human nature leads quite naturally to belief in a violent human nature, which can be controlled, but not changed.

The rise of conservative and neoconservative philosophies of order is some measure of how much the fear of disorder and violence has taken hold. Neoconservatives make ominous connections between "too much democracy" and chaos. This is the classic conservative argument that less freedom really equals more, and that an interventionist state is necessary to protect citizens from one another — a weak theory of legitimacy based on fear. It seems that fear of freedom has become a political bargaining counter in the free society.

It is quite easy to construct a hypothesis which explains away the problem of violent social conflict; less easy to conceive how the violent forces which exist now could be controlled so that such a hypothesis could be tested. The hypothetical solution might run like this:

Social order may be maintained by force (naked power), by authority (legitimated or accepted power), by reciprocity (interdependence), by consensus (general cultural agreement) or by some combination of these.

The prevalence of crime, violence and fear in America demonstrates that force and authority are failing to prevent antisocial behavior, even while they increasingly restrict and control routine social behavior. Thus, citizens are getting a bad bargain; they lose much of their personal freedom to the state while not getting the protection which, under the liberal social contract, the state promises them in return.

Violence is the resource of people who have no other, or who are in some way entirely alienated from their victims. The only ultimate cure is a social order which is more equal, more self-consciously interdependent and more at peace with its fundamental values. What the state cannot do, as a remote arbiter in the economic free-for-all, the community might be able to do by placing citizens once more in organic connection with *one another.*

Even the most democratic society would have to accommodate conflicts of interest between groups and individuals; but it would no longer be alienated conflict. Ideally, each conflict would lead to understanding, compromise and, in the end, to greater cooperation. The emphasis on feminist values in the new politics is part of a search for less conflictual, more cooperative styles of problem solving. So the hypothetical answer to the problem of conflict is that it would take a different and more manageable form in a communal society. Critics of community can't have it both ways. If community diminishes absolute individual freedom, it also must diminish the violent and destructive consequences of such freedom. Which is not to say, by another route, that less freedom equals more; there is a world of difference between social order imposed from above and one which grows organically from the ties of community.

Further, it can be argued that a decentralized, communal society would be less violent precisely *because* of the human capacity for force. As Paul Goodman said, "We must avoid concentration of power precisely because we *are* fallible."

This makes an attractive and symmetrical theory. But what would a noncoercive society do with millions of living individuals thoroughly trained in antisocial violence, and more millions of immigrants from societies with no democratic culture? The only answer is to reeducate them, turning prisons into schools for community rather than schools for more crime. But the term reeducation brings to mind the specter of China in the Cultural Revolution, Vietnam after the war, or Cambodia under the Pol Pot regime. Such an enterprise would be a standing invitation to moral authoritarianism, and it is scarcely imaginable that it could be managed along democratic lines.

Beyond the daunting problem of social violence lurks the still more unmanageable fact of international conflict, terrorism, imperialism and war. The world is militarized and divided by wealth and poverty, by race, by political ideology and by fanatical religiosity. Military readiness for any state entails centralization, control and coercion on a truly monstrous scale. Is it possible to believe that the United States, regarded as an enemy by half the world, as the fattest prize for any conqueror, could give up its military power and survive the consequences? Social anarchists say, quite rightly, that states and military machines do not *defend* citizens, but *cause* wars, and the bigger the states the bigger the wars. But this hardly solves the problem of the existing international standoff. A fully democratic, decentralized society might choose to defend itself, and might even do so successfully against larger forces by making alliances. The American Revolution itself is no bad example. But alliances and their architects have a way of becoming permanent, ever ready for the next external threat.

The apparatus and attitude of defense has a profoundly corrupting effect on democratic aspirations. Internal and external enemies are always there, or can be found. This question — how to maintain the integrity of a democratic, decentralized society against its enemies — remains almost entirely unanswered. Peace movement activists have a point when they claim that all other issues of human progress may hinge on the elimination of international conflict.

BUT YOU CAN'T GET THERE FROM HERE:
THE PROBLEM OF SOCIAL CHANGE

THE GROUPS THAT ARE WORKING for citizen rights and empowerment certainly do not have the feel of a great historic social movement destined to sweep aside the old order. They are small, diverse and loosely linked, fragile and sometimes short-lived, deeply involved with local issues and with their own democratic processes. Socialists, however sympathetic they may be to the humanistic aims of such groups, see their greatest weakness as a theory of social change which devalues class unity, singleness of purpose, and political struggle in favor of a long, uncertain process of public education through alternative institutions.

However, this strategy of change through education is the only one consistent with democratic values. The political state is too powerful, distant and abstract to be attacked; but *society* is loosely integrated by the shared knowledge which forms its culture. This knowledge is socially produced, transmitted and maintained, and may be socially transformed by new ideas which are powerful, useful and widely diffused. It is at this level that the system is vulnerable to pressures for change. Marx debated with the nineteenth-century anarchists and with the Hegelians whether society was shaped by ideas, or by material forces. Technological determinists in the twentieth century staked out a third ground, claiming that we are prisoners of our techniques. Such debates seem sterile as the century draws toward its close, because they are irresolvable and we can hardly avoid admitting that all three forces are significant in the shaping of human society.

The claim for idealism *as a theory of social change in advanced industrial societies* is more bounded, and more modest. Ideas may not be the only driving force of history, but they are the only resource that citizens can use to change history. Citizens cannot, in any imaginable way, transform technology or the organization of production *directly*, other than by rising up and destroying the entire system. And the state has accumulated more than enough power to block any such direct action.

Unable to attack the structure, unwilling to take the reformist line and simply bargain within it, serious radicals have no choice but to work for the transformation of culture. Culture is more malleable, closer to people, and less fiercely defended by the powerful. Any modern movement which aims for massive change becomes, by default, a *countercultural* movement. Social anarchists are countercultural by design.

From the American Revolution on, ideas have been a more significant force in American politics than in the politics of many other societies. The "American creed," expressed most forcefully in the Declaration of Independence, has inspired libertarian and egalitarian movements for more than two centuries, has been a perpetual thorn in the side of conservatives, and shows no sign of losing its ideological power. From time to time, radicals have forced concessions from the system simply by dramatizing the gap between these ideals and the realities of American life, as most recently demonstrated by the civil rights and women's movements. On quite another plane, political culture has proven surprisingly responsive to appeals by fundamentalists, ultra-rightists and others to values labeled "traditional." In short, American society is one in which culture has power in politics.

The most idealistic of all anarchists was William Godwin, who believed that society could be revolutionized by reasoned argument alone. But reasoned argument must be heard, and it must be played out in action to become a force for change. To take the second point first, the action which citizen radicals typically choose is the building of alternative or countercultural institutions which exemplify their ideas.

What must give us pause, and what socialists always remember, is that such alternative institutions have typically been short-lived, and none has seriously challenged the status quo.

The theory of social anarchism suggests a number of responses to this objection. One is that alternative institutions are valuable in themselves, insofar as they promote reciprocity, increase democratic participation, decrease feelings of dependence on the state and in general promote wider and deeper human relations. A second response is that alternative institutions are one building block of democratic change, and not the whole edifice. The small group builds toward wider forms of collective organization, such as neighborhood assemblies and town meetings. To overcome problems of scale and isolation, Benjamin Barber in *Strong Democracy* has suggested "civic communications cooperatives" which would use new technology to allow instant access to debates and instant feedback from citizens. Information access, civic education, campaigns for initiative, referendum and recall are all building block tactics for democratic radicals. And community, workplace and environment are the issues which can most effectively drive those tactics.

Established cultures are immensely difficult to change. But for those who would try, the good news is that nondogmatic knowledge of social change strategies is cumulative, and that this century has brought a vast multiplication of experience, analysis and research about how change actually happens. Activists no longer have to be guided by simplistic, mechanistic theories of change which are almost certainly wrong. They can act with knowledge of the full complexity and indeterminacy of social life.

Culture and its most powerful carriers — the mass media — convey a single political message in the United States, perhaps more than in any other democratic nation. The message is the traditional Good News of liberalism, that the possessive individualist society (though not perfect) is the best of all *possible* worlds, and that any progress beyond it will be achieved by more of the same. Those who have presumed to step outside this consensus, especially in the latter part of this century, have been labeled as utopians, subversives or worse. Democratic, leaderless groups are particularly liable to be ridiculed or ignored by the media because their actions lack drama, and because they offer no power figures for journalists to transform into those heroic, wise or demonic characters who add so much color to a story.

Citizen radicals are not in the confrontation business. Their aim is not to capture the CBS nightly news with mass actions. Yet they need the "media amplification effect" to carry the consciousness of small actions and small victories beyond the circle of the committed. Here, the media's insatiable need for ideas and stimuli to fill their pages and programs can be used to good effect. Local media — far more diverse and more adventurous than the nationals — can always be interested in a local story, if it comes without a heavy dose of political dogma. And even the national media can be captivated by small stories that are cleverly packaged.

From time to time we do see the huge resources of networks, newspapers or newsmagazines mobilized to cover, say, a block rehabilitation project in the Bronx, a work co-op which works, a novel political line-up in local politics, a peaceful antinuclear protest, and so on. The point being made here is elementary but important. The American ideology itself defines this sort of news coverage as evidence of a healthy pluralism, which it is. The radical reflex of revulsion from the media — often based on the sixties experience or an uncritical reading of Marcuse — can prevent them from putting in the time and energy needed to use the media. Society is just not as monolithic or as integrated as many radicals seem to think it is. Like them or not, the media empires are an essential resource for social change. Almost nothing can be accomplished without them. "Communicate! Communicate!" has to be the driving principle of idealistic action.

The weakness of radical movements today reflects a profound failure to communicate their message. Thousands of small, disconnected actions look like a minimalist tactic to change so powerful a system. The localism of these groups, their failure to link up effectively, their failure to take seriously the power of the state and media, and the fantasy that that power is somehow unreal or easily bypassed, all reflect an unwillingness to confront the full scale of the problem.

Changing lives on a small scale is a worthy aim. But in order to change people's minds, social anarchists need to keep their eyes on the larger vision of a democratic society, to build a political identity based on that vision, and to transmit that identity very widely through the culture. Until that identity is sharply drawn and widely understood, the movement cannot be said to have succeeded or failed: it is simply invisible.

CONCLUSIONS: THEORY, ACTION AND OPTIMISM

By the most generous accounting, only half the "hard questions" I posed have convincing answers, leaving the problems of inequality, individual freedom, and social order as massive and daunting practical obstacles. When all the objections are lined up, social anarchism begins to look like the Blithedale Romance in modern dress. It may be beyond the reach of imagination, and therefore without the power to persuade and to mobilize. The most urgent intellectual task therefore is to create a utopian vision and a theory of change which reasonable people can believe in.

Inseparable from the intellectual task is the active task of democratic, countercultural action. Democratic action is satisfying in itself, and it enables groups to claw back some measure of autonomy and self-respect, and to reduce the reach of the state into their lives by the same measure. The self-activity of citizens is the social change which social anarchists are aiming for.

Radicals, like other cultural gadflies, inject a kind of ironic, anarchic consciousness into the system. They make people aware of the fallibility of power and the possibility of change, acting like an anticoagulant in the body politic. By creating countercultures, radicals help

DEMOCRACY WITHOUT ELECTIONS

BRIAN MARTIN

For many a jaded radical, the greens are the most exciting political development for ages. The green movements claim to bring together members of the most dynamic social movements, including the peace, environmental and feminist movements, combining their insights and numbers. This is something that many activists have long sought.

Beyond this, the rapidly achieved electoral success of green parties has really captured the imagination. The German Greens have been the center of attention for a decade precisely because of their election to parliament. A number of other green parties have been electorally successful too.

But wait a moment. Before getting too carried away, isn't it worth asking whether elections are an appropriate way forward? After all, electoral politics is the standard, traditional approach, which has led to those traditional parties which have so frustrated many a radical. Isn't there a danger that participation in the electoral process remains a trap, a bottomless pit for political energy which will pacify activists and masses alike?

My aim here is to take a critical look at elections and their alternatives. I start with a summary of the case against elections and then outline some participatory alternatives. Finally, I present the idea of demarchy, a participatory system based on random selection.

THE CASE AGAINST ELECTIONS

The idea of elections as the ultimate democratic device is a deep-seated one in the West. It is hard to escape it. Children are taught all about elections in school, and may vote for student councils or club officers. Then all around us, especially through the mass media, attention is given to politicians and, periodically, to the elections which put them in power. Indeed, the main connection which most people have with their rulers is the ballot box. It is no wonder that electoral politics is sanctified.[1]

Elections in practice have served well to maintain dominant power structures such as private property, the military, male domination and economic inequality. None of these has been seriously threatened through voting. It is from the point of view of radical critics that elections are most limiting.

Voting doesn't work. At the simplest level, voting simply doesn't work very well to promote serious challenges to prevailing power systems. The basic problem is quite simple. An elected representative is not tied is any substantial way to particular policies, whatever the preferences of the electorate. Influence on the politician is greatest at the time of election. Once elected, the representative is released from popular control but continues to be exposed to powerful pressure groups, especially corporations, state bureaucracies and political party power brokers.

In principle, elections should work all right for moderately small electorates and political systems, where accountability can be maintained through regular contact. Elections can be much better justified in New England town meetings than in national parliaments making decisions affecting millions of people. In these large systems, a whole new set of reinforcing mechanisms has developed: political party machines, mass advertising, government manipulation of the news, government projects in local areas, and bipartisan politics. In essence, voters are given the choice between tweedledee and tweedledum, and then bombarded with a variety of techniques to sway them towards one or the other.

This is a depressing picture, but hope springs eternal from the voter's pen. Some maintain the faith that a mainstream party may be reformed or radicalized. Others look towards new parties. When a new party such as the greens shows principles and growth, it is hard to be completely cynical.

Nevertheless, all the historical evidence suggests that parties are more a drag than an impetus to radical change. One obvious problem is that parties can be voted out. All the policy changes they brought in can simply be reversed later.

More important, though, is the pacifying influence of the radical party itself. On a number of occasions, radical parties have been elected to power as a result of popular upsurges. Time after time, the 'radical' parties have become chains to hold back the process of radical change. Ralph Miliband gives several examples where labor or socialist parties, elected in periods of social turbulence, acted to reassure the dominant capitalist class and subdue popular action.[2] For example, the Popular Front, elected in France in 1936, made its first task the ending of strikes and occupations and generally dampening popular militancy. The experiences of Eurosocialist parties elected to power in France, Greece and Spain in the 1980s have followed the same pattern. In all major areas—the economy, the structure of state power, and foreign policy—the Eurosocialist governments have retreated from their initial goals and become much more like traditional ruling parties.[3]

Voting disempowers the grassroots. If voting simply didn't work to bring about changes at the top, that would not be a conclusive argument. After all, change in society doesn't just come about through laws and policies. There are plenty of opportunities for action outside the electoral system.

It is here that voting makes a more serious inroad into radical social action: it is a diversion from grassroots action. The aim of electoral politics is to elect someone who then can take action. This means that instead of taking direct action against injustice, the action becomes indirect: get the politicians to do something.

On more than one occasion, I've seen a solid grassroots campaign undermined by an election. One example is the 1977 Australian federal election in the midst of a powerful campaign against uranium mining. Another is the 1983 Australian federal election at a crucial point in the campaign against the flooding of the Franklin River in Tasmania.[4]

It should be a truism that elections empower the politicians and not the voters. Yet many social movements continually are drawn into electoral politics. One reason for this is the involvement of party members in social movements. Another is the aspirations for power and influence by leaders in movements. Having the ear of a government minister is a heady sensation for many; getting elected to parliament oneself is even more of an ego boost. What is forgotten in all this 'politics of influence' is the effect on ordinary activists.

The disempowering effect of elections works not only on activists but also on others. The ways in which elections serve the interests of state power have been admirably explained by Benjamin Ginsberg.[5] Ginsberg's basic thesis is that elections historically have enlarged the number of people who participate in 'politics,' but by turning this involvement into a routine activity (voting), elections have reduced the risk of more radical direct action.

The expansion of suffrage is typically presented as a triumph of downtrodden groups against privilege. Workers gained the vote in the face of opposition by the propertied class; women gained it in the face of male-dominated governments and electorates. Ginsberg challenges this picture. He argues that the suffrage in many countries was expanded in times when there was little social pressure for it.

Why should this be? Basically, voting serves to legitimate government. To bolster its legitimacy, if required, suffrage can be expanded. This is important when mass support is crucial, for example during wartime. It can be seen in other areas as well. Worker representatives on corporate boards of management serve to coopt dissent; so do student representatives on university councils.

Ginsberg shows that elections operate to bring mass political activity into a manageable form: election campaigns and voting. People learn that they can participate: they are not totally excluded. They also learn the limits of participation. Voting occurs only occasionally, at times fixed by governments. Voting serves only to select leaders, not to directly decide policy. Finally, voting doesn't take passion into account: the vote of the indifferent or ill-informed voter counts just the same as that of the concerned and knowledgeable voter. Voting thus serves to tame political participation, making it a routine process that avoids mass uprisings.

Voting reinforces state power. Ginsberg's most important point is that elections give citizens the impression that the government does (or can) serve the people. The founding of the modern state a few centuries ago was met with great resistance: people would refuse to pay taxes, to be conscripted or to obey laws passed by national governments. The introduction of voting and the expanded suffrage have greatly aided the expansion of state power. Rather than seeing the system as one of ruler and ruled, people see at least the possibility of using state power to serve themselves. As electoral participation has increased, the degree of resistance to taxation, military service, and the immense variety of laws regulating behavior, has been greatly attenuated.

The irony in all this, as pointed out by Ginsberg, is that the expansion of state power, legitimated by voting, has now outgrown any control by the participation which made it possible. States are now so large and complex that any expectation of popular control seems remote.

Using Ginsberg's perspective, the initial government-sponsored introduction of some competition into elections in the Soviet Union and eastern Europe takes on a new meaning. If the economic restructuring seen as necessary by Communist Party leaders was to have any chance of success, then there had to be greater support for the government. What better way than by introducing some choice into voting? Increased government legitimacy, and hence increased real power for the government, was the aim.

Ginsberg's analysis leads to the third major limitation of electoral politics: it relies on the state and reinforces state power. If the state is part of the problem—namely being a prime factor in war, genocide, repression, economic inequality, male domination and environmental destruction—then it is foolish to expect that the problems can be overcome by electing a few new nominal leaders of the state.

The basic anarchist insight is that the structure of the state, as a centralized administrative apparatus, is inherently flawed from the point of view of human freedom and equality. Even though the state can be used occasionally for valuable ends, as a means the state is flawed and impossible to reform. The nonreformable aspects of the state include, centrally, its monopoly over 'legitimate' violence and its consequent power to coerce for the purpose of war, internal control, taxation and the protection of property and bureaucratic privilege. The problem with voting is that the basic premises of the state are never considered open for debate, much less challenge.

Voting can lead to changes in policies. That is fine and good. But the policies are developed and executed within the state framework, which is a basic constraint. Voting legitimates the state framework.

ALTERNATIVES TO ELECTIONS

What participatory alternatives are there to the state and electoral politics? This is a topic on which there is a large literature, especially by anarchists.[6] So I can do no more than highlight some of the relevant answers and experiences.

Referendums. One set of alternatives is based on direct mass involvement in policy-making through voting, using mechanisms including petition, recall, initiative and referendum. Instead of electing politicians who then make policy decisions, these decisions are made directly by the public.

In practice, referendums have been only supplements to a policy process based on elected representatives. But it is possible to conceive of a vast expansion of the use of referendums, especially by use of computer technology.[7] Some exponents propose a future in which each household television system is hooked up with equipment for direct electronic voting. The case for and against a referendum proposal would be broadcast, followed by a mass vote. What could be more democratic?

Unfortunately there are some serious flaws in such proposals. These go deeper than the problems of media manipulation, involvement by big-spending vested interests, and the worries by experts and elites that the public will be irresponsible in direct voting.

A major problem is the setting of the agenda for the referendum. Who decides the questions? Who decides what material is broadcast for and against a particular question? Who decides the wider context of voting?

The fundamental issue concerning setting of the agenda is not simply bias. It is a question of participation. Participation in decision-making means not just voting on predesigned questions, but participation in the formulation of which questions are put to a vote. This is something which is not easy to organize when a million people are involved, even with the latest electronics. It is a basic limitation of referendums.

The key to this limitation of referendums is the presentation of a single choice to a large number of voters. Even when some citizens are involved in developing the question, as in the cases of referendums based on the process of citizen initiative, most people have no chance to be involved in more than a yes-no capacity. The opportunity to recast the question in the light of discussion is not available.

Another problem for referendums is a very old one, fundamental to voting itself. Simply put, rule by the majority often means oppression of the minority. This problem is more clear-cut in direct voting systems, but also appears in representative systems.

Consensus. Consensus is a method of decision-making without voting that aims for participation, group cohesion, and openness to new ideas. Combined with other group skills for social analysis, examining group dynamics, developing strategies and evaluation, consensus can be powerful indeed.[8]

Yet anyone who has participated in consensus decision-making should be aware that the practice is often far short of the theory. Sometimes powerful personalities dominate the process; less confident people are afraid to express their views. Because objections normally have to be voiced face-to-face, the protection of anonymity in the secret ballot is lost. Meetings can be interminable, and those who cannot devote the required time to them are effectively disenfranchised. The biggest problem for consensus, though, is irreconcilable conflict of interest. The best treatment of this problem is *Beyond Adversary Democracy* by Jane Mansbridge.[9] As a democratic alternative to elections, consensus has severe limitations dealing with large groups.[10]

Small size. One solution to this dilemma is to keep group sizes small.[11] Even voting is not so limiting when the number of voters is so small that everyone is potentially known to everyone else. The use of consensus can be maximized.

Furthermore, small size opens the possibility of a plurality of political systems. Frances Kendall and Leon Louw propose a Swiss-like federation of autonomous political entities, each of which can choose its own political and economic system.[12] With Kendall and Louw's system, the difficulties of trying new methods, and the costs of failures, are greatly reduced.

Small size may make governance easier, but there will still be some large-scale problems requiring solution. Global pollution and local disasters, for example, call for more than local solutions. How are decisions to be made about such issues?

More fundamentally, small size by itself doesn't solve the issue of how decisions are made. There can still be deep conflicts of interests which make consensus inappropriate, and there can still be problems of domination resulting from electoral methods.

Finally, in all but the very tiniest groups, the basic problem of limits to participation remains. Not everyone has time to become fully knowledgeable about every issue. Consensus assumes that everyone can and should participate in decisions; if substantial numbers drop out, it becomes rule by the energetic, or by those who have nothing better to do. Representative democracy, by contrast, puts elected representatives in the key decision-making roles; the participation of everyone else is restricted to campaigning, voting and lobbying. In both cases participation is very unequal, not by choice but by the structure of the decision-making system.

Delegates and federations. A favorite anarchist solution to the problem of coordination and participation is delegates and federations. A delegate differs from a representative in that the delegate is more closely tied to the electorate: the delegate can be recalled at any time, especially when not following the dictates of the electors. Federations are a way of combining self-governing entities. The member bodies in the federation retain the major decision-making power over their own affairs. The members come together to decide issues affecting all of them. In a 'weak federation,' the center has only advisory functions; in a 'strong federation,' the center has considerable executive power in specified areas. By having several tiers in the federation, full participation can be ensured at the bottom level and consultation and some decision making occurs at the highest levels.

Delegates and federations sound like an alternative to conventional electoral systems, but there are strong similarities. Delegates are normally elected, and this leads to the familiar problems of representation. Certain individuals dominate. Participation in decision-making is unequal, with the delegates being heavily involved and others not. To the degree that decisions are actually made at higher levels, there is great potential for development of factions, vote trading and manipulation of the electorate.

This is where the delegate system is supposed to be different: if the delegates start to serve themselves rather than those they represent, they can be recalled. But in practice this is hard to achieve. Delegates tend to 'harden' into formal representatives. Those chosen as delegates are likely to have much more experience and knowledge than the ordinary person. Once chosen, the delegates gain even more experience and knowledge, which can be presented as of high value to the electors. In other words, recalling the delegate will be at the cost of losing an experienced and influential person.

These problems have surfaced in the German Green Party. Although formally elected as representatives, the party sought to treat those elected as delegates, setting strict limits on the length of time in parliament. This was resisted by some of those elected, who were able to build support due to their wide appeal. Furthermore, from a pragmatic point of view, those who had served in parliament had the experience and public profile to better promote the green cause. Thus the delegate approach came under great stress.

The fundamental problem with the delegate system, then, is unequal participation. Not everyone can be involved in every issue. With delegates, the problem is resolved by having the delegates involved much more in decision-making, at the expense of others. This unequal participation then reproduces and entrenches itself. The more layers there are to the federation, the more serious this problem will be. Federations, as well, are not a magical solution to the problem of coordination in a self-managing society.

In this brief survey of some of the more well-known participative alternatives to elections, I've focussed on their limitations. But these and other methods do have many strengths, and are worth promoting as additions or alternatives to the present system. Consensus has been developed enormously over the past couple of decades as a practical decision-making method. The potential of decentralization is undoubtedly great.

Rather than dismissing these possibilities, my aim is to point out some of the problems that confront them. The most serious difficulty is how to ensure participation in a wide range of issues that affect any person. How can the (self-managed) activities of large numbers of people be coordinated without vesting excessive power in a small group of people?

John Zube advocates 'panarchy,' the peaceful coexistence of a diversity of methods for voluntary association.[13] In this spirit, demarchy can be considered as one candidate for organizing society in a participative fashion.

DEMARCHY

Demarchy is based on random selection of individuals to serve in decision-making groups which deal with particular functions or services, such as roads or education. Forget the state and forget bureaucracies. In a full-fledged demarchy, all this is replaced by a network of groups whose members are randomly selected, each of which deals with a particular function in a particular area. The most eloquent account of demarchy is given by John Burnheim in his book *Is Democracy Possible?*[14]

For example, in a population of 10,000 to 100,000, there might be groups dealing with transport, health, agriculture, industry, education, environment, housing, art and so forth, or particular aspects of such functions such as rail transport. Each group would be chosen randomly from all those who volunteer to be on it. The groups could be perhaps 10 or 20 people, large enough to obtain a variety of views but small enough for face-to-face discussion. The groups themselves could use consensus, modified consensus, voting or some other procedure to reach decisions. They could call for submissions, testimony, surveys and any other information they wished to obtain.

Because there are no elections and no representatives, the problems of unequal formal power, disempowerment of electors, regulation of participation and so forth do not apply—at least not in the usual way. Formal participation occurs instead through random selection onto 'functional groups,' namely groups dealing with particular limited areas. Random selection for each group is made only from those who volunteer, just as politicians must volunteer. The difference is the method of selection: random selection rather than election.

Few people would volunteer for every possible group. Most are likely to have special interests, such as postal services, art, manufacture of building materials and services for the disabled. They could volunteer to serve on the relevant groups, and also make submissions to the groups, comment on policies and in other ways organize to promote their favored policies.

Demarchy solves the problem of participation in a neat fashion. Recognizing that it is impossible for everyone to participate on every issue in an informed fashion, it avoids anything resembling a governing body which makes far-reaching decisions on a range of issues. Instead, the functional groups have a limited domain. The people who care most about a particular issue can seek to have an influence over policy in that area. They can leave other issues to other groups and the people most concerned about them. This is basically a process of decentralization of decision-making by topic or function rather than by geography or numbers.

Leaving decision-making to those who care most about a topic has its dangers, of course: self-interested cliques can obtain power and exclude others. That is what happens normally in all sorts of organizations, from governments and corporations to social movement groups. Demarchy handles this problem through the requirement of random selection. No one can be guaranteed a formal decision-making role. Furthermore, the terms of service are strictly limited, so no permanent executive or clique can develop.

Another problem then looms. Won't there be biases in the groups selected, because only certain sorts of people will volunteer? Won't most of the groups, for example, be dominated by white middle-aged men? This poses no problem, given a suitable adaptation of how the random selection is carried out. Suppose, for example, that 80 men and 20 women volunteer for a group of 10, for which it is desired to have an equal number of men and women. The method is simply to select 5 men randomly from the 80 male volunteers and 5 women from the 20 female volunteers. In this way, the sex balance in the group can equal that in the overall population even with different rates of volunteering.

What if people don't volunteer? What if certain groups don't produce enough volunteers for their quota? In some cases this would be a sign of success. If the way things are operating is acceptable to most people, then there would be no urgency about becoming a member of a decision-making group. By contrast, in controversial areas participation is not likely to be a problem. If topics such as abortion or genetic engineering generated passionate debate, then concerned individuals and groups would find it fruitful to educate as many people as possible about the issues and encourage them to stand for random selection. Indeed, any unpopular decision could generate a mobilization of people to stand for selection. Furthermore, the people mobilized would have to span a range of categories: men and women, young and old, etc. As a result, participation and informed comment would be highest in the areas of most concern. In other areas, most people would be happy to let others look after matters.

Of special interest are those who have tried out random selection in practice. Ned Crosby set up the Jefferson Center for New Democratic

Processes, which has carried out practical experiments in random selection of citizens to form 'policy juries' which examine challenging policy issues.[15] Similar projects have been undertaken in West Germany beginning in the 1970s, led by Peter Dienel at the University of Wuppertal.[16] The groups of randomly selected citizens brought together for these projects are called 'planning cells.' The cells have dealt with issues such as energy policy, town planning and information technology.

Between the few experiments with policy juries and planning cells and Burnheim's vision of demarchy is an enormous gulf. What strategy should be used to move towards demarchy?

Burnheim thinks that as various government bodies become discredited, they may be willing to switch to demarchic management in order to maintain community legitimacy. This sounds plausible but provides little guidance for action. After all, there are plenty of unpopular, discredited and corrupt institutions in society, but this has seldom led to significant changes in the method of social decision-making. More specifically, how should demarchy be promoted in these situations? By lobbying state managers? By raising the idea among the general population? One thing is clear. The idea of demarchy must become much more well known before there is the slightest chance of implementation.

The experimentation with policy juries and planning cells is vital in gaining experience and spreading the idea of participation through random selection. The limitation of these approaches is that they are not linked to major social groups which would be able to mobilize people to work for the alternative.

Among the 'major social groups' in society, quite a number are likely to be hostile to demarchy. This includes most of the powerful groups, such as governments, corporate managements, trade union leaders, political parties, militaries, professions, etc. Genuine popular participation, after all, threatens the prerogatives of elites.

In my opinion, the most promising source of support is social movements: peace activists, feminists, environmentalists, etc. Groups such as these have an interest in wider participation, which is more likely to promote their goals than the present power elites. Social movement groups can try to put demarchy on the agenda by the use of study groups, lobbying, leafletting and grassroots organising.

Demarchy, though, should not be seen only as a policy issue, as a measure to be implemented in the community as a result of grassroots pressure. Demarchy can also be used by social movements as a means. In other words, they can use it for their own decision making.

This may not sound like much of a difficulty. After all, many social action groups already use consensus either formally or de facto.

Also, the system of delegates is quite common. It would not seem a great shift to use random selection for decision-making at scales where direct consensus becomes difficult to manage.

Unfortunately, matters in many social movements are hardly this ordered. In many cases, formal bureaucratic systems have developed, especially in the large national organizations, and there are quite a number of experienced and sometimes charismatic individuals in powerful positions. These individuals are possibly as unlikely as any politician to support conversion to a different system of decision-making. (This itself is probably as good a recommendation for random selection as could be obtained. Any proposal that threatens elites in alternative as well as mainstream organizations must have something going for it.)

Nevertheless, social movements must be one of the more promising places to promote demarchy. If they can actually begin to try out the methods, they can become much more effective advocates. Furthermore, the full vision of demarchy, without the state or bureaucracy, stands a better chance within nonbureaucratized social movements than amidst the ruins of bungled government enterprises.

One of the more promising areas for promoting demarchy is in industry.[17] Workers are confronted by powerful hierarchical systems on every side: corporate management, governments and trade union bosses. There is plenty of experience in cooperative decision-making at the shop floor level; difficulties arise at higher levels of decision-making. It is here that random selection presents itself as a real alternative. Works councils, composed of both workers and managers selected randomly to serve a short period, provide a basis for communication and coordination. This approach overcomes the defects of all forms of representation. Workers' representatives on boards of management have served to coopt workers, while representatives in the form of trade union delegates have often become separated from the shop floor. Demarchic groups provide a way to maintain shop floor involvement in large enterprises.

The key point here is that demarchy should not be treated as a policy alternative, to be implemented from the top, but rather as a method of action itself. The ends should be incorporated in the means. It is quite appropriate that groups promoting demarchy use its techniques.

Needless to say, the future of demarchy cannot be mapped out. It is stimulating to speculate about solutions to anticipated problems; Burnheim's general formulations are immensely valuable in providing a vision. But as democracy by lot is tested, promoted, tried out, enjoys successes and suffers failures, it will be revised and refined. That is to be expected.

The message is that the process of developing and trying out alternatives is essential for all those seeking a more participative society. True enough, some worthy reforms can be achieved through the old channels of electoral politics, but that is no excuse for neglecting the task of investigating new structures. Demarchy is one such alternative, and deserves attention.

The greens may be one of the most exciting political developments in decades, but in entering electoral politics they may have limited their potential for bringing about radical change. Ironically, it is the popular, charismatic green politicians who provide least threat to established power structures. Their electoral success will ensure continuing reliance on the old system of politics.

ACKNOWLEDGEMENTS

An earlier version of this paper appeared in *Social Alternatives*, Vol. 8, No. 4, January 1990, pp. 13-18. Valuable comments on a draft were received from Bob James and Ralph Summy.

NOTES

1. These points are well made by Benjamin Ginsberg, *The Consequences of Consent: Elections, Citizen Control and Popular Acquiescence* (Reading, MA: Addison-Wesley, 1982).
2. Ralph Miliband, *The State in Capitalist Society* (London: Weidenfeld and Nicolson, 1969).
3. Carl Boggs, *Social Movements and Political Power: Emerging Forms of Radicalism in the West* (Philadelphia: Temple University Press, 1986).
4. Brian Martin, "Environmentalism and electoralism," *Ecologist*, Vol. 14, No. 3, 1984, pp. 110-118.
5. Ginsberg, *The Consequences of Consent*, op. cit. See also Benjamin Ginsberg, *The Captive Public: How Mass Opinion Promotes State Power* (New York: Basic Books, 1986).
6. A mainstream treatment is Benjamin R. Barber, *Strong Democracy: Participatory Politics for a New Age* (Berkeley: University of California Press, 1984).
7. F. Christopher Arterton, *Teledemocracy: Can Technology Protect Democracy?* (Newbury Park, CA: Sage, 1987); Christa Daryl Slaton, *Televote: Expanding Citizen Participation in the Quantum Age* (New York: Praeger, 1992).
8. Michael Avery, Brian Auvine, Barbara Streibel and Lonnie Weiss, *Building United Judgment: A Handbook for Consensus Decision Making* (Madison,

WI: Center for Conflict Resolution, 1981); Virginia Coover, Ellen Deacon, Charles Esser and Christopher Moore, *Resource Manual for a Living Revolution* (Philadelphia: New Society Publishers, 1981).

9. Jane J. Mansbridge, *Beyond Adversary Democracy* (New York: Basic Books, 1980).

10. See for example Murray Bookchin, "What is communalism? The democratic dimension of anarchism," *Green Perspectives*, No. 31, October 1994, pp. 1-6; Charles Landry, David Morley, Russell Southwood and Patrick Wright, *What a Way to Run a Railroad: An Analysis of Radical Failure* (London: Comedia, 1985); Howard Ryan, *Blocking Progress: Consensus Decision Making in the Anti-nuclear Movement* (Berkeley: Overthrow Cluster, Livermore Action Group, 1985).

11. The case is given by Leopold Kohr, *The Breakdown of Nations* (London: Routledge and Kegan Paul, 1957) and Kirkpatrick Sale, *Human Scale* (New York: Coward, McCann and Geoghegan, 1980).

12. Frances Kendall and Leon Louw, *After Apartheid: The Solution for South Africa* (San Francisco: ICS Press, 1987).

13. Publications available from John Zube, 7 Oxley Street, Berrima NSW 2577, Australia

14. John Burnheim, *Is Democracy Possible? The Alternative to Electoral Politics* (London: Polity Press, 1985). For a short outline, see John Burnheim, "Democracy by statistical representation," *Social Alternatives*, Vol. 8, No. 4, January 1990, pp. 25-28. On decisions on a world scale, see John Burnheim, "Democracy, nation states and the world system," in David Held and Christopher Pollitt (eds.), *New Forms of Democracy* (London: Sage, 1986), pp. 218-239.

15. Ned Crosby, Janet M. Kelly and Paul Schaefer, "Citizen panels: a new approach to citizen participation," *Public Administration Review*, Vol. 46, March-April 1986, pp. 170-178; Ned Crosby, "The peace movement and new democratic processes," *Social Alternatives*, Vol. 8, No. 4, January 1990, pp. 33-37.

16. Peter C. Dienel, "Contributing to social decision methodology: citizen reports on technological projects," in Charles Vlek and George Cvetkovich (eds.), *Social Decision Methodology for Technological Projects* (Dordrecht: Kluwer Academic Publishers, 1989), pp. 133-151.

17. Crucial work on this has been done by Fred Emery. See F. E. Emery, *Toward Real Democracy and Toward Real Democracy: Further Problems* (Toronto: Ontario Ministry of Labor, 1989); Merrelyn Emery (ed.), *Participative Design for Participative Democracy* (Canberra: Center for Continuing Education, Australian National University, 1989).

4

ANARCHAFEMINISM

graphic from **Ecstatic Incisions: The Collages of Freddie Baer**

graphic from **Stealworks: The Graphic Details of John Yates**

Introduction To Anarchafeminism

People who are familiar with feminism and social anarchism are invariably struck by their similarities. Both see social and economic inequality as rooted in institutionalized power arrangements; both stress the necessity of changing those arrangements as a precondition for liberation; and both work for the realization of personal autonomy and freedom within a context of community.

This section features the contributions of four writers: **Elaine Leeder, Susan Brown, Peggy Kornegger,** and **Carol Ehrlich.** Their essays blend in an extraordinary manner, and while they all promote an anarchist feminist position, they all grapple with the differences between that position and other varieties of feminism. That is where we have to start. I think we need to look at the basic statements of feminist theories and observe how people come to endorse some and not others.

All feminist theories start with a set observations about women in society. These three statements represent the core of those observations.

1. The social roles ascribed to women and men are primarily culturally determined.
2. Women are significantly discriminated against in all sectors of society — personally, socially, and politically.
3. Women are physically objectified and, as a consequence, routinely harassed and assaulted sexually.

Given these observations, feminists have had to affirm that:

4. Women and men are equal.

Liberal feminists seek a societal affirmation of their equality by modifying the existing power arrangements in order to eliminate the institutionalized forms of differential treatment. Their goal is not to change the basic structures of society. Further, they make no special claims about women as a class or about a women's culture. Their goal is to obtain equality in the access to resources of power.

The women's movement divided on the problems of existing inequalities *among* women, particularly those of social class, ethnicity and skin color. Both ideologically and from the standpoint of organizing a movement, these divisions proved as difficult for the feminist movement as they were for the larger society. For some feminists, these were not perceived as issues; while for others, they were seen as subordinate to the struggle for power. Still others, mainly radical feminists, split over the process by which matters of class, ethnicity and color should be incorporated into the women's movement.

For the varieties of radical feminists (and anarchists are one of those), there are additional belief statements that make up their theories. Central to all of the radical perspectives is an insistence on the consistency of means and ends, especially in one's everyday life.

5. The personal is the political.

"Politics" are defined as extending beyond the narrow set of events relating to formal government. Politics involves everything we do in our daily lives, everything that happens to us, and every interpretation we make of these things.

In a society that distinguishes people on the basis of gender, females will have a range of experiences that are different from those of males. Even similar experiences will carry different meanings. The consequence is that women (and men) have developed distinctive subcultures. Recognition of this cultural difference is expressed in another belief statement of feminist theory.

6. There is a separate, identifiable women's subculture in every society. The distinctive elements of that culture are usually those centered about activities involving maintenance and components of interpersonal relationships such as nurturance, empathy and solidarity. (Some varieties of thought include spirituality.)

Most radical feminists believe that the elements of women's culture are preferable to their male analogs in the dominant culture. Some radical feminists understandably stop at this point, choosing to live (and work, if possible) within a women's community. Some, claiming the superiority of women's culture, and often, by implication, the superiority of women, have argued that a society controlled by women would not have the oppressive characteristics of patriarchal societies. Some of them have developed matriarchal theories of past and future societies.

Like all political theories, radical feminism has a set of statements on how change is to come about. (Many of these are expressed in Howard Ehrlich's "Building a revolutionary transfer culture," which is reprinted elsewhere in this book.) Central to the feminist transfer culture are two requirements.

7. The individual working collectively with others is the locus of change.
8. Alternative institutions built on principles of cooperation and mutual aid are the organizational forms for this change.

Meaningful social change does not come about by individuals working alone. Change comes through the organization of people in a setting of mutual aid and cooperation. In keeping with this, radical feminists and social anarchists have built an impressive number of organizations and networks: media collectives, clinics, theater groups, alternative schools, antiprofit businesses, and so on. The organizations built by radical feminists are often developed on anarchist principles — although as Peggy Kornegger points out in "Anarchism: The Feminist Connection" — this development is usually intuitive. For the anarchist feminist the linkage is explicit.

Freedom is an important concept in radical feminism, although it is not often explicitly or clearly articulated. One critical belief statement emphasizes what some anarchists have called a "negative" conception of freedom. It is a principle that asserts the necessity of a society to be organized in a manner that people cannot be treated as objects or used as instruments to some end.

9. All people have a right to be free from coercion, from violence to their mind or body.

Perhaps one reason it is not often clearly articulated in radical feminist theories is because its implication moves beyond the bounds of most of those theories into an anarchist feminism. As L. Susan Brown says in her contribution, "Beyond Feminism: Anarchism and Human Freedom":

Just as one can be a feminist and oppose power . . . it is also possible and not inconsistent for a feminist to embrace the use of power and advocate domination without relinquishing the right to be a feminist.

To be free from coercion means that one has to live in a society where institutionalized forms of power, domination and hierarchy no longer exist. For anarchists, the central issue is power.

10. One should neither submit to nor exercise power over other people.

Anarchists disavow the state and see themselves as working for its delegitimation and dissolution. It is the state that lays claim to legitimate authority including the authority, to legitimate power arrangements and the monopoly rights to the mobilization of police and military force. Radical feminists work to end patriarchy, that is, the male domination of women through force and the institutionalized acceptance of masculine authority. To anarchist feminists, the state and patriarchy are twin aberrations. Thus, to destroy the state is to destroy the major agent of institutionalized patriarchy; to abolish patriarchy is to abolish the state as it now exists. Anarchist feminists go further than most radical feminists: they caution that the state by definition is always illegitimate. For this reason, feminists should not be working within the electoral confines of the state nor should they try to substitute *female* states for the present male states. Some radical feminists argue, as we have said, that a society controlled by women would not have the oppressive features of patriarchal society; anarchist feminists respond that the very structure of a state creates inequities. Anarchism is the only mode of social organization that will prevent this from happening.

Anarchist feminists know what other radicals often have to learn from bitter experience: the development of new forms of organization designed to get rid of hierarchy, authority, and power requires new social structures. Further, these structures must be carefully built and continually nurtured so that organizations function smoothly and efficiently, and so that new or informal elites will not emerge. If there is an underlying principle of action it is that we need to cultivate the habits of freedom so that we constantly experience it in our everyday lives.

Elaine Leeder sets the stage for the more theoretical discussions which follow. In her essay, "Let Our Mothers Show the Way," she displays the essential radicalism and currency of the ideas of Voltairine de Cleyre (1866 - 1912) and Emma Goldman (1869 - 1940). As Leeder points out, it was anarchist women who extended the boundaries of male-dominated anarchist thought. To be sure, sexist anarchists existed then, as now, but as Susan Brown noted it is "only by virtue of contradicting their own anarchism."

Carol Ehrlich's essay, "Socialism, Anarchism, and Feminism," concludes this section. The strength of her essay is in her straightforward confrontation with the issues of group structure and her creative merger with situationism. The blending of situationism and anarchist feminism, she writes, "combines a socialist awareness of the primacy of capitalist oppression with an anarchist emphasis upon transforming the whole of public and private life."

Let Our Mothers Show the Way

Elaine Leeder

Where is the women's movement going? Some argue that it is in a period of demise and that we now see the emergence of the "post feminist" generation. Others argue that it is moving into a period of retrenchment, reviewing where it has been and where it is going. While the movement examines itself we continue to exist in a depressed economy where, although women's roles are changing, women are still earning a fraction of men's wages and are assuming much greater responsibility for maintaining their households' economy. In this period of assessment we still see much active work that is being carried out by the various self-help movements. Work in health care, counseling and protection from male violence continue to be vital activities for many of us.

These activities, which often lead to the abandonment of established institutions, may appear to some to be operating in an intellectual and theoretical vacuum. This need now be the case since there is an historical tradition upon which many of the tactics of the women's movement are based. In particular I believe that anarchist women between 1870 and 1920 offer a source of inspiration for a current generation of activists. Many women have been drawn to anarchism because the anarchist belief in freedom of the individual includes the idea of women's freedom. Anarchist ideology holds the belief that all people have the right to complete liberty as long as one's actions do not interfere with the rights of other individuals (Marsh, p. 10). Although this is certainly not an explicit feminist doctrine there are the seeds for women's liberation within the ideology. However, women within the movement also experienced anti-feminist behavior on the part of some anarchist men.

The anarchist tradition of direct resistance to authority, the belief in direct action such as strikes, boycotts and other confrontations with those in power, the conviction that humanity is inherently good and society can change for the better are all themes found in the works of anarchist women. In addition the women sometimes advocated the use of violence. Many of the women who did espouse this tactic did so as young women and changed their thinking or left the movement as they got older. (Marsh, p. 22). Anarchist women, however, added new dimensions to the tradition which can not be found in the teachings of Proudhon, Kropotkin and Bakunin. Anarchist women believed that changes in society had to occur in the economic and political spheres but their emphasis was also on the personal and psychological dimensions of life. They believed that changes in personal aspects of life, such as families, children, sex, should be viewed as political activity. This is a new dimension that was added to anarchist theory by the women at the turn of the century.

The changes that women wanted might be called a "moral revolution," a term used by Voltairine de Cleyre (Avrich, p. 163). This evolution would give freedom to the soul and the body. It was an attempt to free society from the constructions of Victorian morals and, as such, involved developing non-traditional life styles, values and forms of behavior. These women flaunted social norms and thumbed their noses at convention. Emma Goldman lived communally with friends. Some anarchist women lived together with men in "free union" without being married; parents had children and did not raise them. The anarchist women believed that changes had to occur in the institutions of marriage and family, in sexuality, in children's education, to name just a few of the "personal" areas that came under their scrutiny.

Proudhon, Bakunin and Kropotkin had never dealt with the issues that were being raised by anarchist women. All three men had been married and had traditional beliefs about the role of women. Bakunin's marriage was somewhat unusual in that he did not live with his wife for periods of time while she was off living with her lover. In fact, he even assumed responsibility for a child that she had by another man. (Carr, pp. 368, 386, 399). None of the three founders of anarchism wrote of a different role for women other than that of mother, wife and nurturer. Proudhon felt that the patriarchal family was the fundamental unit in his future society (Marsh, p. 19). Believing that women were the domestic force in life, he also opposed divorce. Kropotkin believed that women could do political work but that the working class struggle came first. He assumed that there were natural behaviors for each sex and that women were the dependent sex. Later, anarchist men such as Moses Harmon believed that men's concerns were universal but that women's concerns were selfish (Marsh, p. 56). Other anarchist men were frightened of having any changes made in the domestic situation and thwarted or subverted attempts in that direction (Marsh, pp. 27 and 82).

In dealings with the "woman question," as it was called then, or sexism, as it is called now, anarchist women argued that intellectual and psychological characteristics are not gender based (Marsh, p. 4). They argued that roles in society should be based on capacity and preferences rather than on sex. They believed that women must be economically, sexually and psychologically independent of men. Voltairine de Cleyre spent much of her life educating women to be "industrially independent" (Marsh, p. 158) and to fight against the social constrictions of sex stereotyped roles. She used language that can be found in modern feminist writings such as "she-ro worship" and argued against 'the narrow confines placed on women's behavior in her society (Avrich, p. 159). Not only did de Cleyre argue for economic independence, she also lived it in her life. Having been treated as a sex object and domestic servant by the men in her life, she argued that women should maintain a room or rooms for themselves in order to remain free of the confines of the nuclear family. With much difficulty she maintained economic independence throughout her life.

Anarchist women such as Emma Goldman, Voltairine de Cleyre and others believed that many of women's problems were related to the nature of marriage and the nuclear family. According to Goldman, marriage made women a sex commodity and made them feel they were objects or things (Drinnon, p. 151). It was an economic arrangement that produced jealousy and was not based in love (Goldman, p. 182). In "The Traffic in Women" Goldman argued that marriage made women men's property and that it was no better for women to marry than to be a prostitute since they were in both cases driven by economic need. In making this argument Goldman relied on the anarchist concept of the abolition of private property, true to Proudhon's belief that "property is theft." In this case she was arguing that woman, as private property of a man, was having her freedom and independence stolen.

Anarchist women, often in direct contradiction to anarchist men of the same era, argued for the abolition of the nuclear family and the institution of marriage as direct action against the subordination of women. They reasoned that as women became economically independent of men there would be no need for marriage. They also condemned the institution of monogamy and advocated a concept of "free love" in which individuals were free to choose their sexual partners and to determine how long they would choose to remain with that partner. They believed that people were erotic beings and that sexual relationships concerned only those involved. They held that the state and the church had no right to be involved in these unions (Marsh, p. 69). They believed that marriage made for unhappiness, and that people should be able to enter and leave relationships at their own discretion. In addition, some anarchist writers advocated a concept known as "varietism" or non-exclusive sexual relationships (Marsh, p. 46). Some anarchist women argued that homosexuality was part of the fight to free sexuality of all types and as such was a legitimate sexual alternative. Many of these ideas are strikingly similar to those being made by current feminists and are strangely contemporary in their vision. Many of these women's beliefs, which were considered deviant within their society, are accepted by large segments of our society today.

In keeping with the anarchist tradition of individual freedom and disregard for laws and conventionality, anarchist women were involved in the birth control movement from its beginning. At a time when birth control information was illegal, Emma Goldman spoke publicly on the subject and actually shared her knowledge with interested parties. She and other anarchist women believed that "voluntary parenthood" was a crucial part of women's freedom. She believed that women had a right to determine whether they wanted children and that they had a right to control their own bodies (Drinnon, pp. 166-167). Although she did not make birth control a major part of her work, she popularized the idea through her speeches and assistance in organizing groups to continue educating the public.

Generally anarchist women such as Goldman and de Cleyre scorned the question of the vote and the women's suffrage question. They believed that it was useless to enter the political arena since laws and voting did nothing to change conditions for the powerless in society. Goldman said:

> She can give suffrage or the ballot no new quality, nor can she receive anything from it that will enhance her own quality. Her development, her freedom, her independence must come from and through herself. First, by asserting herself as a personality and not as a sex commodity. Second, by refusing the right to anyone over her body; by refusing to bear children unless she wants them; by refusing to be a servant to God, the State, society, the husband, the family, etc.; by making her life simpler, but deeper and richer. (Goldman, p, 211).

De Cleyre agreed that the ballot could serve no useful purpose for anyone (Marsh, p. 52). Their position was identical with that of Bakunin and Kropotkin who refused to participate in political parties and campaigns.

There was little participation by anarchist women within the larger feminist movement. Some women such as Voltairine de Cleyre organized women's groups for education and "consciousness raising." They did not establish larger organizations for support and education on the woman question (Marsh, p. 63). By not doing so, their views did not become widely known and they had little impact on women of their time. Interestingly enough this question of small decentralized groups versus large mass organizations is one that is currently being discussed within anarchist feminist circles. We are currently questioning the need for larger networks to publicize the anarchist feminist alternative.

While anarchist women differed in some ways from the "patriarchs" of anarchism they also followed many of their teachings. One such example is their involvement in the modern school movement. Anarchist women were involved in this effort to increase public awareness of alternatives in the education of children. Because they were committed to freedom, these women carried this belief into their dealings with children.

The Modern School Movement was started in the U.S. as a result of the death of Francisco Ferrer in Spain in 1909. Ferrer's ideas about education included the beliefs that children need a healthy physical environment in which to learn, and that children need short and interesting instructional periods. Further, he held that there should be respect for the child with no imposition of ideas and no restraint on children's natural inclination to learn. The Modern School emphasized the process of learning, and learning by example rather than by rote. Children were taught to be self-reliant and were not viewed as their parents' property. Kropotkin had written about the need for manual and intellectual work and the need for "integral education" (Avrich, 1980, pp. 16-17). The Modern Schools personified the traditions of the anarchist founders.

Emma Goldman, along with many anarchist men, was a leading force in the establishment of the first Modern School in New York City, as well as the Ferrer Association which promoted education and public forums for adults. She wrote and spoke extensively on the subject, as did Voltairine de Cleyre. de Cleyre taught at the adult programs in the Modern School, feeling that she was unable to handle the aggression of the small children (Avrich, *Voltairine de Cleyre*, p.

222). As de Cleyre became more familiar with the schools she became critical of them, feeling that those who were involved, with the exception of a few teachers, knew little about the educational process and that the schools were chaotic. Although critical, she maintained an active interest in them throughout her life.

Anarchists like Goldman and de Cleyre believed that there should be cooperative communities where those interested in caring for children could do so. They did not address the possibility of mutual child-rearing by both parents. Their positions were somewhat limited and did not deal with the realities of how to handle the day-to-day issues of having a child. They never discussed the question of power relationships between parents and children, although they were discussing the issue of power in other contexts. Some argue that this failure to find a place for children within the anarchist philosophy indicates an inability on the part of anarchists to translate their radicalism into everyday practice (Marsh, p. 99). I disagree. I believe that anarchists were in fact dealing with issues in their own lives but had not yet seen the need to articulate those positions. Because they were involved in such issues as education, suffrage, sexuality, and economics of women, they were not yet ready to consider how they might change their relationships with children. It is possible that they did not see the limits of their thinking about children. I believe that modern anarchist feminists are now ready to address that question.

Anarchist women led in attempting to transcend the social norms that were constricting them. They took the anarchist tradition, but built on it. They attempted to develop a new society within the vestiges of the old. They stretched the vision beyond what was then acceptable. As a result they were regarded with contempt and anger by the larger society.

Anarchist women have provided role models for a current generation of feminists. They lived in communes, developed models for alternative education experiments and made "free unions" the model for current behavior of "living together." They accepted homosexuality and bisexuality. They emphasized the need for economic independence of women. They argued that the vote would not give women what they needed. They even wrote about and took part in affinity groups and consciousness-raising groups which are part of the current political reality for activists (Avrich, p. 165). Emma Goldman, Voltairine de Cleyre and other anarchist women helped bring the domestic sphere of life within the anarchist tradition. Some of their thinking and writing was limited by their time and their position in society. It remains the task of current anarchist feminists to apply their insights to relevant social issues, such as child-rearing. It is also necessary for current anarchist feminists to learn from the failure of our predecessors in establishing far reaching organizations which could educate the public as to the anarchist vision of society.

The anarchist tradition is a long and colorful one. It includes many diverse and unusual personalities who have always held as their ideals the unlimited capacity for human good and the hope for true liberty. It now remains the task for current anarchists and feminists to continue that creative tradition. Modern anarchists are busy applying the ideology to areas that earlier anarchists never imagined. And yet the anarchist tradition, with its belief in the abolition of private property, direct action, resistance to authority, and the reliance on small local groups, is easily applied to today's issues. The issues of nuclear power and disarmament, environmental concerns, women's reproductive rights, and child-rearing all lend themselves to an anarchist analysis. Anarchist feminism may be old in its traditions but it is strangely modern in its relevance to today's world.

REFERENCES

Avrich, Paul. *An American Anarchist: The Life of Voltairine de Cleyre.* Princeton University Press: Princeton, NJ, 1978.

Avrich, Paul. *The Modern School Movement: Anarchism and Education in the U.S.* Princeton University Press: Princeton, NJ, 1980.

Drinnon, Richard. *Rebel in Paradise: A Biography of Emma Goldman.* Harper and Row: New York, 1961.

Goldman, Emma. *Anarchism and Other Essays.* New York: Dover, 1969.

Marsh, Margaret. *Anarchist Women: 1870-1920.* Philadelphia: Temple University Press, 1981.

BEYOND FEMINISM:
ANARCHISM AND HUMAN FREEDOM

L. SUSAN BROWN

It is clear that profound social change has been brought about through feminist struggle, both by the efforts of women belonging to the "first wave" of feminism in the early 1900s and more recently, by the "second wave" of activism that emerged in the 1960s and continues to this day. In general, women today have more freedom of choice than did their mothers or grandmothers before them. While acknowledging these accomplishments, I would like to consider what I see as an inherent limitation of the feminist movement: the lack of an intrinsic critique of power and domination *per se*. The absence of such a critique in the core of feminist thought results in the inability of feminism as a whole to envision or to create a world where all people can be free. I would like to suggest that the political philosophy of anarchism, with its implicit critique of power, offers an alternative to feminism in the ongoing struggle for *human* liberation.

To speak of power as a thing or phenomenon that can exist independent of human consciousness is to profoundly misunderstand the whole problem of power itself. Power exists as a relationship between individual human beings whereby one individual attempts to negate the free will of another. When the will of one has been successfully imposed on another, then there exists a situation of domination. That power is a relationship between two parties — the oppressor and the oppressed — and not something metaphysical or otherwise beyond the beyond the grasp and control of human individuals, is clearly understood by anarchist thinkers.

In the early part of this century, Emma Goldman quoted these lines from John Henry Mackay's poem in her essay "Anarchism: What It Really Stands For":

I am an Anarchist! Where I will
Not rule, and also ruled I will not be![1]

These words clearly and succinctly express the integrity that is fundamental to the anarchist position — integrity born out of the double
imperative to both denounce and renounce the exercise of power.
Anarchist political philosophy is based upon the belief that people are
capable of self-determination, that self-determination is the founda-
tion for human freedom, and that power relationships undermine self-
determination and therefore must be constantly opposed. This uncom-
promising anti-authoritarianism is what makes anarchism so compelling to its adherents, both as a philosophy and as a political movement. Anarchists understand that freedom is grounded in the refusal
of the individual to exercise power over others coupled with the opposition of the individual to restrictions by any external authority. Thus,
anarchists challenge any form of organization or relationship which
fosters the exercise of power and domination. For instance, anarchists
oppose the state because the act of governing depends upon the exercise of power, whether it be of monarchs over their subjects or, as in
the case of a democracy, of the majority over the minority. Anarchists
also rally against the institution of organized religion, which they regard as both implicitly and explicitly engendering relations of hierarchy and domination. Compulsory education, sexual repression, censorship, private property, alienated labor, child abuse — these are all
relationships of power that anarchists critically challenge.

Of course, many expressions of power exist in our society other
than those I have just listed; what distinguishes the anarchist from
other political activists is that the anarchist opposes them all. This condemnation of power *per se* is fundamental to the anarchist position
and gives it a critical impetus that takes it beyond traditional political
movements. The feminist movement, with its central concern the liberation of women, does not contain within itself the larger critique of
power that is basic to anarchism. What I hope to demonstrate below is
that without an implicit condemnation of power *as such*, feminism ultimately fails by limiting itself to an incomplete struggle for liberation.

In my view, it is absolutely necessary that an explicit anti-
authoritarianism be present in a political philosophy if it is to bring
about true human liberation. *No* hierarchy is acceptable, *no* ruler is
allowable, *no* domination is justifiable in a free society. Clearly, if this
anti-authoritarian principle is not fundamental to a political philosophy, then domination and hierarchy can exist in theory and practice
without presenting a crisis. As a movement, feminism does not have

as a defining characteristic an anti-authoritarian critique of power and domination; therefore, as a political philosophy, it is insufficient for the liberation of all people.

Of course, it is possible to point to various groups and individuals within feminism who are critical of power, domination, and hierarchy. The feminist writer Marilyn French, for instance, criticizes power in her book *Beyond Power: On Women, Men, and Morals*, and advocates building a new world on what she argues is the opposite of power: pleasure.[2] Another feminist writer, Starhawk, likewise criticizes the exercise of what she calls "power-over" and advocates the use of consensus decision-making as one means to counter power.[3] Angela Miles, in her essay "Feminist Radicalism in the 1980s," argues for an "integrative" feminism that opposes all forms of domination.[4] These are only three examples of feminist thinkers who consciously oppose the exercise of power and domination; there exist many others.

However, while one can point to examples of feminist thought that focus on the problem of power, this does not indicate in any sense that a critique of power is necessary or integral to feminist theory taken as a whole. In other words, just as one can be a feminist and oppose power like the three writers cited above, it is also possible and not inconsistent for a feminist to embrace the use of power and advocate domination without relinquishing the right to be a feminist. For example, in her essay "The Future — If There Is One — Is Female," Sally Miller Gearheart argues for the establishment of a matriarchy; she says we must "begin thinking of flipping the coin, of making the exchange of power, of building the ideology of female primacy and control."[5] A matriarchy, like patriarchy, is based on power; the fact that in a matriarchy *women* hold the power does not negate the fact that power is still being exercised. Jo Freeman, in her article "The Tyranny of Structurelessness," argues that feminists must abandon their small leaderless groups in favor of delegated power and a strong, centralized feminist organization.[6] In place of small grassroots groups that use consensus to make decisions, Freeman advocates large scale democratic decision making, without questioning the tyranny of the majority over the minority that is inevitable in any democratic form of organization. For Freeman, if feminism is to be successful, then "some middle ground between domination and ineffectiveness can and must be found."[7] Clearly, Freeman sees nothing wrong with women participating in forms of politics which are based on the exercise of domination and power. Betty Friedan, feminist author of *The Feminine Mystique* and *The Second Stage*, argues in both books that the struggle for and the achievement of women's equality should take place without disturbing the existing hierarchies of the state and the capitalist economic systems.[8] Friedan has no quarrel with economic or political power — she simply wants men and women to be able to compete for power on an equal footing. Catharine MacKinnon, in her book, *Toward a Feminist Theory of the State*, suggests that a widening of state power in the form of a feminist state is the only way to counter male sexual domination. MacKinnon does not question power itself; in fact, she advocates investing the state with more power over the individual. MacKinnon's main concern is with *who* exercises power; she believes that feminists must wield power through a strong state in order to achieve the liberation of women.[9] Gearhart, Freeman, Friedan, and MacKinnon — all four are undeniably feminist, and all four accept power as part of their world view. This acceptance of power does not in any way disqualify them from being feminists. Feminism may allow for a critique of power, but a critique of power is not necessary to feminism.

In spite of the fact that some feminists clearly embrace the use of power, the argument has been made by certain theorists that feminism is inherently anarchistic. For instance, Lynne Farrow takes this position when she claims that "Feminism practices what Anarchism preaches."[10] Peggy Kornegger also asserts an identity between the two movements when she states "feminists have been unconscious anarchists for years."[11] She urges feminists to consciously acknowledge "(w)omen"s intuitive anarchism." While it is true that some feminists may in fact embrace anti-authoritarian principles, many feminists have no problem with the exercise of power or the existence of domination. Kornegger herself may very well wish that feminism ought to be explicitly anarchistic, but in reality this is simply not the case. The only way Kornegger can assert an identity between anarchism and feminism is by defining those feminists who accept power (like Gearhart, Freeman, Friedan, and Mackinnon) as not being true feminists at all. Kornegger actually attempts this theoretical slight of hand when she states that "Feminism doesn't mean female corporate power or a woman president; it means *no* corporate power and *no* presidents." This ignores the fact that to Betty Friedan, for instance, feminism is precisely the integration of women into corporate power and the election of a woman president. That Friedan is a feminist cannot legitimately be denied because although she accepts power relationships in her vision of women's liberation, the basic underpinnings of feminist thought do not require a repudiation of power. Kornegger misses this point entirely when she collapses the two movements into one. Once again, Kornegger may legitimately want feminism to mean the dissolution of power, but both in theory and practice this is not what feminism is.

Both Farrow and Kornegger, in their enthusiasm to link feminism with anarchism, ignore groups and individuals within the women's movement who are decidedly "archic," that is who endorse the use of power in both theory and practice. By collapsing anarchism and feminism into one movement, Kornegger and Farrow disregard the rich diversity of perspectives that make up the feminist movement, at the same time committing a grave injustice to anarchism by rendering it redundant. If "feminism practices what anarchism preaches," who needs anarchism anyway? In fact, feminism and anarchism are not identical movements as Farrow and Kornegger suggest; feminism as a whole recognizes the iniquity of the oppression of women by men; anarchism opposes oppression of all kinds. Certainly some feminists look beyond sexism to a wider, anarchistic critique of power; however, this wider critique is not at all necessary to feminism.

Since it is possible, and in fact quite likely, that one could be a feminist without sharing the anarchist sensibility toward power, then it is logical to ask whether it is possible to be an anarchist without being a feminist. In other words, can anarchism accommodate the oppression of women without contradicting itself? As anarchism is a political philosophy that opposes *all* relationships of power, it is inherently feminist. An anarchist who supports male domination contradicts the implicit critique of power which is the fundamental principle upon which all of anarchism is built. Sexist anarchists do exist but only by virtue of directly contradicting their own anarchism. This contradiction leaves sexist anarchists open to criticism on their own terms. Anarchism must be feminist if it is to remain self-consistent.

Not only is anarchism inherently feminist, but also it goes beyond feminism in its fundamental opposition to all forms of power, hierarchy, and domination. Anarchism transcends and contains feminism in its critique of power. This implicit opposition to the exercise of power give anarchism a wider mandate, so to speak, than feminism or other liberatory movements such as Marxism. Anarchist political philosophy and practice is free to critically oppose any situation of oppression. While race, class, age, gender, sexuality, or ability, for instance, may pose analytic problems for other movements, anarchism is capable of dealing with all these issues as legitimate because of its fundamental commitment to freedom for *all* people. No one oppression is given special status in anarchism — *all* oppression is equally undesirable. Anarchism fights for human freedom against each and every form of power and domination, not just a particular historical manifestation of power. This gives anarchism a flexibility not available to other movements. Not only can anarchism address any form of oppression that exists today, it is versatile enough to be able to respond to any form of oppression that may emerge in the future. If tomorrow, for instance, left-handed people were proclaimed criminals for their lack of right-handedness, anarchists would have to oppose such oppression in order to remain true to anarchism's underlying anti-authoritarianism principle. It is this fundamental anti-authoritarianism that leads anarchists to fight for the dignity and freedom of such groups as women, people of color, gays and lesbians, people with AIDS, the differently abled, the poor, and the homeless, among others. Anarchism goes beyond other liberatory movements in opposing oppression in whatever form it takes, without assigning priority to one oppression over another.

Unlike most other political movements, anarchism understands that all oppressions are mutually reinforcing; therefore it urges that the libertarian struggle take place on many fronts at once. Thus some anarchists concentrate on challenging state power, others focus on opposing male domination, and still others spend their energy fight against capitalist exploitation, compulsive heterosexuality, organized religion, and a myriad of other causes. The anarchist movement accommodates a diversity of anti-authoritarian struggles, and while each is recognized as being essential to the establishment of a truly free society, none is placed as prior to or more important than the others. Anarchism fights all oppression in all its forms.

Anarchism goes beyond feminism, indeed beyond most other liberatory movements, in its relentless quest for human freedom. Certainly there are people working within other movements who share anarchism's aversion to power; however, any political movement that does not have at its core an anti-authoritarian critique of power leaves itself open to anarchist questioning. The gift of anarchism lies in this critique — a thoughtful but relentless questioning of authority and power, one which seeks to create a world where all may live in freedom.

Notes

1. John Henry Mackay, quoted in Anar*chism and Other Essays* by Emma Goldman, p.47. New York: Dover, 1969.
2. Marilyn French, *Beyond Power: On Women, Men, and Morals*, pp. 539-540. New York: Summit, 1985.
3. Starhawk, *Dreaming the Dark: Magic, Sex, and Politics*, pp. 110-111. Boston: Beacon, 1982.
4. Angela Miles, *Feminist Radicalism in the 1980s*, p. 5. Montreal: CultureTexts, 1985.

5. Sally Miller Gearheart, "The Future — If There Is One — Is Female," in Pam McAllister, (ed.), *Reweaving the Web of Life: Feminism and Nonviolence,* p. 270. Philadelphia: New Society Publishers, 1982.

6. Jo Freeman, "The Tyranny of Structureless," in *Untying the Knot: Feminism, Anarchism, and Organization.* Montreal: BOA, 1986, Bevy of Anarchist/Feminists, P.O. Box 988, Station Desjardins, Montreal, Quebec, H5B 1C1.

7. Jo Freeman, "The Tyranny of Structureless," p. 14.

8. See Betty Friedan, *The Feminine Mystique,* especially pp. 330, 337-339; New York: Dell, 1974; and Betty Friedan, *The Second Stage,* especially pp. 262, 324, 339; New York: Summit, 1981.

9. Catharine MacKinnon, *Toward a Feminist Theory of the State,* p. 41. Cambridge: Harvard University Press, 1989.

10. Lynne Farrow, Feminism as Anarchism, p. 1. Montreal: BOA, 1988.

11. Peggy Kornegger, "Anarchism: The Feminist Connection."

Anarchism: The Feminist Connection

Peggy Kornegger

Twenty-six years ago, when I was in a small-town Illinois high school, I had never heard of the word 'anarchism' at all. The closest I came to it was knowing that anarchy meant 'chaos.' As for socialism and communism, my history classes somehow conveyed the message that there was no difference between them and fascism, a word that brought to mind Hitler, concentration camps, and all kinds of horrible things which never happened in a free country like ours. I was subtly being taught to swallow the bland pablum of traditional American politics: moderation, compromise, fence-straddling.

I learned the lesson well: it took me years to recognize the bias and distortion which had shaped my entire 'education.' The 'his-story' of mankind (white) had meant just that; as a woman I was relegated to a vicarious existence. As an anarchist I had no existence at all. A whole chunk of the past (and thus possibilities for the future) had been kept from me. Only recently did I discover that many of my disconnected political impulses and inclinations shared a common framework — that is, the anarchist or libertarian tradition of thought. It was like suddenly seeing red after years of colorblind grays.

Emma Goldman furnished me with my first definition of anarchism:[1]

> Anarchism, then, really stands for the liberation of the human mind from the dominion of religion, the liberation of the human body from the dominion of property; liberation from the shackles and restraint of government. Anarchism stands for a social order based on the free grouping of individuals for the purpose of producing real social wealth, an order that will guarantee to every human being free access

to the earth and full enjoyment of the necessities of life according to individual desires, tastes, and inclinations.

Soon, I started making mental connections between anarchism and radical feminism. It became very important to me to write down some of the perceptions in this area as a way of communicating to others the excitement I felt about anarcha-feminism. It seems crucial that we share our visions with one another in order to break down some of the barriers that misunderstanding and splinterism raise between us. Although I call myself an anarcha-feminist, this definition can easily include socialism, communism, cultural feminism, lesbian separatism, or any of a dozen other political labels. As Su Negrin writes: 'No political umbrella can cover all my needs.' [2] We may have more in common than we think we do. While I am writing here about my own reactions and perceptions, I don't see either my life or my thoughts as separate from those of other women. In fact, one of my strongest convictions regarding the women's movement is that we do share an incredible commonality of vision.

WHAT DOES ANARCHISM REALLY MEAN?

Anarchism has been maligned and misinterpreted for so long that maybe the most important thing to begin with is an explanation of what it is and isn't. Probably the most prevalent stereotype of the anarchist is a malevolent-looking man hiding a lighted bomb beneath a black cape, ready to destroy or assassinate everything and everybody in his path. This image engenders fear and revulsion in most people, regardless of their politics; consequently, anarchism is dismissed as ugly, violent, and extreme. Another misconception is the anarchist as impractical idealist, dealing in useless, utopian abstractions and out of touch with concrete reality. The result: anarchism is once again dismissed, this time as an 'impossible dream.'

Neither of these images is accurate (though there have been both anarchist assassins and idealists — as is the case in many political movements, left and right). What is accurate depends, of course, on one's frame of reference. There are different kinds of anarchists, just as there are different kinds of socialists. What I will talk about here is communist-anarchism, which I see as virtually identical to libertarian (i.e. nonauthoritarian) socialism. Labels can be terribly confusing, so in hopes of clarifying the term, I'll define anarchism using three major principles (each of which I believe is related to a radical feminist analysis of society — more on that later):

1) Belief in the abolition of authority, hierarchy, government. Anarchists call for the dissolution (rather than the seizure) of power — of human over human, of state over community. Whereas many socialists call for a working-class government and an eventual 'withering away of the state,' anarchists believe that the means create the ends, that a strong state becomes self-perpetuating. The only way to achieve anarchism (according to anarchist theory) is through the creation of cooperative, anti-authoritarian forms. To separate the process from the goals of revolution is to insure the perpetuation of oppressive structure and style.

2) Belief in both individuality and collectivity. Individuality is not incompatible with communist thought. A distinction must be made, though, between 'rugged individualism,' which fosters competition and a disregard for the needs of others, and true individuality, which implies freedom without infringement on others' freedom. Specifically, in terms of social and political organization, this means balancing individual initiative with collective action through the creation of structures which enable decision-making to rest in the hands of all those in a group, community, or factory, not in the hands of 'representatives' or 'leaders.' It means co-ordination and action via a non-hierarchical network (overlapping circles rather than a pyramid) of small groups or communities. Finally, it means that successful revolution involves unmanipulated, autonomous individuals and groups working together to take 'direct, unmediated control of society and of their own lives.'[3]

3) Belief in both spontaneity and organization. Anarchists have long been accused of advocating chaos. Most people in fact believe that anarchism is a synonym for disorder, confusion, violence. This is a total misrepresentation of what anarchism stands for. Anarchists don't deny the necessity of organization; they only claim that it must come from below, not above, from within rather than from without. Externally imposed structure or rigid rules which foster manipulation and passivity are the most dangerous forms a so-called 'revolution' can take. No one can dictate the exact shape of the future. Spontaneous action within the context of a specific situation is necessary if we are going to create a society which responds to the changing needs of changing individuals and groups. Anarchists believe in fluid forms: small-scale participatory democracy in conjunction with large-scale collective co-operation and co-ordination (without loss of individual initiative).

ANARCHISM AND THE WOMEN'S MOVEMENT

The development of sisterhood is a unique threat, for it is directed against the basic social and psychic model of hierarchy and domination. . . . [Mary Daly[4]]

All across the country, independent groups of women began functioning without the structure, leaders, and other facto-tums of the male left, creating independently and simulta-neously, organizations similar to those of anarchists of many decades and locales. No accident, either. [Cathy Levine[5]]

Anarchist men have been little better than males everywhere in their subjection of women.[6] Thus the absolute necessity of a *feminist* anarchist revolution. Otherwise the very principles on which anarchism is based become utter hypocrisy.

The current women's movement and a radical feminist analysis of society have contributed much to libertarian thought. In fact, it is my contention that feminists have been unconscious anarchists in both theory and practice for years. We now need to become *consciously* aware of the connections between anarchism and feminism and use that framework for our thoughts and actions. We have to be able to see very clearly where we want to go and how to get there. In order to be more effective, in order to create the future we sense is possible, we must realize that what we want is not change but total *transformation*.

The radical feminist perspective is almost pure anarchism. The basic theory postulates the nuclear family as the basis for all authoritarian systems. The lesson the child learns, from father to teacher to boss to God, is to OBEY the great anonymous voice of Authority. To graduate from childhood to adulthood is to become a fully-fledged automaton, incapable of questioning or even thinking clearly. We pass into middle-America, believing everything we are told and numbly accepting the destruction of life all around us.

What feminists are dealing with is a mind-fucking process — the male domineering attitude toward the external world allowing only subject-to-object relationships. Traditional male politics reduces humans to object status and then dominates and manipulates them for abstract 'goals.' Women, on the other hand, are trying to develop a consciousness of 'Other' in all areas. We see subject-to-subject relationships as not only desirable but necessary. (Many of us have chosen to work with and love only women for just this reason — those kinds of relationships are so much more possible.) Together we are working to expand our empathy and understanding of other living things and to identify with those entities outside of ourselves, rather than objectifying and manipulating them. At this point, a respect for all life is a prerequisite for our very survival.

Radical feminist theory also criticizes male hierarchical thought patterns — in which rationality dominates sensuality, mind dominates intuition, and persistent splits and polarities (active/passive, child/adult, sane/insane, work/play, spontaneity/organization) alienate us from the mind-body experience as a whole and the continuum of human experience. Women are attempting to get rid of these splits, to live in harmony with the universe as whole, integrated humans dedicated to the collective healing of our individual wounds and schisms.

In actual practice within the women's movement, feminists have had both success and failure in abolishing hierarchy and domination. I believe that women frequently speak and act as 'intuitive' anarchists; that is, we *approach*, or *verge on*, a complete denial of all patriarchal thought and organization. That approach, however, is blocked by the powerful and insidious forms which patriarchy takes — in our minds and in our relationships with one another. Living within and being conditioned by an authoritarian society often prevents us from making that all-important connection between feminism and anarchism. When we say we are fighting the patriarchy, it isn't always clear to all of us that that means fighting all hierarchy, all leadership, all government, and the very idea of authority itself. Our impulses toward collective work and small leaderless groups have been anarchistic, but in most cases we haven't called them by that name. And that is important, because an understanding of feminism as anarchism could springboard women out of reformism and stop-gap measures into a revolutionary confrontation with the basic nature of authoritarian politics.

If we want to 'bring down the patriarchy,' we need to talk about anarchism, to know exactly what it means, and to use that framework to transform ourselves and the structure of our daily lives. Feminism doesn't mean female corporate power or a woman president; it means no corporate power and no presidents. The Equal Rights Amendment will not transform society; it only gives women the 'right' to plug into a hierarchical economy. Challenging sexism means challenging all hierarchy — economic, political, and personal. And that means an anarcha-feminist revolution.

Specifically, when have feminists been anarchistic, and when have we stopped short? As the second wave of feminism spread across the country in the late 1960s, the forms which women's groups took frequently reflected an unspoken libertarian consciousness. In rebellion against the competitive power games, impersonal hierarchy, and mass organization tactics of male politics, women broke off into small, leaderless, consciousness-raising (C-R) groups, which dealt with personal issues in our daily lives. Face-to-face, we attempted to get at the root cause of our oppression by sharing our hitherto unvalued perceptions and experiences. We learned from each other that politics is not 'out there' but in our minds and bodies and between individuals. Personal relationships could and did oppress us as a political class. Our misery and self-hatred were a direct result of male domination — in home, street, job, and political organization.

So, in many unconnected areas of the U.S., C-R groups developed as a spontaneous, direct (re)action to patriarchal forms. The emphasis on the small group as a basic organizational unit, on the personal and political, on anti-authoritarianism, and on spontaneous direct action was essentially anarchistic. The structure of women's groups bore a striking resemblance to that of anarchist affinity groups within anarchosyndicalist unions in Spain, France, and many other countries. Yet, we had not called ourselves anarchists and consciously organized around anarchist principles. At the time, we did not even have an underground network of communication and idea-and-skill sharing. Before the women's movement was more than a handful of isolated groups groping in the dark toward answers, anarchism as an unspecified idea existed in our minds.

I believe that this puts women in the unique position of being the bearers of a subsurface anarchist consciousness which, if articulated and concretized, can take us further than any previous group toward the achievement of total revolution. Women's intuitive anarchism, if sharpened and clarified, is an incredible leap forward (or beyond) in the struggle for human liberation. Radical feminist theory hails feminism as the ultimate revolution. This is true if, and only if, we recognize and claim our anarchist roots. At the point where we fail to see the feminist connection to anarchism, we stop short of revolution and become trapped in 'ye olde male political rut.' It is time to stop groping in the darkness and see what we have done and are doing in the context of where we ultimately want to be.

C-R groups were a good beginning, but they often got so bogged down in talking about personal problems that they failed to make the jump to direct action and political confrontation. Groups that did organize around a specific issue or project sometimes found that the 'tyranny of structurelessness' could be as destructive as the 'tyranny of tyranny.'[7] The failure to blend organization with spontaneity frequently caused the emergence of those with more skills or personal charisma as leaders. The resentment and frustration felt by those who found themselves following sparked in-fighting, guilt-tripping, and power struggles. Too often this ended in either total ineffectiveness or a backlash adherence to 'what we need is more structure' (in the old male up/down sense of the word).

Once again, I think that what was missing was a verbalized anarchist analysis. Organization does not have to stifle spontaneity or follow hierarchical patterns. The women's groups or projects which have been the most successful are those which experimented with various fluid structures: the rotation of tasks and chairpersons, sharing of all skills, equal access to information and resources, non-monopolized decision-making, and time slots for discussion of group dynamics. This latter structural element is important because it involves a continued effort on the part of group members to watch for 'creeping power politics.' If women are verbally committing themselves to collective work, this requires a real struggle to unlearn passivity (to eliminate 'followers') and to share special skills or knowledge (to avoid 'leaders'). This doesn't mean that we cannot be inspired by one another's words and lives; strong actions by strong individuals can be contagious and thus important. But we must be careful not to slip into old behavior patterns.

On the positive side, the emerging structure of the women's movement in the last few years has generally followed an anarchistic pattern of small project-oriented groups continually weaving an underground network of communication and collective action around specific issues. Partial success at leader/'star' avoidance and the diffusion of small action projects (Rape Crisis Centers, Women's Health Collectives) across the country have made it extremely difficult for the women's movement to be pinned down to one person or group. Feminism is a many-headed monster which cannot be destroyed by singular decapitation. We spread and grow in ways that are incomprehensible to a hierarchical mentality.

This is not, however, to underestimate the immense power of the Enemy. The most treacherous form this power can take is co-optation, which feeds on any short-sighted unanarchistic view of feminism as mere 'social change.' To think of sexism as an evil which can be eradicated by female participation in the way things are is to insure the continuation of domination and oppression. 'Feminist' capitalism is a contradiction in terms. When we establish women's credit unions, restaurants, bookstores, etc., we must be clear that we are doing so for our own survival, for the purpose of creating a counter-system whose processes contradict and challenge competition, profit-making, and all forms of economic oppression. We must be committed to 'living on the boundaries,'[8] to anti-capitalist, non-consumption values. What we want is neither integration nor a *coup d'etat* which would 'transfer power from one set of boys to another set of boys.'[9] What we ask is nothing less than total revolution, revolution whose forms invest a future untainted by inequity, domination, or disrespect for individual variation — in short, feminist-anarchist revolution. I believe that women have known all along how to move in the direction of human liberation; we need only to shake off lingering male political forms and dictums and focus on our own anarchistic female analysis.

WHERE DO WE GO FROM HERE? MAKING UTOPIA REAL

'Ah, your vision is romantic bullshit, soppy religiosity, flimsy idealism.' 'You're into poetry because you can't deliver concrete details.' So says the little voice in the back of my (your?) head. But the front of my head knows that if you were here next to me, we could talk. And that in our talk would come (concrete, detailed) descriptions of how such and such might happen, how this or that would be resolved. What my vision really lacks is concrete detailed human bodies. Then it wouldn't be a flimsy vision, it would be a fleshy reality. [Su Negrin[10]]

Instead of getting discouraged and isolated now, we should be in our small groups — discussing, planning, creating, and making trouble . . . we should always be actively engaging in and creating feminist activity, because we all thrive on it; in the absence of [it], women take tranquilizers, go insane, and commit suicide. [Cathy Levine[11]]

Those of us who lived through the excitement of sit-ins, marches, student strikes, demonstrations, and *revolution now* in the sixties may find ourselves disillusioned and downright cynical about anything happening now. Giving up or in ('open' marriage? hip capitalism? the Guru Maharaji?) seems easier than facing the prospect of decades of struggle and maybe even ultimate failure. At this point, we lack an overall framework to see the process of revolution. Without it, we are doomed to deadended, isolated struggle or the individual solution. The kind of framework, or coming-together-point, that anarcha-feminism provides would appear to be a prerequisite for any sustained effort to reach utopian goals. True revolution is 'neither an accidental happening nor a coup d'etat artificially engineered from above.'[12] It takes years of preparation: sharing of ideas and information, changes in consciousness and behavior, and the creation of political and economic alternatives to capitalist, hierarchical structures. It takes spontaneous direct action on the part of autonomous individuals through collective political confrontation. It is important to 'free your mind' and your personal life, but it is not sufficient. Liberation is not an insular experience; it occurs in conjunction with other human beings. There are no individual 'liberated women.'

So what I'm talking about is a *long-term process*, a series of actions in which we unlearn passivity and learn to take control over our own lives. I am talking about a 'hollowing out' of the present system through the formation of mental and physical (concrete) alternatives to the way things are. The romantic image of a small band of armed guerrillas overthrowing the U.S. Government is obsolete (as is all male politics) and basically irrelevant to this conception of revolution. We would be squashed if we tried it. Besides, as the poster says, 'What we want is not the overthrow of the government, but a situation in which it gets lost in the shuffle.' Whether armed resistance will be necessary at some point is open to debate. The anarchist principle of 'means create ends' seems to imply pacifism, but the power of the state is so great that it is difficult to be absolute about nonviolence.

The actual tactics of preparation are things that we have been involved with for a long time. We need to continue and develop them further. I see them as functioning on three levels: 1) 'educational' (sharing of ideas, experiences); 2) economic/political; and 3) personal/political.

'Education' has a rather condescending ring to it, but I don't mean 'bringing the word to the masses' or guilt-tripping individuals into prescribed ways of being. I'm talking about the many methods we have developed for sharing our lives with one another — from writing (our network of feminist publications), study groups, and women's radio and TV shows to demonstrations, marches, and street theater. The mass media would seem to be a particularly important area for revolutionary communication and influence — just think of how our own lives were misshaped by radio and TV.[13] Seen in isolation, these things might seem ineffectual, but people do change from writing, reading, talking, and listening to each other, as well as from active participation in political movements. Going out into the streets together shatters passivity and creates a spirit of communal effort and life energy which can help sustain and transform us. My own transformation from all-American girl to anarcha-feminist was brought about by a decade of reading, discussion, and involvement with many kinds of people and politics — from the Midwest to the West and East Coasts. My experiences may in some ways be unique, but they are not, I think, extraordinary. In many, many places in this country, people are slowly beginning to question the way they were conditioned to acceptance and passivity. God and government are not the ultimate authorities they once were. This is not to minimize the extent of the power of church and state, but rather to emphasize that seemingly inconsequential changes in thought and behavior, when solidified in collective action, constitute a real challenge to the patriarchy.

Economic/political tactics fall into the realm of direct action and 'purposeful illegality' (Daniel Guerin's term). Anarcho-syndicalism specifies three major modes of direct action: sabotage, strike, and boycott. Sabotage means 'obstructing by every possible method, the regular process of production.'[14] More and more frequently, sabotage is practiced by people unconsciously influenced by changing societal values. For example, systematic absenteeism is carried out by both blue- and white-collar workers. Defying employers can be done as subtly as the 'slowdown' or as blatantly as the 'fuck-up.' Doing as little work as possible as slowly as possible is common employee practice, as is messing up the actual work process (often as a union tactic during a strike). Witness habitual misfiling or loss of 'important papers' by secretaries, or the continual switching of destination placards on trains during the 1967 railroad strike in Italy.

Sabotage tactics can be used to make strikes much more effective. The strike itself is the workers' most important weapon. Any individual strike has the potential of paralyzing the system if it spreads to other industries and becomes a general strike. Total social revolution is then only a step away. Of course, the general strike must have as its ultimate goal workers' self-management (as well as a clear sense of how to achieve and hold on to it), or the revolution will be still-born (as in France, 1968).

The boycott can also be a powerful strike or union strategy (e.g. the boycott of non-union grapes, lettuce, and wines, and of Farah pants). In addition, it can be used to force economic and social changes. Refusal to vote, to pay war taxes, or to participate in capitalist competition and over-consumption are all important actions when coupled with support of alternative, non-profit structures (food co-ops, health and law collectives, recycled clothing and book stores, free schools, etc.). Consumerism is one of the main strongholds of capitalism. To boycott buying itself (especially products geared to obsolescence and those offensively advertised) is a tactic that has the power to change the 'quality of everyday life.' Refusal to vote is often practiced out of despair of passivity rather than as a conscious political statement against a pseudo-democracy where power and money elect a political elite. Nonvoting can mean something other than silent consent if we are simultaneously participating in the creation of genuine democratic forms in an alternative network of anarchist affinity groups.

This takes us to the third area — personal/political, which is of course vitally connected to the other two. The anarchist affinity group has long been a revolutionary organizational structure. In anarcho-syndicalist unions, they functioned as training grounds for workers' self-management. They can be temporary groupings of individuals for a specific short-term goal, more 'permanent' work collectives (as an alternative to professionalism and career elitism), or living collectives where individuals learn how to rid themselves of domination or possessiveness in their one-to-one relationships. Potentially, anarchist affinity groups are the base on which we can build a new libertarian, non-hierarchical society. The way we live and work changes the way we think and perceive (and vice versa), and when changes in consciousness become changes in action and behavior, the revolution has begun.

Making Utopia real involves many levels of struggle. In addition to specific tactics which can be constantly developed and changed, we need political tenacity: the strength and ability to see beyond the present to a joyous, revolutionary future. To get from here to there requires more than a leap of faith. It demands of each of us a day-to-day, long-range commitment to possibility and direct action.

THE TRANSFORMATION OF THE FUTURE

> The creation of female culture is as pervasive a process as we can imagine, for it is participation in a vision which is continually unfolding anew in everything from our talks with friends, to meat boycotts, to taking over storefronts for child care centers, to making love with a sister. It is revelatory, undefinable, except as a process of change. Women's culture is all of us exorcising, naming, creating toward the vision of harmony with ourselves, each other, and our sister earth. In the last ten years our having come faster and closer than ever before in the history of the patriarchy to overturning its power . . . is cause for exhilarant hope — wild, contagious, unconquerable, crazy hope! . . . The hope, the winning of life over death, despair and meaninglessness is everywhere I look now — like taliswomen of the faith in womanvision. . . . [Laurel[15]]

I used to think that if the revolution didn't happen tomorrow, we would all be doomed to a catastrophic (or at least catatonic) fate. I don't believe anymore that that is necessarily true. In fact, I don't even believe in that kind of before-and-after revolution, and I think we set ourselves up for failure and despair by thinking of it in those terms. I do believe that what we all need, what we absolutely require in order to continue struggling (in spite of the oppression of our daily lives), is hope, that is, a vision of the future so beautiful and so powerful that it pulls us steadily forward in a bottom-up creation of an inner and outer world both habitable and self-fulfilling for *all*. (And by self-fulfilling I mean not only in terms of survival needs [sufficient food, clothing, shelter, etc.] but psychological needs as well [e.g., a non-oppressive environment which fosters total freedom of choice before specific, concretely possible alternatives].) I believe that that hope exists — that it is in Laurel's 'womanvison,' in Mary Daly's 'existential courage'[16] and in anarcha-feminism. Our different voices describe the same dream, and 'only the dream can shatter stone that blocks our mouths.' [17] As we speak, we change, and as we change, we transform ourselves and the future simultaneously.

It is true that there is no solution, individual or otherwise, *in this society.* [18] But if we can only balance this rather depressing knowledge with an awareness of the radical metamorphoses we have experienced in our consciousness and in our lives — then perhaps we can have the courage to continue to create what we dream is possible. Obviously, it is not easy to face daily oppression and still continue to hope. But *it is our only chance.* If we abandon hope (the ability to see connections, to dream the present into the future), then we have already lost. Hope is woman's most powerful revolutionary tool; it is what we give each other every time we share our lives, our work, and our love. It pulls us forward out of self-hatred, self-blame, and the fatalism which keeps us prisoners in separate cells. If we surrender to depression and despair now, we are accepting the inevitability of authoritarian politics and patriarchal domination ('Despair is the worst betrayal, the coldest seduction: to believe at last that the enemy will prevail.' [19] — Marge Piercy). We must not let our pain and anger fade into hopelessness or short-sighted semi-'solutions.' Nothing we can do is enough, but on the other hand, those 'small changes' we make in our minds, in our lives, in one another's lives, are not totally futile and ineffectual. It takes a long time to make a revolution: it is something that one both prepares for and lives now. The transformation of the future will not be instantaneous, but it can be total . . . a continuum of thought and action, individuality and collectivity, spontaneity and organization, stretching from what is to what can be.

Anarchism provides a framework for this transformation. It is a vision, a dream, a possibility which becomes 'real' as we live it. Feminism is the connection that links anarchism to the future. When we finally see that connection clearly, when we hold to that vision, when we refuse to be raped of that hope, we will be stepping over the edge of nothingness into a being now just barely imaginable. The womanvision that is anarcha-feminism has been carried inside our women's bodies for centuries. 'It will be an ongoing struggle in each of us, to birth this vision,'[20] but we must do it. We must 'ride our anger like elephants into battle': [21]

We are sleepwalkers troubled by nightmare flashes
In locked wards we closet our vision, renouncing. . . .
Only when we break the mirror and climb into our vision,
Only when we are the wind together streaming and singing,
Only in the dream we become with our bones for spears, we
are real at last and wake.

NOTES

1. Emma Goldman, 'Anarchism: What It Really Stands For,' *Red Emma Speaks* (Vintage Books, 1972), 59.
2. Su Negrin, *Begin at Start* (Times Change Press, 1972), 128.
3. Murray Bookchin, 'On Spontaneity and Organization,' *Liberation*, March 1972, 6.
4. Mary Daly, *Beyond God the Father* (Beacon Press, 1973), 133.
5. Cathy Levine, 'The Tyranny of Tyranny,' *Black Rose* I, 56.
6. Temma Kaplan of the UCLA history department has done considerable research on women's anarchist groups (esp. 'Mujeres Liberes') in the Spanish Revolution.
7. See Joreen's 'The Tyranny of Structurelessness,' *Second Wave*, vol. 2 no. 1, and Cathy Levine's 'The Tyranny of Tyranny,' *op. cit.*
8. Daly, *op. cit.*, 55.
9. Robin Morgan, speech at Boston College, Boston, MA, November 1973.
10. Negrin, op. cit., 171.
11. Levine, op. cit., 50.
12. Dolgoff ed., *The Anarchist Collectives* (Free Life, 1974), 19.
13. The Cohn-Bendits state that one major mistake in Paris 1968 was the failure to take complete control of the media, especially the radio and TV.
14. Goldman, 'Syndicalism: Its Theory and Practice,' *Red Emma Speaks*, 71.
15. Laurel, 'Toward a Woman Vision,' *Amazon Quarterly*, vol. I, issue 2,40.
16. Daly, *op. cit.*, 23.
17. Marge Piercy, 'Provocation of the Dream.'
18. Fran Taylor, 'A Depressing Discourse on Romance, the Individual Solution, and Related Misfortunes,' *Second Wave*, vol. 3., no. 4.
19. Marge Piercy, 'Laying Down the Tower,' *To Be of Use* (Doubleday 1973), 88.
20. Laurel, *op. cit.*, 40.
21. Piercy, *op. cit.*

Socialism, Anarchism, and Feminism

Carol Ehrlich

You are a woman in a capitalist society. You get pissed off: about the job, about the bills, about your husband (or ex), about the kids' school, the housework, being pretty, not being pretty, being looked at, not being looked at (and either way, not listened to), etc. If you think about all these things and how they fit together and what has to be changed, and then you look around for some words to hold all these thoughts together in abbreviated form, you'd almost have to come up with 'socialist feminism.'[1]

From all indications a great many women have 'come up' with socialist feminism as the solution to the persistent problem of sexism. 'Socialism' (in its astonishing variety of forms) is popular with a lot of people these days, because it has much to offer: concern for working people, a body of revolutionary theory that people can point to (whether or not they have read it), and some living examples of industrialized countries that are structured differently from the United States and its satellites.

For many feminists, socialism is attractive because it promises to end the economic inequality of working women. Further, for those women who believe that an exclusively feminist analysis is too narrow to encompass all the existing inequalities, socialism promises to broaden it, while guarding against the dilution of its radical perspective.

For good reasons, then, women are considering whether or not 'socialist feminism' makes sense as a political theory. For socialist feminists do seem to be both sensible and radical — at least, most of them evidently feel a strong antipathy to some of the reformist and solipsistic traps into which increasing numbers of women seem to be stumbling .

To many of us more unromantic types, the Amazon Nation, with its armies of strong-limbed matriarchs riding into the sunset, is unreal, but harmless. A more serious matter is the current obsession with the Great Goddess and assorted other objects of worship, witchcraft, magic and psychic phenomena. As a feminist concerned with transforming the structure of society, I find this anything but harmless.

- Item One. Over 1,400 women went to Boston in April 1976 to attend a women's spirituality conference dealing in large part with the above matters. Could not the energy invested in chanting, swapping the latest pagan ideas and attending workshops on belly-dancing and menstrual rituals have been put to some better and more feminist use?

- Item Two. According to reports in at least one feminist newspaper, a group of witches tried to levitate Susan Saxe out of jail. If they honestly thought this would free Saxe, then they were totally out of touch with the realities of patriarchal oppression. If it was intended to be a light-hearted joke, then why isn't anyone laughing?

Reformism is a far greater danger to women's interests than are bizarre psychic games. I know that 'reformist' is an epithet that may be used in ways that are neither honest nor very useful — principally to demonstrate one's ideological purity, or to say that concrete political work of any type is not worth doing because it is potentially co-optable. In response, some feminists have argued persuasively that the right kinds of reforms can build a radical movement.[2]

Just the same, there are reformist strategies that waste the energies of women, that raise expectations of great change, and that are misleading and alienating because they cannot deliver the goods. The best (or worst) example is electoral politics. Some socialists (beguiled by the notion of gradualism) fall for that one. Anarchists know better. You cannot liberate yourself by non-liberatory means; you cannot elect a new set of politicians (no matter now sisterly) to run the same old corrupt institutions — which in turn run you. When NOW's Majority Caucus — the radical branch of that organization — asks women to follow them 'out of the mainstream, into the revolution' by means that include electoral politics, they will all drown in the depths of things as they are.

Electoral politics is an obvious, everyday kind of trap. Even a lot of non-radicals have learned to avoid it. A more subtle problem is capitalism in the guise of feminist economic power. Consider, for example, the Feminist Economic Network (FEN). The name might possibly fool you.

Ostensibly it was a network of alternative businesses set up to erode capitalism from within by creating economic self-sufficiency for women. That is an appealing idea. Yet FEN's first major project opened in Detroit in April 1976. For an annual membership fee of $100, privileged women could swim in a private pool, drink in a private bar, and get discounts in a cluster of boutiques. FEN paid its female employees $2.50 per hour to work there. Its director, Laura Brown, announced this venture as 'the beginning of the feminist economic revolution .'[3]

When two of the same old games — electoral politics and hip capitalism — are labeled 'revolution,' the word has been turned inside out. It's not surprising that a socialist brand of feminism seems to be a source of revolutionary sanity to many women who don't want to be witches, primitive warriors, senators or small capitalists, but who do want to end sexism while creating a transformed society. Anarchist feminism could provide a meaningful theoretical framework, but all too many feminists either have never heard of it, or else dismiss it as the ladies' auxiliary of male bomb-throwers.

Socialist feminism provides an assortment of political homes. On the one hand, there are the dingy, cramped quarters of Old Left sects such as the Revolutionary Communist Party (formerly the Revolutionary Union), the October League and the International Workers Party. Very few women find these habitable. On the other hand, a fair number of women are moving into the sprawling, eclectic establishments built by newer Left groups such as the New American Movement, or by various autonomous 'women's unions.'

The newer socialist feminists have been running an energetic and reasonably effective campaign to recruit nonaligned women. In contrast, the more rigid Old Left groups have largely rejected the very idea that lesbians separatists and assorted other scruffy and unsuitable feminists could work with the noble inheritors of Marx, Trotsky (although the Trotskyists are unpredictable), Stalin and Mao. Many reject the idea of all autonomous women's movement that cares at all about women's issues. To them, it is full of 'bourgeois' (most damning of all Marxist epithets!) women bent on 'doing their own thing,' and it 'divides the working class,' which is a curious assumption that workers are dumber than everyone else. Some have an hysterical antipathy to lesbians: the most notorious groups are the October League and the Revolutionary Communist Party (RCP), but they are not alone. In this policy, as in a many others, the anti-lesbian line follows that of the communist countries. The RCP, for example, released a position paper in the early 1970s (back in its pre-party days, when it was the plain old Revolutionary Union) which announced that homosexuals are 'caught the mire and muck of bourgeois decadence,' and that gay liberation is 'anti-working class and counter revolutionary.' All the Old Left groups are uneasy with the idea that any women outside the 'proletariat' are oppressed at all. The working class, of course, is a marvelously flexible concept. In the current debates on the Left, it ranges from point-of-production workers (period) to an enormous group that takes every single person who sells her or his labor for wages, or who depends on someone else who does. That's almost all of us. (So, Papa Karl, if 90 percent of the people of the United States are the vanguard, why haven't we had the revolution yet?)

The newer socialist feminists have been trying in all manner of inventive ways to keep a core of Marxist-Leninist thought, update it, and graft it to contemporary radical feminism. The results are sometimes peculiar. In July 1975, the women of the New American Movement and a number of autonomous groups held the first national conference on socialist feminism. It was not especially heavily advertised in advance, and everyone seemed to be surprised that so many women (over 1,600, with more turned away) wanted to spend the July 4 weekend in Yellow Springs, Ohio.

On reading the speeches given at the conference, as well as extensive commentary written by other women who attended,[4] it is not at all clear what the conference organizers thought they were offering in the name of 'socialist feminism.' The Principles of Unity that were drawn up prior to the conference included two items that have always been associated with radical feminism, and that in fact are typically thought of as antithetical to a socialist perspective. The first principle stated: 'We recognize the need for and support the existence of the autonomous women's movement throughout the revolutionary process.' The second read: 'We agree that all oppression, whether based on race, class, sex, or lesbianism, is interrelated and the fights for liberation from oppression must be simultaneous and co-operative.' The third principle merely remarked that 'socialist feminism is a strategy for revolution;' and the fourth and final principle called for holding discussions 'in the spirit of struggle and unity.'

This is, of course, an incredible smorgasbord of tasty principles — a menu designed to appeal to practically everyone. But when 'socialist' feminists serve up the independent women's movement as the main dish, and when they say class oppression is just one of several oppressions, no more important than any other, then (as its Marxist critics say) it is no longer socialism.

However, socialist feminists do not follow out the implications of radical feminism all the way. If they did, they would accept another principle: that non-hierarchical structures are essential to feminist prac-

Reinventing Anarchy, Again

tice. This, of course, is too much for any socialist to take. But what it means is that radical feminism is far more compatible with one type of anarchism than it is with socialism. That type is social anarchism (also known as communist anarchism), not the individualist or anarchocapitalist varieties.

This won't come as news to feminists who are familiar with anarchist principles — but very few feminists are. That's understandable, since anarchism has veered between a bad press and none at all. If feminists were familiar with anarchism, they would not be looking very hard at socialism as a means of fighting sexist oppression. Feminists have got to be skeptical of any social theory that comes with a built-in set of leaders and followers, no matter how 'democratic' this centralized structure is supposed to be. Women of all classes, races and life circumstances have been on the receiving end of domination too long to want to exchange one set of masters for another. We know who has power, and (with a few isolated exceptions) it isn't us.

Several contemporary anarchist feminists have pointed out the connections between social anarchism and radical feminism. Lynne Farrow said, 'feminism practices what anarchism preaches.' Peggy Kornegger believes that 'feminists have been unconscious anarchists in both theory and practice for years.' And Marian Leighton states that 'the refining distinction from radical feminist to anarcho-feminist is largely that of making a step in self-conscious theoretical development.'[5]

We build autonomy
The process of ever growing synthesis
For every living creature.
We spread
Spontaneity and creation
We learn the joys of equality
Of relationships
Without dominance
Among sisters.
We destroy domination
In all its forms.

This chant appeared in the radical feminist newspaper, *It Aint Me Babe*, [6] whose masthead carried the line, 'end all hierarchies.' It was not labeled an anarchist (or anarchist-feminist) newspaper, but the connections are striking. It exemplified much of what women's liberation was about in the early years of the reborn movement. And it is that spirit that will be lost if the socialist feminist hybrid takes root; if goddess worship or the lesbian nation convince women to set up new forms of dominance-submission.

RADICAL FEMINISM AND ANARCHIST FEMINISM

All radical feminists and all social anarchist feminists are concerned with a set of common issues: control over one's own body; alternatives to the nuclear family and to heterosexuality; new methods of child care that will liberate parents and children; economic self-determination; ending sex stereotyping in education, in the media and in the workplace; the abolition of repressive laws; an end to male authority, ownership and control over women; providing women with the means to develop skills and positive self-attitudes; an end to oppressive emotional relationships; and what the Situationists have called 'the reinvention of everyday life.'

There are, then, many issues on which radical feminists and anarchist feminists agree. But anarchist feminists are concerned with something more. Because they are anarchists, they work to end all power relationships, all situations in which people can oppress each other. Unlike some radical feminists who are not anarchists, they do not believe that power in the hands of women could possibly lead to a non-coercive society. And unlike most socialist feminists, they do not believe that anything good can come out of a mass movement with a leadership elite. In short, neither a workers' state nor a matriarchy will end the oppression of everyone. The goal, then, is not to 'seize' power, as the socialists are fond of urging, but to abolish power.

Contrary to popular belief, all social anarchists are socialists. That is they want to take wealth out of the hands of the few and redistribute it among all members of the community. And they believe that people need to co-operate with each other as a community, instead of living as isolated individuals. For anarchists, however, the central issues are always power and social hierarchy. If a state — even a state representing the workers — continues, it will re-establish forms of domination, and some people will no longer be free. People aren't free just because they are surviving, or even if they are economically comfortable. They are free only when they have power over their own lives. Women, even more than most men, have very little power over their own lives. Gaining such autonomy, and insisting that everyone have it, is the major goal of anarchist feminists:[7]

Power to no one, and to every one: To each the power over his/her own life, and no others.

On Practice

That is the theory. What about the practice? Again, radical feminism and anarchist feminism have much more in common than either does with socialist feminism.[8] Both work to build alternative institutions, and both take the politics of the personal very seriously. Socialist feminists are less inclined to think either is particularly vital to revolutionary practice .

Developing alternative forms of organization means building self-help clinics, instead of fighting to get one radical on a hospital's board of directors; it means women's video groups and newspapers, instead of commercial television and newspapers; living collectives, instead of isolated nuclear families; rape crisis centers; food co-ops; parent-controlled day-care centers; free schools, printing co-ops; alternative radio groups, and so on.

Yet, it does little good to build alternative institutions if their structures mimic the capitalist and hierarchical models with which we are so familiar. Many radical feminists recognized this early: that's why they worked to rearrange the way women perceived the world and themselves (through the consciousness-raising group), and why they worked to rearrange the forms of work relationships and interpersonal interactions (through the small, leaderless groups where tasks are rotated and skills and knowledge shared). They were attempting to do this in a hierarchical society that provides no models except ones of inequality. Surely, a knowledge of anarchist theory and models of organization would have helped. Equipped with this knowledge, radical feminists might have avoided some of the mistakes they made — and might have been better able to overcome some of the difficulties they encountered in trying simultaneously to transform themselves and society.

Take, for example, the still current debate over 'strong women' and the closely related issue of leadership. The radical feminist position can be summarized the following way.

1. Women have been kept down because they are isolated from each other and are paired off with men in relationships of dominance and submission .

2. Men will not liberate women; women must liberate themselves. This cannot happen if each woman tries to liberate herself alone. Thus, women must work together on a model of mutual aid.

3. 'Sisterhood is powerful,' but women cannot be sisters if they recapitulate masculine patterns of dominance and submission.

4. New organizational forms have to be developed. The primary form is the small, leaderless group; the most important behaviors are egalitarianism, mutual support, and the sharing of skills and knowledge.

If many women accepted this, even more did not. Some were opposed from the start; others saw first-hand that it was difficult to put into practice, and regretfully concluded that such beautiful idealism would never work out. Ideological support for those who rejected the principles put forth by the 'unconscious anarchists' was provided in two documents that quickly circulated through women's liberation newspapers and organizations. The first was Anselma dell'Olio's speech to the second Congress to Unite Women, which was held in May 1970 in New York City. The speech, entitled 'Divisiveness and Self-Destruction in the Women's Movement: A Letter of Resignation,' gave dell'Olio's reasons for leaving the women's movement. The second document was Joreen's 'Tyranny of Structurelessness,' which first appeared in 1972 in *The Second Wave.* Both raised issues of organizational and personal practice that were, and still are, tremendously important to the women's movement. [9]

> I have come to announce my swan-song to the women's movement. . . . I have been destroyed. . . . I learned three and one-half years ago that women had always been divided against one another, were self-destructive and filled with impotent rage. I never dreamed that I would see the day when this rage, masquerading as a pseudo-egalitarian radicalism under the 'pro-woman' banner, would turn into frighteningly vicious anti-intellectual fascism of the Left, and used within the movement to strike down sisters singled out with all the subtlety and justice of a kangaroo court of the Ku Klux Klan. I am referring, of course, to the personal attack, both overt and insidious, to which women in the movement, who have painfully managed any degree of achievement, have been subjected. . . . If you are . . . an achiever you are immediately labeled a thrill-seeking opportunist, a ruthless mercenary, out to get her fame and fortune over the dead bodies of selfless sisters who have buried their abilities and sacrificed their ambitions for the greater glory of Feminism. . . . If you have the misfortune of being outspoken and articulate, you are accused of being power-mad, elitist, racist, and finally the worst epithet of all: a MALE IDENTIFIER.

When Anselma dell'Olio gave this angry farewell to the movement, it did two things: For some women, it raised the question of how women can end unequal power relationships among themselves without destroying each other. For others it did quite the opposite —

it provided easy justification for all the women who had been dominating other women in a most unsisterly way. Anyone who was involved in women's liberation at that time knows that the dell'Olio statement was twisted by some women in exactly that fashion: call yourself assertive, or strong, or talented, and you can re-label a good deal of ugly, insensitive and oppressive behavior. Women who presented themselves as tragic heroines destroyed by their envious or misguided (and, of course, far less talented) 'sisters' could count on a sympathetic response from some other women.

Just the same, women who were involved in the movement at that time know that the kinds of things dell'Olio spoke about did happen, and they should not have happened. A knowledge of anarchist theory is not enough, of course, to prevent indiscriminate attacks on women. But in the struggle to learn new ways of relating and working with each other, such knowledge might — just might — have prevented some of these destructive mistakes.

Ironically, these mistakes were motivated by the radical feminist aversion to conventional forms of power, and the inhuman personal relationships that result from one set of persons having power over others. When radical feminists and anarchist feminists speak of abolishing power, they mean to get rid of all institutions, all forms of socialization, all the ways in which people coerce each other — and acquiesce to being coerced.

A major problem arose in defining the nature of coercion in the women's movement. The hostility towards the 'strong' woman arose because she was someone who could at least potentially coerce women who were less articulate, less self-confident, less assertive than she. Coercion is usually far more subtle than physical force or economic sanction. One person can coerce another without taking away her job, or striking her, or throwing her in jail.

Strong women started out with a tremendous advantage. Often they knew more. Certainly they had long since overcome the crippling socialization that stressed passive, timid, docile, conformist behavior — behavior that taught women to smile when they weren't amused, to whisper when they felt like shouting, to lower their eyes when someone stared aggressively at them. Strong women weren't terrified of speaking in public; they weren't afraid to take on 'male' tasks, or to try something new. Or so it seemed.

Put a 'strong' woman in the same small group with a 'weak' one, and she becomes a problem: How does she not dominate? How does she share her hard-earned skills and confidence with her sister? From the other side — how does the 'weak' woman learn to act in her own behalf? How can one even conceive of 'mutual' aid in a one-way situation? Of 'sisterhood' when the 'weak' member does not feel equal to the 'strong' one?

These are complicated questions, with no simple answers. Perhaps the closest we can come is with the anarchist slogan, 'a strong people needs no leaders.' Those of us who have learned to survive by dominating others, as well as those of us who have learned to survive by accepting domination, need to resocialize ourselves into being strong without playing dominance-submission games, into controlling what happens to us without controlling others. This can't be done by electing the right people to office or by following the correct party line; nor can it be done by sitting and reflecting on our sins. We rebuild ourselves and our world through activity, through partial successes, and failure, and more partial successes. And all the while we grow stronger and more self-reliant.

If Anselma dell'Olio criticized the personal practice of radical feminists, Joreen raised some hard questions about organizational structure. 'The Tyranny of Structurelessness'[10] pointed out that there is no such thing as a 'structureless' group, and people who claim there is are fooling themselves. All groups have a structure; the difference is whether or not the structure is explicit. If it is implicit, hidden elites are certain to exist and to control the group — and everyone, both the leaders and the led, will deny or be confused by the control that exists. This is the 'tyranny' of structurelessness. To overcome it, groups need to set up open, explicit structures accountable to the membership.

Any anarchist feminist, I think, would agree with her analysis — up to this point, and no further. For what Joreen also said was that the so-called 'leaderless, structureless group' was incapable of going beyond talk to action. Not only its lack of open structure, but also its small size and its emphasis upon consciousness-raising (talk) were bound to make it ineffective.

Joreen did not say that women's groups should be hierarchically structured. In fact, she called for leadership that would be 'diffuse, flexible, open, and temporary;' for organizations that would build in accountability, diffusion of power among the maximum number of persons, task rotation, skill-sharing, and the spread of information and resources. All good social anarchist principles of organization! But her denigration of consciousness-raising and her preference for large regional and national organizations were strictly part of the old way of doing things, and implicitly accepted the continuation of hierarchical structures.

Large groups are organized so that power and decision-making are delegated to a few — unless, of course, one is speaking of a horizontally co-ordinated network of small collectives, which she did not mention. How does a group such as NOW, with its 60,000 members in 1975, rotate tasks, share skills, and ensure that all information and resources are available to everyone? It can't, of course. Such groups have a president, and a board of directors, and a national office, and a membership — some of whom are in local chapters, and some of whom are isolated members. Few such groups have very much direct democracy, and few teach their members new ways of working and relating to one another.

The unfortunate effect of 'The Tyranny of Structurelessness' was that it linked together large organization, formal structure, and successful direct action in a way that seemed to make sense to a lot of people. Many women felt that in order to fight societal oppression a large organization was essential, and the larger the better. The image is strength pitted against strength: you do not kill an elephant with an air gun, and you do not bring down the patriarchal state with the small group. For women who accept the argument that greater size is linked to greater effectiveness, the organizational options seem limited to large liberal groups such as NOW or to socialist organizations which are mass organizations.

As with so many things that seem to make sense, the logic is faulty. 'Societal oppression' is a reification, an over-blown, paralyzing, made-up entity that is large mainly in the sense that the same oppressions happen to a lot of us. But oppressions, no matter how pervasive, how predictable, almost always are done to us by some one — even if that person is acting as an agent of the state, or as a member of the dominant race, gender or class. The massive police assaults upon our assembled forces are few; even the police officer or the boss or the husband who is carrying out his allotted sexist or authoritarian role intersects with us at a given point in our everyday lives. Institutionalized oppression does exist, on a large scale, but it seldom needs to be attacked (indeed, seldom can be attacked) by a large group. Guerrilla tactics by a small group — occasionally even by a single individual — will do very nicely in retaliation.

Another unfortunate effect of the 'Tyranny of Structurelessness' mentality (if not directly of the article) was that it fed people's stereotypes of anarchists. (Of course, people don't usually swallow something unless they're hungry.) Social anarchists aren't opposed to structure: they aren't even against leadership, provided that it carries no reward or privilege, and is temporary and specific to a particular task. However, anarchists who want to abolish a hierarchical structure are almost always stereotyped as wanting no structure at all. Unfortunately, the picture of a gaggle of disorganized, chaotic anarchist women, drifting without direction, caught on.

SITUATIONISM AND ANARCHIST FEMINISM

> To transform the world and to change the structure of life are one and the same thing.[12]

> The personal is political.[13]

Anarchists are used to hearing that they lack a theory that would help in building a new society. At best, their detractors say patronizingly, anarchism tells us what not to do. Don't permit bureaucracy or hierarchical authority; don't let a vanguard party make decisions; don't tread on me. Don't tread on anyone. According to this perspective, anarchism is not a theory at all. It is a set of cautionary practices, the voice of libertarian conscience — always idealistic, sometimes a bit truculent, occasionally anachronistic, but a necessary reminder.

There is more than a kernel of truth to these objections. Just the same, there are varieties of anarchist thought that can provide a theoretical framework for analysis of the world and action to change it. For radical feminists who want to take that 'step in self-conscious theoretical development,'[14] perhaps the greatest potential lies in situationism.

The value of situationism for an anarchist-feminist analysis is that it combines a socialist awareness of the primacy of capitalist oppression with an anarchist emphasis upon transforming the whole of public and private life. The point about capitalist oppression is important. All too often anarchists seem to be unaware that this economic system exploits most people. But all too often socialists — especially Marxists — are blind to the fact that people are oppressed in every aspect of life: work, what passes for leisure, culture, personal relationships — all of it. And only anarchists insist that people must transform the conditions of their lives themselves — it cannot be done for them. Not by the party, not by the union, not by 'organizers,' not by anyone else.

Two basic situationist concepts are 'commodity' and 'spectacle.' Capitalism has made all of social relations commodity relations: the market rules all. People are not only producers and consumers in the narrow economic sense, but the very structure of their daily lives is based on commodity relations. Society 'is consumed as a *whole* — the ensemble of social relationships and structures is the central product of the commodity economy.'[15] This has inevitably alienated people from their lives, not just from their labor; to consume social relationships makes one a passive spectator in one's life. The *spectacle*, then, is the culture that springs from the commodity economy — the stage is set, the action unfolds, we applaud when we think we are happy, we yawn when we think we are bored, but we cannot leave the show, because there is no world outside the theater for us to go to.

In recent times, however, the societal stage has begun to crumble, and so the possibility exists of constructing another world outside the theater — this time a real world, one in which each of us directly participates as subject, not as object. The situationist phrase for this possibility is 'the reinvention of everyday life.'

How is daily life to be reinvented? By creating situations that disrupt what seems to be the natural order of things — situations that jolt people out of customary ways of thinking and behaving. Only then will they be able to act, to destroy the manufactured spectacle and the commodity economy — that is, capitalism in all its forms. Only then will they be able to create free and unalienated lives.

The congruence of this activist, social anarchist theory with radical feminist theory is striking. The concepts of commodity and spectacle are especially applicable to the lives of women. In fact, many radical feminists have described these in detail, without placing them in the situationist framework. [16] To do so broadens the analysis, by showing women's situation as an organic part of the society as a whole, but at the same time without playing socialist reductionist games. Women's oppression is part of the overall oppression of people by a capitalist economy, but it is not less than the oppression of others. Nor — from a situationist perspective — do you have to be a particular variety of women to be oppressed; you do not have to be part of the proletariat, either literally, as an industrial worker, or metaphorically, as someone who is not independently wealthy. You do not have to wait breathlessly for socialist feminist manifestoes to tell you that you qualify — as a housewife (reproducing the next generation of workers), as a clerical worker, as a student or a middle-level professional employed by the state (and therefore as part of the 'new working class'). You do not have to be part of the Third World, or a lesbian, or elderly, or a welfare recipient. All of these women are objects in the commodity economy; all are passive viewers of the spectacle. Obviously, women in some situations are far worse off than are others. But, at the same time, none are free in every area of their lives.

WOMEN AND THE COMMODITY ECONOMY

Women have a dual relationship to the commodity economy — they are both consumers and consumed. As housewives, they are consumers of household goods purchased with money not their own, because not 'earned' by them. This may give them a certain amount of purchasing power, but very little power over any aspect of their lives. As young, single heterosexuals, women are purchasers of goods designed to make them bring a high price on the marriage market. As anything else — lesbians, or elderly single, or self-sufficient women with 'careers' — women's relationship to the market place as consumers is not so sharply defined. They are expected to buy (and the more affluent they are, the more they are expected to buy), but for some categories of women, buying is not defined primarily to fill out some aspect of a woman's role .

So what else is new? Isn't the idea of woman-as-passive-consumer, manipulated by the media, patronized by slick Madison Avenue men, an overdone movement cliche? Well, yes — and no. A situationist analysis ties consumption of economic goods to consumption of ideological goods, and then tells us to create situations (guerrilla actions on many levels) that will break that pattern of socialized acceptance of the world as it is. No guilt-tripping; no criticizing women who have 'bought' the consumer perspective. For they have indeed bought it: it has been sold to them as a way of survival from the earliest moments of life. Buy this: it will make you beautiful and lovable. Buy this: it will keep your family in good health. Feel depressed? Treat yourself to an afternoon at the beauty parlor or to a new dress. Guilt leads to inaction. Only action, to reinvent the everyday and make it something else, will change social relations.

THE GIFT

> Thinking she was the gift
> they began to package it early.
> They waxed its smile
> they lowered its eyes
> they tuned its ears to the telephone
> they curled its hair
> they straightened its teeth
> they taught it to bury its wishbone
> they poured honey down its throat
> they made it say yes yes and yes
> they sat on its thumbs.
>
> *That box has my name on it,*
> said the man, It's *for me.*
> And they were not surprised.

While they blew kisses and winked
he took it home.
He put it on a table
where his friends could examine it
saying *dance* saying *faster*.
He plunged its tunnel
he burned his name deeper.
Later he put it on a platform
under the Kleig lights
saying *push* saying *harder*
saying *just what I wanted*
you've given me a son.

— Carole Oles [17]

Women are not only consumers in the commodity economy; they are consumed as commodities. This is what Oles's poem is about, and it is what Tax has labeled 'female schizophrenia.' Tax constructs an inner monologue for the housewife-as-commodity: ' "I am nothing when I am by myself. In myself, I am nothing. I only know that I exist because I am needed by someone who is real, my husband, and by my children."[18]

When feminists describe socialization into the female sex role, when they point out the traits female children are taught (emotional dependence, childishness, timidity, concern with being beautiful, docility, passivity, and so on), they are talking about the careful production of a commodity — although it isn't usually called that. When they describe the oppressiveness of sexual objectification, or of living in the nuclear family, or of being a Supermother, or of working in the kinds of low level, under-paid jobs that most women find in the paid labor force, they are also describing woman as commodity. Women are consumed by men who treat them as sex objects; they are consumed by their children (whom they have produced!) when they buy the role of the Supermother; they are consumed by authoritarian husbands who expect them to be submissive servants; and they are consumed by bosses who bring them in and out of the labor force and who extract a maximum of labor for a minimum of pay. They are consumed by medical researchers who try out new and unsafe contraceptives on them. They are consumed by men who buy their bodies on the street. They are consumed by church and state, who expect them to produce the next generation for the glory of god and country; they are consumed by political and social organizations that expect them to 'volunteer' their time and energy. They have little sense of self, because their selfhood has been sold to others.

WOMEN AND THE SPECTACLE

It is difficult to consume people who put up a fight, who resist the cannibalizing of their bodies, their minds, their daily lives. A few people manage to resist, but most don't resist effectively, because they can't. It is hard to locate our tormentor, because it is so pervasive, so familiar. We have known it all our lives. It is our culture.

Situationists characterize our culture as a *spectacle*. The spectacle treats us all as passive spectators of what we are told are our lives. And the culture-as-spectacle covers everything: we are bom into it, socialized by it, go to school in it, work and relax and relate to other people in it. Even when we rebel against it, the rebellion is often defined by the spectacle. Would anyone care to estimate the number of sensitive, alienated adolescent males who a generation ago modeled their behavior on James Dean in 'Rebel Without a Cause?' I'm talking about a *movie*, whose capitalist producers and whose star made a great deal of money from this Spectacular.

Rebellious acts, then, tend to be acts of *opposition* to the spectacle, but seldom are so different that they *transcend* the spectacle. Women have a set of behaviors that show dissatisfaction by being the opposite of what is expected. At the same time these acts are cliches of rebellion, and thus are almost prescribed safety valves that don't alter the theater of our lives. What is a rebellious woman supposed to do? We can all name the behaviors — they appear in every newspaper, on prime time television, on the best-seller lists, in popular magazines — and, of course, in everyday life. In a setting that values perfectionist housekeeping, she can be a slob; in a subculture that values large families, she can refuse to have children. Other predictable insurgencies? She can defy the sexual double standard for married women by having an affair (or several); she can drink; or use what is termed 'locker room' language; or have a nervous breakdown; or — if she is an adolescent — she can 'act out' (a revealing phrase!) by running away from home and having sex with a lot of men.

Any of these things may make an individual woman's life more tolerable (often, they make it less so); and all of them are guaranteed to make conservatives rant that society is crumbling. But these kinds of scripted insurrections haven't made it crumble yet, and, by themselves they aren't likely to. Anything less than a direct attack upon all the conditions of our lives is not enough.

When women talk about changing destructive sex role socialization of females, they pick one of these possible solutions: 1) girls should be socialized more or less like boys to be independent, competitive, aggressive, and so forth. In short, it is a man's world, so a woman who wants to fit it has to be 'one of the boys', 2) we should glorify the female role, and realize that what we have called weakness is really strength. We should be proud that we are maternal, nurturant, sensitive, emotional, and so on; 3) the only healthy person is an androgynous person: we must eradicate the artificial division of humanity into masculine' and 'feminine,' and help both sexes become a mix of the best traits of each.

Within these three models, personal solutions to problems of sexist oppression cover a wide range. Stay single; live communally (with both men and women, or with women only). Don't have children; don't have male children; have any kind of children you want, but get parent and worker-controlled child care. Get a job; get a better job; push for affirmative action. Be an informed consumer; file a lawsuit; learn karate; take assertiveness training. Develop the lesbian within you. Develop your proletarian identity. All of these make sense in particular situations. for particular women. But all of them are partial solutions to much broader problems, and none of them necessarily requires seeing the world in a qualitatively different way.

So. We move from the particular to more general solutions. Destroy capitalism. End patriarchy. Smash heterosexism. All are obviously essential tasks in the building of a new and truly human world. Marxists, other socialists, social anarchists, feminists — all would agree. But what the socialists, and even some feminists, leave out is this: we must smash all forms of domination. That's not just a slogan, and it is the hardest task of all. It means that we have to see through the spectacle, destroy the stage sets, know that there are other ways of doing things. It means that we have to do more than react in programmed rebellions — we must act. And our actions will be collectively taken, what each person acts autonomously. Does that seem contradictory? It isn't — but it will be very difficult to do. The individual cannot change anything very much; for that reason, we have to work together. But that work must be without leaders as we know them, and without delegating any control over what we do and what we want to build.

Can the socialists do that? Or the matriarchs? Or the spirituality-trippers? You know the answer to that. Work with them when it makes sense to do so, but give up nothing. Concede nothing to them, or to anyone else: [19]

> The past leads to us if we force it to.
> Otherwise it contains us
> in its asylum with no gates.
> We make history or it
> makes us.

NOTES

1. Barbara Ehrenreich, 'What is Socialist Feminism?', *WIN Magazine* (6/3/76), 4.
2. The best of these arguments I've encountered are 'Socialist Feminism: A Strategy for the Women's Movement,' by the Hyde Park Chapter, Chicago Women's Liberation Union (1972); and Charlotte Bunch, 'The Reform Tool Kit,' *Quest*, 1:1 (Summer 1974), 37-51.
3. Reports by Polly Anna, Kana Trueblood, C. Corday and S. Tufts, *The Fifth Estate* (May 1976), 13, 16. The 'revolution' failed: FEN and its club shut down.
4. People who are interested in reading reports of the conference will find them in almost every feminist or socialist newspaper that appeared in the month or so after July 4. Speeches by Barbara Ehrenreich, Michelle Russell, and the Berkeley-Oakland Women's Union are reprinted in *Socialist Revolution*, no. 26 (Oct.–Dec. 1975); and the speech by Charlotte Bunch, 'Not For Lesbians Only,' appears in *Quest*, 2:2 (Fall 1975). A 30-minute audiotape documentary is available from the Great Atlantic Radio Conspiracy, 2743 Maryland Avenue, Baltimore, MD 21218.
5. Lynne Farrow, 'Feminism as Anarchism,' *Aurora*, 4 (1974), 9; Peggy Kornegger, 'Anarchism: The Feminist Connection,' *The Second Wave*, 4:1 (Spring 1975), 31 and reprinted here; Marian Leighton, 'Anarcho-Feminism and Louise Michel,' *Black Rose*, 1 (April 1974), 14.
6. Dec. 1, 1970, p. 11.
7. 'Lilith's Manifesto,' from the Women's Majority Union of Seattle, 1969. Reprinted in Robin Morgan (ed.), *Sisterhood is Powerful* (New York: Random House, 1970), 529.
8. The best and most detailed description of the parallels between radical feminism and anarchist feminism is found in Kornegger, *op. cit.*
9. The speech is currently available from KNOW, Inc.
10. Joreen, 'The Tyranny of Structurelessness,' *The Second Wave*, 2:1 (1972).
11. 'What Future for Leadership?,' *Quest*, 2:4 (Spring 1976), 2-13.
12. Strasbourg Situationists, *Once the Universities Were Respected*, (1968), 38. Reprinted in *Reinventing Anarchy*, 1979.
13. Carol Hanisch, 'The Personal is Political,' *Notes from the Second Year* (New York: Radical Feminism, 1970), 76-8.
14. Leighton, *op. cit.*
15. Point-Blank!, 'The Changing of the Guard,' in *Point-Blank!* (Oct. 1972), 16.
16. For one of the most illuminating of these early analyses, see Meredith Tax, 'Woman and Her Mind: The Story of Everyday Life,' (Boston: Bread and Roses Publications, 1970).
17. Carole Oles, 'The Gift,' in *13th Moon*, II: I (1974), 39.
18. Tax, *op. cit.*, 13.
19. Marge Piercy, excerpt from 'Contribution to Our Museum,' in *Living in the Open* (New York: Knopf, 1976), 74-5.

5
WORK

graphic from Ecstatic Incisions: The Collages of Freddie Baer

graphic from **Ecstatic Incisions: The Collages of Freddie Baer**

Introduction To
WORK

Work and the liberation of people from work they do not want to do has been a central concern of all anarchists. Obviously, to live in community requires that some maintenance work be done. Living in an urban community requires even more work. And if the appropriate technology for your community is a bicycle or a photovoltaic cell or a radio station or computer, even more work will be called for. The paradox of work in this society is that it has become tied to economic survival at the same time that it is often mind-deadening and dangerous to one's health and safety. The tragic aspect of this paradox is that many workers have been so "oversocialized" that they seldom perceive, and often deny, what their work is doing to them. For most people, paid employment is perceived as a necessary means to other ends. It is the sociability and friendships at work, the after-hours socializing, the weekends and vacations that one works for. Few people can conceptualize alternatives to current systems of work, and as one American corporate executive, intrigued by my ideas of self-management, told me "It wouldn't matter anyway because most people won't accept it." In part, he was correct. Hierarchical work arrangements with differential rewards and privileges are simply considered as the way things are done. It is "truth," and other ways of thinking simply don't come up. Furthermore, the ideology of work is so strong that alternative views are too threatening to think about and too terrifying to risk their actualization.

The literature of anarchism is redundant with questions about work. Here are some of the compelling issues.

1. How much work is really necessary in society? We know that most goods and services produced are truly unnecessary and

wasteful, but are people really aware of the magnitude of waste? For example, 22.5 percent of the U.S. nonfarm workforce is employed in "guard labor," that is, as supervisors, police, judicial employees, security personnel, makers of security equipment, military, and Pentagon-dependent civilian jobs. What about the advertising industry, the packaging industry, the marketing and public relations firms? How much of this work is truly productive? How much of this work helps to build a better society?

2. Can we rationally allocate work to provide for the shared requirements of a community — at the least, the production of food, energy, and shelter, the growth and nurturance of its people, and the conservation of resources and the nonpolluting disposal of garbage and other wastes?

3. How can we allocate work in order to achieve goals that go beyond the local community? For example, we need to be able to have people work at mail delivery, the upkeep of the roads, and trade in goods and services.

4. How is the workplace itself to be organized? Is there an optimum size for different types of work units? How are decisions to be made? And, how shall we deal with dirty work and boring work ? Can play be built into work? Or work into play?

5. How are people to be rewarded for their work? Can we exchange labor credits? What kinds of systems of exchange and accounting are congruent with the principles of an anarchist society?

6. How do we deal with a division of labor, with differences in skill, authority and expertness?

The answers to these questions have been plotted on paper and, in many cases, actualized by anarchists around the world in settings as different as heavy industry and the university. What we need to consider in organizing transitional forms is how well they contain the seeds of their own destruction and rebirth.

David DeLeon, George Benello, and **Colin Ward**, in the next three contributions, are all dealing with transitional forms. Each in his own way has addressed some of the questions we ask here.

David DeLeon's essay, "For Democracy Where We Work," is the departure for this section. DeLeon codifies many of the standard criticisms of union reform and the failures of state socialism. He concludes with consideration of alternatives, from moderate reforms to complete democracy at the workplace.

George Benello's description and analysis of the Mondragon network presents a practical and successful example of a step toward the liberation of labor. While short of the anarchist mark, the organization of the Mondragon cooperatives goes beyond most capitalist and socialist workplaces.

Colin Ward looks in a different direction, that of the "informal economy." Like DeLeon and Benello, he is looking for fertile ground to plant the seeds of anarchy.

Bob Black, in contrast to the other contributors in this section, is more of a guerrilla gardener. He addresses himself to what so many writers and workers refuse to acknowledge: For most people and at most times, jobs are the equivalent of part-time slavery. As one writer put it, the ring of the alarm clock is the first humiliation of the work day. "I say we should end employment," Black provokes us at the beginning of his essay. Look more closely and you will see that what he really wants is to create new forms of work, to turn work into play. "Workers of the world — relax."

For Democracy Where We Work:
A Rationale for Social Self-Management

David DeLeon

While some of us work in offices, and others in factories, we frequently have common complaints.

First, capitalism has tended to reduce us to simple interchangeable parts that can be readily replaced. It's the same if our jobs are on an assembly line, or in row-after-row of telephone operators or secretaries. Our labor is usually a treadmill of routine that requires speed and mental concentration at an immediate task. For example, if you worked at the auto factory in Lordstown, Ohio, in 1976, the cars went by you at the rate of 101 an hour. Every thirty-three seconds you had to mechanically repeat certain motions. If you were a telephone operator, a keypuncher or a steelworker you might have the same response to such a division of labor:

> You're there just to handle the equipment. You're treated like a piece of equipment.

> You do it automatically, like a monkey or a dog would do something by conditioning. You feel stagnant; everything is over and over and over. . . . This makes the average individual feel sort of like a vegetable.

> That's mechanical; that's not human.. We sweat, we have upset stomachs, and we're not about to be placed in the category of a machine.

The images are all non-human: a vegetable, a monkey, a dog, a machine. Already in the 1840s, Emerson observed that industrial capitalism had destroyed the independence and satisfactions of craft labor, turning the workers into commodities to be bought, sold and 'used' — into a collection of walking monsters, here 'a good finger, a neck, a stomach, an elbow,' but never a whole person.

Second, our jobs are often in dirty, noisy, unpleasant, and sometimes dangerous places. Capitalism is concerned primarily with profit, not with providing us with an attractive workplace (unless this might increase productivity enough to offset the expense). We are expected to put up with the bad lighting, noise pollution, chemical hazards, radiation, and poor ventilation that produce a host of occupational diseases from asbestosis, through black lung, brown lung, and the rest of the alphabet. While the Department of Labor reported, in 1975, that the number of job-related health threats had declined (partly because of unemployment!), it still noted 5,300 deaths and 5 million non-fatal injuries.

Government regulations are usually minimal and are generally avoided or subverted by the companies. Federal laws such as the Occupational Safety and Health Act seldom have a dramatic impact since the government does not wish to hinder the profitability of business. Thus, by the mid-1970s, the national government employed only fifty-five industrial hygienists: one for every one million workers. The typical factory is still likely to have the following conditions:

The presses leaked oil. The roof leaked. [Forklifts] drove with faulty brakes. Scraps accumulated in the aisles. The high pressure air-lines screeched through the plant as leaks were left unrepaired. In late '72 when a die setter was killed by a bolster plate blowing loose cutting off his head, the flashpoint was provided that set up an unofficial safety committee. On 7 June 1973 a walkout of the second shift in the press room protested the conditions that removed two fingers from a woman working a bad press.

Third, our jobs deny us many basic rights. While many believe that there is democracy in politics, few would argue that there is democracy where we work. Most factories are like military dictatorships. Those at the bottom are privates, the supervisors are sergeants, and on up through the hierarchy. The organization can dictate everything from our clothing and hair style to how we spend a large portion of our lives, during work. It can compel overtime; it can require us to see a company doctor if we have a medical complaint; it can forbid us free time to engage in political activity; it can suppress freedom of speech, press and assembly — it can use ID cards and armed security police, along with closed-circuit TVs to watch us; it can punish dissenters with 'disciplinary layoffs' (as GM calls them), or it can simply fire us. We are forced, by circumstances to accept stances, to accept much of this, or join the millions of unemployed. Herbert Marcuse once called our society a 'nonterroristic totalitarianism.' In almost every job, we have only the 'right' to quit. Major decisions are made at the top and we are expected to obey, whether we work in an ivory tower or a mine shaft.

Fourth, our jobs are making others wealthy, although we have less than we want. We are living in a society where we are forced to sell ourselves, producing profits for a few, and administering their property and power. Capitalism is a form of institutionalized robbery, depriving us of the full value of our labor, and selling our products back to us for a profit. As one writer has commented: 'laborers can be robbed twice — at the point of production and at the market place.' In a more significant sense, we are really being deprived of the fullness of our lives. Even when capitalists are compelled to make concessions, they have more to give. As one character in *Marat/Sade* remarked: 'even if it seems to you that you never had so much — that is only the slogan of those who still have more than you.' Most of these complaints are found in this depiction of the world of the assembly line worker:

> Try putting 13 little pins in 13 little holes 60 times an hour, eight hours a day. Spot-weld 67 steel plates an hour, then find yourself one day facing a new assembly-line needing 110 an hour. Fit 100 coils to 100 cars every hour; tighten seven bolts three times a minute. Do your work in noise 'at the safety limit,' in a fine mist of oil, solvent and metal dust. Negotiate for the right to take a piss — or relieve yourself furtively behind a big press so that you don't break the rhythm and lose your bonus. Speed up to gain time to blow your nose or get a bit of grit out of your eye. Bolt your sandwich sitting in a pool of grease because the canteen is 10 minutes away and you've only got 40 for your lunch-break. As you cross the factory threshold, lose the freedom of opinion, the freedom of speech, the right to meet and associate supposedly guaranteed under the constitution. Obey without arguing, suffer punishment without the right of appeal, get the worst jobs if the manager doesn't like your face. . . . Wonder each morning how you're going to hold out until the evening, each Monday how you'll make it to Saturday. Reach home without the strength to do anything but watch TV, telling yourself you'll surely die an idiot.

While I've stressed that life is not much better for the white-collar worker, there are differences between those who work with tools and those who, in effect, administer people. Although neither experiences much dignity or satisfaction, the white-collar worker may be less oppressed. One student from a blue-collar family made this comparison between the factory worker and the college professor who is compelled to 'produce' scholarship:

> The professor would begin to understand how a factory worker feels if he had to type a single paragraph, not papers, from nine to five, every day of the week. Instead of setting the pace himself, his typewriter carriage would begin to move at nine and continue at a steady rate until five. For permission to go to the bathroom or to use the telephone, the professor would have to ask a supervisor. His salary [would be cut in half], and his vacations reduced to two weeks a year. Finally, if he faced the grim conclusion that his job was a dead end, his situation would then approximate that of an unskilled young worker in a contemporary auto factory.

Still, it must be said that all workers tend to feel little sense of meaning in their work. Few would disagree with the worker who said that 'the things I like best about my job are quitting time, pay day, days off, and vacations.' The nature of capitalism — however reformed and prettified — has not changed since Marx criticized it in the 1840s as 'coerced labor' because it was prompted not by 'the satisfaction of a need; it is merely the means to satisfy needs external to it. Its alien character emerges clearly in the fact that as soon as no physical or other compulsion exists, labor is shunned like the plague.' Or as Marx later summarized the attitude of the worker: '*I work in order to live* and provide for myself the means of living. Working is *not* living.'

Does this mean that all workers are, at all times, seething with resentment against capitalism? No, this essay is not the script for a radical melodrama. Many workers, if they are unhappy or unemployed, believe the official ideology that it is somehow their fault and not that of 'free enterprise.' Others tolerate work because their pay buys them a sense of freedom through being a consumer. It is easy to be narcotized by the vision and partial reality of consumption. Consumerism becomes a kind of spectacle that controls people by convincing them that they have meaning through products: 'come alive, you're in the Pepsi generation,' 'Suzuki [motorcycle] conquers boredom,' and 'take a puff and it's springtime.' Even those who become disillusioned are often caught in 'the golden chains' of installment buying; they now have something to lose if they rebel.

Many observers of the surface of advanced capitalist society see only a rather placid working class. Failing to perceive the fundamental inhumanity of capitalism, such commentators say that all fundamental problems have been solved by the beneficent welfare state and a people's capitalism.' Events such as the May-June days in France in 1968 have always startled these pundits, because such events were presumably impossible. For example, in the early 1960s a sociology professor analyzed class consciousness among the Vauxhall auto workers in England. Dr Goldthorpe concluded that the workers had adjusted to the inevitability and necessity of their jobs and were quite apathetic. The workers unexpectedly began to discuss his views. At the same time, Vauxhall issued its yearly report of substantial profits. This discussion, combined with the 'provocation' that the company had made several thousand dollars from each worker, prompted an explosion of anger. As the London Times reported:

> Wild rioting has broken out at the Vauxhall car factories in Luton. Thousands of workers streamed out of the shops and gathered in the factory yard. They besieged the management offices, calling for the managers to come out, singing the 'Red Flag' and shouting 'string them up!' Groups attempted to storm the offices and battled the police which had been called to protect them.

This rioting continued for two days, no doubt to the astonishment of poor Dr Goldthorpe! Similar examples of workers being ignited by studies proving their indifference have occurred in such diverse areas as Oslo, Norway and Cologne, Germany.

Yet such open violence is uncommon. While most of us feel a 'diffuse hostility' toward our work, this hostility is seldom so dramatically explicit. Although we have always fought back against monotony, speed-ups, dangerous work conditions and arrogant bosses, we may not go beyond indolence and bad work, just as the slaves often responded to their masters. This level of resistance is easily understandable. Capitalism limits our interest in our jobs. If we produce more, we threaten other workers and ourselves, since the quotas will probably be raised. If we develop a more efficient way to do our work, the time and motion experts may suddenly appear. While we usually adjust to 'doing time' in the industrial prison, our frequent passivity should not be confused with contentment.

Some forms of 'striking back' are more obvious, such as stealing from work, stores and supermarkets ($1 billion a year in the early 1970s), or wildcat strikes, sabotage and other types of spontaneous protest. Sabotage can be one brake to a speed-up in an auto factory. The workers begin to make scratches, cut wires, break instruments, fail to tighten bolts, and similar acts. As cars pile up in the repair lot, management is likely to get the message. Of course, sabotage tends to be individualized and may threaten or irritate other workers since it could bring down more supervision and firings. But it will undoubtedly continue, so long as the circumstances of capitalism continue. Such acts are important for what they symbolize. Take the case of a black worker who was fired at a Detroit Chrysler plant in 1969. He went home, got a gun, returned to the factory and killed two foremen and a UAW committeeman. The next day, many foremen got anonymous newspaper clippings about this event. The worker's defense was that the brutal conditions of the plant had driven him insane. After the judge and jury visited the factory, he was acquitted!

Most employers are aware of such undercurrents of hostility. Employers are concerned about low productivity, lack of interest, sabotage, absenteeism, and other signs of what was called in the early 1970s 'the revolt against work' or 'the blue-collar blues.' Soon, the Department of Health, Education and Welfare had funded a study on 'work in America,' Senator Edward Kennedy chaired an investigation into 'worker alienation,' and President Nixon declared that 'the need for job satisfaction' was one of the great issues of the day. In 1975, the Hart poll indicated that about 80 percent of Americans believed that capitalism had reached its peak and was in decline. American capitalism has been able to respond to such challenges with moderate reforms, seeking to convince us that our best interests are served by capitalism. Business has been able to adjust to 'responsible' unionism, and to such techniques as profit-sharing, company pensions, teams of workers, and more flexible hours of work. These are all excellent forms of social control: 'quit and you lose your pension!;' 'We're speeding up the line to increase your profit-sharing;' or, 'buy a share in your company!' While most of these changes are cosmetic, merely giving the appearance of 'humanistic management,' most radicals have been insensitive to the power of such devices to minimally meet human needs. Elinor Langer soon realized that the 'busy little world' of small rewards and loyalties can assuage the impersonality of most existing work situations. For business, 'the pattern of cooptation . . . rests on details: hundreds of trivial, but human details.' Business people have generally understood this better than radicals.

Other business experiments have offered some real elements of workers' control. In 'job enlargement,' a petty job is made more complex and thus (presumably) more interesting. In 'job enrichment,' the worker is permitted to make a few decisions, rather than being completely under the thumb of the supervisor. Job redesign involving both of these factors has included a team of workers building individual cars instead of turning one screw or tying three wires. Elinor Langer noticed other cases in a phone company which had created a mass of minor supervisors and an elaborate system of limited mobility, thus fostering the impression of power and progress. AT&T has allowed those who do the sorting and coding of checks and invoices to vary their pace, work with the same clients continuously (thus developing a sense of 'my' customers) and arrange different hours of work. This resulted in a 27 percent increase in productivity and a saving of $558,000 a year. General Foods, in the early 1970s, granted a number of rights to the workers in its Topeka, Kansas, factory: they could interview and hire new workers, form teams for particular work projects, and make various decisions. This stimulated 30 percent higher productivity. Obviously, the workers were more satisfied.

Nevertheless, job redesign will not solve the basic problems of capitalism. While it might alleviate some difficulties, it causes others. Job enlargement usually means doing more work (often in a higher 'skill' classification) without more money; more efficiency will mean fewer jobs; 'team leaders' are, in effect, foremen; and what happens when these novelties are no longer new? After all, the major goal is still profit: 'I participate, you participate, they profit.'

In Europe, pressure from the working class has forced the capitalists to try even more advanced reforms. In Germany, workers have representation on all boards of directors and management committees of major industries. Under this policy of 'codetermination,' labor and business have regular get-togethers to discuss health, safety and production. Such involvement or consultation, of course, does not mean control — it is pseudo-participation. American reformers like Ralph Nader are naturally attracted to such moderation, and have also called for consumer and 'public' members on U.S. corporate boards. Some capitalists will make such changes because they want to decrease worker resentment and to increase productivity, but this will not eliminate the fact that capitalism is based upon the exploitation of labor. It will remain true that, in the class struggle, nice guys finish last. Capitalism has changed, and may still change, but it will always be divided into the owners of the means of production and the rest of us, wage laborers.

What about unions? Won't they protect us? Aren't they for workers' control? No, they are essentially for the control of workers. While unions began as self-defense organizations for workers to limit the power of capital, they have become junior partners of business. Even during the 1920s, intelligent capitalists like Gerard P. Swope, the president of General Electric, had praised 'businesslike' unions that insured a stable, orderly work force. Many other liberals and conservatives became convinced of the need for a new form of discipline when 8.2 million workers struck in 1933, and federal troops were used in sixteen states in 1934. Frances Perkins, FDR's Secretary of Labor, reiterated the values of unions to capitalism: 'You don't need to be afraid of unions. . . . They don't want to run the business. You will probably get a lot better production and happiness if you have a good union organization and a contract.' By the 1960s, Clark Kerr agreed that unions were major 'disciplinary instruments,' Daniel Bell lauded them as part of 'the control system of management,' C. Wright Mills denounced them as 'managers of discontent,' and Paul Jacobs characterized them as 'an integral part of the system of authority.' How do unions keep the workers in line, and facilitate long-term capitalist planning?

1) *The contract.* Companies are pleased by contracts that promise a predictable labor force. Unions are pleased by the prospect of their own organizational stability. Walter Reuther of the UAW once even stressed a five-year contract (which union militants ridiculed as the equivalent of Stalin's five-year plan), and I. W. Abel of the steelworkers urged a three-year contract with a no-strike provision. Of course, the average worker may not share all of this enthusiasm. It is his or her freedom that has been limited.

The content of these long-term contracts may also be unattractive to many workers. 'Responsible unionists' have tended to limit bargaining to industry-wide issues of wages and hours. Workers at a particular factory or office may be more disturbed about work conditions, but the distant bureaucracy negotiates on other issues. While the contract may win certain concessions, it is at the price of the workers' guaranteed passivity. If work conditions deteriorate, if a speed-up eliminates time benefits, if inflation destroys wage gains — the worker is still bound by the contract. The contract is a basic validation of the company's legal authority. It is the legal mortgage or bill of sale of the workers.

Once the leadership has negotiated a contract, the members are seldom given a chance to knowledgeably discuss it, or even, sometimes, to vote on it. The whole process has become so remote and legalistic that most workers are turned off. A recent contract at Lordstown was representative: it was 166 pages long, and written in a language that would require a team of interpreters to tell the average person what was happening. By the end of bargaining, the majority of workers are pathetic, confused or possibly hostile — leaving about 10-14 percent of contracts rejected. The contract has become a maze of 'proper channels' that baffles the worker.

2) *The right to strike.* Just as the contract is handed down from above, so are strike orders. Most unionized workers have lost the power to strike over local issues. Even the CIO of the 1930s vigorously discouraged sitdowns and direct action. Strikes, under union direction, are supposed to be controlled, quiet, legal actions occurring only at the end of a contract, if at all. Instead of masses of workers outside and inside the plant, there are a few 'official' pickets. Instead of occupying plant, it is surrendered to the employer. Instead of spontaneous struggle, the strike is planned and announced to the enemy in advance. The workers are virtually expected to be passive spectators during their own strike. The unions say 'go home! We are negotiating for you.' Union struggles have become so ritualized that 'most official strikes resemble a badminton game more than a boxing match.'

When workers become impudent and act by themselves, the modern union often responds as a strike-breaker. In 1974, a wildcat at one of Chrysler's truck plants was defeated when the union called the police to throw the workers out of the union hall that had been built with their own dues! The sanctity of the contract was everything. In 1976 nearly one-half of the miners of the UMW wildcatted against the contract negotiated by one of the darlings of liberal unionism, Arnold Miller. His response to the rebellious miners was typical of any bureaucrat: if they don't like it, they can quit.

3) *Grievance procedures.* Let us say that a contract has been 'accepted' and the company follows the pattern described in the UMW Journal: it begins 'violating the contract on the day it's signed and continues until the day it expires.' If the workers can't officially strike, why don't they protest through the grievance process?

Suppose that a worker is idle and the foreman tells him or her to push a broom across the floor to 'make work.' The worker may reply: 'shove it up your . . . ,' but the order will probably have to be obeyed. If the worker wants to refuse, s/he may be required to ask the foreman to call the union representative to file a complaint. This, in itself, prevents many from acting. If not, the union rep may be slow in arriving since the number of them has declined over the years. Then, the rep will inform the worker that the order must be obeyed, although a grievance can be filed. If so, the event will be recorded on a piece of paper. Months or years later, you may 'win' your grievance, but it will no longer make any difference. This system is obviously too cumbersome to be effective, and even if the union official is sympathetic s/he is really a kind of cop who compels the worker to continue working while the lawyers or the officials do something — or nothing. In 1974 the St. Louis local of the UAW had 18,000 unresolved grievances. Since the union hesitates to endanger its own privileges (even the lowly committeeman often has special pay, no blue-collar work and the right to leave the workplace during the day), it has holstered its most threatening weapons such as the strike, and speaks in soft, legalistic tones. The union is seldom a watchdog for workers' rights. As one militant has said, 'Your dog don't bark no more.'

4) *Dues checkoff.* Well, if workers don't like what's going on, can't they refuse to pay their dues? No, they can't. One of the first goals of many unions was to have all dues automatically deducted from the worker's paycheck *by the company.* The workers then became passive dues payers. 'The union no longer had to come down to the ranks and hustle your dollars.' This tied the union bureaucracy closer to the company and made it more remote from the workers. In the 1880s, the officers of the American Railway Union 'rode the rails' like paupers; today, AFL leaders have private jets. They are 'tuxedo unionists.' The uncontrolled wealth generated by the dues checkoff, along with the closed shop (which has limited the necessity for organizing), has fostered the corruption documented by the Kefauver and McClellan investigations, and such magnificent salaries as the $100,000 a year received by seventeen officers of the Teamsters in 1975. Unions have become big business. In 1976 they had 170,000 contracts and $3 billion a year in dues and assessments. The money, cars, clothes and status of these 'workers' place them in the same physical context and intellectual perspective as the capitalist — riding the backs of labor. Where was the average worker at one of the 1976 meetings of this elite:

> Somehow they didn't look like formidable political foes of reaction as they relaxed in their shorts and colorful sports shirts around the pool of the Americana Hotel in Bal Harbour, a rather swank Florida resort where they had been gathering each winter for more than two decades. And they didn't look like tough leaders of America's workers as they ordered escargots and rack of lamb or thick steaks in the dining rooms of Miami Beach, or when they sipped Dry Sack Sherry and talked quietly among themselves at the nightly receptions given for them by supplicants of their

good will. With salaries of $50,000 or more, they might not be expected to voice the concerns of the average worker.

Indeed, historically the unions have 'protected' mainly the aristocrats of labor (the better paid occupations), and locked out minorities and the unskilled. Herbert Hill, the national labor director of the NAACP, lamented that the unions were no longer a social movement, but had disintegrated into 'narrow protective service agencies for their duespayers,' ignoring the masses of unorganized workers — which means especially the black, Puerto Rican and Chicano laborer. Existing unions are more concerned about their bank accounts than about the general interests of the working class. George Meany regretted the money given to the United Farm Workers because they 'make a lot of noise' but 'few contributions to the working of this organization.' Walter Reuther, despite his own limitations, recognized this as 'the banker mentality in the American labor movement.'

5) *Bureaucracy*. If all of this is true, why don't the workers rise up and vote the rascals out of office? This is not impossible, but extremely difficult since most unions are police states. There is little or no local autonomy; there are no legitimate parties or factions within unions; the bureaucracy controls the union press, union patronage, and union treasury; the bureaucracy has few traditions or 'due process' in union disputes; power is concentrated in the office of the president; dissidents can be broken easily. Frank Marquart, of the auto workers, recalls that when he tried to use the union hall to discuss local issues, the union locked the doors. Jordan Sims claimed that he hadn't seen a contract in ten years, and the union constitution in eighteen — and that the president of the local told him that 'you don't want to read something like this. It'll just mix up your mind and get you into trouble.' Such bureaucrats turn union meetings into puppet shows:

> The tricks of the trade are numerous. They include all-inclusive resolutions that blunt an opposition view; lengthy and technical committee reports which are difficult to follow; stacking convention committees with 'safe' members, advised by experts whose function is to sell predetermined policy; careful choice of speakers from the floor; overloading the guest list as a form of filibuster against too much time for delegates' discussion; postponing controversial resolutions to the last minute, when delegates are increasingly impatient, so that the discussion is either too brief, or

else is 'referred to the incoming board'; and finally using the staff's power of patronage to keep things under control.

Sometimes, militants do win, like Arnold Miller of the UMW. Then, because of the imperatives of 'working within the system,' they become rapidly transformed into 'respectable leaders.' Even the election of radicals may change little of the essentially oligarchic structure of trade unionism. Consider the case of the UAW. All three of the Reuthers were once members of the Socialist Party — Walter Reuther had even been a tool-and-die worker in the U.S.S.R. during the 1930s (and had no basic criticisms of the labor discipline). Emil Mazey, the secretary-treasurer, once belonged to the Proletarian Party and the SPA. Leonard Woodcock (born in England) came out of the sectarian Independent Labor Party and the SPA! Nevertheless, the UAW remains a dictatorship, though, perhaps, a benevolent one. Whatever the case, it suffers from all of the problems that have been mentioned.

This doesn't mean that unions are all alike. It can be argued that, while George Meany represents a kind of narrow 'business as usual unionism,' Walter Reuther was a champion of 'social unionism' — favoring more social planning or engineering. While one type could be said to be more reformist than the other, both are basically pro-capitalist, although Reuther tended toward state capitalism.

Both kinds of unions have some positive qualities. They do make some quantitative if not qualitative differences in society. Workers may derive certain benefits in wages and hours, along with the power of mass organization. Unions may foster a sense of solidarity — as in the ritual use of 'brother' and 'sister' at some meetings — and the inclusion (though often minimal) of women, blacks and minorities. Union officials may, like old-time political bosses, perform certain minor favors: notarizing documents, finding jobs, and influencing local judges and politicians. But, in essence, unions have been accepted by much of capitalism because they insure 'social peace,' divide the workers into organizations (each with its own jealous bureaucracy), and allow for long-term planning.

Of course, it is also true that business remains hostile to the organization of non-militant workers, who can be controlled by other means. While unions and capital can work compatibly, business is still reluctant to concede any wage gains, improvements in physical working conditions, 'interference' with management powers, and workers' rights. Many companies still resist union elections or engage in 'surface bargaining' in the hope of defeating the ratification of any contract.

Nevertheless, there are many circumstances where unions can act as buffers or shock absorbers between the workers and the company. Trade unions, after all, accept capitalist legality, private property, the 'harmony of class interests' and strike limitations. Such union officials function as the agents of capital, mediating as middlemen with the workers. If the company is prosperous (for example, if the workers are more exploited), the union — that is, generally, the bureaucracy — also prospers. Unions like the United Steel Workers, the International Ladies Garment Workers, and the United Rubber Workers have preached productivity to their members. The UMW has promoted automation that has eliminated the jobs of thousands of people. Within the values of capitalist competition, these were all reasonable and responsible actions.

It is understandable, then, that many people are skeptical about unions. Only about 32 percent of American labor is unionized, and the percentage has been dropping in recent years. Why join a union? In 1975, the California Poll and a study by Gallup revealed that, while business ranked lowest in public esteem, labor unions vied for this distinction. In 1965 unions won 60 percent of NLRB elections; in 1976, 49 percent. Many blacks consider the unions racist, many women have been excluded or oppressed by union sexism. And American workers are not unique in this pessimism. Over 40 percent of British labor votes Conservative! Does this prove that they are content, stupid or misled, as many radicals claim? Perhaps — but it may also illustrate that, in many cases, people can see no difference between Conservative candidate and a Labour one.

Although many of us are unhappy about our jobs, our unions and our politics, there are few alternatives. Radical parties are usually quite as repressive. Radical unions will not succeed at this moment, and circumstances are not conducive to mass organization. American capitalism has been able to make concessions because of the unique wealth of North American farmlands and circumstances are not conducive to mass organization. It has been able to maintain its profits by a high rate of return from foreign investment or by raising prices (ultimately lowering the workers' real gains). But revoluions abroad and competition from such countries as Japan and West Germany limit these options. What remains is to 'rationalize' the work process through automation and a reduction in the number of workers, along with intensified exploitation (making us work harder). American labor, in the future, may be forced to go beyond trade unionism.

Many workers doubt that the major existing alternative, socialism, would be much better, and they are justifiably suspicious of American radical parties. They have heard of the lack of even political democracy in most socialist countries, and many know something about the military battles against the working class in Hungary, East Germany, Poland and Czechoslovakia. They sense that in most socialist systems the working class does not rule. Instead, a single party dominates all, supposedly 'in the interests of the working class.' None of the Marxist-Leninist states — and this includes China — permits the formation of any open opposition, or the printing of opposition literature, or the holding of opposition meetings. The total life of the workers is subject to the will of a few. Now and then, the 'happy proletarians' rebel, as did many Polish workers in 1970 and 1976 when various Communist Party buildings were sacked. Even in China, the struggle for power after the death of Mao Tse-tung was not openly debated. Most socialist countries are a sad parody of socialist ideals.

This is most obvious in the workplace.

First, the division of labor has been maintained with few exceptions. Marx had condemned this fragmentation of life, saying that it 'converts the laborer into a crippled monstrosity' and that 'the subdivision of labor is the assassination of a people.' Yet conventional socialism has not challenged the organization of work. At best, some argue that 'alienation' is less under socialism because the worker may feel that s/he is working for a higher standard of living for all. But this is not enough. As one critic has stated the proper goal of liberation: 'socialism is not a backyard of leisure attached to the industrial prison. It is not transistors for the prisoners. It is the destruction of the industrial prison itself.'

Second, the immediate aims of state socialism and capitalism are the same: efficiency and productivity. If these conflict with happiness, then happiness is sacrificed. Russia, for example, invented Stakhanovite socialism, named after the ox-like worker who always overfulfilled his quota. What laborer is going to applaud the prediction of André Gorz that 'after the communist revolution we will work more, not less'? Or the special homes, clothing, food and status of the socialist elites? What worker who hears of Soviet productivity will not think 'speed-up'? Consider the description of a Russian factory where the main work area was dominated by a gigantic poster of Lenin ('Lenin is eternally with us'), surrounded by such thrilling banners as 'every day of shock labor is a stride toward communism' and 'discipline is the precondition of success.' Shock labor? Discipline? Or the North Korean newspaper that proudly informed us that 'Fierce Flames of Speed-Up Campaign [are] Raging at Every Construction Site' (onward, comrade serfs!). What all Marxist-Leninist parties call 'the Communist attitude toward work' is apparently marching, rank after rank, toward tomorrow. Yet the denial of democracy today means the defeat of democracy tomorrow. The workers' rights have been subordinated to capital accumulation, just as they are under capitalism, although individual capitalists have been replaced by a collective capitalist, the state. In either case, productivity comes first, people second. While Chinese communism has been a partial exception, with its refusal to repeat the Russian model of rapid industrialization based upon brutal coercion, it may still be bureaucratized in the era following Mao Tse-tung.

Third, the atomized and oppressive work that is generally maintained under socialism is not democratically organized. If it were, it might be abolished. Instead, workers have little voice in what happens in their workplace. They are still subject to appointed managers, their unions are usually powerless, and they cannot strike against 'their' state. Nationalization has failed to replace what Marx called 'the barracks discipline' of industrial civilization. Nationalization is not synonymous with democratization. Rather, power has become more remote. One British coal miner complained that it was 'like working for a ghost' instead of a definite group of capitalists. Another Yorkshire miner added: 'Why is it we must always work under management and never with it?' Michael Polanyi was probably correct when he observed that a worker in a nationalized mine no more felt that he 'owned' the mine than he felt that he owned the Royal Navy.

Nationalization has not solved inequalities of power; it has merely substituted officials for owners. These officials are the realization of Bakunin's fear of a 'red bureaucracy,' what one modern radical has called 'a red bourgeoisie.' Under the direction of this new elite, an enormous and highly centralized bureaucracy rigidly plans everything. The local unit is, in practice, reduced to insignificance. This is bureaucracy, not democracy . . . and Fabians are as guilty of it as Leninists, Trotskyists as much as Stalinists. For all, the workers are still treated like draftees into the industrial army. This is a socialism of five-year plans, growth rates, and dams and factories, but it is not everyday democracy. These criticisms have been summarized by one author this way:

> People can no longer satisfy themselves with the system of the U.S.S.R. 'Here is a state factory, and the state is the Party, and the Party is the masses, thus the factory belongs to the workers. Q.E.D.' No, this is no longer tenable. If someone says to me: 'This factory is yours, it belongs to the people,' but I blindly obey the orders of the directors, I understand nothing of my machine and still less about the rest of the factory, if I

do not know what becomes of my product when it is finished nor why it was produced, if I work quickly, very quickly for a bonus, and if, in the meantime, I am bored to death by it all week, Sunday and each holiday, if I am, besides, more neglected after years of work than at the beginning — in that case this factory is not mine, it does not belong to the people.

We must study the alternatives to both traditional capitalism and socialism. We must draw upon such history as the Paris Commune of 1871, Russia during 1905 and 1917-21, examples of wildcats, the IWW, the Socialist Labor Party, the sit-ins of the 1930s, Spain during 1936-9, Hungary in 1956, direct action during the 1960s, Algeria in the early 1960s, France in 1968, Chile in 1972, and Portugal in 1975. Libertarian theories must be analyzed, such as syndicalism, anarcho-communism, Oscar Lange's 'market socialism' of the 1930s, the idea of the general strike, cooperative movements, the 'ultra-Left critique of Leninism, and the Council Communism of Karl Korsch, Anton Pannekoek, Herman Gorter, Paul Mattick, Serge Mallet and André Gorz. Not least, we must understand existing models in West Germany, Scandinavia, Israel (*kibbutzim*), Algeria, Yugoslavia and the United States. From all of this, we may find answers to what Bakunin called the greatest problem of socialism, 'to integrate individuals into situations which they can understand and control.'

Not all illustrations of workers' control occur in foreign countries. The United States also has some examples of worker-run factories, businesses and coops. We could cite the eighteen worker-owned plywood factories of the Northwest, producing 12 percent of U.S. plywood. Some of these began in the 1930s. Workers elect the 'managers' of the firm, retain considerable control, create special benefits like dental and health care, gas at wholesale, lunches, insurance paid by the company, along with greater concern for safety, 35 percent higher salaries, and job security in slack times. Other cases include a multi-million-dollar asbestos factory (the Vermont Asbestos Group), the Saratoga Knitting Mills, clothing factories in the Southeast, and various coops. In additions to these attempts — often flawed — to achieve workers' control, there are numerous small libertarian associations.

While there are no perfect models of workers' control, these still cause us to reconsider such 'facts of life' as hierarchy, domination and constraining social roles. By comparison, labor unions are social workers for capitalism; radical parties are ideological junkshops, cluttered with overstuffed Victorian social democracy, faded Orthodox icons and cracked china. It is time, perhaps to follow the advice of one of the maniacs' in *Marat/Sade*: 'pull yourself up by your own hair, turn yourself inside out and see the whole world with fresh eyes.'

In our radical vision, the very nature of work and the use of technology must be questioned. Our first motto might be: let the machines do the work! Automated trains, printed circuits rather than hand-wiring, prefabricated houses, car factories with only a few workers, and the general application of computers to production are all possible. Machines should be workers, rather than workers machines.

This libertarian society could guarantee, as a simple matter of justice, a minimum of food, shelter, medicine and clothing free to all. Perhaps you say that no one would work. 'Those committed to the present state of affairs will ask, "How will we eat, how will we get rid of garbage how will we fly to Italy, if we get rid of wage labor? People only work because of coercion".' This is not self-evident. One study indicated that 80 percent of the employed would continue to work even if they didn't have to, although many added that they would quickly change jobs if it were possible. Most people feel a sense of well-being when something has been accomplished. If they felt self-realization through their jobs, it is improbable that they would abandon them. This would be more likely in a world where jobs were not as trivial, or were more equitably rewarded (to give Fourier's example, garbage collectors should be the highest paid people in any society). None the less, a free society must allow the option of not working, at a socially guaranteed subsistence. As one free spirit proclaimed: 'I don't believe in work; I believe in the no-work ethic. . . . If you have to work for something it's not worth having' (that is, why work for the future, why not live now?). Our model is not the society of the ascetic revolutionary, but a culture of celebration, festival, pleasure and play.

This libertarian perspective would encompass all of life, from the person's earliest years to old age. Domestic functions, for example, should be communalized, since housework can be as stultifying as factory work. Charlotte Perkins Gilman once suggested collective laundries, dining areas, child-care and cleaning facilities. These could all be organized by their workers, men and women. In the school, the ideal must be 'self-teaching' and the 'self-managed child,' not the student as passive consumer, note-taker and spectator, and the teacher as cop. The school, too is a workplace; it needs student and faculty syndicalism. The same is true of the office, or the factory.

Each libertarian organization can be founded and sustained only by a conscious, well-informed public. Each person would be able to vote where he or she works or is active, on all issues of significant concern. It is vital that people who have direct experience make the decisions, not some remote bureaucracy. Such elections would occur when necessary, since in the era of TV, radio and rapid communication there should be instantaneous democracy. Participation would mean greater experience and thus, in a general way, greater competence. Meetings should discuss all issues, and votes can be taken on local, regional and 'national' questions. Since the individual has the option of refusal, and a socially guaranteed minimum, this 'democracy' does not violate libertarian principles.

By democracy, I do not mean 'state.' The political system as we know it could be abolished as archaic and parasitic. Instead, people might be organized at local units, electing delegates (if representation could not be avoided) with limited mandates which could be immediately revoked. 'Managers' of all sorts would be directly accountable, and their actions subject to initiative, referendum and recall. Technicians and specialists would still be necessary also, but their status would be transformed. It would not be enough for the workers to decide what to do, and then have the technicians tell them how to do it. Rather, the technicians would be involved in the original discussions about both the what and the how.

This might function in the following way. Auto workers could vote for people to speak for their particular shop, for others who would be general representatives for their factory, for industry-wide spokespeople and for members of a central council of labor that would be necessary for dlscussion, statistics, and the coordination of production. The workers would have direct, continuous control over their representatives Delegates for general community interests should sit on all of these committees, to speak for those who do not work (including the young and the aged), and to criticize activities that might be racist, sexist, concerned only with local profit, or harmful to the overall community such as air and water pollution.

Gar Alperovitz has called this system a pluralist commonwealth combining both diversity and some unity of values. This would not be a state in any usual sense. There would be no geographic capital, but wherever the General Council of Labor was meeting. It would not be a union of states, but a union of unions; it would achieve the goal that Marx stated in the *Communist Manifesto*: a free association of people in which the free development of the individual is the condition of the free development of all, where organization exists to administer things rather than people.

That leaves one final question: can we achieve these ideals? Sartre once belittled surrealism's call for total revolution, saying that it does not harm anybody precisely because it is total,' and unattainable. We must have both a maximum program (our radical vision) and a minimum program of immediate criticisms and solutions. Within unions, we should waste no energy seeking to have the AFL declare the general strike! Instead, efforts should be made to foster rank-and-file caucuses and to form newsletters in which people could share their experiences. Committees can demand that the company 'open the books' — that is, reveal its true finances and organizational practices. Committees could also discuss grievances, and agitate on issues of speed, scheduling, the right to strike during a contract, hiring, firing and safety and health issues. Libertarians should, whenever possible, use schools, unions and other groups to agitate and inspire. These can be transitional means to move toward radical goals.

Even today, there are small working models of alternative institutions: producers' co-operatives, free schools, co-ops for food and services, tax resistance funds, communes, and community control movements for education, tenant organizing and many other local concerns. These go beyond the rhetoric of democracy to day-to-day reality. While they are small and disorganized, they represent the IWW dream of 'building the new society within the shell of the old.' But such radicals can still learn from Marx's critique of the social limits of such individual projects. While Marx praised the coops, in 1866, as a 'beneficent system of the association of free and equal producers,' he realized that their political consciousness was limited, and that they often starved because of the lack of capital, were attacked by large businesses, or, if economically successful, were absorbed into capitalist values. Like Marx, modern libertarians must educate themselves and others to understand the problems of the existing order, the potential for a new society, and the difficulties in achieving it.

Still, revolutions are not planned. Even 'vanguard' intellectuals and parties are usually stunned by such events as the Paris Commune, the Russian Revolution, the precipitous collapse of the Chinese Nationalists, or the French upheavals in 1968. We can only predict that, just as the feudal world died in wars and revolutions, so will the capitalist world. But while change may be abrupt, we can prepare for it. Otherwise, when tomorrow brings the equivalent of the Commune or the Soviets, our hopes will once again be suppressed by reaction or becom perverted into some new autocracy.

BIBLOGRAPHIC NOTE

The original publication contains references to all of the quotations as well as extensive documentation. These are available from the author or editor.

THE CHALLENGE OF MONDRAGON

GEORGE BENELLO

IN THE BEGINNING . . .

THE BASQUE REGION OF SPAIN HAS, in recent years, seen the rise of a system of cooperatives that is unparalleled in its dynamism, growth, and economic impact on a region. The system, which spreads throughout the surrounding Basque region, is named after Mondragon, a town in the mountains of Guipuzkoa Province near Bilbao, the place where the first cooperatives started. Since its start over thirty years ago, it has gained an international reputation, with similar models now being developed in England, Wales, and the United States.

While its explicit connections to the anarchist tradition are unclear, the Mondragon system is an example of liberatory organization which, like its predecessors in the Spanish Civil War, has achieved success on a scale unequaled in any other part of the world.

The Mondragon network was founded by a Catholic priest, Don Jose Maria Arizmendi, a man who had narrowly missed being put to death by Franco as a result of his participation in the Spanish Civil War on the Republican side. With the help of collections from citizens of Mondragon, he founded an elementary technical school in 1943. The first graduates numbered among them five men who, in 1956, founded a small worker-owned and managed factory named ULGOR, numbering initially 24 members, and given to the manufacture of a copied kerosene stove.

This cooperative venture proved successful and developed into the flagship enterprise of the whole system which later was to come into being. At one point ULGOR numbered over 3,000 members, although this was later recognized as too large and was reduced. The structure of this enterprise served as the model for the latter enterprises forming the system. Following the Rochedale principles, it had one member-one vote; open membership; equity held by members and hence external capitalization by debt, not equity; and continuing education.

ADDITIONAL PRINCIPLES

IT ADAPTED AND ADDED ADDITIONAL PRINCIPLES which are responsible for its dynamism and success, in contradistinction to almost all industrial cooperatives which preceded it. The additions can be summarized as follows:

1. It developed a system of individual internal accounts into which 70 percent of the profits (a more accurate term is *surplus*) of the cooperative were placed. Each member had such an internal account. 30 percent were put into a collective account for operating capital and expansion, with a portion of that being earmarked for the community. The individual internal accounts noted receipt of the potion of the surplus earmarked for it, but this was then automatically loaned back to the cooperative, with interest paid. Upon leaving, members receive 75 percent of the accumulated funds credited to their internal account, while 25 percent is retained as the capitalization which made the job possible. This system essentially allows the cooperative to capitalize close to 100 percent of its yearly profit and gives it a capacity for internal capital accumulation unequaled by any capitalist enterprise. It also establishes an ongoing flow-through relation between the individual and collective portions of the surplus.

2. A membership fee was determined, now about $3,000, which represents a substantial investment in the cooperative, and which could be deducted from initial earnings. This too is credited to the internal account. Both the membership fee and the share of the surplus represent methods of ensuring commitment through financial incentives. Unlike older cooperatives, which often determined the membership fee on the basis of dividing the net worth into the number of shares, hence making the membership fee prohibitive, the fee is arbitrary and fixed at an affordable amount.

3. Unlike traditional cooperatives, members are considered to be worker-entrepreneurs, whose job is both to assure the efficiency of the enterprise but also to help develop new enterprises. They do this in their deliberative assemblies and also by depositing their surplus in the system's bank, described below, which is then able to use it to capitalize new enterprises. There is a strong commitment on the part of the membership to this expansive principle, and it is recognized

that the economic security of each cooperative is dependent on their being part of a larger system.

4. A probationary period of one year was instituted, to ensure that new members were not only appropriately skilled, but possessed the necessary capacity for cooperative work. Whereas in a capitalist enterprise workers are considered *factors of production*, in a cooperative they are members of an organization with both the rights and duties of membership, sharing also in the ownership of the organization. Thus while there is open membership, members must be able to participate not simply as hired hands but must be able to discharge their membership duties by sharing in the management of the enterprise. This requires a capacity for responsibility and group participation that in turn implies a certain level of maturity.

5. The *anticipo* or earnings that would in a conventional enterprise be considered as wages, was fixed at prevailing wage levels, minimizing conflict with other local enterprises. Also, the wage differential — the difference between the lowest and highest wage — was set at 1 to 3. This ensures an egalitarianism between workers and the management (selected by the General Assembly of workers) that makes for high morale. Wage levels are determined by a formula which takes into account the difficulty of the job, personal performance, experience, and interpersonal skills. Relational skills have been given greater weight recently out of a recognition that in cooperative work they significantly affect group performance. *(Editors' note: the wage differential was subsequently increased.)*

6. Above all, Mondragon represents a *systems approach* to cooperative development. In addition to the base-level industrial cooperatives there are a set of so called second degree cooperatives which variously engage in research, financing, technical training and education, technical assistance, and social services. In addition there are housing and consumer cooperatives which collectively are able to create a cooperative culture in which the basic activities of life take place. Members can operate within a context of interdependent and cooperating institutions which follow the same principles; this makes for enhanced efficiency.

A CREDIT UNION IS ADDED

TO CONTINUE THE STORY, three years after ULGOR was founded, Don Arizmendi suggested the need for a financial institution to help fund and give technical assistance to other start-up cooperatives. As a result, the Caja Laboral Popular (CLP), a credit union and technical assistance agency was founded. The CLP contains an Empressarial Division, with a staff of over 100, which works intensively with groups desiring to start cooperatives or in rare cases to convert an existing enterprise. It does location studies, market analysis, product development, plans the buildings, and then works continuously for a number of years with the start-up group until it is clear that its proposal is thoroughly developed and financially and organizationally sound. In return, the CLP requires that the cooperative be part of the Mondragon system, via a *Contract of Association*, which specifies the already proven organizational and financial structure and entails a continuing supervisory relation on the part of the CLP. The surplus of the industrial cooperatives is deposited in the CLP and reinvested in further cooperatives. This close and continuing relationship with the financial and technical expertise of the CLP is both unique and largely responsible for the virtually 100 percent success rate within the system.

The CLP is considered a second degree cooperative, and its board is made up of a mix of first level or industrial cooperative members and members from within the CLP itself. In addition to the CLP there are a number of other second degree cooperatives: a social service cooperative which assures 100 percent pension and disability benefits, a health care clinic, and a women's cooperative which allows for both flex-time and part-time work; women can move freely from this to the industrial cooperatives. Also there is a system of educational cooperatives, among them a technical college which includes a production cooperative where students both train and earn money as part-time workers. This, too, is operated as a second degree cooperative with a mixed board made up of permanent staff and students.

Mondragon also features a large system of consumer cooperatives, housing cooperatives, and a number of agricultural cooperatives and building cooperatives. Today the total system's net worth is in the billions. Mondragon consists of 86 production cooperatives averaging several hundred members, 44 educational institutions, seven agricultural cooperatives, 15 building cooperatives, several service cooperatives, a network of consumer cooperatives with 75,000 members, and the bank. The Caja Laboral has 132 branches in the Basque region and recently opened an office in Madrid. This is significant, since it indicates a willingness to expand beyond the Basque region. The CLP's assets are over a billion dollars.

Mondragon produces everything from home appliances — it is the second largest refrigerator manufacturer in Spain — to machine tool factories and ferry boats, both of which it exports abroad. It represents over one percent of the total Spanish export product. With its

18,000 workers, it accounts for about 15 percent of all the jobs in Guipuzkoa Province and five percent in the Basque country. Although a major part of its products are in middle level technologies, it also produces high technology products. Its research institute, Ikerlan, regularly accesses U.S. data bases including that of M.I.T., and has developed its own industrial robots for external sale and for use in its own factories. This is typical of its approach to technology, which is to assimilate new technologies and make them its own. Mondragon has spent considerable time studying and implementing alternatives to the production line; its self-managed organizational system is now being complemented with the technology of group production.

The internal organization of a Mondragon cooperative features a General Assembly which ordinarily meets annually and selects management. In addition there is a Social Council which deals specifically with working members' concerns. There is also a Directive Council, made up of managers and members of the General Assembly, in which managers have a voice but no vote. This system of parallel organization ensures extensive representation of members' concerns and serves as a system of checks and balances. Mondragon enterprises are not large; a deliberate policy now limits them to around 400 members. ULGOR, the first coop, grew too large and at one point in its early history had a strike, organized by dissidents. The General Assembly voted to throw the ringleaders out. But they learned their lesson: size of its own accord can breed discontent.

To obtain the benefits of large scale, along with the benefits of small individual units, Mondragon has evolved a *system* of cooperative development. Here, a number of cooperatives constitute themselves as a sort of mini-conglomerate, coordinated by a management group elected from the member enterprises. These units are either vertically or horizontally integrated and can send members from one enterprise to the other as the requirements of the market and the production system change. They are able to use a common marketing apparatus and have the production capacity to retain a significant portion of a given market. This system was started initially by a set of enterprises in the same market banding together for inter-enterprise cooperation. Now Mondragon develops such systems from the outset.

EFFECTIVENESS OF MONDRAGON

IF ONE ENTERS A MONDRAGON FACTORY, one of the more obvious features is a European style coffee bar, occupied by members taking a break. It is emblematic of the work style, which is serious but relaxed.

Mondragon productivity is very high — higher than in its capitalist counterparts. Efficiency, measured as the ratio of utilized resources — capital and labor — to output, is far higher than in comparable capitalist factories.

One of the most striking indications of the effectiveness of the Mondragon system is that the Empressarial Division of Mondragon has continued to develop an average of four cooperatives a year, each with about 400 members. Only two of these have ever failed. This amazing record can be compared with business start-ups in this country, over 90 percent of which fail within the first five years. I have seen a feasibility study for a new enterprise. It is an impressive book-length document, containing demographics, sociological analysis of the target population, market analysis, product information — just about everything relevant. When a new prospective cooperative comes to Mondragon seeking help, it is told to elect a leadership. This leadership studies at the Empressarial Division for two years before they are allowed to start the cooperative; they thus learn every aspect of their business and of the operation of a cooperative.

Mondragon is not utopia. While it does not produce weapons, useless luxury goods, or things that pollute the environment, it does produce standard industrial products using a recognizable technology of production. It does not practice job rotation, and management is not directly elected from the floor — for good reason, since experiments elsewhere that have tried this have not worked. Members vary in the nature of their commitment. In fact there is something of a split in Mondragon between those who see Mondragon as a model for the world and those who prefer to keep a low profile and have no interest in proselytizing beyond their confines.

Mondragon has also been faulted for failing to produce mainly for local consumption. It is in the manufacturing, not community development business, and, while it creates jobs, its products are exported all over the world. It has exported machine tool factories to eastern European countries, to Portugal and to Algeria; a Mondragon furniture factory is now operating in New York State. Mondragon does not export its system with the factories however; they are simply products, bought and run by local owners. In general, it makes little attempt to convert the heathens; at present, it is swamped by visitors from all over the world, and it finds this hard enough to deal with without going out and actively spreading the word.

Mondragon has awakened worldwide interest. The Mitterand government in France has a special cabinet post for the development of cooperatives, the result of its contact with Mondragon. In Wales, the Welsh Trade Union Council is engaged in developing a system of cooperatives patterned after Mondragon. In England, the Job Owner-ship Movement along with numerous local governments, developed both small and large cooperatives on the Mondragon model. Progressives in the Catholic Church, seeing Mondragon as an alterna-tive to both capitalism and communism, have helped establish indus-trial cooperatives in Milwaukee and in Detroit; and in Boston this writer worked with the local archdiocese to develop a system of coop-eratives based on the same model.

Why does Mondragon work so well? Part of the answer lies in the unique culture of the Basque region. Members of the staff of Mondragon with whom I have talked (those of Ikerlan, the research institute, and of ULARCO, the first of the mini-conglomerates) have doubts about whether the model can be exported, arguing that the cohesiveness and communitarian traditions of the Basque culture alone make it possible. But Anna Gutierrez Johnson, a Peruvian sociologist who has studied Mondragon extensively, believes that basically it is the *organizational pattern* that makes the whole system work, and that this is exportable. I share her opinion, but also believe that in the United States our culture of individualism and adversary worker-manage-ment relations is a major impediment. Workers have little ideological consciousness in this country; moreover, they have very largely bought into the capitalist system and often see work as a ticket into the middle class. But their lack of ideology is nonetheless a plus in one way, for *the secret of Mondragon is, above all, organizational, not ideological: it is how-to knowledge that makes it work.* Knowledge, for example, of how specific industry sectors work, of how to facilitate cooperation between the CLP and worker-entrepreneurs, of how to ensure that individual enterprises are integrated into the Mondragon community.

Mondragon has revolutionary implications, primarily because its structure of democratic governance, with worker ownership and control, challenges the capitalist system at its very heart. Where capi-talism awards profit and control to capital and hires labor, Mondragon awards profit and control to labor. In the process, it has developed a worker-centered culture which, rather than infantilizing, empowers. Mondragon members are citizens of a worker commonwealth, with the full rights that such citizenship confers. This can be seen best in the steps that have been taken to make the formal system of participa-tion into a working reality: different systems of leadership have evolved, and with them, a growing sense of teamwork. For example, a furniture factory now operates completely through work teams. Thus the formal system has led to the ongoing evolution of a democratic process which is the real indicator of its success in revolutionizing the relations of production.

Also, Mondragon has created a *total system* where one can learn, work, shop, and live within a cooperative environment. (On such total systems, see Antonio Gramsci.) In such an environment motivation is high because members share an overall cooperative culture which integrates material and moral incentives, and which extends into every aspect of life — work, community, education, consumption, and family. A member of the Empresserial Division has underlined the uniqueness of Mondragon viewed as a total system, pointing out that this system goes far beyond what can be found in the Basque culture. The proof of this is to be found in the efforts needed to socialize new workers into the system; the simple fact of being Basque is hardly enough to guarantee effective participation.

LESSONS OF MONDRAGON

PERHAPS ONE OF THE MOST BRILLIANT achievements of the Mondragon organizational system is the way in which it has combined collective ownership with the incentives of individual ownership in a mixed system which recognizes both the individual and the collective side of human motivation. The system of individual accounts with automatic loan-back, along with the partitioning of the surplus into an individual component and a collective component, represents a method of giving the worker a sense of individual ownership along with a sense of collective participation in an organization which provides more than simply a meal ticket, even as it expects more than simply job performance.

A strong argument can be made for the importance of creating more networks like Mondragon — if one is to move toward social liberation. Its systems approach to job creation confronts the problems of economic organization and development head-on, managing at once to create freedom in work and enough jobs to have a powerful impact on a regional economy. Until it happened, it was easy to write off experiments in economic democracy as marginal and unrealistic utopian ventures, totally irrelevant to the task of affecting any sizable portion of an existing economy. This can no longer be said, and hence both state socialist and capitalist arguments for the economic necessity of oppressive work are given the lie.

Moreover, Mondragon contains an important lesson: it demonstrates that to achieve freedom in work, a high level of organizational skill is needed, and that when such skills are present, the traditional opposition of democracy and efficiency vanish, and the two reinforce rather than oppose each other. Mondragon is important because it serves as a model of how this can be done. Here, ideological debate gives way to concrete know-how and another false dilemma bites the dust. Centralization in concert with modern technologies, entirely apart from the further coercions of capitalist ownership, contains pressures toward an oppressive machine form of organization. This is true both because of its large scale and its productivity requirements; these pressures are greatest in the case of mass production.

Taming this contemporary organizational beast thus represents a challenge which must be met if one is to create freedom in work. This type of organization, moreover, is central to advanced industrial societies. It would be nice, utopian fashion, to simply be able to leap over the problem and go back to small-scale craft production, thereby, admittedly, eliminating piles of semi-useless junk. But the first step in deciding what is to be produced or not produced is to regain control of the system. What should or should not be produced is after all not a given but a decision to be democratically arrived at. If the control is there, people may indeed decide in good time that mass production simply is not worth the effort — or they may not.

With control of the production process one can then at least begin the process of educating consumers to better products, or less products, or craft products, or whatever one happens to feel is an improvement over the present system. Moreover, one cannot change a whole culture in a day; if one wishes to wean people from an over-dependence on cars, for example, one way is to build better trains, which is at least a step beyond building more fuel-efficient cars. The fact that one cannot do everything should not be made into an argument for doing nothing.

I recall a debate a few years ago in the pages of *Social Anarchism* where Len Krimerman described his efforts to create a poultry processing cooperative. In the main his anarchist respondents were horrified: he had borrowed money from the government (the Small Business Administration)! Also, he had foremen and supervisors, rather than pure and total self-government! He trafficked with capitalist distributors! The whole thing was a desecration of anarchist principles, being centrally involved with capitalism, hierarchy, and the state. This is of course an old debate, but it is reminiscent of the Marxist's argument that, until the *objective conditions* for revolution exist, nothing can (and hence need) be done.

One can indeed preach purity, but talk is cheap, and moreover, people know that. The significance of Mondragon is twofold: it represents a positive vision of freedom in work, a community that is democratically controlled by its members. The ideal of democracy, to which everyone gives lip service, is actually practiced here. But it also represents something that works, and that in turn constitutes a statement about human nature, establishing beyond controversy that people can manage complex social tasks via democratic organization. *If a picture is worth a thousand words, an effective working model is worth at least a thousand pictures.*

Probably the most frequent criticism of utopian thinking is that it flies in the face of human nature, which has powerful propensities for evil as well as good. This argument is not one that can be settled in the abstract. The value of Mondragon is that it speaks to the claim of the weakness and fallibility of human nature in specific and concrete ways. Whereas the Webbs and others have long argued against the viability of worker cooperatives on the basis that they tend to degenerate into capitalist enterprises, Mondragon has clearly shown that this is not true. Not only does Mondragon work, but it works a lot better than its capitalist counterparts, and it grows faster. By showing that one can combine democracy with efficiency, it gives the lie to a basic article of capitalist dogma about human nature: that people are naturally lazy and irresponsible and will work only when given the twin incentives of the carrot and the stick.

Another objection has been raised: Structure is brainlessly equated with hierarchy and bureaucracy, and hence the complex organizational structure of a system such as Mondragon is written off out of hand. But structurelessness breeds tyranny: informal cliques develop, hidden leaders emerge who wield power behind the cloak of an espoused equality.

Mondragon is worth studying because it works, and the argument can be made that utopian theory must always confront the practical since the burden of proof is on the theorist. The problem with capitalism and, more generally, with coercive industrial systems of whatever persuasion, is not that they don't work; they do deliver the goods, but in the process grind up human beings. The only answer to this state of affairs is to prove that a better system also works; theory alone simply will not do. And, if we wish to claim that something better than Mondragon needs to be built, then it is incumbent on us to do it.

Reinventing Anarchy, Again

Anarchism and the Informal Economy

Colin Ward

One hundred thirty-eight years ago Marx and Engels claimed that the specter haunting Europe was the specter of Communism. Having lived for many decades in a world in which the larger part of the earth's surface is governed by Marxist regimes, most of us have lost our fear of this specter. We don't actually worry about the redistribution of property that communism implies, because most of us have so little of it individually that it isn't worth worrying over. What we do fear is something which has nothing to do with social justice, and that is the deprivation of ordinary civil liberties which government by technocrats, theologians and ideologists implies. Not one of the innumerable exiles from Marxist countries has complained that they have lost the freedom to exploit other people. That particular freedom was reserved for the ruling elite of the regimes they had escaped from.

It would be closer to the truth to say that the specter that is haunting us all is that of nuclear war. War is the ultimate weapon of governments against peoples, and it doesn't matter whether we are thinking of our own or other nations' peoples. But if you were a citizen of, say, Austria, Algeria, Tanzania, Uruguay or Burma, you would be obliged to realize that there was no conceivable action you could take to remove this threat, short of a world-wide revolution of people against governments — something which would make a change but is not remotely on anyone's political agenda. It's like the situation of those people who live on the slopes of a volcano: people shrug their shoulders and attend to the problems of daily life.

The computer games of the military and governmental establishments of the great powers pass us by: it's appalling but it's true. The specter that really is haunting us all in the countries of the East and

West, the rich and the poor, whether employment is provided by capitalists or communists, is the specter of mass unemployment. It is more than a specter. In most countries of the world it is the ordinary condition that people live in all their lives. Ivan Illich remarks that 'unemployment, a term first introduced in 1898 to designate people without a fixed income, is now recognized as the condition in which most of the world's people live anyway.'

In the rich countries we have been bludgeoned into indifference by forecasts of the millions of permanently unemployed adults expected by the year 2000. Somehow we feel it won't happen to us, or that its effect will be mitigated by the welfare machinery which is intended to ensure that nobody actually starves. But what is to happen when, as long-term, large-scale unemployment grows, the privileged, employed section of the population shrugs off the responsibility of providing an income for those who cannot get a job and are never likely to have one? There have been glimpses of such a future in the taxpayers' revolt signaled by Proposition 13 in California in 1978 and in the return of a crudely fundamentalist Conservative government in Britain the following year, as well as in the increasingly vicious harassment of 'social parasites' in the Soviet Union and its satellites. The governor of California was elected as President of the United States with an overwhelming popular vote, and re-elected for a second term. Mrs. Thatcher's welfare-bashing government in Britain was similarly endorsed.

The town-planner Graeme Shankland, attempting to grapple with the unemployment problems of British cities, saw a prospect of 'increasing impoverished, depressed and demoralized millions, barely sustained by supplementary benefits and on pensions paid for by a diminishing, powerful and resentful elite work-force,' just as André Gorz in his *Farewell to the Working Class* envisages a society where the majority will be 'marginalized by an unholy alliance of unionized elite workers with managers and capitalists.'

We have already moved a long way from the expansive 1950s when our prophets were urging us to sever, at last, the connection between work and purchasing power. In those days Robert Theobald was demanding a 'guaranteed annual income' to be paid to every American as a constitutional right, and John Kenneth Galbraith was arguing for what he called Cyclically Graduated Compensation — a dole which went up when the economy took a down-turn, so that people could go on spending, as Keynes before him urged, and consequently keep other people employed, and which went down when full employment was approached. But have you noticed that nobody talks about full employment any more?

'One day,' Galbraith forecast, 'we shall remove the economic penalties and also the social stigma associated with involuntary unemployment. This will make the economy much easier to manage.' But, he added, in 1960, 'we haven't done this yet.' Nor have we by the 1980s. Two decades of radicalism and reaction have gone by, and some of the same people who in the 1960s were urging us that the work ethic was obsolete in the days of automation and cybernetics, are by the 1980s protesting as governments cut back on their token job creation schemes, when faced by the era of micro-processors.

All those ingenious calculations of how short a working day, or working week, or working lifetime could be in a rationally organized society were made in the days of relatively full employment. They began to lose their attractiveness as unemployment grew. The prophecies are still being made, all the same. In a paper commissioned by the British Cabinet Office, Professor Tom Stonier of Bradford University declares that by early in the next century only 10 percent of the present labor force will be required to provide a technologically advanced society with all its material wants or needs.

None of the prophecies are plausible enough to banish the specter that is haunting the world of work. Still less comforting are the short-term forecasts of politicians and economists. We don't really believe that British or American manufacturing industries are going to recover lost markets. We don't really believe that robots or microprocessors are going to create more than a small proportion of the jobs that they eliminate. Nor do we believe that big business has any answers for us. Even our faith that the tertiary or service economy is bound to expand to replace the jobs lost in the productive sector has been shattered by the demonstration by Jonathan Gershuny of the Science Policy Research Unit at Sussex University that employment in service industries in Western societies is already declining. Dr Gershuny, however, does provide a ray of hope that could lead us to look at the future of work in a quite different way. He sees the decline of the service economy as accompanied by the emergence of a self-service economy in the way that the automatic washing machine in the home can be said to supersede the laundry industry. His American equivalent is Scott Burns, author of *The Household Economy*, with his claim that 'America is going to be transformed by nothing more or less than the inevitable maturation and decline of the market economy. The instrument for this positive change will be the household — the family — revitalized as a powerful and relatively autonomous productive unit.'

The only way to banish the specter of unemployment is to break free from our enslavement to the idea of employment. The pre-industrial economy was, after all, a domestic economy, and the old American phrase for an employee, a 'hired man' carries with it the notion that he was something less than a free citizen, as does the old socialist definition of the working class as those with nothing to sell but their labor power. The very word 'employment' has only been used in its modern sense since the 1840s, just as 'unemployment' in the sense in which we use it is even more recent.

We do need of course to remind ourselves that wage labor and even factory production existed before the industrial revolution. Adam Smith in the mid-eighteenth century told readers of *The Wealth of Nations* that in every part of Europe twenty workmen served under a master for one that was independent, and he gave us the classic account of the division of labor. A century after him, Marx concluded that the condition he called alienation resulted from the worker's loss of ownership of his skills, tools, products, time and space. Any account of the Industrial Revolution in this country tells how workers were driven by starvation to accept the disciplines of employment. For me, the classic description was that of J.L. and Barbara Hammond in their book *The Town Laborer*. The home worker in domestic industry, they observed, 'worked long hours, but they were his own hours; his wife and children worked, but they worked beside him, and there was no alien power over their lives; his house was stifling, but he could slip into his garden; he had spells of unemployment, but he could use them for cultivating his cabbages. The forces that ruled his fate were in a sense outside his daily life; they did not overshadow and envelop his home, his family, his movements and habits, his hours for work and his hours for food.' They declared that:

> No economist of the day, in estimating the gains and the losses of factory employment, ever allowed for the strain and violence that a man suffered in his feelings when he passed from a life in which he could smoke or eat or dig or sleep as he pleased, to one in which someone turned the key on him, and for fourteen hours he had not even the right to whistle. It was like entering the airless and laughterless life of a prison. Unless we keep this moral sacrifice in mind, we shall not understand why the hand-loom weavers refused to go into the power-loom factories, where they would have earned much higher wages: a refusal that is an important fact in the history of the cotton industry.

It is enlightening to compare their picture of the horrors of early factory life with the interviews that the sociologist Ferdinand Zweig had with car workers in Coventry. He said: 'It is interesting to note that quite often the worker comes to work on Monday worn out from his weekend activities, especially from "do-it-yourself". Quite a number said that the weekend is the most trying and exacting period of the whole week, and Monday work in the factory, in comparison, is relaxing.' This, of course, leads us to ask what is work and what is leisure, if we work harder at our leisure than at our work.

The first distinction we have to make then is between work and employment. The world is certainly short of jobs, but it has never been, and never will be, short of work. William Morris grasped this a hundred years ago when he contrasted useful work with useless toil. The second distinction is that between the regular, formal, visible and official economy, and the economy of work which is not employment. In the United States, Louis Ferman and his colleagues at the University of Michigan, and in Britain Jason Ditton of the University of Glasgow, have attempted to sort out the various words we use for the disparate kinds of activities which are not part of the formal, measurable economic system. *Irregular* is one of these words, subsuming such concepts as *secondary* or *shadow* or *secret*. *Informal* is the most widely used word, taking in adjectives like *social, peasant, subsistence, natural, domestic, household, communal, cottage* and *ghetto*, as descriptions of these various economies. The final range of words, carrying implications of crime and illegality, includes *hidden, black, underground* and *subterranean.*

The four main kinds of informal economy are illustrated in a homely example by Professor Pahl, taking the options available to someone who wants to get a broken window repaired. They might:

- Firstly, hire a glazier through the formal economy, paying the full cost including a share of the overheads of the building firm and value-added tax;

- Secondly, find someone nearby who is known to be able to mend windows and pay cash for the job, possibly thereby entering the underground economy because s/he would not know whether such a person was declaring all his or her income, paying all his or her tax, or working in time already paid for by another employer;

- Thirdly, s/he might ask a neighbor to do it within the communal economy, either in exchange for specific goods or services now or in the future, or as part of a broader ongoing relationship;

- Or, fourthly, s/he might do the job in his or hir own time and own tools, within the household economy.

Now, with some honorable exceptions, public discussion of the informal economy has concentrated on the Underground Economy aspect: tax evasion, fiddles, and so on. Efforts are made to calculate what proportion of the Gross Domestic Product is in this aspect of the economy. They differ enormously, just because it is so unquantifiable, but they aren't at all helpful, because the greater part of activities and transactions outside the measurable economy have no tax-evasion aspect.

Let me repeat that the Underground Economy is the creation of fiscal policy and is not a moral issue. Many of us, for a whole variety of reasons, do not accept the unspoken doctrine that the state is all-powerful and all-wise. If you make it a moral issue you have to cope with the fact that the governments of the world spend more than a million dollars of their tax income every ninety seconds on their armed forces and on war preparations. Was this what their citizens wanted?

The Underground Economy is part, and not the most important part, of the Informal Economy, which I use as a blanket word to cover all the possible conceptions of alternative economies listed above, including ordinary self-employment, which is the official designation of two million workers in Britain and millions more in the United States, and including that multitude of mutual services where money doesn't change hands at all. But each of the descriptions I have listed has its own particular connotations, and they add up to an enormous range of human activities without which life on this planet would be impossible. The Formal Economy *depends* on the Informal Economy, but the reverse is also true. The household economy depends on manufactured articles produced in the regular economy. So does the hidden economy of illicit sales, the communal economy of joint use of expensive equipment, or the enormous variety of sub-contracting which is combined in the finished and measurable product of the official economy.

It *does* in fact make sense to help people on the way to employing themselves, not as a temporary, bankrupt gesture, but because, whether we like it or not, this is the only discernible pattern of the future economy. In what other possible light can you read the daily newspaper headlines? 'Productivity up and the number in work falls,' reports the business editor. 'Half those being trained on youth programs returning to dole queues' is the headline for the social services correspondent. Victor Keegan remarks that 'the most seductive theory of all is that what we are experiencing now is nothing less than a movement back towards an informal economy after a brief flirtation of 200 years or so with a formal one.'

We are talking about the movement of work back into the domestic economy. There are certainly class divisions in the assumptions we make about this. People selling high technology often fantasize about this when persuading business executives that there was no need for that tedious commuter journey to work, since their personal computer outlet, word processor and videophone would enable them to do all their work from the comfort of home. Since one of the alleged privileges of that station of life is to do most of your work from the company car by radiotelephone anyway, we don't have to worry about them.

What about ordinary productive work at home? Home-working has always been a byword for exploitation, low pay and sweated labor. This is why the trade unions are so hostile towards it. But it is by no means a declining industry, and it is possible to reduce its least desirable aspects. The most suggestive illustration of one of the preconditions for effectively moving industrial production back into the home comes from the many studies of the informal economy in Italy. Sebastino Brusco claimed that it was only the existence of a vast informal sector of small workshops that saved the Italian economy from ruin in the 1970s. He points to the phenomenon of whole villages of small workshops with power tools sub-contracting for the industrial giants of the motor industry, and when hit by recession, turning to other kinds of industrial components.

A BBC film took us to another Italian industrial village where 80 percent of the women's tights made in Italy are produced. It illustrated two aspects of the informal economy there: the woman who, using a hand machine, earns a pittance from the contractor who brings her the unfinished goods for assembly and collects them finished, in the classic sweatshop situation; and, as a completely contrasted example, the woman who, with her mother, makes a good living assembling tights in her home, using a sophisticated machine which cost them £5,000 and is now paid for. Brusco claimed that what we were seeing was the decentralization of manufacturing industry in a way which for him, as for Kropotkin, foreshadowed the pattern of a post-industrial society. Even Kropotkin's combination of industry and agriculture can be found, and is in fact traditional, in Italy. Philip Mattera reports: 'There are even people who have been moonlighting in agriculture. Studies of employees of the few large factories of the South, especially the huge Italsider plant at Taranto, have found that many are using their free time to resume their prior occupation as small farmers.'

The key difference between Brusco's two examples of the tights-makers was that one was trapped in the sweated labor situation and the other was freed from it by increased productivity, in just the same way as do-it-yourself users of power tools have increased theirs. It is of course a matter of access to a very modest amount of credit. This is the lesson of the Informal Economy in the exploding cities of the Third World too. Kenneth King, studying the multitude of small-scale producers in Nairobi, reminds us that the enterprising artisans do not use improvised equipment from choice: 'Many would be anxious to obtain and use lathes if power were available, but the most popular brands now cost £3,000-£5,000. Although Western observers may admire the cheapness and in-genuity of the various Heath Robinson machines, their inventors re-gard them very differently. They know precisely what sort of Czecho-slovakian center-lathe they would buy first, what it would cost, and why they cannot afford it.' He contrasts the millions of pounds worth of credit advanced for the high-technology plastics industry with the extraordinary difficulties experienced in raising any kind of credit in the artisan sector. 'It is not principally the technical dimension which constitutes the obstacle, but rather the lack of basic credit infrastruc-ture, security of tenure in the urban areas, and a technology policy that would support the very small-scale entrepreneur.'

In the rich world, where we have fallen so far under the spell of capitalist ideology, and of Marxist ideology too, which can only see petty trades as some kind of primitive left-over from some less advanced stage in industrial evolution, the informal society is similarly neglected, apart from token aid to the people who start small businesses in the expectation that they will become big business. Yet while we have be-gun to look at its implications and its potential simply out of despair at the irreversible decline of employment, we tend to forget that it also represents an aspiration for millions of employed people. Ask anyone employed by someone else what he or she would do if a legacy or a gambling win suddenly provided working capital. In four cases out of five the answer would not be an aspiration to live a life of idleness on a sun-drenched island in the sun. It would be to set up on one's own, individually or collectively, to be one's own boss, to start a little busi-ness, a shop, a workshop, a small-holding or a country pub. It may be just a matter of dreams, but even a survey conducted by the Consum-ers' Association and published in its journal WHICH? indicated that the happiest and most satisfied workers were the self-employed.

What poor people in the world's poor cities do out of necessity, the poor and the securely employed in the rich world aspire to. The obstacle in both cases is the same: lack of access to capital or credit;

lack of security, since in all countries social security is geared to the employed, controllable workers, not to the self-employed; and the absence of a social infrastructure which could automatically favor the small, local provider.

I often wonder how we reached the situation when honorable words like 'enterprise,' 'initiative' and 'self-help' are automatically associated with the political right and the defense of capitalism, while it is assumed that the political left stands for a Big Brother State with a responsibility to provide a pauper's income for all and an inflation-proof income for its own functionaries. Ninety years ago people's mental image of a socialist was of a radical self-employed cobbler, sitting in his shop with a copy of William Morris's *Useful Work versus Useless Toil* on the workbench, his hammer in his hand, and his lips full of brass tacks. His mind full of notions of liberating his fellow workers from industrial serfdom in a dark satanic mill. No doubt the current mental picture is of a university lecturer with a copy of *The Inevitable Crisis of Capitalism* in one hand, and a banner labeled 'Fight the Cuts' in the other, while his mind is full of strategies for unseating the sitting Labor candidate in the local pocket borough.

Whatever did happen to all those aspirations for the liberation of work? Clive Jenkins at least wrote a book called *The Collapse of Work* about the way the micro revolution was going to destroy jobs at a terrifying rate, and urging us to outgrow the work ethic. But he got it all wrong, as usual. In the first place, who actually wants a cradle-to-grave contract with some Mitsubishi type employer just for the privilege of being put out to grass at 55 instead of 65, which is essentially what Clive is advocating? In the second place, he has got the language wrong. He is talking, perfectly correctly, about the collapse of *employment*. There will never be a shortage of work in the sense of coping with useful tasks.

I asked a man who had just, unwisely as I thought, bought the local franchise for a photocopy shop what was in it for him. He replied: 'It's the only way open to me to be my own boss.' But surely you're completely in their hands, I asked. 'Yes,' he replied, 'but the feeling of independence is the most important thing in life for me. That this was not total deception can be gauged from the fact that in that arcane specialty known as job-evaluation, a crucial test is the time-span spent without supervision, or that in the Mondragon cooperatives in the Basque country, the absence of supervisors is regarded by workers as the great triumph of the enterprise.

But merely to mention cooperatives is to raise another tricky ideological use of language. If one man and his dog set up a workshop to make rocking-horses and three-legged stools, it is merely petit-bourgeois individualism, and to prove it our local craftsman of this kind is president of the Chamber of Commerce. But if two or three are gathered together to do just the same thing, with the assistance of the Manpower Services Commission, it becomes a worthy example of socially significant job creation. Co-operative production has become an OK phrase once more, in spite of the bashing it got sixty years ago from Sidney and Beatrice Webb.

One of the sad truths about life, which was impressed on me by a veteran of cooperative building enterprises, is that often those who are most in love with the idea of cooperation are those most lacking in the market skills of getting the job done on time at the right price, while those best endowed with entrepreneurial skills are often the least able to master the delicate art of working, without coercion, with others. I don't get any pleasure from citing this fact: I merely want to stress that there is room in the garden of the informal economy for both cooperators and individualists. Pierre-Joseph Proudhon, the paradoxical anarchist, would have taken this for granted. His vision of industrial organization was that of a federation of self-employed craftsmen. We certainly get echoes of the Proudhonian view in Robert Frost's observation, 'Men work together, I told him from the heart / Whether they work together or apart.'

Prophecies seldom come true in the way their originators anticipate. But the idea that I mooted in my edition of Kropotkin's *Fields, Factories and Workshops*, that his decentralist and anarchist vision of the future of work will come true through the collapse of employment and the growth of the informal economy, is less absurd than the faith of his socialist contemporaries that the humanization of work would come about through the conquest of the power of the state by a political party claiming to be the proletariat. Communism, as some Polish wit said, is a conspiracy by the unemployed intelligentsia to complete the enslavement of the workers.

The French socialist André Gorz argues that the political left has become frozen into authoritarian collectivist attitudes belonging to the past:

> As long as the protagonists of socialism continue to make centralized planning . . . the linchpin of their program, and the adherence of everyone to the 'democratically formulated' objectives of their plan the core of their political doctrine, socialism will remain an unattractive proposition in industrial societies. Classical socialist doctrine finds it difficult to come to terms with political and social pluralism, under-

stood not simply as a plurality of parties and trade unions but as the coexistence of various ways of working, producing and living, various distinct cultural areas and levels of social existence. . . . Yet this kind of pluralism precisely conforms to the lived experience and aspirations of the post-industrial proletariat, as well as the major part of the traditional working class.

How on earth, he asks, has the socialist movement got itself into the position of dismissing as petit-bourgeois individualism all those freedoms which people actually value: everything that belongs to the private niche that people really cherish? This is important for anyone who has grown beyond the notion that a desirable society is one in which everyone else has exactly the same view of life as himself or herself. We, as anarchists, however, are not, I hope, lumbered with all that out-of-date luggage of the socialist movement. How do we approach the Informal Economy?

Anarchism has many different strands, but the thing that unites us is a hostility towards the institution of the State, and a desire to creep out from under it as much as we can. I have always admired the way in which many anarchists have contrived to scrape a living outside the official economy or in its interstices. I have a good anarchist friend who has always lived that way, but regards the informal economy with great suspicion, because he equates it with tax evasion. He believes that to approve tax evasion is to encourage a selfish individualism which ignores the need to pay for socially necessary services which in our society are provided by the state: the health service, unemployment insurance, education and so on. 'I wouldn't feel happy living in a society of such people,' he says. Of course he, like me, pays so little income tax that we don't make any difference, but he is always attempting to draw the Inspector of Taxes into a dialogue about the principles of taxation, about the need to be empowered to transfer to other purposes the portion (13 percent) of government revenue spent on so-called defense. He is mortified by the computerization of the tax system, of course.

Another anarchist friend of mine is hostile to the informal economy because he regards those who earn cash in it as scabs, undermining trade union rates of pay and labor protection legislation. He sees it as a conspiracy against working class solidarity. Both these friends look upon the operators in the informal economy as would-be businessmen, little capitalists — the kind of people who believe in the Thatcherite rhetoric about entrepreneurial enterprise.

Now, outside our assumptions, for or against, very little actual study has been made of the psychology and sociology of the small businessperson. The only study I know of is a book by Richard Scase and Robert Goffee called *The Real World of the Small Business Owner*. The historian Paul Thompson reports on their findings thus:

> It turns out that far from being an especially purposeful breed of men, Samuel Smiles' heroes a hundred years on, many small businessmen are closer to a kind of drop-out. They disliked the whole modern capitalistic ethic, and especially being employed by others; instead they preferred to feel the satisfaction of providing a 'service' and doing a 'good job.' Quite often it was a mere chance which allowed them to find their present vocation. Moreover, they will not provide the basis for our next industrial revolution, because they don't want to expand: that would imply employing people and losing the personal relationships they like to have with a small number of workers. Nor are they in the least discouraged by taxation: on the contrary, tax avoidance through the 'hidden' economy set many of them going, and once started, tax has simply been a 'given' within which they operate. And, most revealingly of all, the real burden of struggle in their earlier years fell as much on their wives as themselves: for it was the wife who had to turn the bedroom into an office and double up as company secretary and accountant for no pay at all.

It's an indication of how research changes stereotypes. Sad to say, the comforting stereotype that the informal economy helps the poorest most takes rather a dent from Ray Panl's investigation reported in his book *Division of Labor*. He finds that the families who benefit most from the informal economy are not the 'welfare scroungers' that preoccupy the government and the popular press, but the 'moonlighters' in households with at least one formal income. Obviously tools and travel, and even the chance to sit around in a pub and pick up jobs, are expensive and depend on *some* basic income above the welfare minimum.

Well, I've taken you for a tour around the ideas in circulation about the informal economy. I think it's important from an anarchist point of view, and I am pleased that Freedom Press, an anarchist publishing house, has just brought out an anarchist interpretation of it. This is the little book *The Employment Question* by Denis Pym. He seeks to question the legitimacy of the employing institutions, and the monopoly we ascribe to them of creating wealth.

We already have a dual economy, with capital on the one side, whose object is to do without labor, while the other, which is Pym's view is the unofficial, unmeasured and domestic economy, 'offers people the opportunity to reunite their social and economic lives and use the tools and techniques which suit their personal and social requirements.' Pym's hero is the bricoleur, the local fixer, the man or woman who uses resourcefulness to cater directly and reciprocally for human needs in the interstices of the allegedly 'real' economy.

The entrepreneur, the big-time captain of industry and commerce, not the small-time wheeler-dealer, he sees as an egocentric, bullying, imposing public figure. The bricoleur, or bricoleuse, the person we know who actually keeps things going — relationships, machines and the natural world — is our warmer, closer, private, indispensable neighbor.

Revolutionary letter no. 19
(for The Poor People's Campaign)

Diane di Prima

if what you want is jobs
for everyone, you are still the enemy,
you have not thought thru, clearly
what that means

if what you want is housing,
industry
    (G.E. on the Navaho
    reservation)
a car for everyone, garage, refrigerator,
TV, more plumbing, scientific
freeways, you are still
the enemy, you have chosen
to sacrifice the planet for a few years of some
science fiction utopia, if what you want

still is, or can be, schools
where all our kids are pushed into one shape, are taught
it's better to be 'American' than black
or Indian, or Jap, or PR, where Dick
and Jane become and are the dream, do you
look like Dick's father, don't you think your kid
secretly wishes you did

if what you want
is clinics where the AMA

can feed you pills to keep you weak, or sterile
shoot germs into your kids, while Mercke & Co
grows richer

if you want
free psychiatric help for everyone
so that the shrinks
pimps for this decadence, can make
it flower for us, if you want
if you still want a piece
a small piece of suburbia, green lawn
laid down by the square foot
color TV, whose radiant energy
kills brain cells, whose subliminal ads
brainwash your children, have taken over
your dreams

degrees from universities which are nothing
more than slum landlords, festering sinks
of lies, so you too can go forth
and lie to others on some greeny campus

THEN YOU ARE STILL
THE ENEMY, you are selling
yourself short, remember
you can have what you ask for, ask for
everything

The Abolition of Work

Bob Black

No one should ever work.

Work is the source of nearly all the misery in the world. Almost any evil you'd care to name comes from working or from living in a world designed for work. In order to stop suffering, we have to stop working.

That doesn't mean we have to stop doing things. It does mean creating a new way of life based on play; in other words, a *ludic* revolution. By "play" I mean also festivity, creativity, conviviality, commensality, and maybe even art. There is more to play than child's play, as worthy as that is. I call for a collective adventure in generalized joy and freely interdependent exuberance. Play isn't passive. Doubtless we all need a lot more time for sheer sloth and slack than we ever enjoy now, regardless of income or occupation, but once recovered from employment-induced exhaustion nearly all of us want to act. Oblomovism and Stakhanovism are two sides of the same debased coin.

The ludic life is totally incompatible with existing reality. So much the worse for "reality," the gravity hole that sucks the vitality from the little in life that still distinguishes it from mere survival. Curiously — or maybe not — all the old ideologies are conservative because they believe in work. Some of them, like Marxism and most brands of anarchism, believe in work all the more fiercely because they believe in so little else.

Liberals say we should end employment discrimination. I say we should end employment. Conservatives support right-to-work laws. Following Karl Marx's wayward son-in-law Paul Lafargue I support the right to be lazy. Leftists favor full employment. Like the surrealists — except that I'm not kidding — I favor full unemployment. Trotskyists agitate for permanent revolution. I agitate for permanent revelry. But if all the ideologues (as they do) advocate work — and not only because they plan to make other people do theirs — they are strangely reluctant to say so. They will carry on endlessly about wages, hours, working conditions, exploitation, productivity, profitability. They'll gladly talk about anything but work itself.

These experts who offer to do our thinking for us rarely share their conclusions about work, for all its saliency in the lives of all of us. Among themselves they quibble over the details. Unions and management agree that we ought to sell the time of our lives in exchange for survival, although they haggle over the price. Marxists think we should be bossed by bureaucrats. Libertarians think we should be bossed by businessmen. Feminists don't care which form bossing takes so long as the bosses are women. Clearly these ideology-mongers have serious differences over how to divvy up the spoils of power. Just as clearly, none of them have any objection to power as such and all of them want to keep us working.

You may be wondering if I'm joking or serious. I'm joking and serious. To be ludic is not to be ludicrous. Play doesn't have to be frivolous, although frivolity isn't triviality: very often we ought to take frivolity seriously. I'd like life to be a game — but a game with high stakes. I want to play *for keeps*.

The alternative to work isn't just idleness. To be ludic is not to be quaaludic. As much as I treasure the pleasure of torpor, it's never more rewarding than when it punctuates other pleasures and pastimes. Nor am I promoting the managed time-disciplined safety-valve called "leisure"; far from it. Leisure is nonwork for the sake of work. Leisure is the time spent recovering from work and in the frenzied but hopeless attempt to forget about work. Many people return from vacation so beat that they look forward to returning to work so they can rest up. The main difference between work and leisure is that at work at least you get paid for your alienation and enervation.

I am not playing definitional games with anybody. When I say I want to abolish work, I mean just what I say, but I want to say what I mean by defining my terms in non-idiosyncratic ways. My minimum definition of work is forced labor, that is, compulsory production. Both elements are essential. Work is production enforced by economic or political means, by the carrot or the stick. (The carrot is just the stick by other means.) But not all creation is work. Work is never done for its own sake, it's done on account of some product or output that the worker (or, more often, somebody else) gets out of it. This is what work necessarily is. To define it is to despise it. But work is usually even worse than its definition decrees. The dynamic of domination intrinsic to work tends over time toward elaboration. In advanced work-riddled societies, including all industrial societies whether capitalist or "Communist," work invariably acquires other attributes which accentuate its obnoxiousness.

Usually — and this is even more true in "Communist" than capitalist countries, where the state is almost the only employer and everyone is an employee — work is employment, *i.e.*, wage-labor, which means selling yourself on the installment plan. Thus 95 percent of Americans who work, work for somebody (or something) else. In the USSR or Cuba or Yugoslavia or any other alternative model which might be adduced, the corresponding figure approaches 100 percent. Only the embattled Third World peasant bastions — Mexico, India, Brazil, Turkey — temporarily shelter significant concentrations of agriculturists who perpetuate the traditional arrangement of most laborers in the last several millennia, the payment of taxes (= ransom) to the state or rent to parasitic landlords in return for being otherwise left alone. Even this raw deal is beginning to look good. All industrial (and office) workers are employees and under the sort of surveillance which ensures servility.

But modern work has worse implications. People don't just work, they have "jobs." One person does one productive task all the time on an or-else basis. Even if the task has a quantum of intrinsic interest (as increasingly many jobs don't) the monotony of its obligatory exclusivity drains its ludic potential. A "job" that might engage the energies of some people, for a reasonably limited time, for the fun of it, is just a burden on those who have to do it for forty hours a week with no say in how it should be done, for the profit of owners who contribute nothing to the project, and with no opportunity for sharing tasks or spreading the work among those who actually have to do it. This is the real world of work: a world of bureaucratic blundering, of sexual harassment and discrimination, of bonehead bosses exploiting and scapegoating their subordinates who — by any rational-technical criteria — should be calling the shots. But capitalism in the real world subordinates the rational maximization of productivity and profit to the exigencies of organizational control.

The degradation which most workers experience on the job is the sum of assorted indignities which can be denominated as "discipline." Foucault has complexified this phenomenon but it is simple enough. Discipline consists of the totality of totalitarian controls at the workplace — surveillance, rotework, imposed work tempos, production quotas, punching in- and out-, etc. Discipline is what the factory and the office and the store share with the prison and the school and the mental hospital. It is something historically original and horrible. It was beyond the capacities of such demonic dictators of yore as Nero and Genghis Khan and Ivan the Terrible. For all their bad intentions they just didn't have the machinery to control their subjects as thoroughly as modern despots do. Discipline is the distinctively diabolical modern mode of control, it is an innovative intrusion which must be interdicted at the earliest opportunity.

Such is "work." Play is just the opposite. Play is always voluntary. What might otherwise be play is work if it's forced. This is axiomatic. Bernie de Koven has defined play as the "suspension of consequences." This is unacceptable if it implies that play is inconsequential. The point is not that play is without consequences. This is to demean play. The point is that the consequences, if any, are gratuitous. Playing and giving are closely related, they are the behavioral and transactional facets of the same impulse, the play-instinct. They share an aristocratic disdain for results. The player gets something out of playing; that's why he plays. But the core reward is the experience of the activity itself (whatever it is). Some otherwise attentive students of play, like Johan Huizinga (*Homo Ludens*), *define* it as gameplaying or following rules. I respect Huizinga's erudition but emphatically reject his constraints. There are many good games (chess, baseball, Monopoly, bridge) which are rule-governed but there is much more to play than game-playing. Conversation, sex, dancing, travel — these practices aren't rule-governed but they are surely play if anything is. And rules can be *played with* at least as readily as anything else.

Work makes a mockery of freedom. The official line is that we all have rights and live in a democracy. Other unfortunates who aren't free like we are have to live in police states. These victims obey orders or else, no matter how arbitrary. The authorities keep them under regular surveillance. State bureaucrats control even the smaller details of everyday life. The officials who push them around are answerable only to higher-ups, public or private. Either way, dissent and disobedience are punished. Informers report regularly to the authorities. All this is supposed to be a very bad thing.

And so it is, although it is nothing but a description of the modern workplace. The liberals and conservatives and libertarians who lament totalitarianism are phonies and hypocrites. There is more freedom in any moderately de-Stalinized dictatorship than there is in the ordinary American workplace. You find the same sort of hierarchy and discipline in an office or factory as you do in a prison or monastery. In fact, as Foucault and others have shown, prisons and factories came in at about the same time, and their operators consciously borrowed from each other's control techniques. A worker is a part-time slave. The boss says when to show up, when to leave and what to do in the meantime. He tells you how much work to do and how fast. He is free to carry his control to humiliating extremes, regulating, if he feels like it, the clothes you wear or how often you go to the bathroom. With a few exceptions he can fire you for any reason, or no reason. He has you spied on by snitches and supervisors, he amasses a dossier on every employee. Talking back is called "insubordination," just as if a worker is a naughty child, and it not only gets you fired, it disqualifies you for unemployment compensation. Without necessarily endorsing it for them either, it is noteworthy that children at home and in school receive much the same treatment, justified in their case by their supposed immaturity. What does this say about their parents and teachers who work?

The demeaning system of domination I've described rules over half the waking hours of a majority of women and the vast majority of men for decades, for most of their lifespans. For certain purposes it's not too misleading to call our system democracy or capitalism or — better still — industrialism, but its real names are factory fascism and office oligarchy. Anybody who says these people are "free" is lying or stupid. You are what you do. If you do boring, stupid monotonous work, chances are you'll end up boring, stupid and monotonous. Work is a much better explanation for the creeping cretinization all around us than even such significant moronizing mechanisms as television and education. People who are regimented all their lives, handed off to work from school and bracketed by the family in the beginning and the nursing home at the end, are habituated to hierarchy and psychologically enslaved. Their aptitude for autonomy is so atrophied that their fear of freedom is among their few rationally grounded phobias. Their obedience training at work carries over into the families they start, thus reproducing the system in more ways than one, and into politics, culture and everything else. Once you drain the vitality from people at work, they'll likely submit to hierarchy and expertise in everything. They're used to it.

We are so close to the world of work that we can't see what it does to us. We have to rely on outside observers from other times or other cultures to appreciate the extremity and the pathology of our present position. There was a time in our own past when the "work ethic" would have been incomprehensible, and perhaps Weber was on to something when he tied its appearance to a religion, Calvinism, which if it emerged today instead of four centuries ago would immediately and appropriately be labeled a cult. Be that as it may, we have only to draw upon the wisdom of antiquity to put work in perspective. The ancients saw work for what it is, and their view prevailed, the Calvinist cranks notwithstanding, until overthrown by industrialism — but not before receiving the endorsement of its prophets.

LET'S PRETEND FOR A MOMENT that work doesn't turn people into stultified submissives. Let's pretend, in defiance of any plausible psychology and the ideology of its boosters, that it has no effect on the formation of character. And let's pretend that work isn't as boring and tiring and humiliating as we all know it really is. Even then, work would *still* make a mockery of all humanistic and democratic aspirations, just because it usurps so much of our time. Socrates said that manual laborers make bad friends and bad citizens because they have no time to fulfill the responsibilities of friendship and citizenship. He was right. Because of work, no matter what we do we keep looking at our watches The only thing "free" about so-called free time is that it doesn't cost the boss anything. Free time is mostly devoted to getting ready for work, going to work, returning from work, and recovering from work. Free time is a euphemism for the peculiar way labor as a factor of production not only transports itself at its own expense to and from the workplace but assumes primary responsibility for its own maintenance and repair. Coal and steel don't do that. Lathes and typewriters don't do that. But workers do. No wonder Edward G. Robinson in one of his gangster movies exclaimed, "Work is for saps!"

Both Plato and Xenophon attribute to Socrates and obviously share with him an awareness of the destructive effects of work on the worker as a citizen and as a human being. Herodotus identified contempt for work as an attribute of the classical Greeks at the zenith of their culture. To take only one Roman example, Cicero said that "whoever gives his labor for money sells himself and puts himself in the rank of slaves." His candor is now rare, but contemporary primitive societies which we are wont to look down upon have provided spokesmen who have enlightened Western anthropologists. The Kapauku of West Irian, according to Pospisil, have a conception of balance in life and accordingly work only every other day, the day of rest designed "to regain the lost power and health." Our ancestors, even as late as the eighteenth century when they were far along the path to our present predicament, at least were aware of what we have forgotten, the underside of industrialization. Their religious devotion to "St. Monday" — thus establishing a *de facto* five-day week 150-200 years before its legal consecration — was the despair of the earliest factory owners.

They took a long time in submitting to the tyranny of the bell, predecessor of the time clock. In fact it was necessary for a generation or two to replace adult males with women accustomed to obedience and children who could be molded to fit industrial needs. Even the exploited peasants of the *ancien regime* wrested substantial time back from their landlords' work. According to Lafargue, a fourth of the French peasants' calendar was devoted to Sundays and holidays, and Chayanov's figures from villages in Czarist Russia — hardly a progressive society — likewise show a fourth or fifth of peasants' days devoted to repose. Controlling for productivity, we are obviously far behind these backward societies. The exploited *muzhiks* would wonder why any of us are working at all. So should we.

To grasp the full enormity of our deterioration, however, consider the earliest condition of humanity, without government or property, when we wandered as hunter-gatherers. Hobbes surmised that life was then nasty, brutish and short. Others assume that life was a desperate unremitting struggle for subsistence, a war waged against a harsh Nature with death and disaster awaiting the unlucky or anyone who was unequal to the challenge of the struggle for existence. Actually, that was all a projection of fears for the collapse of government authority over , communities unaccustomed to doing without it, like the England of Hobbes during the Civil War. Hobbes' compatriots had already encountered alternative forms of society which illustrated other ways of life — in North America, particularly — but already these were too remote from their experience to be understandable. (The lower orders, closer to the condition of the Indians, understood it better and often found it attractive. Throughout the seventeenth century, English settlers defected to Indian tribes or, captured in war, refused to return. But the Indians no more defected to white settlements than Germans climb the Berlin Wall from the west.) The "survival of the fittest" version — the Thomas Huxley version — of Darwinism was a better account of economic conditions in Victorian England than it was of natural selection, as the anarchist Kropotkin showed in his book *Mutual Aid, A Factor of Evolution*. (Kropotkin was a scientist — a geographer — who'd had ample involuntary opportunity for fieldwork whilst exiled in Siberia: he knew what he was talking about.) Like most social and political theory, the story Hobbes and his successors told was really unacknowledged autobiography.

The anthropologist Marshall Sahlins, surveying the data on contemporary hunter-gatherers, exploded the Hobbesian myth in an article entitled "The Original Affluent Society." They work a lot less than we do, and their work is hard to distinguish from what we regard as play. Sahlins concluded that "hunters and gatherers work less than we do; and, rather than a continuous travail, the food quest is intermittent, leisure abundant, and there is a greater amount of sleep in the daytime per capita per year than in any other condition of society." They worked an average of four hours a day, assuming they were "working" at all. Their labor, as it appears to us, was skilled labor which exercised their physical and intellectual capacities; unskilled labor on any large scale, as Sahlins says, is impossible except under industrialism. Thus it satisfied Friedrich Schiller's definition of play, the only occasion on which man realizes his complete humanity by giving full "play" to both sides of his twofold nature, thinking and feeling. As he put it: "The animal *works* when deprivation is the mainspring of its activity, and it *plays* when the fullness of its strength is this mainspring, when superabundant life is its own stimulus to activity." (A modern version — dubiously developmental — is Abraham Maslow's counterposition of "deficiency" and "growth" motivation.) Play and freedom are, as regards production, coextensive. Even Marx, who belongs (for all his good intentions) in the productivist pantheon, observed that "the realm of freedom does not commence until the point is passed where labor under the compulsion of necessity and external utility is required." He never could quite bring himself to identify this happy circumstance as what it is, the abolition of work — it's rather anomalous, after all, to be pro-worker and anti-work — but we can.

THE ASPIRATION TO GO BACKWARDS or forwards to a life without work is evident in every serious social or cultural history of preindustrial Europe, among them M. Dorothy George's *England in Transition* and Peter Burke's *Popular Culture in Early Modern Europe*. Also pertinent is Daniel Bell's essay, "Work and Its Discontents," the first text, I believe, to refer to the "revolt against work" in so many words and, had it been understood, an important correction to the complacency ordinarily associated with the volume in which it was collected, *The End of Ideology*. Neither critics nor celebrants have noticed that Bell's end-ofideology thesis signaled not the end of social unrest but the beginning of a new, uncharted phase unconstrained and uninformed by ideology. It was Seymour Lipset (in *Political Man*), not Bell, who announced at the same time that "the fundamental problems of the Industrial Revolution have been solved," only a few years before the post- or meta-industrial discontents of college students drove Lipset from UC Berkeley to the relative (and temporary) tranquillity of Harvard.

As Bell notes, Adam Smith in *The Wealth of Nations*, for all his enthusiasm for the market and the division of labor, was more alert to (and more honest about) the seamy side of work than Ayn Rand or the Chicago economists or any of Smith's modern epigones. As Smith observed: "The understandings of the greater part of men are necessarily formed by their ordinary employments. The man whose life is spent in performing a few simple operations . . . has no occasion to exert his understanding. . . . He generally becomes as stupid and ignorant as it is possible for a human creature to become." Here, in a few blunt words, is my critique of work. Bell, writing in 1956, the Golden Age of Eisenhower imbecility and American self-satisfaction, identified the unorganized, unorganizable malaise of the 1970s and since, the one no political tendency is able to harness, the one identified in HEW's report *Work in America*, the one which cannot be exploited and so is ignored. That problem is the revolt against work. It does not figure in any text by any laissez-faire economist — Milton Friedman, Murray Rothbard, Richard Posner — because, in their terms, as they used to say on *Star Trek*, "it does not compute."

If these objections, informed by the love of liberty, fail to persuade humanists of a utilitarian or even paternalist turn, there are others which they cannot disregard. Work is hazardous to your health, to borrow a book title. In fact, work is mass murder or genocide. Directly or indirectly, work will kill most of the people who read these words. Between 14,000 and 25,000 workers are killed annually in this country on the job. Over two million are disabled. Twenty to twenty-five million are injured every year. And these figures are based on a very conservative estimation of what constitutes a work-related injury. Thus they don't count the half million cases of occupational disease every year. I looked at one medical textbook on occupational diseases which was 1,200 pages long. Even this barely scratches the surface. The available statistics count the obvious cases like the 100,000 miners who have black lung disease, of whom 4,000 die every year, a much higher fatality rate than for AIDS, for instance, which gets so much media attention. This reflects the unvoiced assumption that AIDS afflicts perverts who could control their depravity whereas coal-mining is a sacrosanct activity beyond question. What the statistics don't show is that tens of millions of people have their lifespans shortened by work — which is all that homicide means, after all. Consider the doctors who work themselves to death in their 50s. Consider all the other workaholics.

Even if you aren't killed or crippled while actually working, you very well might be while going to work, coming from work, looking for work, or trying to forget about work. The vast majority of victims of the automobile are either doing one of these work-obligatory activities or else fall afoul of those who do them. To this augmented body-count must be added the victims of auto-industrial pollution and work-induced alcoholism and drug addiction. Both cancer and heart disease are modern afflictions normally traceable, directly or indirectly, to work.

Work, then, institutionalizes homicide as a way of life. People think the Cambodians were crazy for exterminating themselves, but are we any different? The Pol Pot regime at least had a vision, however blurred, of an egalitarian society. We kill people in the six-figure range (at least) in order to sell Big Macs and Cadillacs to the survivors. Our forty or fifty thousand annual highway fatalities are victims, not martyrs. They died for nothing — or rather, they died for work. But work is nothing to die for.

Bad news for liberals: regulatory tinkering is useless in this life-and-death context. The federal Occupational Safety and Health Administration was designed to police the core part of the problem, workplace safety. Even before Reagan and the Supreme Court stifled it, OSHA was a farce. At previous and (by current standards) generous Carter-era funding levels, a workplace could expect a random visit from an OSHA inspector once every 46 years.

State control of the economy is no solution. Work is, if anything, more dangerous in the state-socialist countries than it is here. Thousands of Russian workers were killed or injured building the Moscow subway. Stories reverberate about covered-up Soviet nuclear disasters which make Times Beach and Three-Mile Island look like elementary-school air-raid drills. On the other hand, deregulation, currently fashionable, won't help and will probably hurt. From a health and safety standpoint, among others, work was at its worst in the days when the economy most closely approximated laissez-faire. Historians like Eugene Genovese have argued persuasively that — as antebellum slavery apologists insisted — factory wageworkers in the Northern American states and in Europe were worse off than Southern plantation slaves. No rearrangement of relations among bureaucrats and businessmen seems to make much difference at the point of production. Serious enforcement of even the rather vague standards enforceable in theory by OSHA would probably bring the economy to a standstill. The enforcers apparently appreciate this, since they don't even try to crack down on most malefactors.

What I've said so far ought not to be controversial. Many workers are fed up with work. There are high and rising rates of absenteeism, turnover, employee theft and sabotage, wildcat strikes, and overall goldbricking on the job. There may be some movement toward a conscious and not just visceral rejection of work. And yet the prevalent feeling, universal among bosses and their agents and also widespread among workers themselves is that work itself is inevitable and necessary.

I disagree. It is now possible to abolish work and replace it, insofar as it serves useful purposes, with a multitude of new kinds of free activities. To abolish work requires going at it from two directions, quantitative and qualitative. On the one hand, on the quantitative side, we have to cut down massively on the amount of work being done. At present most work is useless or worse and we should simply get rid of it. On the other hand — and I think this the crux of the matter and the revolutionary new departure — we have to take what useful work remains and transform it into a pleasing variety of game-like and craft-like pastimes, indistinguishable from other pleasurable pastimes, except that they happen to yield useful end-products. Surely that shouldn't make them *less* enticing to do. Then all the artificial barriers of power and property could come down. Creation could become recreation. And we could all stop being afraid of each other.

I don't suggest that most work is salvageable in this way. But then most work isn't worth trying to save. Only a small and diminishing fraction of work serves any useful purpose independent of the defense and reproduction of the work-system and its political and legal appendages. Twenty years ago, Paul and Percival Goodman estimated that just five percent of the work then being done — presumably the figure, if accurate, is lower now — would satisfy our minimal needs for food, clothing, and shelter. Theirs was only an educated guess but the main point is quite clear: directly or indirectly, most work serves the unproductive purposes of commerce or social control. Right off the bat we can liberate tens of millions of salesmen, soldiers, managers, cops, stockbrokers, clergymen, bankers, lawyers, teachers, landlords, security guards, ad-men and everyone who works for them. There is a snowball effect since every time you idle some bigshot you liberate his flunkies and underlings also. Thus the economy *implodes*.

Forty percent of the workforce are white-collar workers, most of whom have some of the most tedious and idiotic jobs ever concocted. Entire industries, insurance and banking and real estate for instance, consist of nothing but useless papershuffling. It is no accident that the "tertiary sector," the service sector, is growing while the "secondary sector" (industry) stagnates and the "primary sector" (agriculture) nearly disappears. Because work is unnecessary except to those whose power it secures, workers are shifted from relatively useful to relatively useless occupations as a measure to assure public order. Anything is better than nothing. That's why you can't go home just because you finish early. They want your time, enough of it to make you theirs, even if they have no use for most of it. Otherwise why hasn't the average work week gone down by more than a few minutes in the last fifty years?

Next we can take a meat-cleaver to production work itself. No more war production, nuclear power, junk food, feminine hygiene deodorant — and above all, no more auto industry to speak of. An occasional Stanley Steamer or Model-T might be all right, but the auto-eroticism on which such pestholes as Detroit and Los Angeles depend is out of the question. Already, without even trying, we've virtually solved the energy crisis, the environmental crisis and assorted other insoluble social problems.

Finally, we must do away with far and away the largest occupation, the one with the longest hours, the lowest pay and some of the most tedious tasks around. I refer to *housewives* doing housework and child-rearing. By abolishing wage-labor and achieving full unemployment we undermine the sexual division of labor. The nuclear family as we know it is an inevitable adaptation to the division of labor imposed by modern wage-work. Like it or not, as things have been for the last century or two it is economically rational for the man to bring home the bacon, for the woman to do the shitwork to provide him with a haven in a heartless world, and for the children to be marched off to youth concentration camps called "schools," primarily to keep them out of Mom's hair but still under control, but incidentally to acquire the habits of obedience and punctuality so necessary for workers. If you would be rid of patriarchy, get rid of the nuclear family whose unpaid "shadow work," as Ivan Illich says, makes possible the work-system that makes it necessary. Bound up with this no-nukes strategy is the abolition of childhood and the closing of the schools. There are more full-time students than full-time workers in this country. We need children as teachers, not students. They have a lot to contribute to the ludic revolution because they're better at playing than grown-ups are. Adults and children are not identical but they will become equal through interdependence. Only play can bridge the generation gap.

I haven't as yet even mentioned the possibility of cutting way down on the little work that remains by automating and cybernizing it. All the scientists and engineers and technicians freed from bothering with war research and planned obsolescence should have a good time devising means to eliminate fatigue and tedium and danger from activities like mining. Undoubtedly they'll find other projects to amuse themselves with. Perhaps they'll set up world-wide all-inclusive multimedia communications systems or found space colonies. Perhaps. I myself am no gadget freak. I wouldn't care to live in a pushbutton paradise. I don't want robot slaves to do everything; I want to do things myself. There is, I think, a place for laborsaving technology, but a modest place. The historical and prehistorical record is not encouraging. When productive technology went from hunting-gathering to agriculture and on to industry, work increased while skills and self-determination diminished. The further evolution of industrialism has accentuated what Harry Braverman called the degradation of work. Intelligent observers have always been aware of this. John Stuart Mill wrote that all the labor-saving inventions ever devised haven't saved a moment's labor. Karl Marx wrote that "it would be possible to write a history of the inventions, made since 1830, for the sole purpose of supplying capital with weapons against the revolts of the working class." The enthusiastic technophiles — Saint-Simon, Comte, Lenin, B.F. Skinner — have always been unabashed authoritarians also; which is to say, technocrats. We should be more than skeptical about the promises of the computer mystics. *They* work like dogs; chances are, if they have their way, so will the rest of us. But if they have any particularized contributions more readily subordinated to human purposes than the run of high tech, let's give them a hearing.

What I really want to see is work turned into play. A first step is to discard the notions of a "job" and an "occupation." Even activities that already have some ludic content lose most of it by being reduced to jobs which certain people, and only those people are forced to do to the exclusion of all else. Is it not odd that farm workers toil painfully in the fields while their air-conditioned masters go home every weekend and putter about in their gardens? Under a system of permanent revelry, we will witness the Golden Age of the dilettante which will put the Renaissance to shame. There won't be any more jobs, just things to do and people to do them.

The secret of turning work into play, as Charles Fourier demonstrated, is to arrange useful activities to take advantage of whatever it is that various people at various times in fact enjoy doing. To make it possible for some people to do the things they could enjoy it will be enough just to eradicate the irrationalities and distortions which afflict these activities when they are reduced to work. I, for instance, would enjoy doing some (not too much) teaching, but I don't want coerced students and I don't care to suck up to pathetic pedants for tenure.

Second, there are some things that people like to do from time to time, but not for too long, and certainly not all the time. You might enjoy baby-sitting for a few hours in order to share the company of kids, but not as much as their parents do. The parents meanwhile, profoundly appreciate the time to themselves that you free up for them, although they'd get fretful if parted from their progeny for too long. These differences among individuals are what make a life of free play possible. The same principle applies to many other areas of activity, especially the primal ones. Thus many people enjoy cooking when they can practice it seriously at their leisure, but not when they're just fueling up human bodies for work.

Third — other things being equal — some things that are unsatisfying if done by yourself or in unpleasant surroundings or at the orders of an overlord are enjoyable, at least for awhile, if these circumstances are changed. This is probably true, to some extent, of all work. People deploy their otherwise wasted ingenuity to make a game of the least inviting drudge-jobs as best they can. Activities that appeal to some people don't always appeal to all others, but everyone at least potentially has a variety of interests and an interest in variety. As the saying goes, "anything once." Fourier was the master at speculating how aberrant and perverse penchants could be put to use in post-civilized society, what he called Harmony. He thought the Emperor Nero would have turned out all right if as a child he could have indulged his taste for bloodshed by working in a slaughterhouse. Small children who notoriously relish wallowing in filth could be organized in "Little Hordes" to clean toilets and empty the garbage, with medals awarded to the outstanding. I am not arguing for these precise examples but for the underlying principle, which I think makes perfect sense as one dimension of an overall revolutionary transformation. Bear in mind that we don't have to take today's work just as we find it and match it up with the proper people, some of whom would have to be perverse indeed. If technology has a role in all this it is less to automate work out of existence than to open up new realms for re/creation. To some extent we may want to return to handicrafts, which William Morris considered a probable and desirable upshot of communist revolution. Art would be taken back from the snobs and collectors, abolished as a specialized department catering to an elite audience, and its qualities of beauty and creation restored to integral life from which they were stolen by work. It's a sobering thought that the Grecian urns we write odes about and showcase in museums were used in their own time to store olive oil. I doubt our everyday artifacts will fare as well in the future, if there is one. The point is that there's no such thing as progress in the world of work; if anything it's just the opposite. We shouldn't hesitate to pilfer the past for what it has to offer, the ancients lose nothing yet we are enriched.

The reinvention of daily life means marching off the edge of our maps. There is, it is true, more suggestive speculation than most people suspect. Besides Fourier and Morris — and even a hint, here and there, in Marx — there are the writings of Kropotkin, the syndicalists Pataud and Pouget, anarchocommunists old (Berkman) and new (Bookchin). The Goodman brothers' *Communitas* is exemplary for illustrating what forms follow from given functions (purposes), and there is something to be gleaned from the often hazy heralds of alternative/appropriate/intermediate/convivial technology, like Schumacher and especially Illich, once you disconnect their fog machines. The situationists — as represented by Vaneigem's *Revolution of Everyday Life* and in the *Situationist International Anthology* — are so ruthlessly lucid as to be exhilarating, even if they never did quite square the endorsement of the rule of the workers' councils with the abolition of work. Better their incongruity, though, than any extant version of leftism, whose devotees look to be the last champions of work, for if there were no work there would be no workers, and without workers, who would the left have to organize?

So the abolitionists would be largely on their own. No one can say what would result from unleashing the creative power stultified by work. Anything can happen. The tiresome debater's problem of freedom vs. necessity, with its theological overtones, resolves itself practically once the production of use-values is coextensive with the consumption of delightful play-activity.

Life will become a game, or rather many games, but not — as it is now — a zero/sum game. An optimal sexual encounter is the paradigm of productive play. The participants potentiate each other's pleasures, nobody keeps score, and everybody wins. The more you give, the more you get. In the ludic life, the best of sex will diffuse into the better part of daily life. Generalized play leads to the libidinization of life. Sex, in turn, can become less urgent and desperate, more playful. If we play our cards right, we can all get more out of life than we put into it; but only if we play for keeps.

No one should ever work. Workers of the world . . . relax!

6

THE CULTURE
OF ANARCHY

graphic from **Fifth Estate**, *July 1981 #306*

graphic from **Stealworks: The Graphic Details of John Yates**

INTRODUCTION TO
THE CULTURE OF ANARCHY

There are two separate themes to be explored here. One is the relation of anarchists to the existing culture. Generally speaking that relationship takes the form of analysis, criticism, and revolt. The essay by **George Bradford** takes that form. To Bradford, we have already been overwhelmed by the mass media; we may not be able to escape.

His provocative position is that the media transmit an underlying signal that tells people that meaning can only be found in transmissions which are designed and packaged by the media controllers themselves. In that sense, Bradford argues, the mass media undermine what is really necessary in society, namely "unmediated, face-to-face dialogue."

What the media do is *simulate* meaning. For Bradford there are two realities — human meaning and mediatization. The two, he says, cannot coexist. Even publishing his essay in an anarchist alternative periodical, the *Fifth Estate*, Bradford says is "an act of desperation."

Although Bradford reifies the media and devalues the ability of people to learn to decode its messages, thus overstating its force; his argument is still compelling. It is apparent that the simulated meanings of the mass media of news and entertainment have had an indelible impact on society and the ability of many people to distinguish the authentic from the inauthentic in human experience.

While our first theme is the relation between an anarchist culture and the dominant culture, our second theme is that of creating of an anarchist culture. This is, in part, the role of the cultural worker. Let's remind ourselves that "culture" refers to the totality of norms, beliefs, values and the technology of the society which are transmitted from generation to generation. In this conventional anthropological sense, anarchism is a subculture within the larger society in which anarchists live. The problematic for anarchists is whether that subculture can survive the constant attempts at its domination, the centralized technology and social forms of expression, and the institutionalized mechanisms of oppression. While one could argue, if only by looking at this publication, that it has survived; one could also argue that this is merely a token serving as a safety valve for some anarchists who are permitted to continue — but only at certain historical periods and under highly controlled conditions.

This problematic aside, we look here at an aspect of the culture itself: the communication of ideas through the media of the written, performing, and visual arts. (For the moment, I ignore the "transfer culture," namely that subset of beliefs and values that instructs us in how to get from here to there, from this society to an anarchist society.)

We look first at the production and display of anarchist ideas *within* the dominant culture's media. **Susan White** examines, for example, how anarchist ideas have been portrayed in current film. Her perceptive viewing comes through in this essay. Especially revealing is the way she uncovers antianarchist themes which are presented so negatively as to imply their opposite. This is illustrated powerfully in the case of "The Brig" where the relentless subordination to arbitrary authority and the resocialization of the prisoners leads the viewer (inescapably?) to an antiauthoritarian attitude. White makes no claim that these themes were necessarily the intent of the producer or performer. She deals solely at the level of manifest content.

We do need to ask, however, what is the efficacy of this insinuation of anarchist ideas in popular cultural forms? Obviously, some analysts would claim it to have negative value — a cooptation of radical symbols. But I think that the matter is still open. On the one hand, the delegitimation of formal authority or the modeling, or even didactic presentation, of alternative forms of behavior, are messages that may be received by some members of the audience. Just the same we need to admit that the density of these symbols of opposition is low, so low that it is not interpreted as a threat to the elite consensus by those who are its gatekeepers. On the other hand, I am also concerned that because the messages are imbedded within the conventional media's system of symbols, they may be discounted as media fantasy. In fact, in order for people to survive in this mass media environment, they have to develop ways of insulating themselves from the often conflicting and self-denying messages which are ubiquitous. It may be that only a traumatic break in a medium's form and structure will enable a radical message to come through. This may be especially true the more politically radical the deviant message is.

Let's stay with the issue of anarchist themes in cultural productions, but move to an even more subtle, almost subliminal level. Here is a mundane example. **Glenda Morris** and I wrote a book about the baking of nonyeast (quick) breads (Crossing Press, 1989). The book was informed by our political concerns. It actually came out of our experiences teaching baking and cooking in an adult alternative school which emphasized self-help and survival skills. For example, we devised a technique to speed preparation and adapted recipes to single loaf baking in keeping with the schedules and size of today's households. We did not include breads which were very expensive to create and we were quite conscious of nutrition in developing our recipes. In our text, we shared our baking secrets and encouraged readers to use their own taste and judgement, and even ignore our expert advice. All of these decisions we made were deliberate on our part and were made as a result of our anarchist perspective. However, I submit that no one would know that this book had been so informed. (I even sign my culinary writing with a pseudonym, a *nom de pan*.)

Fast Breads is not a very direct or important contribution to the creating of an anarchist subculture. I use this example to highlight my argument, namely, that just because a cultural production is devised by an anarchist — even along anarchist principles — it does not in some self-propelled manner become an anarchist production. The same is true for any politic: lesbian or gay, ecological, marxist, even fascist.

To be sure, astute literary or artistic critics may be able to look at a work and discern how the author's background or commitment made that work *different* from others. And, as a teacher, that critic may be able to inform students of the underlying difference and its social significance. But that teacher is then creating a meaning that was not accessible or recognized beforehand. So it is that my explicit discussion of my bread book may change the way people read it.

Let's move out of the kitchen for another example, the case of Noam Chomsky. Chomsky is clearly one of the most prolific writers of political criticism in the English-speaking world. His critique of United States policy in Central America (*On Power and Ideology*, 1987), his critique of American and Soviet policies in the Middle East (*Pirates and Emperors*, 1987), his writings on the news media (*Manufacturing Consent*, 1988), among other productions, have all been outstanding in clarity and documentation and in exposing the cruelties and conspiracies of capitalism. Nowhere in these writings does Chomsky put forward an explicit anarchist critique or offer an anarchist solution or model, or even identify himself as an anarchist. (In less public contexts, he has written and spoken about anarchism and identified himself as an anarchosyndicalist.) There is no question that his writing is an attempt to delegitimize the existing regimes of imperialist states, but I claim that neither *Fast Breads* nor the *Managua Lectures* make a substantial contribution to the development of an anarchist subculture.

I do not mean to imply that the anarchist must always write a political preface or program note. The anarchist as writer and artist should be free as any artist to create with spontaneity and individuality. But the anarchist as *cultural worker* needs to put forward an anarchist vision. That act is the first step in building the substructure of an anarchist culture.

In this context, maybe we should distinguish three kinds of cultural productions. First, there are works produced by people who don't identify themselves with anarchism which nevertheless reveal an anarchist analysis and present, although unlabeled, anarchist concepts and ideas. Second, are works produced by anarchists which do not put forward an explicit anarchist analysis. Finally, there are works produced by anarchists which present anarchist ideas in an explicit and identifiable fashion. I think the term "cultural worker" should be limited to this third group. Clearly people do move in and out of these last two categories. I think it is important that we recognize that and be clear when we are or are not functioning as cultural workers.

For these reasons, many anarchists seek the *direct* display of their ideas in whatever medium they work in, although this often limits their ability to display their work in establishment contexts. Furthermore, though all art may be political, the ability to compose an *explicitly* political work, as **Glenda Morris'** "Poetry" asserts, is not an automatic outcome of writing. In fact, that is the dilemma of the anarchist as cultural worker.

Some artists have challenged the reigning authorities of their field or the dominant conventions of form or structure in an effort to express themselves. Robert Motherwell's room-sized fringed carpet pad (which hangs by itself on a wall at the Museum of Modern Art) or his red-painted drainpipe (which stands in the National Museum) may be a classic antiauthoritarian statement, and one that was critical in developing modern art, but it is not much more than that. One might contrast this with the music of John Cage who, like Motherwell, broke with conventional form and, like Motherwell, achieved considerable recognition and influence in his field. Unlike Motherwell, Cage had an explicit anarchist approach to music, and he publicly articulated his position as **Richard Kostelantz** points out in his essay. The history of the arts is filled with creative acts which generated a revolution within the discipline, but those radical changes had little impact beyond their domains.

Charles Keil, writing about the role of "song" in everyday life moves us to a still different way of looking at the issue. As a cultural worker, an anarchist musicologist, he views song and music as essentially liberating. It is this authoritarian society with its rigid dualisms, he maintains, that prevents us from using this liberatory form. By getting people to sing and make their own music, they take an active role in breaking down the mediatization of music. **Terri Clark**, writing from the perspective of a jazz vocalist, talks of learning her politics from her music and of the integral connection of jazz and anarchy. Just as some technology may be liberating, so it is we might consider whether some artistic, cultural forms may be more liberatory than others.

There is still another dimension to any discussion of anarchy and art, and that is how the production of art is organized. As cultural workers, anarchists can work to delegitimize the authoritarian overlay to most cultural productions within society and to elaborate upon their imagery of a good society. They can introduce elements of collectivity into cultural productions, and help break down the distance between artists and the spectator. Perhaps, ultimately, an "anarchist realism" is needed. In contrast to socialist realism that required art to serve the needs of the state, an anarchist realism would be a movement to develop the music, art and literature of everyone. I think that it is far more important that everyone in the community can make their own artistic productions if and as they choose than that the community sponsor an elite group of artists to do so. Of course the two are not mutually exclusive, but what is critical is that art not be organized into an elite grouping or that it be transformed into a commodity. And above all, it is important that an elitist view of art not be permitted to dominate and intimidate people so that they can not express themselves freely.

MEDIA: CAPITAL'S GLOBAL VILLAGE

GEORGE BRADFORD

These are tentative, unfinished remarks about the mass media. They should be taken as a series of questions rather than as definitive answers. They do start from the recognition that the media have come to usurp reality, representing the structure and the content of mass society as it spins around its own unstable axis. It is precisely because life itself has become mediatized that any discussion of media and our assumptions about their operation is so problematic.

In a previous article on communications technology, I pointed out this problem, remarking that human communication has come to resemble the model imposed by the standardized transmission and reception of messages between machines. "The discourse has shifted," I wrote, since "all of human intercourse tends to be restructured along the lines of this petrified information and its communication." (See "1984: Worse Than Expected?" in the Spring 1984 issue of the *Fifth Estate*.)

Jean Baudrillard, after Argentine author Jorge Luis Borges, takes as his metaphor for this state of affairs the fable of a map "so detailed that it ends up covering the territory." Whereas with the decline of the Empire comes the deterioration of the map, tattered but still discernible in some remote places, "this fable has come full circle for us," writes Baudrillard, "and if we were to revive the fable today, it would be the territory whose shreds are slowly rotting across the map. It is the real, and not the map, whose vestiges subsist here and there, in the deserts which are no longer those of the Empire, but our own." (*Simulations*).

I would like to make some observations on the nature of communications technology and media with this fable in mind. These are fragmentary notes, but perhaps they will help to elaborate on some questions raised by the previous articles on technology and mass society. I would also like to make some observations on the media and social control, in particular their alleged potential for resisting social domination when utilized by radicals.

But more importantly, I want to explore the fable raised by Baudrillard, and the sense that it suggests of having come full circle, the notion that media are more than a machine which transmits messages. Rather, a fundamental mutation has taken place or is taking place — in Baudrillard's words, "Everything is obliterated only to begin again." The media are an entire universe which simulates meaning, communication, community. These simulations have covered the real, or have duplicated it so that even a nostalgia for that territory which crumbles into dust beneath the map loses coherence.

THE NATURE OF THE FACT

INFORMATION IS CENTRAL to this new "hyperreality." The demand for information, the "democratic" distribution of "facts," is the battle cry of the radicals who struggle to capture the machinery of media. "If only we could present people with the facts," goes the refrain. But it is the nature of the fact, and finally of masses of facts transmitted on a mass scale as information, which lies behind the problem of the media. Not that facts have no reality at all, but they have no intrinsic relation to anything: They are weightless.

Modern technological society, of course, sees in the fact something akin to the Holy Ghost: they are the repositories of the truth, and it is only by facts, happily provided by communications media, that we can find our way. Indeed, the fact is the stuff of media. True or false, meaningless or significant, it can be reduced to a signal because it arrives already diminished. The fact is a great mystery: in and of itself it is nothing until combined with other facts and presented by media. Yet it is also *everything*, since truth can only be conveyed by such facts in the eyes of the believer. The fact achieves its ultimate manifestation in trivia and in statistics, to which society is madly addicted. No action can take place without the justification of statistics, while trivia fills every corner of the media.

The fact is a selection, hence an exclusion. Its simplification is a mutilation of a subtle reality which refuses to be efficiently packaged. One set of facts confronts another in different configurations of information employed by competing rackets. Facts are organized to conform to technological necessities, production values, and the principles of media rhetoric. Facts are hoarded, and they are disseminated. They reproduce like cells. Finally, they are orchestrated as propaganda and advertising — the official language of capital which finds itself reproduced miraculously on the lips of the individual.

One would think that this inchoate, exponential growth and availability of facts would have helped people find their way out of the mass totalitarian structures of society. On the contrary, the formation of the individual conscience is more affected by powerful forces of domination than it was in previous periods. As Jacques Ellul wrote in his book *Propaganda: The Formation of Men's Attitudes*, "Excessive data do not enlighten the reader or listener, they drown him." People are "caught in a web of facts."

Whatever specific message is transmitted by the media, the central code is affirmed: meaning must be designed, packaged, and distributed by technicians and administrators. Truth and meaning can no longer flow from the complex interaction which takes place face to face among human beings — they are delivered by media, and their power and their validity are unquestionable because they are media. "Everywhere," writes Ellul in language evocative of Orwell or Reich, "we find men who pronounce as highly personal truths what they have read in the papers only an hour before . . ." The result is an amputated being — "nothing except what propaganda has taught him."

A Ballast To Established Power

Even the desire to transform society is itself colonized by becoming one media message, one competing repertory of facts among many, to be consumed alongside of those which support the entrenched powers. Thus, in spite of their intent, alternative media tend to reinforce an artificial sense of plurality (when in reality it is the universal act of media consumption, of channel switching, which is affirmed). They provide a ballast to established power and its media by taking part in its technological discourse.

This is why the media radical's notion of "democratic" access and the necessity of "rational" selection is a pathetic wish. The selection of a program implies the acceptance of an entire set of conditions. Imagine, for example, the arrival of television programming to an isolated community. Certainly, the members of that community can select one program over another, a documentary on ecology or a ballet over a cop show or porno tape. But in the process they are changing their way of life to that of television viewers. They have surrendered to the discourse of media — they are silenced. It talks. They listen. When they resume their speech, it will resemble that of the machine.

They are also plugged into the information industry, and are suddenly in need of ever greater amounts of information.

It is the same with politics, that degraded, binary discourse of power and its opposition. It is Baudrillard's brilliant insight that universal suffrage is the first mass medium, based on negative/positive, question/response oppositions, and epitomized in the referendum. Here once again "selection" takes place within a series of simulations, of pseudo-choices posed by capital. A and not-A. Politics is an "operational Theater," a Pavlovian program. One year the citizen, pummeled and prepped by the media, sallies forth to fulfill his duty, voting in favor of Political Reason. At the next cycle, he votes it out. Such a binary model obliterates any genuine human discourse.

In a world dominated by loudspeakers, in which human action is reduced to the pulling of lever A or lever B, the argument is to develop or obtain bigger and better loudspeakers for "our side" in order to "reach the masses," or to get "our cause" represented by one of the levers. Sharply drawn contrasts, flashing lights and melodrama are called upon to move the viewer/citizen already desensitized by the wondrous techniques of media. Profound beliefs, shaded by intuition, ambivalence and social interaction, must be stereotyped into easily identifiable signals which correspond to the familiar world of everyday, banalized experience — the experience of the laboratory test, of the media.

When the subtle nuances and complex values of a genuinely radical resistance to this epoch are treated by media, nuance is lost and its profound sense is drowned out. Only the media are affirmed. Events happening to real people in the real world are reduced to "good media." But in the media, what moves the receiver (to passivity and to passive aggression, that is) is not truth, is not nuance, is not ambivalence, but technique. And technique is the domain of Power and of established ideology — the domain of simulated meaning. Real meaning — irreducible to a broadcast — disintegrates under such an onslaught. People who accept this counterfeit as reality will follow the lead of the organization with the biggest and best loudspeakers.

The media appeal to the masses is simply that — an appeal to masses formed by the media. Where they make no such appeal, they remain marginalized and incoherent, unassimilable to the mass society in whose functions they participate. Information is noise, truth becomes a trick done with mirrors. As Nazi leader Goebbels remarked, "We do not talk to say something, but to obtain a certain effect."

THE LOSS OF AURA

THE ALIENATED BEING who is the target of Goebbels' machinery can most of all be found in front of a television set — this ubiquitous reality-conjuring apparatus which is the quintessential mass medium and the centerpiece of every household, the emblem of and key to universality from Bali to Brooklyn. Everywhere people receive the simulated meaning generated by television, which everywhere duplicates and undermines, and finally colonizes what was formerly human meaning in all its culture-bound and symbolic manifestations. Finally only television contains or generates meaning. Even the old shell of the host is burst for the parasite to emerge in its own image. Television, mass media *become* culture. The diminished reality spewing from the media reflects and aggravates our own diminished condition.

People and events captured by communications media, and especially by television, have lost what Walter Benjamin referred to as their "aura," their internal, intersubjective vitality, the specificity and autonomous significance of the experience — in a sense, their *spirit*.

Only the external aspects of the event can be conveyed by communications media, not experiential meaning or context. Jerry Mander's *Four Arguments for the Elimination of Television* shows how boring and two-dimensional nature is rendered by television, how incoherent the subtle expressions of emotion become, how the ceremonial mood of a group of primal people is lost when the camera captures it. Such a sense cannot be conveyed by media, and it is rendered absurd by television.

Although television, through its illusion of immediacy and transparency, seems to represent the most destructive, the most glaring example of the media, the same can be said of all other forms. At the cinema, for example, social meaning is generated both in the so-called content of the film (as manipulation), and by the act of film-going itself (as alienation) — a spectacularized social interaction mediated by technology. In a movie theater, modern isolation is transposed by the passive reception of images into the false collectivity of the theater audience (which can also be said of modern mass sporting events). As in modern social life itself, like all media, film-going is "a social relation mediated by images" (Debord).

Siegfried Kracauer, in his books *Theory of Film* and *From Caligari to Hitler: A Psychological History of the German Film*, discussed in great detail the fragmented consciousness which simultaneously seeks community and escape, fleeing social atomization not in practical collective activity (which could only have revolutionary implications) but in isolated voyeurism. He quotes a student: "Some days a sort of 'hunger for people' . . . drives me into the cinema." Kracauer adds, "He misses 'life'. And he is attracted to the cinema because it gives him the illusion of vicariously partaking of life in its fullness."

Even the latest technological fad among anarchists — pirate radio — may serve as an example. People using such technology have two choices: to become like the mass media by relying more on techniques of propaganda, by packaging their "message"; or to liquidate technique for genuine communication, to become unlike radio, more local and communitarian.

But such forms can never compete with technology — there is nothing more boring than radio or television trying to be human, trying to deny technique. People turn it off and turn to disco-mojo with lasers. If technological principles are not obeyed, no listener will be reached; but following such technological demands undermines reality, substituting a flattened propaganda. Unmediated, face-to-face dialogue can only take place locally — in people's houses or in the street, where it is still possible to transgress the code of the media.

MEDIA AND MEANING CANNOT LONG COEXIST

WHAT I AM SUGGESTING FLIES IN THE FACE of the logic of technology and the pervasiveness of the model of meaning which it has imposed. To most people, the utter volume of artistic, intellectual, and scientific production — of films, recordings, books, magazines, gadgets, scientific discoveries, art, all of it — seems to imply that subtle human values and plenitude of meaning and well-being are accumulating at a tremendous rate, that we can now experience life more rapidly, in greater depth, and at a greater range.

We can know more, thanks to the phenomenal growth of information, and we can feel and experience more, with the boom in the arts. As one reviewer wrote in the *New York Times Book Review*, "If the average person can have access to information that would fill the Library of Congress or can control as much computing power as a university has today, why should he be shallower than before?" (Paul Delany, "Socrates, Faust, Univac," NYTBR, 3/18/84)[1]

Linked with this notion is the sense that computers and the media simply aren't meant for communicating subtle meaning, but that nevertheless they have a place, and information has its role. The human values generated by family, community and culture still can remain while at the same time electronic communications can link us with others. In fact, the two enhance one another, according to this argument. McLuhan: "Our new environment compels commitment and participation. We have become irrevocably involved with, and responsible for, each other." (*The Medium is the Massage.*) Human beings can autonomously generate meaning, and transmit this meaning (or minimally make appointments to share it with others) by way of the radio, video, camera and computer available to everyone.

I do not want to repeat what I wrote in my previous article — that such computer power is not available in any significant way to most people. Let us assume that people do have equal access to the media. This in no way alters the fact that, quite simply, two realities — human meaning and mediatization, the territory and the map — cannot long coexist, a truth which daily becomes more obvious. There is a certain incommensurability between them which cannot be bridged. The media undermine and destroy meaning by simulating it. The fact that everywhere people accept this simulation as genuine, that they seem to lack that sense of loss necessary to keep the diminishing world outside of capital alive, brings to mind the metaphor of the completed circle.

What happens when there cannot be said to be any sense of loss, or when nostalgia is simulated as a sense of loss of some other mode of technology itself.[2] When we can no longer be said to be victims of a powerful, centralized media (which could be subverted, captured, made to "serve the masses"). We are no longer free to resist the messages of the media or autonomously create our own; we are becoming the media, or it has collapsed into the mass, what Baudrillard calls the collapse of two poles and their merging.

"We are no longer in the society of spectacle which the situationists talked about," he writes in *Simulations*, "nor in the specific types of alienation and repression which this implied. The medium itself is no longer identifiable as such, and the merging of the medium and the message (McLuhan) is the first great formula of this new age. There is no longer any medium in the literal sense: it is now intangible, diffuse and diffracted in the real, and it can no longer even be said that the latter is distorted by it.

"Such immixture, such a viral, endemic, chronic, alarming presence of the medium, without our being able to isolate its effects — spectralized, like those publicity holograms sculptured in empty space with laser beams, the event filtered by the medium — the dissolution of TV into life, the dissolution of life into TV — an indiscernible chemical solution: we are all . . . doomed not to invasion, to pressure, to violence and to blackmail by the media and the models, but to their induction, to their infiltration, to their illegible violence."

How can authentic discourse take place when our own language and our being has become so dependent on, molded by this centralized and yet also diffused, molecular apparatus and its code? It is no longer a question of the loss of aura in artistic images. What happens when human beings begin to be denuded of their aura? What happens when the problem is no longer one of representation, but rather that duplication has turned both what is real and the spectacle into indistinguishable modes of a simulation?

A SURFEIT OF INFORMATION AND EXPERIENCE

THE SURFEIT OF INFORMATION CORRESPONDS to an equal excess of experiences or emotions in the media. Modes of being are expanded and imploded by their constant surveillance. One can today experience emotions and drama every day for the price of a ticket (one is reminded of the "feelie movies" in Huxley's *Brave New World*). But how can these emotions and human values resist being trivialized when they are not grounded in anything but the mechanical transmissions of images which are themselves exchanged as a commodity? When we imitate those models — noble or reprehensible as the case may be — we are recreating, or rather duplicating, a simulation. We surveil ourselves, luridly, as on a screen.

Yet isn't it also true that the media are much more appropriate to the duplication of high contrast, rapid, and superficial modes, which is precisely why the new cultural milieu is infused not with the silences of meditation or of the gardener who slowly places seeds in the ground along a freshly dug furrow, but rather of the speed of machines, of violence and weapons, of that hard-edged, indifferent nihilism of a degraded, artificial environment? The fascination with machines, the technofascist style so prevalent today, carries well on the media, until there is no separation between brutalization by Power and the brutalization we carry within.

Even where other values creep through, we see people judging their own experiences by that of the media. "Pretty as a picture" — a sky reminds us of a film, the death of a human being finds meaning in a media episode. Hence, an irreal experience becomes our measure of the real: the circle is completed. The real experience is called into question; there is only duplication, only a *hyperreality* (Baudrillard).[3]

The very formation of the subject, once the result of a complex interaction of human beings participating in a symbolic order, has been replaced by the media. Modernists argue that by replacing the symbolic order with the nihilism of machines, we become free to create our own reality — a naïve appraisal of our transformations. Instead, we are becoming machine-like rather than animal-like, and what we are is more and more determined by a technological roulette. We now make our covenant with commodities, demand miracles of computers, see our world through a manufactured lens rather than the mind's eye. One eye blinds the other — they are incommensurable, absolutely incompatible. I think of a photograph I saw recently, of a New Guinea tribesman in traditional dress taking a photograph with an instamatic camera. What is he becoming, if not exactly another duplication, another clone of what we are all becoming?

The fact that everyone has "access" to media, that we have all to some degree or another become carriers of media, is far from being a defense against centralized power. In actuality it is perhaps the final logic of centralization as it spins out of orbit, the final reduction of the prisoner, when the realization occurs that, yes, he truly does love Big Brother. Or the realization that nature does not exist but is only what we arbitrarily decide to organize or that you do not experience a place until you have the photograph. The age of the genuine imitation.

The paleolithic cave walls are redone to protect the originals which are themselves shut off forever — these imitations are "authentic," of course, but the spirit of the cave has fled; this is "art," do you have your ticket, sir? "Take a photograph, it lasts longer." You are capturing what is already only a frozen picture, devoid of symbolic and spiritual meaning — an "aesthetic hallucination," in Baudrillard's words. There is no aura. For a primitive, the mountain speaks, and a communication is established. For the tourist, it is tamed, desiccated. It is a dead image before the camera is aimed.

READING THE NEWSPAPERS

I will not exempt print media and newspapers from my criticism, though I tend to think that they are being eclipsed by television and computers. Nevertheless, they function similarly. The greater the scope, the more frequent the publication, the more the newspapers impose their model of fragmented, ideologized reality. Their spurious claim to "objectivity," their mutilating process of selection and editing, their automatic reinforcement of the status quo (or their official manipulation if they serve as propaganda tools for competing rackets who are contesting only the present alignment of power), their banalization of real events happening to real human beings, all parallel television.

On the one hand, they are instruments of a vast, centralized lying machine. On the other, they distort even the information they transmit both in the way they present it and in the context they provide. The daily affair of the news is impossible to integrate even when one sets out to become informed by careful reading of the newspapers. Only extensive research would present any kind of reliable picture, but most people do not have the time or inclination to conduct such a project. Indeed, very few people read newspapers to be informed. Most people glance at the little news they might encounter, then head for so-called "features" — the actual reason people buy newspapers. They would be just as well off illiterate — they are just as much the creatures of rumor, manipulation and advertising as they were over a hundred years ago, when universal education and literacy were being touted as the foundations for an informed and free populace. In fact, as the techniques and scope of media have developed, people have become more manipulated than ever.[4]

I recognize the contradictions in publishing this essay in the *Fifth Estate*, which is media — alternative, not necessarily assimilable to the larger media discourse, perhaps, but nevertheless media. I am not sure how to move beyond the code; I am raising the possibility of doing so, and suggesting how far we have to go. I am not writing this to convince people of the truth of these feelings, but to put my own thoughts in order, and to invite response. From a discussion in a marginalized media operation about the nature of the media, to actually overthrowing the form of life which we have adopted, is a leap that won't be made here. But I would like to undermine the official religion of technology and media, and in order to do so, with tremendous ambivalence and doubt, I partake in it in a small, awkward, conditional way. Quite frankly, it is an act of desperation.

MACHINES OF DECEIT

BUT HOW DO WE CONFRONT the centralized machines of deceit? Am I suggesting that people stop producing media which expose the lies of the mass media on Central America, the Middle East, the nuclear threat, and the rest? Not necessarily. We are in desperate straits. But the "facts" aren't going to make the difference. What will is people's capacity to resist capital and the structures of domination — *for their own reasons*? Do people need to know the horrible facts about Central America in order to resist the coming war? Can we possibly beat the Power in this penny-ante game of facts when a single pronouncement by that media image called a "president" — that Nicaragua is destabilizing, terrorist, and all the rest, for example — drowns out the truth? If people were willing to turn off the media they might have fewer facts to win arguments, but they might not accept media-manufactured images of "strength," "security," and "well-being" — all delivered through the advertising techniques of propagandists — as reality. Real well-being, real peace, could not be reduced to a commodity sign to be consumed along with other signs. If only media can move people to resist domination, and they can only be signaled to resist as they are now to obey, what can this portend for human freedom?

Perhaps to some degree it is a question of balance; it is fair to say that there is a difference between using old technical means to communicate, and uncritically cheering on the latest technological developments and even volunteering for the regiments which will bring them about. I am writing this on a typewriter (with help from a pencil) because they are at hand; I am not shopping around for a word processor simply because it is available and is touted as the wave of the future. I am trying to figure out how to become less dependent on these machines, less linked to "world communications," not more. The "global village" is capital's village; it is antithetical to any genuine village or community.[5]

Finally, I cannot help but suspect that people who promote communications technology for its potential community applications are much more fascinated by technology than they are by community. Thus, they affirm the technolatry which is the ideological linchpin of modern technological civilization. I think that for many such people, only a major technological catastrophe that affected them directly could change their minds. They are not predisposed to relinquish their illusions, which stem not only from a mystical faith in the salvation promised by technological development, but also from an utter fatalism which views the technological runaway as inevitable. This essentially religious viewpoint is shared by anarchist and authoritarian, scientific rationalist and religious fundamentalist. Bound to this is a complete surrender to media, in which even rebellion becomes mediatized and hence recuperated to the functional operation of technology — a self-operating feedback.

An "Epistemological Luddism"

EVEN WHERE PEOPLE ARE CRITICAL of the blatantly negative effects of mass technics and media, they tend to argue that technology does not *have* to be as it is; in a different, more perfect world. it could be different. This hypothetical justification of some mystical potentiality for technology refuses to face reality. Certainly, if human beings were radically different, if society had built-in defenses against technological runaway, if everyone had the superhuman ability to learn every specialization in order to make decisions, if this were a different planet with a different history, if, if, if . . . . Meanwhile, what is legitimized is the material reality of a technological system which demands social stratification and compartmentalization, technological hierarchy and domination, runaway development, deadening labor, passivity, stupefaction and the ever-present risk — or certainty? — of disaster.

Contrary to McLuhanesque fantasies, the wheel is not an extension of the foot, but a simulation which destroys the original. Media do not extend meaning, but duplicate it, rendering any contrast between authenticity and inauthenticity, between a genuine experience rooted in human symbolic activity and a simulated meaning manufactured by technology, both absurd and deadly. The emerging hyperreality is completing the circle, replacing the symbolic integration of human beings in autonomously generated culture, with a functional integration within the technological universe. Little of the original territory now remains.

Abolishing mass media means abolishing a way of life, of learning to live in a different way. I don't know where to begin, or if there is an "anywhere" (or nowhere) from which we can begin, if only catastrophe — a word which I ponder and which evades me — awaits us. [6]

And so in desperation, I look for "solutions," for "strategies" towards a way out. In his book *Autonomous Technology*, Langdon Winner suggests that a possible beginning to stopping this decaying juggernaut would be to begin dismantling the problematic technological structures and to refuse to repair those systems that are breaking down. This would also imply refusing to accept newly devised technological systems meant to fix or replace the old.

"This I would propose not as a solution in itself," he writes, "but as a method of inquiry." In this way we could investigate where our dependency lies and how we can find our way to autonomy and self-sufficiency. Such an "epistemological Luddism," in Winner's words, could help us break up the structures of daily life and make it possible for us to discover new ways to live. Perhaps then we could take meaning back from the meaning-manufacturing apparatus of the mass media, stop talking its speech and create our own speech and meaning which are rooted in community life.

A primary decision would be to refuse the "sacred communion" of technolatry, to give up our illusions about technology and the false promise of mass communications, to begin to *turn off the media* and start thinking, creating, seeing for ourselves. I think it is all possible — paradise lies just beyond these walls. Is there enough courage and imagination left in us to topple them?

FOOTNOTES

1. And another writer, in the *Village Voice*, discusses the increasingly rapid breakdown of visual narrative by television, now exploded by the simultaneous use of several video screens. "Why not be cheerful about it for a change, and view it as an increase of the speed at which information is taken in?" says Julie Talen (in "Beyond Monovision," *VV* 3/27/ 84). "How long do you have to watch Mrs. Olson [a character in a television commercial] . . . before you know what she'll say? We couldn't keep operating at a slower pace, we'd never keep up with the amount of information we're expected to choose and process. ["Choice" — as in mechanized testing or voting; and "to process," as meat is eviscerated, as "raw materials" are processed for distribution — two fundamental components of modern capital.] That's what multiplier effects are all about: attention spans, increasing information." The Pavlovian implications are clear, apart from the inevitable anxiety about what is happening to attention spans. Ellul writes in *Propaganda*, ". . . Though it is true that after a certain time the individual becomes indifferent to the propaganda content, that does not mean that he has become insensitive to propaganda, that he turns from it, that he is immune. It means exactly the opposite. . . . He continues to obey the catchwords of propaganda, though he no longer listens to it. His reflexes still function. . . . He no longer needs to see and read the poster; the simple splash of color is enough to awaken the desired reflexes in him. In reality, though he is [rendered immune] to ideological content, he is sensitized to propaganda itself."

2. As in gentrification of cities, the mania for collection, reconstruction of historical sites, and folklore tamed and televised to be consumed as entertainment.

3. The completion of the circle can be seen in modern music. At one time, synthesizers and electronic music were used experimentally to imitate acoustic instruments and the human voice. More recently, however, modern composers have used completely acoustic ensembles and choirs to imitate electronic sounds, so that the two are indistinguishable: there is no longer any distinction between the "real" and the simulacrum

4. Ellul writes, "Let us not say: 'If one gave them good things to read . . . if these people received a better education. . . .' Such an argument has no validity because things just are not that way. Let us not say, either: 'This is only the first stage; in France, the first stage was reached half a century ago, and we still are very far from attaining the second. There is more, unfortunately. This first stage has placed man at the disposal of propaganda. Before he can pass to the second stage, he will find himself in a universe of propaganda. Actually, the most obvious result of primary

education in the nineteenth and twentieth centuries was to make the individual susceptible to propaganda."

5. Which is why the argument that an increasingly complex world renders computers necessary is so fallacious; computerization can only make things even more complicated and intangible, and us more dependent on computers.

6. Baudrillard writes, "We all live by a fanatical idealism of meaning and communication, by an idealism of communication through meaning, and, in this perspective, it is very much *a catastrophe of meaning* which lies in wait for us.

But it must be seen that the term 'catastrophe' has this 'catastrophic' meaning of the end and annihilation only in a linear vision of accumulation and productive finality that the system imposes on us. Etymologically, the term only signifies the curvature, the winding down to the bottom of a cycle leading to what can be called the 'horizon of the event,' to the horizon of meaning, beyond which we cannot go. Beyond it, nothing takes place *that has meaning for us* — but it suffices to exceed this ultimatum of meaning in order that catastrophe no longer appear as the last nihilistic day of reckoning, such as it functions in our current collective fantasy." And elsewhere: "Are the mass media on the side of power in the manipulation of the masses, or are they on the side of the masses in the liquidation of meaning, in the violence done to meaning and in the fascination that results? Is it the media which induce fascination in the masses, or is it the masses which divert the media into spectacle? . . . The media carry meaning and nonsense; they manipulate in every sense simultaneously. The process cannot be controlled, for the media convey the simulation internal to the system and the simulation destructive of the system according to a logic that is absolutely Moebian and circular — and this is exactly what it is like. There is no alternative to it, no logical resolution. Only a logical *exacerbation* and a catastrophic resolution." ("The Implosion of Meaning in the Media," in *In the Shadow of the Silent Majorities*)

Anarchist Perspective on Film

Susan White

What does it mean to watch, or, for that matter, make films from an anarchist perspective? Although some films effectively present anarchist ideas (Jean Vigo's *Zero for Conduct*) or recount the history of an anarchist episode (Pacific Street's *The Free Voice of Labor* or Hector Olivera's *La Patagonia Rebelde*), too often the films rely on stereotypes about anarchism (Lena Wertmuller's *Love and Anarchy* or Louis Malle's *Le Voleur*). Some widely distributed films such as Giulano Montaldo's *Sacco and Vanzetti* ignore the political identity of the characters depicted, and some films are simply not distributed in mainstream theaters.

We can look to European and Latin American cinema for anarchistic approaches — The anti-bourgeois films of Luis Bunuel (*The Discreet Charm of the Bourgeoisie, That Obscure Object of Desire, The Andalousian Dog, The Golden Age*) reflect a strongly anarchistic approach to the Spanish (and French, and Mexican) society they lampoon. Even the films of Jean-Luc Godard, though they sometimes seem more Marxist than anarchist in perspective, often escape the narrow boundaries of Maoism to embrace a broader vision (*Alphaville, Hail Mary*). Margarethe von Trotta's *Marianne and Juliane* concerns a Marxist terrorist and her sister, but can be read for anarchist overtones. And almost every film by Rainer Werner Fassbinder can be read for anarchist content, though often in a very problematic form. But to answer the second part of the opening question, to *make* films from a truly anarchist point of view, and to have them widely distributed requires political insight, personal vision, an understanding of prevailing economic circumstances, perseverance, and luck. It is rare that all of these factors coincide, though there are many films that successfully portray actions that must be called anarchistic, even if the participants would not describe themselves as such — environmental and con-sumer activism, resistance of the corporate structures, women and minorities taking oppressive situations into their own hands in order to "take back the night." Fortunately, watching films, even mainstream films, anarchistically is not as difficult as making them. Indeed, ac-tively anarchistic spectatorship can be cheap, easy, and fun. You may even trick people into questioning their own values by discussing films with them from an anarchist perspective — a perspective that is the most powerful available tool for analysis.

Why is anarchism such a powerful investigatory tool? Because it lays bare the fundamental power structures at work in any cultural production — including film — without privileging any particular determinants, such as the economy (as does Marxism) or the person-ality of the filmmakers (as do many critics). Anarchism uses what's there, focusing on current situations rather than on dogma. This does not mean that anarchists ignore history. On the contrary: anarchists view history as a living entity and recognize the fluidity of social forces. There is no waiting until the "right moment" to effect political change. Every moment, and every person, can be a means of contributing to the empowerment of ordinary people, the dissolution of oppressive structures, the enhancement of world justice. And these ends (the shift-ing of power structures, the achievement of justice) cannot be brought about through "temporary" denial of human rights or at the expense of "expendable" minorities (as can happen in democracies). Such tem-porary devices of change rigidify, becoming permanent wounds in the psyche of the people.

How can principles such as the ones outlined above be brought to bear on film criticism? And — a question relevant to my own life and practice — what is the effect of performing such criticism within the context of academic institutions, the Hollywood film industry, or the popular press? If we are functioning within what Marxists have called the "ideological apparatuses of the state," how can we really critique its cultural products? In the last twenty years, academic film criticism has been "radicalized" by feminism, deconstructionism, and Marxism. I will discuss some of the important contributions made by radical academics to the study of film. Still, a rule of thumb (sustained by my own experience) is that these are fundamentally conservative (and self-perpetuating) institutions. It's not that the analyses made in them are inaccurate, though if one limits oneself to an academic audi-ence or to a discourse that is radically chic among academics but not available to others, one's influence will likely be negligible outside those circles. Still, although a radical film teacher in a college setting or a protester of a racist commercial film may only get so far working within the confines of these institutions, it seems nevertheless consistent with anarchist philosophy to make the effort to erode those institutions from within. Indeed, deconstructive critics would hold that the dominant discourses of the West (its philosophies, literature, scientific language, etc.) by definition do erode themselves from within, just as Marxism sees the capitalist system as ultimately falling prey to its inner "contradictions." Anarchist thought can use the insights provided by these points of view, without either confining itself to the hallowed few or waiting for those contradictions to "ripen." What most academics (and Hollywood producers) underestimate is the curiosity people have about the conditions of their own lives, and their ability to understand the structures that produce those conditions. I have seen this hundreds of times in the classroom: students who thought they were indifferent to the political agenda of the science fiction film, or the sexual politics of melodrama suddenly see how their own way of thinking has been formed by these narratives. They want to know more; their relation to visual images is forever changed.

Obviously, people other than college students and readers of *Variety* and *The Village Voice* should be given the ability to understand the visual images bombarding them daily. Thus, it's important to open dialogues outside the academy. People can learn how films both reflect and impact on their lives even if they have only the most minimal understanding of film technique and political history. Coffeehouses and bars, alternative and even mainstream presses, classrooms, and living rooms are the proper setting for such discussions. Unfortunately, there is much about the medium of film that can be seen as *resistant* to analysis. Spectators are herded, for the most part, into large "multiplexes," where conversation can take place only in the (overpriced) popcorn line, and where viewers sit passively before enormous screens, drinking in whatever image offers itself. But this horrifying vision, reminiscent of the Marxist Frankfurt School's notion (during the 40s-70s) that, under capitalism, popular culture is irredeemably an apparatus for state control of the masses, can be, and indeed *is* subverted on a daily basis. More and more critics think that it is demeaning to dismiss utterly the popular forms that have somehow provided entertainment and comfort for the majority of people. We are learning to look for revolutionary messages in soap operas — and they are there! Although the "heartbeat of America" can have conservative, sexist, racist, even fascist rhythms, there are also impulses of justice and a suspicion of being manipulated that can grow into a strong perception of the political realities. One might even find cause to be optimistic in observing incidents such as the following: groans often accompany the visually hypnotic American Express commercials now appended to the previews at many theaters around the U.S. As was the case with pay toilets (now almost obsolete), Americans' resistance of poorly disguised commercials in movie theaters may prevent this additional channeling of our attention onto consumerism from becoming entrenched. The large foyers of multiplexes would be a great forum for protest or discussion of films — the mind boggles at the possibilities.

Before the reader thinks that he or she can only respond anarchistically to a film by creating a furor in the popcorn line of a multiplex theater, let's return to the more mundane picture of film analysis/criticism we were sketching above. In trying to open discussion about a film with friends or family members, one often comes up against another form of resistance characteristic of peoples' attitudes towards film: that one's pleasure is diminished if the film is analyzed too closely. The opposite is in fact true, but discussion must proceed gently and address people's real reactions to the film in question (I have to resist yelling at my sisters for liking *Steel Magnolias*, for example. And why do I like *Dragnet*? Are these only guilty pleasures?). One notion recent feminist criticism has brought to film study is that films that seem to portray women as masochistically obsessed with male approval often actually express the frustrations of women with male oppression. This would be, then, the opposite of the "Frankfurt School" approach in that it assumes that people are not taken in by the defeatist messages of the films they watch, but may be using the films (and television) in a way that is not obviously apparent. Many melodramas that depict a suffering heroine (*Steel Magnolias, Stella Dallas, Mary Hartman. Mary Hartman*) actually dwell on her strength — if only the strength for sacrifice — and emphasize her emotional superiority over the man she loves. The women in 1940s film noir (*Gilda, Double Indemnity, Out of the Past*) are vilified as "black widow spiders" who prey on men, yet they are also vital and sexually-alive women, whose forceful images linger in our memories even after their demise.

On the other hand, not every film can be rescued from the negative messages it conveys, though there's always room for argument (a good reason why censorship is so problematic). Sociological and psychoanalytic film criticism have taught us to see hostility towards women and ethnic minorities in films that seem superficially to be about space aliens, successful career women, and other familiar cinematic figures. In *Invasion of the Body Snatchers* (particularly the 1956 version), people's bodies are being taken over by giant pods which replicate them and then destroy the "original." A close look at the film reveals many subliminal cues that women — especially sexually active women — are really the "alien force" that is to be feared. In the recent film *Working Girl*, the lower-class career "girl" makes her way up the ladder of success, but only at the expense of her (female) yuppie boss. One might look at this as a triumph of the working class over the ruling class — but an even stronger implication is that women become evil ballbreakers when they are "given" any power. *Dances With Wolves* depicts the life of the Sioux in a way that has almost never been achieved for any Native American group in the history of the U.S. film industry. However, the Sioux are presented as admirable in contrast to the Pawnees, who are "bad Indians" sold out to the whites, in Costner's interpretation. An anarchist vision can discern this subtle denigration of what the film seems to praise, while recognizing that even a partial victory (the use of a genuine Indian language in a mainstream U.S. film, even though it was the wrong language) may have real significance.

Film and television are excellent media for the exercising of anarchist theory. Even the slightest bit of visual awareness gives people the ability to control the kind of information, and ultimately the ideologies that are forming their thoughts, opinions, and desires. Anarchism can take advantage of its flexibility to incorporate theory and approach from many disciplines and walks of life, all in the interest of self-determination, equality and justice.

Poetry

Glenda Morris

I want to write political poetry.
Propaganda to change the world.
Poems about nuclear power,
imperialism, racism and capitalism.

Instead I write:
love poems,
personal poems
celebrating life,
exposing my worries.

Will I every write poems
to change people's lives?
Will I ever write real poetry
or just prose
chopped into lines?

(October, 1982)

ANARCHOMUSICOLOGY AND PARTICIPATION

CHARLES KEIL

Musicking is practical action and an ultimate mystery as it models anarchy in cultures all over the world: the jam session, the polka party (Keil, Keil and Blau 1992), the tribal ceremony. It is this leaderless grooving (Feld and Keil 1994) on each other and on the natural world through music which can give all of us the best possible understanding of the participatory consciousness which was all of consciousness before civilization and its attendent oppressions/alienations distorted our thoughts and feelings in ways that thousands of books on capital accumulation and mental illness have not adequately described.

"The Bororo (neighboring tribe) boast that they are red araras (parakeets). This does not merely signify that after their death they become araras, nor that araras are metamorphosed Bororos, and must be treated as such. It is something entirely different. 'The Bororos', says Von den Steinen, who would not believe it, but finally had to give in to their explicit affirmations, 'give one rigidly to understand that they are araras *at the present time*, just as if a caterpillar declared itself to be a butterfly."

Levy-Bruhl in *How Natives Think* (1966).

＊＊＊

"Bo Diddley Bo Diddley have you heard
My pretty baby said she was a bird."

Bo Diddley in "Bo Diddley"

***

"Participation begins by being an activity, and essentially a communal or social activity. It takes place in rites and initiation ceremonies resulting in (quoting Durkheim) 'collective mental states of extreme emotional intensity, in which representation is as yet undifferentiated from the movements and actions which make the communion towards which it tends a reality to the group. Their participation is so effectively *lived* that it is not yet properly imagined.

This stage is not only pre-logical, but also pre-mythical. It is anterior to collective representations themselves, as I have been using the term. Thus, the first development Durkheim traces is from symbiosis or active participation (where the individual feels he is the totem) to collective representations of the totemic type (where the individual feels that his ancestors were the totem, that he wil be when he dies, etc.) From this symbolic apprehension he then arrives at the duality, with which we are more familiar, of ideas on the one hand and numinous religion on the other."

Owen Barfield in Saving the Appearances (1965)

***

"doin' the do. . . . "

James Brown

I have chosen "participation" as the key term, but almost any term from the left column in the following page of contrasts could serve as well because that's the name of the game or the game of the name: conceptual merging and consubstantiation are what participatory consciousness is all about.

food vs. famine (F.M. Lappe)
dromenon vs. drama (J.E. Harrison)
participation vs. alienation (O. Barfield)
antiabolitionism vs. progressivism (K. Burke)
pleasure vs. power (M. French)
players vs. professionals (Airto)
life vs. death (Freud/Brown/Dinnerstein)
natural world vs. legal world (Haudenosaunee)
spiritual vs. utilitarian (J. Rifkin)

material vs. ideal (K. Marx)
sacrament vs. entropy (G. Bateson)
culture vs. civilization (E. Sapir)
process vs. product (R. Williams)
incorporative vs. exclusionary (C. Ellis)
system B vs. system A (S. Gooch)
immanence vs. transcendence (S. de Beauvoir)
mind and nature enough vs. projects (A. Keil)
intensional vs. extensional (A. Chester)
process & texture vs. syntax (C. Keil)
lift-up-over-sounding vs. unison (S. Feld)
downtown vs. uptown (S. Feld)
the beach and cold beer vs. taking inventory (Olavo Alen Rodriguez)
discrepancies vs. addiction to perfection
speaking-in-unknown-tongues vs. writing in insider jargon
song & dance routines vs. serious music
(coated) feelings vs. meanings (coded)
associational brain vs. logical brain
audio vs. visual
acoustic vs. amplified
live vs. mediated
rites vs. rights
wrights vs. writes
crafts vs. arts
hack vs. genius
humility vs. hubris
interlocking vs. vivisection
"changing same" vs. "contrived variation"
repetition vs. innovation
pre-Dionysian vs. post-Apollonian
pre-Socratic vs. post-Platonic
felicitous merging vs. control over
"present time" vs. false pasts/futures
(suspended time, Dreamtime) vs. (His-story, tech fixes)
ancestors/7th generation vs. "gimme now"
we belong to land vs. land belongs to us
synthetic vs. analytic
organic vs. formal
flux vs. fixity
diversity vs. monomania
ecology vs. cancer
equality vs. hierarchy

what it is vs. dualisms
party time vs. trance-in-dance

These dualities are not presented here in order to be dialectically struggled into higher syntheses. The stuff on the left is mostly good and part of the solution. The stuff on the right is mostly bad and part of the problem. I am urging you to put more thought, energy, feeling into the left side and to simply leave the other side alone for a while. Participate. Do what feels good for you. Celebrate life. Move on down the left hand column affirming and encouraging and don't even bother to "critique" or protest the stuff on the right; if you do, it will suck you into its orbit quickly and before you know it you'll be making Faustian deals to compose and conduct great symphonies of transcendence and liberation. Some of the stuff on the right is very powerful and magnetic; it can keep you from developing your best instincts and insounds year after year after year and it has kept a participatory paradigm shift from occuring for some decades.

Participate. Break out the drums, sing for the unborn 7th generation and try to get everybody dancing. Is this mosaic of notes and quotes (or anything else you see in print) moving us toward a revitalization of human rites in tune with the natural world, toward a world in which no children starve to death and ALL children learn to sing, dance, and drum superlatively well? If it isn't, put it aside and participate.

I believe that a major and long overdue paradigm shift is underway. An alternative and applied sociomusicology as earthshaking as plate tectonics in geology is emerging, finally. Conceivably it could have emerged with the Parisian polkamania in March of 1844. A pamphlet was published soon after the polkamania broke loose which described a ballerina kicking off her shoes to join the crowd, but the revolutions of 1848 turned bourgeois nationalist and failed. The paradigm might have emerged with the collapse of serious music in the early 20th century, if there had been a supranational revolution then. It might have emerged with the collapse of jazz and rock in the late 1960s, if the Paris spring of 1968, or the New Left, had been able to trigger a transformation of the world order.

Where has the evidence been piling up for a paradigm shift? Keil and Chester articles ask for it in the 60s. Blacking's *How Musical is Man?* (1976) almost asks the right question. If Dorothy Dinnerstein had steeped herself in the ethnomusicology of classless societies, *The Forest People* (Turnbull 1961) and ecological thinking, her *Mermaid and Minotaur* (1976) might have done the job. The nearly simultaneous publication of *Whose Music?*(Shepherd et al), Chris Small's wonderful ecological chapters in *Music: Society: Education* and R. Murray Schafer's *Tuning of the World* in 1977 might be considered the shift itself, so many minds arriving near the same place at the same time. But again, this seems more of a chorus calling for new ways of understanding and making music, rejecting many of the Western definitions and conventions to be sure, but without putting a new paradigm in place. Much that has been written since 1977 has further clarified what is fundamentally wrong about written down visually fixated departmentalized music on the one hand and what is promising but continually commodified by the consciousness industry on the other. But moving back and forth between deconstructing high culture's music and criticizing popular culture's music, is to stay stuck in negation. The participatory paradigm is elsewhere.

What we have to put together is not just a theory of music-and-society as they are, but enactments of music-society-environment (environment including here the surrounding mosaic of societies) **as we would like it to be in our neighborhood**. Locality by locality. All over the globe and soon.

More recently I have been getting this participatory approach or paradigm from Colin Turnbull's chapter "The Politics of Non-Aggression" (in A. Montagu, *Learning Non-Aggression* 1978), from Steve Feld's *Sound and Sentiment* (1982), the Kaluli picking up their music from the birds and neighboring peoples, from Catherine Ellis' *Aboriginal Music: Education for Life* (1985), from Morris Berman's *The Reenchantment of the World* (1981), and finally, constantly, from the ecocatastrophe, our civilization in crisis, and the green movement's response to all this.

✳ ✳ ✳

It hit me hard during the funeral service for a young man who committed suicide, that Christianity is about killing a young man in the springtime, a Father sacrificing his son for mysterious higher purposes. (Out of womb envy? Pretending to control fertility? "Holy Mary Mother of God. . . blessed is the fruit of thy womb, Jesus.") Dionysius. Osiris. The king must die in these "first kingdoms." And those middle eastern monotheisms somehow keep this patriarchal death trip going today.

The relatively egalitarian Tiv people of central Nigeria, whom I lived with for a year or so in the 1960s, also believe that fathers sacrifice children by sorcery. This patriarchal human sacrifice idea goes deep, as deep as settling down to do agriculture and animal "husbandry," to plant and breed for surpluses. As deep as not resolving conflicts when they occur but harboring grievances, projections, displacements, witchcraft accusations.

In otherwise egalitarian societies in Papua New Guinea and in the Amazon, men learn to fear women's menstruation, to envy women's wombs, and they hide themselves away in the flute house to initiate boys, often brutalize would be a more accurate verb, into becoming men like themselves. Music, songs to learn and sacred tubes to blow, is at the very heart of these man-making processes. Girls in their blessed immanence become women automatically.

Hence "*pre*-Dionysian" on the good list. We need local interlocked, incorporative, music rites that celebrate a forest we no longer live in, that affirm a nomadic exploration of that remembered forest, that accept a wildness and wilderness we can rarely experience first hand; pre-sacrificial rites of passage to and from our human nature. Lacking enough forests, our very survival may depend on creating these musics that "remind" us.

✳✳✳

Groove AS grove! And not the grove of academe.

✳✳✳

Are men still lost in the flute house today? Ellen Koskoff came to a "Music in Daily Life" class I was teaching and toward the end of her talk began to speak of how important it was for her to listen to music by herself, how hard it was to share a listening experience with someone. This struck a responsive chord with a couple of women in the class, a guy piped up to say sharing was what it was about for him, I remembered how very much I enjoyed sharing jazz records as a kid, etc. So we went around the room of twenty students and every woman had some deep convictions about listening alone and every man declared that listening with others was more satisfying. Getting into the specifics of men's experience it became clear that "male-bonding" might be a better description than "sharing" and the specifics of women's experience revealed much living room space fully occupied with men's music and women listening only after the men have left or "mostly when I'm alone in the car."

✳✳✳

"The last three thousand years of mankind have been an excursion into ideals, bodilessness, and tragedy and now

the excursion is over. . . . it is a question, practically, of relationship. We *must* get back into relation, vivid and nour-
ishing relation to the cosmos. . . . The way is through daily
ritual, and the reawakening."

D. H. Lawrence

✳ ✳ ✳

The "critical" path to follow from the pile of polarities might be
to explore the terms in the right column that you think still have some
socially redeeming virtues e.g. "transcendence," "meanings," "serious music," "civilization" or even "power." But I'll leave that to those
persevering deconstructionists who can't take time to get into a local
participatory groove.

✳ ✳ ✳

"Who needs transcendence if you have glorious immanence?"
says Angie Keil. Musical experience is not like science-in-service-to-
technology with its narrow goals in linear sequences of historical
progress. Music is phatic, saying 'we are here and now.' Good music
is emphatic, 'we are here in ways that feel good to everyone, bound
by the group to present time, enjoying the sound of each person and
all together.' Science-serving-technology segments the continuum and
tries to innovate at every segment. This may be where our ideas about
"transcendence" are coming from. But science-as-appreciation-of-wild-
ness, all the interconnectedness, the interlocking, is about immanence
and a lot like the good emphatic music we need.

✳ ✳ ✳

Those Reich and Glass versions of "interlock" are so ugly because they are static white male controlling parodies of responses to
this desperate need of ours. And the mass mediated substitutes for
participation are just as disgusting.

✳ ✳ ✳

It can't be another "project," not even a male enterprise to end
all male enterprises.

✳ ✳ ✳

Translator's Footnote from *The Second Sex*(1949):

"This word [immanence], frequently used by the author,
always signifies, as here, the opposite or negation of tran-

scendence, such as confinement or restriction to a narrow round of uncreative and repetitive duties; it is in contrast to the freedom to engage in projects of ever widening scope that marks the untrammeled existent."

Have eco-feminists or gyn-ecologists reinterpreted all the statements about "transcendence" and "immanence" in Simone de Beauvoir's book in the light of our need for sustainable economies, "cool cultures" and participatory approaches to music and life?

✳ ✳ ✳

Antiabolitionists like Kenneth Burke insist that the agricultural, urban, industrial and electric-atomic revolutions did not abolish our primary human nature. They just distorted, repressed, oppressed, depressed and alienated it. Both the conventional bourgeois or capitalist wisdom about civilization and progress (the arts and sciences continually advancing our understanding and control of the universe, etc.) and the Marxist or communist or "critical" conventional wisdom about civilization and progress (the arts and sciences continually advancing our understanding and control of the universe if only those reactionaries would get out of the way) assume that a "New Man" emerges with each historic phase, that each phase abolishes the previous sociocultural formation, that feudalism abolishes primitive communism, that capitalism abolishes feudalism, and, if you're a Marxist or a utopian socialist, that communism will one day abolish capitalism. We antiabolitionists see this history as a recent layering of distortions and oppressions, and we assume that all of us are aching to get out from under these temporary hierarchical straitjackets and back to our naturally egalitarian and diverse processes. From this perspective, the biggest superstar must still do what the local shaman did five, twenty or fifty thousand years ago and is still doing today in many parts of the world: cure us with an incantation, manipulate the participatory discrepancies that will involve us, suck up the evil within us and spit it out, restore our sense of being in complete solidarity with a corporate group, and so forth (R. Taylor, *The Death and Resurrection Show*, 1985).

✳ ✳ ✳

Thinkers of fine reputation often dismiss the participatory approach as "romantic," "primitivist," "Rousseauian," "mystical," "spiritualist," "idealist," "essentialist" and so forth. Some of these adjectives fit. Barfield's *Saving the Appearances* is certainly the result of long and fruitful meditations on Goethe, Romanticism, Rudolph Steiner's anthroposophical treatises; and if I had to pick one philosophical exercise that grounds a participatory approach to music it would be this Barfield book (with but a few words of warning about the plunge into Christian mysticism toward the end). Yes to "primitivist" in the sense of Stanley Diamond's *In Search of the Primitive*. Yes to Rousseau too.

But these other adjectives need careful definition. When the Haudenosaunee explain what they mean by "the spiritual as the political" it coincides with a broad biodeterminism, respect for all the life forms, a very concrete, practical concern and responsibility for the material conditions that sustain our species in relation to all other species. Isn't this rational? Real science? More in touch with reality than Star Wars planners, NASA engineers, germ-warfare experimenters, gene-splicers, tech-fixers of a thousand different specialties? The principles of interlocking and inclusion, shared by aboriginals and indigenes everywhere, are distinguished as "spiritual," "mysterious," "essential" once the context of hot power-mad societies raping the planet for the last penny of profit becomes clear. I suspect that in their own terms, pre-contact, songs and dromenon (the thing pre-done, done and re-done) about belonging to the land had more to do with what we now call "immanence" (the inherent, the within, the potential) than with what we now call "transcendence."

> "Consubstantiation is not mumbo jumbo. Life is one piece. They say we share a lot of DNA with rabbits and amoebas. We are made of star dust I guess. There is more information in a tree than in the library I am told. 'They say', 'I guess', 'I am told', because I can't quite believe it. Our language makes so many distinctions, more coming all the time, making the oneness of life appear as multiplicity. The multiplicities of language have become unbalanced, every distinction becoming the basis of an exploding technology. While the multiplicity of nature tends toward ecological balance. So language, with its hard-won and addictive distinctions, is lying to us about core reality more and more. We have a deep biological need for the biological truth that our languaged consciousness denies us."

> Angeliki V. Keil

✳ ✳ ✳

rites : rights :: wrights : writes
      REITS
(Real Estate Investment Trusts)

This formula describes how it is. It's time to turn it over and divide up the real estate in terms of our expressive needs.

✳✳✳

If the BaMbuti pygmies have to sing and *molimo* night after night from dusk to dawn for some weeks to wake up the forest and restore equilibrium after a single death or loss, how much singing, dancing and ceremony will we need to rebalance ourselves after Auschwitz, Hiroshima, Biafra, etc.? If the administrative massacres had never occurred and the burden of history did not need to be lifted first, if these atrocities were not continuing in forty countries today, how much song and dance time will it take to cure us of the day-to-day hurts this civilization currently inflicts on each of us?

✳✳✳

The alternative musicology is simply helping people, especially very young people, to make music (play-sing-dance).

I am constantly amazed by how far the music department caste system (singular, there is only one music department) has departed from this obvious mission. Composers sit at the top of the totem pole and create for all us sub-geniuses. Theorists have some importance for trying to explain what composers do. Historians are respectable working-class clerks who chronicle and document the doings of the great men above. Way below historians are mere performers, usually hired part-time, a little lumpen and parasiti,c really; too bad we have to divert resources to them. And finally, in the departments where they have not been kept out altogether, the untouchables, music educators.

In self-defense many music educators armor themselves in the psychological statistics of nearly hard science. They study the statistical procedures appropriate to the measurement of the psychopedagogical techniques used to develop the appreciation skills of kids listening to written-down music as recorded and then played on a record player in a classroom. How many layers of reification is that? Eight? Ten? "Hey Dr. Advanced Music Educator, could I beat this drum a coupla times?"

✳✳✳

Helping children to make music is easy. Just be there. Participate. Do the do. Incorporate the Muses.

Two or three of us Greens were drumming at an anti-styrofoam save-the-ozone demonstration in front of McDonald's when a little girl about 4 came up and took a penny whistle from my bag, figured out how to finger the top hole to get two tones, and began dancing to her own melody in time to the drumming. Her little sister, three, picked up a can full of rice and shook it as she bounced along behind her sister. I was drumming and suddenly realized that all the thinking and speculating I had been doing for years about the "best possible" or "right sequence" of learning for pre-schoolers and primary schoolers had been a waste of time.

✳ ✳ ✳

Wrights. Participatory discrepancies (Feld and Keil 1994). The key to it all. Shaking a little can of rice in time and then shaking it a tiny bit more or less than in time. A twist of the wrist, a slight hitch to it, and everybody wants to dance. Airto's touch on a tambourine: how can one person sound like a whole samba school on the march? Will Kenny Clark's "tap" on a ride cymbal or John Coltrane's "tone" ultimately be considered more of a miracle than all nine Beethoven symphonies?

✳ ✳ ✳

"There is no wrong way to sing. There is no wrong way to dance either. To laugh at someone's singing or dancing would be to laugh at the Creator and who would be so foolish?" I have found these wise thoughts from the Haudenosaunee tradition very encouraging, even after attending an Iroquois social dance and suspecting that the Creator herself might be laughing at some of our sillier paleface footwork. It turns out there is always room for improvement in singing and dancing, a better relation to the people around you and to the natural world. Let us set about finding it, brightening the corners where we are. Participate.

References

Barfield, Owen.1965 *Saving the Appearances: A Study in Idolatry*. New York: Harcourt Brace Jovanovich.

Bateson, Gregory. 1972 *Steps to an Ecology of Mind*. New York: Ballantine.

Blacking, John. 1973 *How Musical is Man?* Seattle: University of Washington Press.

Beauvoir, Simone de. 1949 *The Second Sex*. Paris: Librairie Gallimard.

Berman, Morris. 1984 *The Reenchantment of the World*. New York: Bantam Books.

Brown, Norman O. 1959 *Life Against Death*. Middletown, CT. Wesleyan University Press.

Chester, Andrew. 1970 "Second Thoughts on a Rock Aesthetic: The Band." *New Left Review*, No. 62.

Diamond, Stanley.1974 *In Search of the Primitive.* New Brunswick: Transaction.

Dinnerstein, Dorothy. 1976 *The Mermaid and the Minotaur: Sexual Arrangements and Human Malaise.* New York: Harper and Row.

Ellis, Catherine. 1985 *Aboriginal Music: Education for Living.* St. Lucia: University of Queensland Press.

Feld, Steven. 1988 "Aesthetics as iconicity of style, or, 'Lift-up-over sounding': Getting into the Kaluli groove." *Yearbook of Traditional Music 20.* (Also in Steven Feld and Charles Keil 1994.)

———.1982 *Sound and Sentiment: Birds, Weeping, Poetics and Song in Kaluli Expression.* Philadelphia: University of Pennsylvania Press.

Feld, Steven and Charles Keil. 1994 *Music Grooves.* Chicago: University of Chicago Press.

French, Marilyn. 1985 *Beyond Power.* New York: Summit Books.

Gooch, Stan. 1972 *Total Man: Notes towards an Evolutionary Theory of Personality.* London: Allen Lane, Penguin Press.

Harrison, Jane Ellen. 1903 *Prolegomena to the Study of Greek Religion.* Cambridge.

Haudenosaunee. 1978 *The Basic Call to Consciousness.* Rooseveltown: Akwesasne Notes.

Keil, Charles, Angeliki V. Keil and Richard Blau. 1992 *Polka Happiness.* Philadelphia: Temple University Press.

Levy-Bruhl, Lucien. 1966 *How Natives Think.* New York: Washington Square Press.

Rifkin, Jeremy with Ted Howard. 1980 *Entropy: A New World View.* New York: Viking.

Sapir, Edward. 1924 "Culture, Genuine and Spurious" in *American Journal of Sociology, 29.* (Also in *Selected Writings of Edward Sapir,* David G. Mandelbaum, Ed. Berkeley: University of California Press, 1985.)

Schafer, R. Murray. 1977 *The Tuning of the World.* New York: Alfred A. Knopf.

Shepherd, John et al. 1977 *Whose Music? A Sociology of Musical Languages.* New Brunswick, NJ: Transaction Books.

Small, Christopher. 1977 *Music: Society: Education.* London: John Calder.

Taylor, Rogan. 1985 T*he Death and Resurrection Show.* London: Anthony Blond.

Turnbull, Colin. 1978 "The Politics of Learning Non-Aggression (Zaire)" in Ashley Montagu, Ed. *Learning Non-Aggression: The Experience of Non-Literate Societies.* New York: Oxford University Press.

———. 1961 *The Forest People.* New York: Simon and Schuster.

Williams, Raymond. 1973 "Base and Superstructure in Marxist Cultural Theory" *New Left Review 85.*

Jazz — Circling in Anarchism

Terri Clark

Sh ba bau —. Sh da da da ba ba bau; sh boo boo bau. — Sh bat an day doe, jau um jau jau, um. sh gong gonggg — —. Bau!

I am: third generation heir to the legacy of Lucy Parsons, Black anarchist; inheritor of the Ma Rainey tradition, independent woman, sometimes rowdy, singing my own world blues; seeking to speak in blood and radical politics in the sophisticated Black musical webs of Abbe Lincoln; dreadheaded and renegade singing in the magical rhythms of reggae, sistren to Judy Mowatt; wanting to gather up myself, call up the folk and traditions from Africa to America and telling stories of their resistance like I'm kin to Bernice Reagon; lesbian, child of myself. I face the rising sun of inspiration and I bask in the moonlight of lunacy and I pour libations for the spirits that speak to and through me, ancestral, living sisterkin, and daughter energy. But, what I really be about at this time, in this place is the telling of my jazz politic, that is, the politics of making jazz and the jazz in making politics.

Jazz is the classical music of america. It originated here and nowhere else. It is unique to the soils, soul, and borders of the United States and was invented by Black american people. It is also a social commentary on the constant tension of Black america's conflict to remain separate or to assimilate and serves as an indicator of america's hopes and fears. Most importantly it is a tradition of improvisation, of process, of constantly changing products. It is a music of imagining and being.

When I begin to sing a piece, whether I'm working off of a traditional tune or from my own musings, I must have a vision. I must know where I'm going ultimately because I must direct and control my energy along that path. Now getting there is a process that unfolds more than a process I completely control, at least if I'm doing a good improvisation.

The chord changes or patterns are the structures in which I explore musical questions and resolve them. Sometimes there are strict boundaries and sometimes not. The challenge is to establish webs of communication among musicians and listeners and to engage everyone in the process. Through the changes or patterns I initially sing, I say, "Hey, these are the basic structures, environments, and ground rules I'm using to explore a musical idea." By this greeting, the listener is invited to participate in making the soundscape happen. So as I start my improvisation with a phrase like "sha ba ba bau," the listener will hear the phrase and will imagine several resolutions, or wonder in confusion, or relax and wait. As I start my improvisation I must operate in the past, present, and future all at the same time because I must know where I'm taking the music. I am always thinking, what does this phrase mean? What tones will finish this phrase or answer the musical call? What syllables will bring out these tones? I also wonder, am I making skillful bridges from what's gone before to what's coming? What aspect of this musical idea am I exploring and does that make sense? Or even, will I finish this thought now or come back to it? Will they understand?

Hopefully, I will explore the idea in such a way that the resolution will be understandable but somewhat unpredictable to the listener and to myself. This is the timeless novelty of improvising, especially when I'm scatting.

This is the way I create my politics. Like a jazzwoman I learn history, my roots. I study structures and the mechanics of the processes of change, and I become visionary, knowing where I want to go. I realize my vision through a firm set of principles and an ever-changing process based on respect and responsibility. These principles begin with a celebration of the human spirit, a fostering of cooperation among people and between people and the earth, an appreciation of diversity and difference and move to the creation of environments which encourage human evolution and development.

What jazz teaches me about anarchism and feminism is that nothing remains the same, that living is complex, constant motion with cycles and natural changes. It teaches me the essence of process. We must be goal-directed to reach our visions, but we are meant to experiment, for there is no *one* solution to any problem nor, for that matter, is there a guarantee that any solution will work beyond one time. Jazz teaches me that we must engage each other in our visions knowing fully what we can each bring and listening for what others can bring. It means having faith.

The act of scatting points up many of the contradictions bound up in revolutionary politics, questions like: the balance of work and play, of structures/products and process, of history/tradition and originality, and of individuality and group identity/affiliation. These are tensions inherent in movement.

Loving jazz and scatting brought me a gut understanding of anarchism that no words could've. The many flashes of insight and knowledge spring from material and spiritual sources and most certainly from places of love and passion. This is key if we are about changing our lives and the world, because these are the places which give us pride in our past, hope for our future, and strength in the present. They are the best sources for our visions.

So just as I began this improvisation, I finish it with — Bau, bau, bau . . . bau, bau, bau . . . a-click-click, a click-click, gong-kgong, gong — shboody a bau, bau ch kown, ch kown . . . ch, kown kown.

ANARCHIST ART: THE EXAMPLE OF JOHN CAGE

RICHARD KOSTELANETZ

In surveying his work in music and theater, in poetry and visual art, I have noticed that the American John Cage favors a structure that is nonfocused, nonhierarchic and nonlinear, which is to say that his works in various media consist of collections of elements presented without climax and without definite beginnings and ends. This is less a negative structure, even though I am describing it negatively, than a visionary esthetic and political alternative. In creating models of diffusion and freedom, Cage is an anarchist libertarian.

What makes Cage's art special, and to my senses politically original, is that his radical politics are expressed in decisions not of content but of form. For instance, one quality of most works of his for large ensembles is that they do not need a conductor. By extension, Cage is implying that outside of music, as well as in, it is possible to create social mechanisms that likewise can function without conductors, without chiefs. In other words, in the form of his art, in the form of performance, is a representation of an ideal polity.

It is precisely in relinquishing traditional opportunities for authority that Cage is making essentially political decisions. His scores are designed to encourage a greater variety of interpretations than usual. There is no "right way" to do them, though there are wrong ways, especially if a performer violates the instructions that are not left to chance. A second reflection of Cage's politics is writing music for an ensemble of equals, even when he is one of the performers, thereby resisting such conventional hierarchical forms as a soloist with a backup group. (The fact that this last feature was always true indicates to me that Cage subscribed to his egalitarian politics long before he was conscious of them.) Thirdly, the principle of equality extends to the materials of his art. Not only are all notes equal, but all instruments are equal, regardless of their rank in the musical tradition. In *Credo in Us* (1942), for instance, the piano has no more presence than the home radio; all are equidistant from the audience. Fourth, he has performed his music in gymnasiums as well as opera houses, the assumption being that all venues are equally legitimate.

In his book *Notations* (1968), where Cage presents in alphabetical order a single page apiece of scores chosen by contributing composers, the radical assumption is that the editor has no more authority than the reader in assigning value. Nothing is featured by being put ahead of the others, or having its name on the book's cover. The absence of hierarchy and of editorial discrimination in this book likewise reflects his politics. A traditional editor would huffily characterize a book like *Notations* as "an abdication of professional responsibility.") Anyone who has ever worked in theater with Cage knows that he believes every performance venue should have convenient exits so that spectators can leave whenever they wish. Capturing anyone's attention, as we say, is to him no more justifiable in art than in life. One truth of Cage's own functioning is that no one loses anything by relinquishing power, but the essence of his method is not to tell but to show.

With that last point in mind, it is instructive to contrast the anarchism of Cage's art with another masterpiece of anarchist art in our time, the Living Theater's production of *Paradise Now* (1968). Those of us who saw it two decades ago will remember that *Paradise Now* was structured as a series of sketches designed to elicit audience participation. Thus, it opened with the performers reciting testimony of their own imprisonment: "I can't travel without a passport," they repeatedly proclaimed, confronting and challenging the audience to respond with argument or shocked acceptance. "I am not allowed to take off my clothes." "I don't know how to stop the war," they kept on repeating. From this purgatory the performers progress to sketches of liberation, which is paradise, culminating with members of the audience being invited onstage to leap into the locked arms of male company members. Structurally, this play is dialectical, moving from antithesis to synthesis; and in this respect, it differs from Cage who hasn't presented any antitheses, as far as I can tell, in at least forty years.

Another difference is that *Paradise Now* is preachy, Julian Beck even telling us that we've been offered glimpses of the postrevolutionary age. Cage, by contrast, shows instead of tells, for his assumption is that, in the world represented by his art, the Promised Land has come. When asked about his response to such programmatic political music as Frederic Rzewski's, he has said, "I have difficulty with it, because it's so pushy. It has precisely in it what government has in it: the desire to control; and it leaves no freedom for me. It pushes me toward its conclusion, and I'd rather be a sheep, which I'm not, than be pushed along by a piece of music. I'm just as angry, or refusing to go along with the 'Hallelujah Chorus' as I am with the Attica one [by Rzewski]. The moment I hear that kind of music I go in the opposite direction. And they use the technique of repetition, and of sequence, incessantly [as did the Living Theater, I should add]. And I can do without that."

One thing that fascinates me about Cage is the purity of his anarchism. His perceptions are true to his politics; in neither his speech nor his behavior do you find the kinds of contradictions and compromise that some political people think are opportune for ultimate ends. He is utterly free of pretenses to superior humanity and thus false snobbism (and in these respects so utterly different from his sometime protege Morton Feldman). I've always regarded Cage as epitomizing the noncompetitive life, where no one is regarded as a threat who must be eliminated, where you can afford to be generous with your own work as well as your possessions, and to do work so extreme and idiosyncratic that plagiarism need not be feared. As he has always made a point of publishing his writings in small magazines as well as large, assuming that the putative "reputation" of any venue affects him not, it is not surprising that his recent creative piece on the Satie Society bypasses book-publishing entirely to become available gratis, but only through the modem on your home computer. Even his philosophy is true to his politics, at a time when, to paraphrase Barnett Newman, philosophy is for the artist, especially for some painters nowadays, much as the Bible is to the minister, which is to say a respectable source that can be used to justify anything. I recently read scores of interviews with him and have never found Cage saying anything about his art that was demonstrably false.

It is scarcely surprising that in his own professional life he has resisted not only titles and accompanying power but servility, being neither a boss nor an employee, but instead both, or more precisely, a small businessman with a peripheral relation to another small business that didn't give him much power (or until recently make much money) — I'm thinking of the Merce Cunningham Dance Company. In other words, even in his own life there has been an absence of antitheses. In 1989 Harvard offered him a professorship, which gives him one of those titles purportedly raising its bearer above the nonprofessors; but this is false to our politics, comrade. Especially if, John, you are to be talking about anarchy, as I've heard, you must insist upon being called the Charles Eliot Norton *Person* of Poetry. (Remember, John, that England's anarchist movement went through a divisory crisis in 1953, when Herbert Read accepted a knighthood!)

Another quality I admire about Cage is that, especially in contrast to many postsocialists of his generation, he has never doubled back. He has never said that an earlier position of his was now unacceptably radical. As a result, he's never been an ex-anything in either esthetics or politics. His art, as I noted before, has always displayed the anarchist characteristics I'm defining here. I would judge that one reason for his confidence now, in politics as well as esthetics, is that he knew from the beginning that he was never wrong, which I hasten to add is not the same thing as being always right, especially in politics.

One Cagean tactic that always puzzled me in reading interviews with him is how he will often rationalize an esthetic move in terms not of ideology but simply of social benefit. Let me quote an example from my new Cage book, *Conversing with Cage*, where he says of his *Freeman Etudes* for violin: "They are intentionally as difficult as I can make them, because I think we're now surrounded by very serious problems in the society, and we tend to think that the situation is hopeless and that it's just impossible to do something that will make everything turn out properly. So I think that this music, which is almost impossible, gives an instance of the practicality of the impossible. "

Once I recognized this tendency toward social rationalization in Cage's commentary, I was skeptical about it, thinking it might represent a certain opportunism; but the more often I see it, I have come to recognize Cage as someone who came of age in the 1930s, when ideas about social betterment through art were more plentiful. To me, Cage is essentially a thirties lefty, more interesting than others who came out of that period because he made some original perceptions not only about art, but especially about the place of politics in art, and then the possible role of art for politics, all the while remaining true to the sentiment of that time. In my sense of Cage, Zen and chance and everything else came afterwards; they are merely icing on this anarchist cake.

7

LIBERATION
OF SELF

Johann Humyn Being; originally appeared in Anarchy #39 Winter 94

He Plays with the Future

The little boy's toys are very real to him. He plays at fueling hostilities between Middle Eastern countries. He sails his ships into the sovereign waters of foreign nations, heightening tensions. His automobiles run on fuel that is constantly fluctuating in price, mostly upwards, due to the increasing costs of policing these foreign waters. All the while, he is being educated in a great modern phenomenon — today's corporate/military power play.

Through his play, he is learning the importance of control and manipulation, military intervention and the art of wielding "the Big Stick.' The ability to pull the strings of everyone from his Dad to foreign heads of state. That's the power of petroleum.

Right now, his learning process is steadily being twisted and maneuvered into believing that this sort of total control from petroleum manipulation is usual and necessary for the effective money and power gains connected with a multinational dominated superpower. This indoctrination will continue and heighten until he is eligible to enter the corporate or military world of which he now fantasizes. When the little boy grows up, he will be fully prepared to play with the future and manipulate it to his own ends.

Petroleum helps to build a better life, for those who control it.

graphic from **Stealworks: The Graphic Details of John Yates**

INTRODUCTION TO
LIBERATION OF SELF

Anarchists have always stressed the dual importance of liberating themselves as well as transforming society. For anarchists, the revolutionary process takes place in everyday life. How is it that some people become anarchists or can sustain themselves in a society that regards such beliefs with condescension if not hostility? In part, the answer to this question is to be found in the biographies of anarchists. In part it is to found in how people are socialized in society.

There are three elements of political socialization into a capitalist or state socialist society. On a personal level, this means the acceptance of authority as a guide to behavior. The first is to get people to accept the inequalities and hierarchies of the society. The cohesiveness of a society depends largely on how well people are socialized into the automatic acceptance of its dominant social arrangements and legitimate authorities.

The second is to teach people how to deal with others as objects or, as some analysts would put it, as commodities. If in social relationships people deal with others, and with their relationships, as something to be exchanged for something else, then they have reduced themselves and their relationships to objects. When people become objects, they can be bought and sold; they can be used. When categories of people are no longer or never were people, we can have racism and we can have war.

The third element of political socialization is the inculcation of self-rejection. This may be the most controversial, yet it is the most well-grounded psychologically. Teaching people to dislike themselves may be the single most significant mechanism of political control in contemporary society. People who reject themselves come to reject others — and vice-versa (people who reject others come to reject themselves).

One nonobvious example of how these three elements of political socialization work may be found in how people take care of and confront their own bodies. At a fundamental level, learning about one's body can be political and provide a basis for personal liberation. We all live in a body, yet we do not have much understanding of how it works, how to care for it, or even its potential. Because of this we find it difficult to make intelligent decisions about our physical selves.

Modern advertising focuses on the physical inadequacies of the consumer. The consumer is told that s/he is unattractive, unappealing, unsatisfied and unsatisfying, and unquestionably unworthy. The cure to this unwholesome state is to be found in the advertiser's product. Images of beauty and symbols of success are set out as desirable *and* attainable. (The average American viewer of television sees 35,000 such representations a year.)

Few people can live up to the physical ideals projected in popular culture because they are mythic creations. However, as long as people are concerned about the inadequacies of their bodies, and hold to this fictive imagery, it is difficult to feel physically at ease or to be motivated to learn how to optimally use what you have.

This alienation from our bodies also leads to having little knowledge of health care or the confidence to treat ourselves when it is appropriate. It is not surprising that the "free clinic" movement was a deliberate tactic in the political organizing of the new left. Nor is it surprising that the women's movement of that period focused strongly on health care. Women who joined gynecological self-help groups found that coming to know their bodies in a supportive group setting helped them to understand that they could learn enough about their bodies and medical treatment to make intelligent decisions about health care. It also led many women to understand that in learning how to control this one aspect of their lives they had the potential for control in other aspects.

Another aspect of alienation from our bodies is to be observed in the norms of sexual behavior in this culture. The repression of sexual expression and the limits placed on sexual orientations are deeply alienating. The cultural norm is that of a heterosexual relationship between two people, with sex defined as genital sex. To be sure, these norms are built on an essentially religious ideological framework, but that framework couldn't survive without the elements of political socialization we have been discussing.

Another area of alienation from our bodies involves movement. Everyone learns how to walk and we all develop standard ways of moving without giving much thought to the process. We are taught that exercise is good for us. Physical education is part of most school curricula, but the emphasis is on learning competitive sports or calisthenics. People are taught to imitate a model but not to explore different ways of moving or learning about the structure of the body through movement. As a result, most people believe they are clumsy, that exercise is painful and uninteresting, and that someday they should lose some weight and "get into shape." When they do seek out exercises that will supposedly get them into shape, they face the same experiences they had in school. So people often become discouraged and give up trying to use their bodies in new ways.

How people treat their bodies is not merely a result of self-rejection. People treat themselves as they treat others; and much as they are socialized to deal with others as objects, so they come to deal with themselves and their bodies as objects. The consequence is to be further alienated from one's self since "body" and "mind" can only be separated in analytic writing such as this. (One could argue that conceptualizing this dualism is itself a political-ideological act.)

The idea that mind and body are integrally related is not new and there has been a revival of interest in movement disciplines including yoga, aikido, t'ai chi, among others, which attempt to make people aware of these connections. It is possible to use techniques from all movement skills to teach people to break old habits by making conscious decisions about how they want to use their bodies in everyday life.

Certainly one of the limits to people breaking free is their socialized acceptance of authority. Most people have ceded the control of their nutrition, their physical regimen, and their health care to external, legitimate authorities. So it is that the elements of political socialization have ramifications for all of us. Our dealing with our bodies is merely an illustration of how the elements of political socialization work to capture the thoughtways of people. Yet some escape. How it is that this can happen eludes us. Certainly it comes through many experiences. **Kingsley Widmer** discusses how some of his experiences in school, factory, and prison led him to an anarchist identity. Widmer's strategy for change is to build a community of refusal which challenges the authority of institutions. He points out that this community of refusal already exists in the form of folklore and the practice of beating the system — natural anarchism. It remains for us to build on this.

Jay Amrod and **Lev Chernyi** focus on the aspect of socialization that Wilhelm Reich called "character." Character is a structural phenomenon which exists in such diverse forms as chronic muscular tensions, guilt, dogmatism, racism, mysticism and sexism. But just as this character structure limits free human activity in the service of capital, ideology is the limitation and deformation of thought which justifies self-repression. These two, character structure and fixed ideology, support each other. Only an understanding of both will lead to "transparent communication and coherent organization."

The insistence that anarchists evaluate and change their everyday life can be wearing in the context of a hostile society. **Ruthann Robson**'s parodistic treatment of how to live your life is a welcome change. Like all good parody it is built on a structure of reality.

A revolutionary vision must give people a continually revived sense that alternatives are possible. This along with the persistent pain of oppression, creates the strongest initial and lasting commitment to revolutionary change.

To maintain their vision of a better society, anarchists must create new structures and lifestyles that give a sense of renewal. Only a movement that is already living the revolution will be able to inspire people to liberate themselves.

We open this section with a poetic reminder from **Diane di Prima** who cautions that the stakes are ourselves.

REVOLUTIONARY LETTER NO. 1

DIANE DI PRIMA

I have just realized that the stakes are myself
I have no other
ransom money, nothing to break or barter but my life
my spirit measured out, in bits, spread over
the roulette table, I recoup what I can
 nothing else to shove under the nose of the *maitre de jeu*
nothing to thrust out the window, no white flag
this flesh all I have to offer, to make the play with
this immediate head, what it comes up with, my move
as we slither over this board, stepping always
(we hope) between the lines

THREE TIMES AROUND THE TRACK:
AMERICAN WORKOUTS TOWARDS ANARCHISM

KINGSLEY WIDMER

When I was in a midwestern public high school, the genially mean moron who was the gym coach maintained his authority by a graded set of punishing workouts: "Run once around the track" for any deficiency in obedience or enthusiasm, called "poor sports spirit"; "Run twice around the track" for any questioning or criticism of his orders, called "wise-guy back talk"; "Run three times around the track" for sardonically smiling, or otherwise looking rebellious, while being punished for crimes one or two, called "showing your Al Capone character."

That was long ago, and I've done a good bit of bad-character jogging since. But perhaps that early formulation of the rules of American institutions stayed with me because it was so simple and clear. That has not always been true of the corrective workouts in other of our society's organizations — in the infantry platoons, factory shops, business offices, field crews, prison cellblocks, university departments, and other social subordinations I've run through. I don't recall this early coercive style just to attack my particular schooling. In rather different times and places, and supposedly reformed public schooling, my sons found essentially the same pattern of workouts, even graded trips around the track, though the rhetoric of domination shows some changes. So does the iconography of the rebel as the smiling thug; now the defiant are more often treated as psychiatric cases. Incidentally, I finally refused to run the track, which only resulted in moderate hassling; the delayed revenge by the district superintendent, for this and a couple of other defiances, was denying me "honors" at graduation for "poor school citizenship." Big deal.

I do not especially mock the obviously common authoritarian type epitomized by the sports coach. As long as the society exalts hyperorganized and specialized competitive sports, thus corrupting the spirit of games and play, especially in such inappropriate places as schools and colleges, we must expect three-times-around-the-track bosses. My early one, I have been told, later became a highly successful administrator in the schooling bureaucracies. I don't see him as the more vicious sort because "three times around the track!" rather exhausted his imagination for institutional control. The same cannot be said for the coercions and denigrations developed by some of our more ostensibly "liberal" authorities. Still, those run-around workouts remain an appropriate metaphor for what encouraged me to become a "philosophical," and on some more or less prudent occasions, an activist-anarchist.

Though starting with an anecdote from adolescence, I want to put the emphasis not on personality development, such as why I spoke out or smiled or resisted at inconvenient moments, which got me extra laps around the track, but on our institutional order which makes people arbitrarily run. Of course I could instead fashionably sketch a psychological profile. No doubt it would be a fairly commonplace rebellious pattern: first-born child with ambivalent relations to the father (in my case, a poor farm boy self-made into a railroad middling executive and resentful right-winger) with consequent transferred hostilities to authority figures. Equally standard but pertinent might be a marginal sense of social place (in my case, partly engendered by social-class confusions from alternately being raised by poor small-town and ambitiously genteel city relatives). Thus self-definition through counter-roles, resulting in resistance. Add to that a few traumatic experiences for a "bright kid," and the acquiring of critical intellectual responses ("obsessional defenses" in the self-defensive cant of the psychiatrically oriented). Thus to elaborate the personality accounting of an anarchist wouldn't necessarily be wrong, it just wouldn't be enough. For there is a real world outside, a run-the-track social ordering that often demands radical responses, resistances that are reasonable and humane. So let us just assume the usual rebellious psyche — to emphasize only it would be to avoid the public issues — and ask what it may find in our contemporary institutions. Arbitrary impositions, and considerable unnecessary suffering, exist there, in shop and classroom and office and cell and street, not just in my, or your, warped head and wizened heart.

Running the Work Track

I considerably associate "social ordering" less with custodial schooling than with more punitively unpleasant jobs. I did some variety of menial and hard labors for more than half-a-dozen years, and I'm not satisfied to turn my times as a dock-walloper and seaman and sausage packer and scaffold-jack into mere romantic initiation on the way to something else. Many people never get elsewhere. And there are weariness and pain and rage in me still when memory brings back some of those labors. But could I be an exception — a sensitive kid who went to work too soon in field and factory? That won't do, not only because when anyone goes to exploited and subordinated work s/he goes too soon but also because whether one were early or late, tough or tender, those were often arbitrarily harsh and dehumanized jobs. And they often still are. Considerable work is embittering pain and resentment.

What else could come from stoop-hoeing carrots in a hot sun for a few cents an hour, with the sweat-caked peat burning on my skin and the constant scatological threats of the straw-boss burning in my brain? A bitter taste, literally, comes from unloading by hand boxcars of bagged cement, 800 pounds to a dolly, choking on cement dust and a steep ramp. A better job, I then thought, was running a big steam-filler in a canning factory. It paid more — mandatory overtime, usually at least twelve-hour shifts. But I soon learned why such rich, machine-happy work was so available; with the required speed in 120-degree heat not many lasted long. Nor, in spite of inculcated Protestant stoicism, did I. It was a nice company, though, for when I got well they rehired me to tend the newest automatic filler. Much easier, and less pay. But I was irresponsible. After hours of watching thousands of shiny cans wind through the conveyer, I would be so hypnotized that I didn't always punch the reject lever in time to flip out the defective ones. Hot cream-style corn sprayed over everything. Appropriately? Fired, I took off down the anesthetizing road. And then there was. . . .

However, I realize that literate people no longer care for this style of reportage — bathetic old proletarian novel stuff. It just happens to be true, not only of my history but, perhaps with a bit less discontented variety, of the work lives of millions of Americans, not to mention much of the rest of the human world. The rasping sense of arbitrary, monotonous, body-and-mind dulling labor, without autonomy or reasonable reward — the sense of injustice an essential part of the pain — remains a harshly basic noise in my hearing our social reality. It seems to have also made me a bit deaf, not least when I read political moralists, economists and sociologists, on our Gross National Product wealth and our high-tech ordering. Neither affluence nor automation has eliminated a lot of our painful and unjust labors. The human-robotizing tracks still run on.

When it comes to the work many must do, we are still a long way from those fantasies of bureaucratic technology in which suprahuman machines tend other machines in pure, mad productivity. Scientific techniques, and their liberal-or-socialist bureaucratic rationalizations, contain few necessary imperatives for humaneness and individual autonomy. Superior technology promises no product of ordinary justice. My rounds of work convinced me, for example, that for a society to recognize the burdens of labor fairly would mean that no salesman hustling with his hype would receive higher rewards than the field hand hacking with his hoe, and that no exalted professional would merit more money and honor than those mucking out our coal and crap. No artist in the culture centers or entertainer in the media towers should receive more than those in home and shop and street. I know on my nerves, having been both, that the garbage man deserves to be at least as well paid and comforted as the college professor. Such perfectly sensible conclusions, I eventually learned, made me an anarchist. So be it.

Freedom and equality must be testable on the independence and vitality of the body, not just in abstract equations. We must judge a society by the equity and solace and merit it allows for doing our unpleasant and boring labors. A society that does not redeem the Edenic curse will be rotten even in its most polished fruits.

Let me carry the issue of dehumanized laboring beyond the essential physical and moral revulsion. No longer so young, and an academic dropout (any decent person must be reluctant about arbitrary certification in a "profession"), I went back to laboring, this time at the somewhat skilled trade of airframe "template-maker" in various plants and job-shops in three Western states. After some months of fabricating templates in one of the largest, and reputedly most "progressive," plants, my boredom reached such excruciation that some gesture toward critical response seemed imperative. From the better writings on the subject as well as from my co-workers, I know that much of my reaction was unexceptional. Many a factory hand, not just a *poete maudit* with a power drill, finds his routine painful, his conditions of work arbitrary, and his sense of life emptied.

Naïvely combining my responses to the tooling shop with things I had read, I came up with a list of moderate, rational requests for a bit of work humanization. When I then consulted a noted academic specialist in industrial relations at UCLA on how I might initiate these improvements, he exhibited considerable embarrassment. But he did suggest two pieces of wisdom on how I might improve my factory life: I should go back to school to major in Industrial Relations, thus both getting out of the shop and "getting ahead" — the traditional American pseudo-ideal of "opportunity" substituting for justice and meaning — and I should immediately become involved in my spare time in politics, in liberal-Democratic chores in a Republican suburb. That's what often passes for liberal realism.

Next, the union. With some difficulty, I finally presented my critical points to someone at a middling level in that hierarchy. My little suggestions included flexible "breaks" instead of a plant-wide schedule, cooperative decisions on work assignments, and a procedure for electing foremen. All such were indignantly rejected. Flexible, individualized, rules were deemed to lack force as bargaining issues. By a logic that still eludes me, the union also held that work assignments and promotions were purely corporate prerogatives. Though too dumb to say it, the union official's attitude suggested that arbitrary work required arbitrary authority, including his own, rather than any independence and co-operation on the part of those doing the work.

Even raising such issues was suspect: Just what are your politics? I remembered that I better have none. A few years earlier I had put some related questions to an official of a different union (a Teamsters' local) and obtained my answers from two persuasive gentlemen who wanted me to make contact with the hard realities of the issues, and so repeatedly put my head against a brick wall, then got me fired. In addition to my cowardice, I felt some reluctance in pushing the argument with the machinists' union because of my experience in a non-union tooling shop, from which I got fired solely for talking too much: "Trouble-maker."

So I started arguing my way up the aircraft company hierarchy, finally reaching one of the biggest incompetents, the Plant Superintendent. That was a scene of comic pathos in a cubicle high above the assembly line, with the factory Major General trying to get rid of a loquacious third-rate toolmaker inexplicably arguing about perfectly standard shop procedures. He came on with phony geniality, then irritated belligerence, finally collapsing into self-made-boss intimacy, lamenting that he had never understood those "industrial psych" courses the company had made him take in night school back in his foreman days. With a paternal hand on my shoulder, he asked, "What can I really do for you? Put you in for a promotion?" No, I wanted to be able to smoke my pipe at reasonable intervals, work out with the other template men the divvying up of the jobs (it might even be more efficient), have a say in organization, and generally not be trapped by plant schedules and engineering numbers and supervisory caprice. In sum, we wanted to better our work lives by being a bit more our own bosses. Wasn't that reasonable?

He agreed, but wearily assured me that such changes would require getting rid of all those "goddamn personnel people," redoing the company and union contractual procedures, and not only reorganizing the whole plant but the prime contractor, which happened to be the U.S. government. System, indeed! From such experiences, I suspect that many of those in our institutions supposedly running things don't really, except by their acquiescence, their unwillingness to refuse. I had also discovered, though I didn't then know the name or history of it, a version of traditional anarchism's demands for "worker's control." No doubt I was temperamentally disposed to workplace democracy as well as radical egalitarianism before I empirically discovered that various institutions were dehumanizingly run by over-rewarded careerists of dubious competence incapable of much meaningful response. Still, it came as a shock to my naïveté to find repeatedly that those in authority essentially agreed that the system was locked up, and the alternatives were to exploit it or get out.

For me to become, say, an "industrial relations" decorator, or climb the shop (or union) hierarchy, would mostly reinforce what was wrong. I arrived at the obvious libertarian conclusions: In the long run, the productive order must be radically transformed; in the short run, it must be resisted. A good deal, though not nearly enough, of such screwing the system goes on, providing what decency there is in many jobs. Personal and small-group intransigence, though unpopular in pseudogenial American manners, seems essential. And sometimes more: Our great unwritten contemporary works in social thought may be Humanizing Technobureaucracies, by the descendants of Ned Lud. Freedom and equality and community must start where people are, not in distorted political abstractions. Changing our "workout" realities, rather than choosing among the competing rhetorics of political power, provides the authentically radical issues in our society. Says the anarchist, the urbane kept telling me, and so I discovered where I ideologically belonged.

Running Some Total Tracks

If broadly true of what I perceive to be the subordination in our ordinary custodial places, such as schools and factories, how much more it must be true of our "total institutions," which structure Leviathan. A reasonably responsive person forced to spend several years as a private in the U. S. Army infantry can only snigger at many American claims to decency, much less liberty and democracy and justice for all. Though a decorated combat veteran of World War II (honorably discharged in spite of my court-martials for insubordination) and supposedly not subject to immediate further military service, I refused, as a point of moral revulsion and antiauthoritarian principle, to complete re-registration when conscription was Cold War reinstated in 1948. It is a tale of characteristic American righteousness, certainly theirs and, I must now admit, mine. While I innocently lectured the court on the illegitimacy of the draft and the criminality of the U. S. Army that I had directly discovered — with rhetorical appeals to my Swiss grandfather who came in flight from conscription (but ignoring my British grandfather who came to ride with Teddy Roosevelt at San Juan Hill) — the federal prosecutor demanded that I be given appropriately harsh punishment, the maximum years, as "a dangerous and immoral character" who encouraged treason. The judge lectured me, Cold War fashion, on what might happen to me for such misbehavior in Russia, but, in order to demonstrate American liberality toward a purely technical and principled violation, gave me only eight months in federal prison (Sandstone). Just another totally arbitrary run around the custodial track. The judge, too, complained about my sardonically smiling.

The official American, if one really comes up against him or her, can be nastily intolerant. Yet few people that I know who have not experienced time in our total institutions — as soldiers, convicts, mental patients, police victims, and the like — think badly of our institutional character. Thus I am rather less than half-facetious when I now and again argue that the minimum educational certification for any position of prestige and authority in America should be a prison sentence of, say, two-to-five. For proper edification into our basic institutional realities. But I grant that a lottery for many preferences and privileges, from admissions to awards, would more properly reflect basic chance-and-necessity. (My anarchism is finally cosmic!)

Granted, given the innocence of a midwestern, small-town character, such as mine, perhaps nothing less than a convicted act of defiance could create a radicalization that went beyond the abstract-sentimental prejudices of usual "progressivism." Not that the federal prison was so mean; indeed, it was physically better than the county jails and army stockades that I have studied from the inside. Yet that seemingly endless and grim track — the arbitrariness and tedium, the always threatening unlimited repression, which characterizes total institutions — pushes most into doing "hard time."

Still, helped by a short determinate sentence, I could hang tight on resisting a good many things, such as mean job assignments. So I became convict head librarian. Relatively cushy. Yet since I was there for having defied an unjust system, esthetic as well as moral consistency pushed me towards a number of critical responses. For example, the supposed educational system only rarely surfaced as a "rehabilitation" ritual. My trouble-making about it (including writing letters to authorities against other authorities, for the less literate) got me the additional job of teacher of illiterates. But as with most official schooling jobs, the main effects were probably moral solace and co-option. That did discourage me from very vigorous additional complaints about the psychiatric and religious services, for fear that I might be assigned unnecessary additional lessons in humility. After all, in prison all is imprisoning. There is nothing like a closed, total system for checking out the conventional social and political theorists, and for learning that the usual ameliorist notions of improvement are frequently irrelevant. Abolition may be somewhat more practical than reform; certainly resistance is.

But I also came up with a libertarian theory of reform-by-resistance. A psychopathic young con, bright autodidact and compulsive captive, got bumrapped with a bad work assignment (outside in the Minnesota winter). As in most institutions in our society, so in prisons: placements and promotions come about through sycophancy and other corruption, custodial needs to avoid trouble, and, I guess, some unconscious factors such as psychosomatic identifications — not through genuine motives of competence and need and desire. More reasonable standards would not only lessen power but undercut the illicit order that pays off with what pleasures there are to be had. When advantage and avoiding trouble block reform, the basic warping, with its trade-off of power for denied gratification, must be disrupted. To be rationally appropriate, efforts at change must sometimes be *extreme* in style, breaking not only advantage and identification but overall order. Nothing less will work. True politics, then, is the art of trouble-making.

I encouraged my psychopathic friend, after he confided his defiant breakout plans to me, to first refuse to work, which I "unreasonably" backed up by also refusing. Raising the ante included getting other dissidents to "act out," refusing to go to the mess hall as the start of a hunger strike, and making demands about almost everything. These direct actions may have produced less the moral suasion claimed for civil disobedience than such anti-powers as the practical breakdown of the illicit structure of gratification (underground use of the bakery and dispensary), the disproportionate trouble (extra work for the hacks), and the potential psychic explosiveness. Thus are rebellions made.

As I was staring hungrily at the sky, for a last gulp before they dragged me off to windowless solitary, the chief hack sauntered in and announced, "You dumb bastard! You can't win. No con ever does." Generally true enough. But he had just fearfully made some sensible changes in job assignments and privileges, and I soon went back to eating, working, and ineffective liberalism. (My friend later went over the wall anyway and, with proper gesture, stole the warden's personal car.) In the art of drawing the line (as Paul Goodman put it) — something one can learn only by overreaching sometimes — I had been lucky. Partly, I now believe, that was because that joint had considerable history of resistance by "political" prisoners (many Conscientious Objectors). My action was therefore recognized as partly ideological rather than simply sick or self-serving. That may suggest a crucial function for radicals within institutions, creating traditions and dramaturgy for resistance and revolt.

But, on long reflection, I admit that part of my view of what I later came to recognize as variant anarchist theory is indeed problematic. In suggesting not just rational resistance but psychopathic revolt, rather like Bakunin on lumpen revolutions, isn't there obvious destructive danger? Granted, and so qualify it in terms of the situation. Yet with totalizing authorities, "madmen" — the psychopathic dissidents, such as, in libertarian novels, McMurphy and Hayduke — may well be essential. As may be "creative destruction." I am not arguing for violence, nor its systemic form in revolutionism, less because of religious-moral principles than because of pragmatic objections — the wrong people usually get it in the neck. But I am arguing for what anarchists have long identified as "direct action." Since those days, of course, immediate protest and rebellion has been more widely adopted — some of the historical vanguardist role of anarchism.

Retrospectively, I suspect that I was often guilty in my resistance of excessive moderation, of over-selective rebellion in such places as army and prison and factory. Perhaps I am not only arguing for rebellious extremity but even more insisting that we recognize libertarian realities, however sometimes messy and disproportionate the trouble-making fearfully appears. From comic mockery through sabotage and on to total refusal, resistance is usually the more humane response.

TOWARD A COMMUNITY OF REFUSAL

This brief highlighting of some radical-libertarian motifs from my experiences in schools and factories and total institutions — awareness of and resistance to arbitrary institutional coercions, the methods of "workers' control" and "direct action,""spontaneous rebellion," and all sorts of "delegitimatizing" authorities, even unto farce — hardly suggest a complete syllabus of anarchism. They but sketch the personal discovery of a libertarian direction. I grant some variety of additional complexities, and of variations from the basic school and factory and prison templates of domination. For example, I must admit with some intellectual discomfort that while I libertarianly tend to advocate small, communal forms, I have usually ended up opting to be in large and inefficient bureaucracies: big, muddled factories rather than more tightly disciplined job shops; rule-ridden federal prisons rather than brutality-ridden county jails; confusedly massive and mediocre state colleges rather than ruthlessly pretentious and cleverly co-opting prestige universities. (I have tried some of them all.) That is less hypocrisy than taking some degree of autonomy where I can find it, without confusing its present location with a truer and better order. And without forgetting, for long, that every institution I have been part of is less a candidate for reform than for abolition. Consequently, I urge commitment to institutional disloyalty and hierarchical treason.

I haven't even suggested rejecting all authority, though most that I know is dubious when not contemptible. Perhaps we can acknowledge real authority — the ability truly to know, to say, to exemplify, to do-without giving to any authority continuing force and privilege. *Nonce* leadership, only for the specific thing or time, as some anthropologists note of some sensible earlier social forms. Direct democracy, of course, usually with consensus (minus one as proper acknowledgment of human intransigence!). But if we must have other leaders, including such as institutional figureheads and celebrities and legislators and culture heroes, a random drawing would probably give us a better selection than we currently have, and it would properly devalue most claims to prerogative and power. Otherwise, down with them!

Though resistance and refusing obviously do not provide a full liberating ethos and its politics — I am leery of totalistic claims here, too — resistance may well provide the crucial tests. Institutions that cannot bear considerable refusal, often evident in their arbitrarily running us around a track, deserve on that basis alone to go under. We should respond accordingly. Too negative, even unto the destructive? Real destructions follow not from anarchists but from those who never claim it, the "positive" orderings and saviors that advance the local as well as "great historical" crimes. Better, far, the little negations that move us in the direction of a communal order of more voluntary and equal and immediate human proportions. Otherwise, even anarchy-as-chaos is preferable.

My skeptical anarchism, of course, strongly diverges from a leftism with a declared or implied model in political revolutionism. Such subordination to mass external methods of power and institutional manipulation — of course, in the name of le peuple, or the proletariat, or a party, or an ambitious elite, or a materialist dialectic, or "modernization" and other deified historical process — must reject much actual social and cultural freedom. Instead of depowering our institutions, revolutionism heightens their arbitrary and punitive workouts. Political revolutionism is not nearly radical enough.

What just might be would be a community of refusal, a libertarian praxis in which visionary radicalism with its possibilities of an institutionally transformed society, and personal radicalism, from intransigent behavior through Joachimite lifestyles, would work together. The immediate purpose is deconversion from our institutional faiths. The dissident ways, the resistant methods, the selective trouble-making, must be put both against and inside our institutional orderings. Furthering resistant styles constitutes liberating change now. I have often noted of others as well as of myself that defying some arbitrary authority, including a variety of social institutions as well as the omnipresent State, is a positively transforming process, and a downright joy.

This is not just a plea for "bad manners" with the technocracy with which we are subordinatingly meshed, though less "nice day" bullshit would itself be an improvement, nor for tragic martyrdom from the repressive powers, since much of dissolving the ancient curse of authority means turning it into a daily comedy. Anarchy-by-resistance is already evident in that considerable folklore and practice of "beating the bureaucracy," "fighting the system," "fucking-up the bastards," and the like: natural anarchism. It looks to me to be in an expanding way — otherwise many of our institutions would be quite unbearable since patently not designed or run for passionate human freedom and fullness. Natural anarchism — contra some anarchist friends of mine who are such nice, earnest folks — should be encouraged.

The manifold ways of resistance and refusal may redeem the curse of labor by transforming its autonomy and justice, dethrone and decorrupt authority by removing its ease of legitimacy and domination, and humanize power by making it more and more limited and communal and personal. The favorite myth of those who would master others is that denial is bad-bad manners, bad psychology, bad policy. Do they most fear its truth, its effectiveness, or its pleasure? By a fraudulent calculus they conclude that an order of human attritions and arbitrary workouts comes out less destructive than a liberating human negation. My anarchism holds, among other views, to the simple premise that a richer human life often comes from a joyous no, three times over, to running the track.

CODA (1991): RUNNING STIFF? HALF-SPEED ANARCHISM?

These brief reflections on how I came to learn some anarchism (with the prose tightened up but the points unchanged) date from the 1960s, and draw upon my experiences of earlier decades. Do they still apply? Those younger and with parallel running experiences in institutions of more current vintage might be better able to determine their pertinence. Or better replacement, with a better style of trouble-making.

Perhaps with some cowardly hypocrisy, I took the upward-way-down of becoming a *college* professor. I emphasize "college," though the bureaucracies have usually been called universities, because I mostly chose introductory courses for undergraduates (often labeled "General Education"). Though much published in my supposed expertise of modernist literary studies, I had little stomach for "professionalism" and its intellectual fakery and corrupt aggrandizements (literally, the few professional meetings I attended produced in me acute nausea). Have I been a tendentious teacher? Of course, for I never confused responsiveness and intellectual rigor and fairness with the camouflaging claims, mostly untenable, to "objectivity." Have I been "propagandizing," then, in the classroom for atheism and anarchism and nihilism? So it is reported. It has, I insist, been fair labeled, teaching significant literature, with a non-exclusive emphasis on iconoclasm and radical criticism and rebellion. Have I been successful? Not very, but that is no adequate reason for not trying.

For my generation, marginal or minor academic roles provided places for some libertarian dissidents. That may be less so now. The co-optive expansionism, so characteristically American, may have been relatively cushy, though I managed to make it a bit gravely by being thrown out of a few universities, and a bit ostracized at others, for my iconoclasm and resistant manners. In the academic, too, the dominant shits know their own. But now I am through.

About time, says a libertarian friend, for you have long dubiously conflated resistance and refusal. My basic arguments in these memoir-reflections, she says, is halfway-anarchism. What I should have really done is run away from the public schools, never gone to work in field and factory and university, and more promptly told the foremen and captains and deans and other wardens to shove their orders where the sun doesn't shine.

Fair enough. Such heroes as I have, like Diogenes of 5th Century B. C. Athens — in my view one of the first recorded anarchists in the Western tradition — would have put down the authoritarian nonsense much more quickly, and wittily, than I did. Can one even imagine

Thoreau or Tolstoy as a factory hand and an infantry private and a tenured state college professor? But for those of us less brave and wise, intellectual and social resistance against and within institutions, baiting as well as battling the bureaucracies (I have some skill at the counter-memo, etc. and warning students against teachers, including myself), may still have some relevance.

Relevance? says my friend? where is a word of recognition in your account of the oppression of women? Arthritically, I reply that I published at about the same time as this account a bit of the story of my women's rights grandmother (an early woman journalist, deserted by her publisher husband) explaining to childish me at her knee how men exploited women. Besides, the ships and platoons and jails I was mostly ruminating about were then all male (though, admittedly, not the schools and factories). Women, I insist, in Enlightenment manner, are implicitly included because I held, and still hold, that humankind is equally one. Still, I grant that my libertarian perspective was not sufficiently ranging.

An even more obvious deficiency for these days is that I say not a word about the physical environment. Wasn't I aware of at least a few of the ecological ravages by our technocracy? Well, I do recall my vehement arguments in the 1950s about over-population with Catholics and Marxists, the latter disdainfully calling me a "reactionary neo-Malthusian." Radical ecologists now insist that lunatic over-production of kids as well as cars and rockets is much of our destructive and oppressive problem. Again, I admit that even my negative population impetus was partly rooted in personal experience, without this time much support in anarchist traditions, such as my shocked adult learning that my mother had not died of god- given complications in childbirth but, after defiantly announcing that two children were enough, of complications from a forbidden and illegal, botched abortion. And I am not so doctrinaire as to deny that reactionary Malthus also had some good points, in spite of their anti-egalitarian misuse. As radical environmentalists now argue, decency, ecological as well as social, requires the anti-expansionary movement towards a lesser steady-state population as well as a lesser steady-state economy. My long-term personal preference might be towards the neolithic, but I sympathize with many negative emphases. I don't doubt that a libertarian now developing similar issues to mine would say much, indeed, about how authoritarian orderings tend to exploit viciously the physical as well as social world. Our technocracy makes all the more imperative the fair and simple life. And perhaps the best anarchism, and the kind that has certainly increased since my bitter-salad days, is what goes under the name of "alternative lifestyles," understood as variant and defiant ways of seeking daily autonomy.

For, historically as well as currently, anarchism has been, sometimes paradoxically, the theory and practice of limits. It denies legitimacy and authority and power on the principles of more free and equal human scale. The opposite of the State is less confusion than community. Preferably small scale and direct. Community, of course (as we ex-midwestern small towners know too well), can be oppressive. So anarchism, at least implicitly, partly holds to utopian senses of community, though hoping to find elements of them realized in various co-operative and communal efforts, including appropriate "intentional communities." Now "utopian" is often a curse word, for impractical, abstract, and (appropriately enough in some cases) totalitarian fantasies, and many anarchists disavow it. While my temperament and taste incline to the critical and satiric, the dystopias, even they are grounded (as I have argued in various studies) in the positive utopian. Given the predominant evil of the history of human institutions of authority and power, anarchism — indeed, any large claim for freedom and equality — is probably inevitably utopian. But then it may be that the long survival of homo sapiens is, too.

In the meantime, in an anarchism not bedded with presumptuous optimism, something this side of sweeping utopianism also seems essential. Hence, some of my emphasis on resistance and refusal. That, I am aware, is too skeptical, pessimistic, and hostile for many people. Let them at least keep their faiths off my back! But my acknowledgment should also include that in my perspective the libertarian is always a minority view, a permanent disloyal opposition, a beleaguered "saving remnant." I would like to think that I would have the perception and courage to make trouble even in utopia. Of course, I define a "good place" as one where I have more liberty to be effectively troublesome. But, the earnest may counter, you are not sufficiently helping us get there — your methods are too individualistic, anti-social, unprogrammatic, ahistorical, off-putting, arrogantly vulgar, rooted more in immediate anger than in enduring love. Ah! but then you essentially agree with me as to the world we live in, and would but teach me better than my half-way methods of resistance and refusal, as you completely opt out of our institutions. Just don't expect me to run any custodial tracks, earnestly loving or not, in the meantime, even in the name of anarchism.

BEYOND CHARACTER AND MORALITY: TOWARDS TRANSPARENT COMMUNICATIONS AND COHERENT ORGANIZATION

JAY AMROD AND LEV CHERNYI

1

TO CREATE A REVOLUTIONARY ORGANIZATION, it is not sufficient mechanically to link up a number of people with revolutionary pretensions. The creation of such an organization must involve the conscious project of aggressively destroying all barriers to communication, thought, and action both from within and from outside the organization. It involves the conscious elaboration of a theory and practice adequate to its task. And it involves a commitment to change which never questions the need for self-change. You can't change the world if you expect to remain unchanged.

2

THE FIRST STEP IN THE DESTRUCTION of all barriers to communication, thought, and action is logically the identification of these barriers. When we examine our situation closely we inevitably find that these obstacles can all be subsumed under the general label of 'capital,' understood as the coherent totality of all the aspects that together make it up. It is only logical that what restrains all our attempts to destroy capitalist society is in the end only capital itself.

3

FOR OUR THEORETICAL AND PRACTICAL PURPOSES we will focus our attention on that moment or aspect of capital that Wilhelm Reich called 'character.' Character is 'capital' as it appears to us within the individual. It is the totality of all the internalized or habitual incapacities and limitations of action within the individual. It is not an aggregate sum of arbitrary limitations, but a coherent structure of incapacities and limitations which, as an organized whole, serves its function within the framework of capitalist society. Character must never be viewed as a thing in itself, detached from any other social reality. It only exists as one moment of the totality of capital. To act on any other perception of character is to miss the whole point.

4

RECALL YOUR CHILDHOOD. In doing so you will recall the formation of your character structure, the formation of the pattern taken by your defeat at the hands of (and your submission to) the logic of capital as it was presented to you by your family, your peers, your church or temple, the media, and your school. You can see the same process going on every day if you observe the lives of the children around you. They are learning the logic of capital the hard way, just as we all did. Each time a child is born her/his capacity for self-regulation is systematically attacked by the people who are closest to him/her. It usually begins with rigid feeding times, which are not only a convenience to mothers and hospitals, but serve the added function of introducing the child early in the game to the 'reality principle' ('You'll eat on schedule, not when you're hungry'), otherwise known as the logic of character and capital. For most newborn males there is the added trauma of circumcision which serves him notice as to the kind of care to expect from his parents. In quick succession the child is exposed to more and more types of conditioning when s/he is least able to understand and fight it. Often children who cannot yet walk are 'potty-trained.' Any touching of the genitals is quickly punished by most conscientious parents, and children are taught always to wear clothes ('It's not nice for people to see you naked'). Parents impose rigid sleeping schedules on children, who know well enough when they are tired and when they want to get up. And in general, children are allowed to investigate their environment and exercise their powers only within the limits allowed by their captors — whether their captors be parents, schools, etc.

5

THE ONE BASIC MESSAGE that is always received with each conditioning is that the child isn't in control; someone else is. Children react to this in the only way they can, they adapt themselves to the situation through a trial-and-error process. The first time a child is slapped for what s/he thought was a natural act, there is a look of astonishment and wonder. After being punished more than a few more times for the mysteriously simple act, the child learns to avoid it when in the presence of the seemingly irrational aggressor. The child eventually acquires a deference to figures of authority (arbitrary power) within the family. This is eventually generalized to a 'respect' for and deference to all authority as the child is exposed to ever-wider spheres of perception and action. One thing that needs to be made clear is that few people consciously condition children. The pervasive conditioning that takes place is usually a result of a whole organization of forces working through the parents and others. These forces include those of the economy, the parents of the parents, social mores, etc. Capital must continually reproduce itself or it will cease to exist.

6

We live in a society without natural scarcity. Our natural desires are often temporarily frustrated by the natural world. This usually has no lasting effect on our lives, though, since we eventually learn what we did wrong, or the natural circumstances change such that we are then able to fulfill our wish. Unfortunately, we also live in a society dominated by capital, which is to say that we live in a society dominated by chronic, socially enforced (artificial) scarcities. These scarcities result in chronic frustrations of certain desires. And when important natural desires are chronically frustrated, not just denied but also often punished, we are soon forced to collaborate with this denial. In order to avoid the punishment that we will receive for trying to satisfy this need, we learn to suppress it as soon as it begins to intrude upon our awareness. We use some of the energy that would otherwise have been used to fulfill our desire to suppress it in order to satisfy our secondary desire to avoid punishment. Once this self-repression exists for any prolonged period, it becomes a habit, an unconscious habitual attitude of our character structure. Our awareness of the original situation of chronic frustration is repressed because it is too painful to maintain. We learn that our desire is 'irrational,' 'bad,' 'unhealthy,' etc. We internalize the logic of capital as character traits, and they become 'natural' for us and the original desires become 'irrational' desires. Even when there is no longer a threat of punishment for acting within the logic of the original desire, we continue to suppress it automatically. We have learned to cripple ourselves and *like it*.

7

Throughout the first years of our lives we were forced not just to internalize a few aspects of capital, but to build up a structure of internalizations. As our capacity for coherent natural self-regulation was systematically broken down, a new system of self-regulation took its place, a coherent system, incorporating all the aspects of self-repression. We participated in capital's ongoing project of colonization by colonizing ourselves, by continually working at the construction of a unitary character-structure (character armor), a unitary defense against all the drives, feelings, and desires which we learned were dangerous to express. In the place of our original transparent relations to our world, we created a structure of barriers to our self-expression which hides us from ourselves and others.

8

THE RAMIFICATIONS OF CHARACTER can be found in all aspects of our behavior because character is a unitary deformation of the entire structure of our existence. It produces a deterioration of our capacity to live freely and fully by destroying the structural basis of free life. Character is not a mental phenomenon. It is a structural phenomenon of our entire existence. It exists as: inhibitions, chronic muscular tensions, guilt, perceptual blocks, creative blocks, psychosomatic or psycho-genetic diseases (in many of the cases of 'illnesses' as diverse as chronic insomnia, arthritis, obsessive-compulsive neuroses, chronic headaches, chronic anxiety, etc.). It exists as: respect for authority, dogmatism, mysticism, sexism, communications blocks, insecurity, racism, fear of freedom, role-playing, belief in 'God,' etc., ad nauseam. In each individual these character traits take on a coherent structure which defines that person's character.

Just as character is a limitation and deformation of the free human *activity* in general in the service of capital, so ideology is the limitation and deformation of *thought* in the service of capital. Ideology is always the acceptance of the logic of capital at some level. It is the form taken by alienation in the realm of thought.

9

Wɪᴛʜ ɪᴅᴇᴏʟᴏɢɪᴇs, I ᴊᴜsᴛɪғʏ my complicity with capital, I justify my self-repression (my submission, my guilt, my sacrifice, my suffering, my boredom, etc. — in other words, my character). On the other hand, my character structure, by existing as fixed, conditioned behavior, naturally tends to express its existence in thought as fixed ideas which dominate me. Neither character nor ideology could exist without the other. They are both parts of one unitary phenomenon. All ideology is revealed as the impotence of my thought, and all character is revealed as the impotence of my activity.

10

A ᴘᴀʀᴛɪᴄᴜʟᴀʀʟʏ ɪɴsɪᴅɪᴏᴜs ғᴏʀᴍ ᴏғ ɪᴅᴇᴏʟᴏɢʏ is the pervasive moralism which has always plagued the libertarian revolutionary movement. It destroys possibilities for transparent communication and coherent collective activity. To limit one's behavior according to the proscriptions of a morality (to seek the 'good' or the 'right') is to repress one's own will to satisfaction in favor of some ideal. Since we cannot possibly do anything else but seek our own satisfaction, alienation results, with one part of ourselves subduing the rest — one more instance of character. Wherever morality exists, communication is replaced by manipulation. Instead of speaking to me, a moralist tries to manipulate me by speaking to my internalizations of capital, my character, hoping that his brand of ideology may give him a hold on my thought and behavior. 'The projections of my subjectivity, nurtured by guilt, stick out of my head like so many handles offered to any manipulator, any ideologue, who wants to get a hold of me, and whose trade skill is the ability to perceive such handles' *(The Right To be Greedy)*. The only really transparent, and thus revolutionary, communication is that which takes place when our selves and our desires are out in the open, when no morals, ideals, or constraints cloud the air. We will be amoralists, or we will be manipulators and manipulated. The only coherent organization is that in which we unite as individuals who are conscious of our desires, unwilling to give an inch to mystification and constraint, and unafraid to act freely in our own interests.

LIVING OUR LIVES

RUTHANN ROBSON

Emma Goldman's two-volume autobiography *Living My Life* spans the years from her birth in 1869 until 1931, and treats many significant historical events including the Haymarket Massacre, the assassination of McKinley, and the Russian Revolution. Yet when I think of Goldman's book, it is the scenes of daily life that I remember: her account of receiving violets from Johann Most which prompted Alexander Berkman to exclaim: "violets at the height of winter, with thousands out of work and hungry"; her account of enthusiastic dancing provoking a controversy about whether such was appropriate to "the Cause." While one could construct plausible expositions of such scenes as "capturing the quintessential conflict of practical anarchism with theory," I remember such scenes precisely because of their dailiness. There is a great deal of theoretical work on anarchism, but precious little apart from autobiographies and biographies (and these are often dated) about how we live our lives.

This piece is an attempt to explore some aspects of anarchist living. The premise is that our theory permeates our practice, though not always in predictable ways. While it has been said that only white, heterosexual businessmen (with a slight gray at the temples) have lives, and the rest of us have "life-styles," I have yet to encounter an anarchist life-style article. Rather than allowing some mainstream editor to define us, I have taken it upon myself to become a media spokesperson and elucidate our trends and habits. Only portions of this piece will be facetious, and in accordance with anarchist tenets, all "prescriptions" are to be randomly violated.

What We Look Like

We are women and men. We are Black, Asian, White, Native American, Hispanic, and that category on surveys I've always longed to check "other." We are bodies with various measurements. We may have bones that have been broken or MS or blond hair. Most of the way we appear is beyond our control and is therefore equally acceptable in our anarchist communities. However, there are wide areas in which we can exercise personal choices.

Let's talk body hair. Razors are simply not anarchist. It's not merely the problems with steel and exploitation of workers and survival of the planet; it is symbolism. Beards are *de rigueur* for men. Women should avoid shaving their legs or "bikini areas." Neither gender should use wax depilatories, burning chemicals or professional services. However, for tropical anarchists of both genders, it is permissible to scrape off armpit hair with a dull knife.

Dressing is a valuable means of anarchist self-expression. Except for synthetic materials processed from petroleum and animal fur coats, almost anything goes. Yet I confess to longing for the days when we thought we could tell something about people by the way they were dressed: dungarees and work shirts used to mean something. Not that we should have a uniform, but perhaps we should have a sense of anarchist fashion. I would like to see more fuchsia and lavender, crop pants, cotton sandals and vinyl boots with feathers. Clothes with labels on the outside, children's outfits advertising franchised foods, tee shirts from resorts and Budweiser sneakers are all irredeemable.

Anarchist jewelry can be bartered for at craft shows. Gold chains and South African diamonds are inappropriate. Silver not mined from Native American sacred lands is fine. String rings and bracelets are quite acceptable. Watches should be shunned unless necessary or childhood gifts, although in no case is a digital watch tolerable. At least one earring is virtually required. Nose rings are anarchically exquisite. Beads, shells and amulets dangling from the hair are very admirable.

What We Eat

Anarchists are vegetarians, of course, but what type? Some subscribe to the "face theory" (i.e., if it doesn't have a face, it's ethically edible). Others debate the concept of sentience. More serious vegetarians divide themselves into many sects including lacto-vegetarians, vegans and fruititarians. Moving between the serious realms is encouraged.

Tap water is the drink of choice, preferably lukewarm. Other acceptable choices include watermelon juice, Chinese beer, mother's milk and vodka.

Who We Love

Anarchists love everyone. Therefore, when we express our sexuality, we are most often bisexuals. Being bisexual does not mean that we engage in sexual relations with everyone; it just means that we recognize the potential so to engage. Usually, however, we become erotically engaged with thinking through the political ramifications of any contemplated liaison, and miss our chance.

For anarchists, the issue of homosexual marriage is akin to the issue of conscripting women. No, homosexuals should not "be allowed" to marry, but then neither should heterosexuals, and no one should be drafted. Sorry, but "living together contracts" are also impolitic.

Children raise themselves in communal households. They attend "free schools" or are home-schooled. They take part in all household decisions from birth. They are never punished or vaccinated.

How We Make Money

Surviving in a capitalist world is a problem for anarchists if one is not by birth a prince. Since we believe in the ultimate nonexistence of the state, a state job is the most anarchist option because it's really not like working at all. And a state paycheck is not exactly a lure to become either a statist or a capitalist.

To get that state paycheck, an anarchist can have various "career positions" within government. Education remains popular because it gives a constant, if limited, platform to the anarchist for dissemination of revolutionary theory. Positions with access to sophisticated technology are encouraged in preparation for worldwide orchestration of "pulling the plug." In most other cases, bureaucratic jobs are unacceptable. Also to be shunned by the practicing anarchist are titles such as: correctional officer (though wouldn't it be wonderful if all our prison guards were anarchists?), quasi-military auxiliary, research assistant in a drug approval agency, executioner, chief lottery executive, and Secretary of "Defense." The best jobs are in "field work": transportation, horticulture, oceanography and artistic affairs are good bets.

Where We Live and How We Get Around

We live in cities and use public transportation, even when it rains.

We live in the country and drive borrowed four wheel drives.

We hitchhike from coast to coast and then get to other continents and ride rails or walk.

We rent apartments (painting one wall black) or we rent an old farmhouse and keep a cow on our porch in winter. I once heard of an anarchist who owned an oceanfront condominium, but that was a long time ago.

WHAT WE DO IN OUR SPARE TIME

Nothing — we have no spare time. We are too busy bringing about the revolution to have time for frivolity. However, we encourage what we call "cultural work," which is what my parents call "pretentious shit." Thus, anarchists may be devotees of music (anything but Wagner), poetry (structuralist), visual art (primitive women artists are currently in vogue), dance (French/Mozambique jazz), theater (either without words or without gestures), gardening (African violets are favored, bonsai are not).

We also read a great deal. In addition to all the anarchist classics, we read current novels that are not on the *New York Times* Bestseller List, nonfiction that does not concern aerobics, investments or actualizing ourselves, and periodicals printed on newsprint.

We listen to public radio or alternative radio. We never watch television, unless we are in a group of more than ten people gathered to discuss media manipulation.

HOW WE COMMUNICATE

We like to stay up all night, drinking (see above) and talking. Esperanto is no longer required. It is permissible to resort to English, if heavily peppered with slang and words such as "hegemonous" are avoided.

Postcards are absolutely anarchist — so egalitarian and public! The writing should be particularly tiny and florid, however, and using a water soluble ink is recommended for risk enhancement. All letters (including ones to persons within the same commune) should be written on airmail stationery. Typewriters are never used as the paper would tear.

For emergencies, the use of black rotary phones is acceptable. For nonemergencies, those with state jobs may use autodex 2300 pana fax.

And, of course, the indispensable organ of communication among anarchists is *Social Anarchism*.

REINVENTING ANARCHIST TACTICS

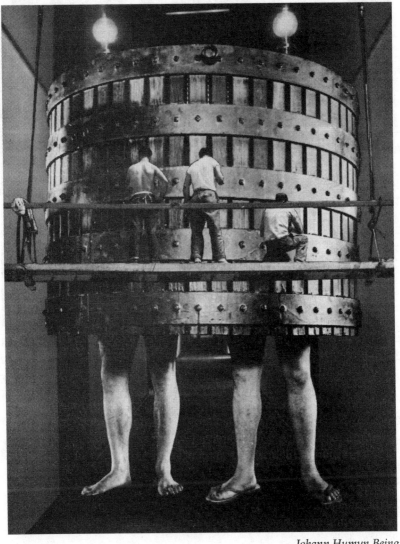

Johann Humyn Being

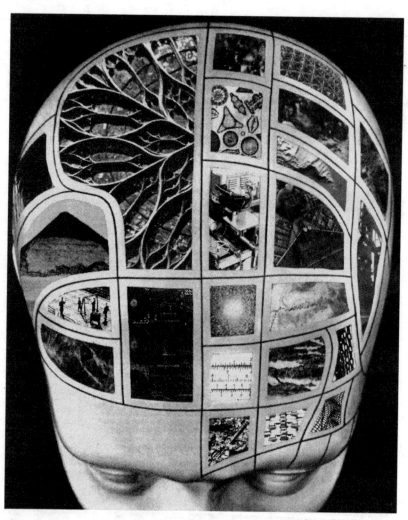

Johann Humyn Being

INTRODUCTION TO
REINVENTING ANARCHIST TACTICS

The keynote of this section is my essay on a revolutionary "transfer culture." A transfer culture is that agglomeration of ideas and practices that guide people in making the trip from the society here to the good society there in the future. The essay is both a philosophical statement and a practical guide. It is critical, I believe, that we self-consciously understand that we are building a transfer culture. That is, we are developing a set\of institutions and intergroup and interpersonal processes that are consistent with our image of a good society, though it is not that society itself. As part of the accepted wisdom of that transfer culture we understand that we may never achieve anything that goes beyond the culture itself. It may be, in fact, that it is the very nature of anarchy that we shall always be building the new society within whatever society we find ourselves. But anarchists recognize that it is the *process* of change that is critical. Whether we are organizing to oppose another aggressive war being waged by the government or some oppressive new legislation, whether we are organizing within our community to provide needed services, or whether we are organizing within our work or living unit, *how* we organize is inseparable from the *outcome*.

I begin with a radical catechism:

- *We must view revolutionary change as a process, not an end.*
- *We must develop a view of the good society.*
- *We must act on the principles of the society we would like to see.*
- *Our means must be consistent with our ends.*
- *We must act as if the future is today.*

In the first two parts I consider leftist obstacles to building a transfer culture and the varieties of escapism employed by the left, including the rhetoric of failure. In the remainder of the essay, I sketch the elements of a transfer culture. These, then, are echoed in the selections which follow.

If we were to write a handbook for building a transfer culture, **Tom Knoche**'s principles of community organizing would be central. These 14 principles are an extraordinary compilation. They are based on his 10 years of organizing experiences in a multicultural and bilingual community in New Jersey. These principles are clearly responsive to the "hard questions" raised earlier by Bouchier (see part three).

Caroline Estes's introduction to the practice of consensus decision-making may be the best single statement on the subject. "Consensus," she reminds us, "refers to agreement (on some decision) by *all* members of a group. The consensus *process* is the process the group goes through to reach this unity of agreement." In principle, consensual decisions represent a pure anarchist practice, and Estes details the complexities of this process.

David Wieck's succinct statement on direct action closes the didactic portion of this section, and the book. Direct action is the anarchist imperative. As Wieck states, direct action is "that action which, in respect to a situation, realizes the end desired. In contrast, indirect action realizes an irrelevant or even contradictory end, presumably as a means to a good end." This is not an abstract moral issue: social anarchists should realize that some frequently used tactics are not only inconsistent with their aims, but may even be harmful. Perhaps the largest category of bad tactics include those that rely on the government to bring about desired changes or on terrorist activities. The terrorists in their attack on ordinary citizens take the position that their concern was to generate an interest in the issues by the class of persons who were deemed to be unconcerned. In both instances, the elector or the terrorist, the actor sought changes which were not directly attainable by their actions. In the case of the terrorist action in the pursuit of justice, we see also a serious breach in the relation of means and ends.

HOW TO GET FROM HERE TO THERE: BUILDING REVOLUTIONARY TRANSFER CULTURE

HOWARD J. EHRLICH

Like all of you, I am concerned with building a "transfer culture." I know that you never heard that term before, and obviously didn't know you were concerned with it. But you are. You are, that is, if you see yourself as working for fundamental social change, if you see yourself as a radical. What I want, what we want, is to be able to construct a programmatic sketch of a theory that informs people what to do and how to do it in order to bring about the new society.

A transfer culture is, of course, a part of a theory of revolutionary change. A complete theory includes two other parts: a critique of the existing society and a view of the kind of new society one would like. The transfer culture is that guide that tells us how to get from here to there. The distinctive part of a social anarchist culture, of my theory, is that we build "there" right here. But let's begin at the beginning.

THE UNDERLYING ASSUMPTIONS

The beginning, as I see it, is the laying out of some of the basic assumptions of social anarchism.

I suppose we can start simply enough by recognizing as our first assumption that revolution is not an end. That is an important principle because it directs us to three anarchist assumptions not always incorporated in other leftist theories. If revolution is not an end, then what is it? What are our ends? And what are the means of revolution, and how do they relate to our ends?

Our end is a "good society." Throughout this paper I will present some of my ideas as to what that good society might look like. Our second assumption, then, is that we need to have in mind what kind of society we are attempting to build. We need to put forward a view of the future. What kind of world would we like to see? The details should be filled in only as a sketch. We are ourselves probably incapable of presenting much more than that anyway. What we want is limited by what we have. We can imagine the possible. But if the possible were what we had, then could we not imagine something still more?

Revolution is a process. That is an important assumption. It is not that point in time when the old regime vacates the capitol. It is all of those years and years and years of struggle. We are revolutionaries because we identify ourselves as being engaged in that struggle.

Oppression is a state of being where past and future meld with the present and go no further. Revolution is the process, we assume, of acting as if the future is the present. This is no simple task; there are no easy guidelines. In fact we are sketching those guidelines as we go along. If we are not actively involved in building the new society today, it is unlikely that we will be involved tomorrow.

In living in and working towards the new society we must try to live by the principles we advocate. While we can all agree that the revolutionary process should be consistent with our ends in view, not everyone has recognized that "consistency" isn't always apparent. We will not always know how to act consistently; we will not always be very consistent. But we do try. Like first-generation immigrants to a strange culture, first-generation revolutionaries will have a high casualty rate.

Let me recapture the assumptions I have just put forward. They are so simple that their power is deceptive. For if you have found yourself in agreement so far, you have become engaged in a social anarchist framework and it will be difficult for you to reject its transfer culture. I have said the following:

> We must view revolutionary change as a process, not an
> end.
> We must develop a view of the "good society."
> We must act on the principles of the society we would
> like to see.
> Our means must be consistent with our ends.
> We must act as if the future is today.

The kind of society we choose to live in is one in which freedom and equality are maximized. Here we confront the major dilemma of anarchist organization. All social organization places some constraint on individual behavior. But we can not have an egalitarian society unless we are all free. And we cannot be free without equality. Our transfer culture, then, will be based on experiments in social arrangements, arrangements in which we will consistently be testing new principles of collective social organization. We are attempting uniquely to build freedom in community.

Our transfer culture will also be based on patterns of resistance — resistance to the agents of the state and resistance to the residues of the state that are in our heads. It is in our resistance that our major casualties will occur. And it is in our ability to withstand repression that our collective social arrangements will meet their critical test.

Is there a revolutionary sector of society? Who will make the revolution?—These are standard questions of revolutionary theory. The social anarchist response is that if there is a revolutionary sector it is to be found among those who are de-classed. Those who have voluntarily unleashed themselves from the bonds of social integration as well as those whose release was more traumatic. It is an open sector, and anyone can join.

As to recruitment, the social anarchist knows that you cannot *liberate* people. You may free people from constraints of an oppressive set of institutions, but unlocking even prison doors does not automatically liberate them. The central problem of freeing people is that they cannot cope necessarily just because they have been freed.

Liberation requires self-education and autonomy. Autonomous behavior and the regular practice of educating oneself are habits (in the old-fashioned sense of habits) built up over years. To be free is not to be liberated, but merely one necessary condition for liberation to occur.

Can people be liberated in a society in which they are not free? I doubt it strongly. Certainly some people can behave in a more autonomous manner than others, and some people can behave in a manner that enhances their self-development more than others, but in a society that is not free — liberating activities must necessarily have narrow limits. An "unfree" society cannot permit too much deviance— at least not in a liberating direction. Liberal societies, for example, are far more tolerant of rightist and conservative deviance than they are of deviation on the left.

Freeing people, while surely important, carries with it an often tragic burden. Those bestowing freedom run the serious risk of making their free subjects passive instruments. For the newly freed want, often above all, to be told what to do.

It is for these reasons that social anarchists do not organize as do others on the left. If there is an anarchist vanguard, it is a vanguard of teachers — and not a cadre of a secret army.

Obstacles to a Transfer Culture

More people today have less confidence in American government, and less confidence in its economy, and less of a sense of "well-being," than perhaps ever before. No matter what criteria you use, no matter how you assemble the formal evidence — voting, public opinion polls, standard sociological indicators of alienation and social disintegration — they all present the same readings through the 1960s and 1970s. People have a genuine sense that they are not in control of significant aspects of their own lives. And they are more convinced that there is a power elite in this country, and that neither political leaders nor the mass media of communication are to be trusted.

All of this should give us on the left some encouragement. But political and social attitudes are easy to change. And "building confidence" is an essential and day-to-day activity of the managers and agents of the State. When Jimmy Carter, as President, toured the control room of the disabled nuclear power plant at Three-Mile Island, he restored the confidence of perhaps hundreds of thousands of people. Not only did his presence transmogrify that smoldering reactor, but in what was one of the major ploys of political public relations of this country—his bringing his wife with him — he demonstrated to patriarchal America that the nuclear plant was safe.

Cynicism, alienation, and escape are the reactions of many. One of my more gloomy scenarios for the remainder of this century depicts more and more people opting out, encapsulating themselves in shells of despair, retreating into the drug of the day, or mindlessly pursuing themselves through eck and est and other fantasies of becoming. Should that happen, we will all have lost. It can only result in the polarization of the left and right. And in that struggle the left will lose. For in order to transcend capitalism in this country the majority of people will have to embrace principles of libertarian socialism.

As the left grows more visible and more successful, we will be met with increased repression. Can we seriously have any other expectation? The grounds for that repression are already here. We are already known and on file. (My own FBI record goes back over 25 years, beginning with a public talk I gave on the right wing in America.) The apparatus for political surveillance is well-developed, and the legislative legacies of Richard Nixon and his attorney-general are still with us.

The new left of the 1960s was *new*. New, because the old left had been destroyed by open repression. But the old left was destroyed also by itself, and today's left is also a major obstacle to its own growth. It is these left obstacles to the left that I want to discuss now.

Avoiding Community. Let us begin by admitting that there is no Left in America. There is no left community, nor is there a feminist community, a black community, a Marxist community, an anarchist community. There is, rather, an extraordinary number of people who embrace some principles of leftist opposition to capitalism. But they do not embrace each other. Some on the left are organized, but most of their formal organizations are either so rigid or so fragile that they cannot engage in mutual actions without threatening their own organizational integrity. Keep in mind that no group can act without a clear sense of its own identity. The absence of stable alliances and coalitions is not the cause of left weakness; it is the result.

When we talk of "the left" we run the risk of self-delusion. Let us be clear that we are talking about an amorphous mass, perhaps several million today. Some of them live and work in organized and satisfying collectives; some work in small, disciplined political groupings and some in amorphous, barely structured political groups and in marginal counter institutions. But it is my observation that the majority of Americans who hold to some identity as leftists belong to no formal organization Most of them see themselves as socialists or Marxists, but their participation in political actions is typically limited to giving money, participating in study groups, attending occasional demonstrations or rallies and other polite activities, usually those associated with the amenities of middle class life or their career or job. Their main direction is their job or career.

The liberal left, if I may call them that, participate even less. They are basically "free riders" on the currents of leftist political movements. They genuinely agree with the vision of a socialist society. If it comes, they will embrace it. But they also embrace the life they have. Most of them are quite aware that working for social change means changing their personal life. That they are not willing to do. When the going gets rough, most of them will change course. Their main direction is personal survival.

Other people (including many leftists) see themselves as being without effective power. Even though they may feel strongly about achieving a political objective, it appears nonrational for them to invest their time or to pay the costs of participation. If the objective is achieved by political activists, the free riders can join in the benefits and celebration; if the objective isn't obtained, the free rider hasn't lost anything.

The independent leftist and the free riders are left obstacles to the development of a leftist community. Their involvement and participation in affairs on the left have a profound impact on the kind of agenda that the American Left puts forward. At its most benign, their influence has not been very productive. At its worst, I think their influence impedes the development of leftist community, and that development is high on my agenda. The obsolete *class analysis* of the Marxist and the equally obsolescent belief in *progress* of the liberal analyst permit them both an ideological rationalization for not working on the development of leftist community.

These segments of the left are not engaged in revolutionary struggle, and this is especially true of the independent Marxists despite their rhetoric. And both segments exert a conservatizing influence: they opt out of acts and situations that call for commitment. They cannot engage in community-building because they have no community with which to identify.

As someone who has been an organizer of leftists for over ten years (although it took me a long while to recognize what I was doing) I have found few things more demoralizing to a group than the almost capricious participation or support of those who profess their comradeship.

Negativism, Amateurism and Voluntarism. Negativism, voluntarism, and amateurism are the hallmarks of the American left.

"Sure, I know you're against racism, sexism, capitalism and imperialism, but what do you people stand for?" That was the caption of a popular cartoon during the late 1960s. It was a fair question then. The campus-based movement was a movement of opposition and resistance. It ended before it could formulate an answer. Unfortunately, much of the agenda of the left is still negative. We act in response to ruling-class accidents and scandals. We act in opposition to the pathologies of the society. A left without an articulated vision of a good society is trapped in the capitalist trick-bag.

The agenda of the American left is written invariably by its opposition. The government acts, the media dramatize the action, the left responds.

A left response is, of course, necessary. But a response shouldn't always be limited to an act of opposition. Take, for example, the issue of nuclear power. We cannot successfully oppose it without at the same time demonstrating the viability of other energy options. A local "energy alliance" without a local program of conservation and the demonstration of alternative energy resources may effect more sociological damage than political good. That is, if you educate people about the dangers of nuclear accidents and radiation without presenting workable alternatives, you may, in effect, increase personal alienation, cynicism, and withdrawal. Similarly, opposition to the military budget and new weapons production must at the same time show people how disarmament can occur and how more jobs can be created through the conversion of war industries. An act of opposition must carry with it a political proposition.

Once upon a time I attended a meeting of socialist scholars. The second and final evening session was to be devoted to the topic of "socialist socializing." The session was to end by 9 P.M. A band was waiting and we were to end the weekend with a party. Now that's not bad practice. But the discussion of socialist socializing became very heavy — there were, it turned out, many ideological differences — and the participants, all survivors of academic jungles and totally intolerant of political differences, began circling each other for the kill. I left after twenty minutes and went to the mezzanine overlooking the meeting hall. The band, bartenders, a few children and I witnessed one of the most brutal discussions I've ever seen at any academic or political meeting. They were supposed to have been talking about comradeship and sociability. Instead, that rare opportunity to talk about comradeship became an occasion to vent all of the personal angers and frustrations of repressed middle-class political academics. The meeting ended only by direct action. I did try the formal channels first. I returned to the meeting and made a brief statement about theory and practice, recommending that having the party would lead to a better understanding than continuing the discussion. I was shouted down. The subject was too important to be halted by a party. An hour after the session was to end, I recruited the band and several friends and assaulted the enraged scholars with several squadrons of paper airplanes launched from the mezzanine. The moral to my story has two parts. You cannot build a movement for liberation on the basis of negativism. Moreover, a movement built on negativism will destroy itself.

An amateur is a dabbler, a superficial or unskillful worker. Left groups have a high density of amateurs. There are many reasons for it, and certainly the most important is that most people working in left groups have only a limited amount of time they can devote to their work. Obviously, there's more to it than that. Some "part-timers" are highly skilled; they're "professionals" in the best sense of that term.

Many left groups do not offer much systematic training, and there are often internal conflicts over applying standards of competency or standards of organizational equality. Often the outcome has been to de-emphasize competency. To be sure, it is a difficult conflict to manage. But I think it can be managed without a reduction to amateurism. And its result for the left has certainly been disastrous.

There are few people on the left who can give their full time to political work. There are perhaps millions of people who are salaried to devote their work day to promoting capitalism and to suppressing leftist ideas.

Many on the left, as you all know, are engaged in straight jobs in corporate, bureaucratic settings that are alienating and energy-draining. *All* are sometimes co-opted. Some on the left have deliberately chosen part-time work and its marginal income to free themselves for political work. And in political organizations, "movement wages" are still offered —and not always paid regularly.

If capitalists snicker at the impoverished left, they are not alone. Once I had been invited to talk to a regional group of political academics on alternatives to careers in the academy. In the discussion following, one participant — the "president" of a national Marxist organization —said in what was meant to be a total put-down of me that he could not take me seriously because he wasted more money in a year than I earned.

But the problem of voluntarism is not that people won't take us seriously, it is that we are not taking ourselves seriously. Political workers have a personal obligation to feed themselves healthfully and to live in some comfort. If we are engaged in political work, we need money and resources to do that work. Voluntarism is necessary, but there is no such thing as a free lunch.

Varieties of Escapism

Leftists have many ways of avoiding revolutionary work. Some ploys are escapist, some are retreatist, but the end result is the same. That result isn't merely political inaction. For if it were only inaction, it would be no more problematic for the left than any other organizing. Rather, retreatist and escapist ploys on the left misdirect people and exhaust their energies while presenting the facade of political activity The end result is burn-out and disillusionment. Cataloging these ploys is important. These are major forms of escape from social anarchist activity.

Afghanistanism. To illustrate the first ploy, I should begin by deploring the state of affairs in Afghanistan. Let me explain. In the jargon of journalists, the editorial practice of *Afghanistanism* is that of deliberately ignoring conditions close at home, while deploring those far away. This keeps the newspaper from offending their sponsors or the local elites, while at the same time presenting the appearance of social concern. It works the same way for leftists, too. It is generally a safe form of political opposition. (Since the Soviet involvement in Afghanistan, practicing journalists may seek another country.)

Fighting other people's battles. This is, in fact, a descriptive definition of liberalism. The left, because of its liberal origins, is very good at that. The decisions about where or how to lend your support to other struggles is always very difficult. Consider one major form of leftist struggle — the economic boycott. It is a form of social noncooperation that is a direct attack upon those who hold economic power. It has been used in civil rights movements and in national liberation struggles. It is an important tactic. But there are differences when I boycott and picket a local merchant, say to stop sexist advertising. I am in some control of the end result. When I boycott, say, a national clothing manufacturer to help the workers gain union recognition, I have no control over that outcome. That is, the outcome is mediated by all of the contesting groups. Take for example the Farah Pants boycott of 1973-74. It was so effective that Farah had to shut down four of his eight American plants, and Farah stock fell from $30 a share to $3.25. And while unionization was achieved, 4,000 workers lost their jobs, and the union officers signed a "no strike" contract and ignored almost all of the demands that led to the strike and boycott to begin with. So much for fighting other people's battles.

Getting one's head together. For some on the left, the study group has become a surrogate therapy group. Others haven't moved out of therapy as yet. I have observed leftists who expend most of their political energies in study groups, and I have also observed leftists moving from therapy to therapy in an almost desperate attempt to avoid self-examination. Study groups and therapy may not sound like a parallelism, but for some leftists they are. They are yet another way to appear to be engaged in meaningful self-directed activity when, in fact, they are a means of rationalizing the avoidance of political work.

The ordinal fallacy. Many leftists justify their not working as a matter of expedience. They are involved, they will tell you, "in preparation" for their revolutionary future so they will be able to work effectively. First, they will master their craft, then they will use their skills for change. First they will get tenure, then they will bring their revolutionary agenda to the campus. First they will achieve a position of power, then they will use their power for the good of all.

The philosopher Abraham Kaplan called this the "ordinal fallacy." First I will do this, then I will do that. It is a disorder of thought. It usually strikes the young adult; it almost never leaves. For after all, we are what we do. And if we do not do what we believe to be true today, it is the nature of life that we will probably not do it tomorrow.

Electoral politics. Within the capitalist state, the electoral road to radical reform has become a dead-end. Most persons on the left recognize that statement to be true — although, as we all know, the residues of liberalism are hard to get out of your mind. Just the same, some leftists use the electoral arena as a place for recruiting people into left organizations. For them, it is the deliberate manipulation of the sacred symbols of the society. It is, of course, a cynical and dishonest manipulation of people.

The theory for involvement and recruitment through straight politics is this. When you bring people into reformist electoral struggles, they soon learn the limits of reformism. As the participants gain experience in working together and gain self-confidence they become, through this collective experience of the failure of reformism, willing recruits to the left.

To me, this theory has never been demonstrated to be true. And all of my experience tells me it is false. Moreover, we need to realize that when the left tries to recruit people into working through established political structures, they undercut involvement in alternative institutions and in the building of a left community. What is more is that they recruit on the basis of deceit or self-delusion. And all of these actions, camouflaged by their rhetoric, legitimize participation in electoral politics and reaffirm to those who may have had their doubts about the efficacy of the system that this is probably the only way to go. After all, even the left is doing it.

THE RHETORIC OF FAILURE

STILL ANOTHER LEFT OBSTACLE TO THE LEFT is its rhetoric of failure. That is, much of the way in which some leftists conceptualize and talk about the world is demoralizing and self-defeating.

Let me give some illustrations. I have on several occasions heard people talk about "the time not being right" or "the nature of the times" as if what they were analyzing were a chronograph and not a complex of social factors. Almost always when I have questioned people about their criteria, I have found them inarticulate and defensive. "The time is not right" is a socially acceptable rationalization for many. It permits people to justify their inaction. Consider other rationalizations such as "getting my head together" or "my shit together" or "it together" — or being "burned out!' All of these, of course, have a kernel of meaning but they are basically verbal ploys to rationalize failure and avoid self-knowledge.

Take another illustration from the Marxist left. I have heard many Marxist intellectuals tell me that the reasons that they are not active politically is because "there is no mass movement in the United States."

Now I don't want to quibble over that ancient (and misleading) concept of a "mass movement." But I do want to argue that if everyone insisted that a movement be a certain size, or be in some condition related to size, *before* they joined it, then that movement would never come about. So you see the search for the mass movement is almost inherently self-defeating.

A final illustration — take the very idea of "revolution" itself. Conceptualized as an event, as something that occurs at some point in time it is always distant, often hopelessly so. Have you ever noticed how depressive some revolutionaries are? Conceptualized as a process, as a relationship among people who are working in opposition to the state, the response to the idea of revolution changes.

The language we use to analyze our political life is critical to how we then act on our analysis.

THE FAILURE OF IMAGINATION

MANY OF YOU MAY REMEMBER the first "energy crisis," that initial period of 1973 of long gas station lines and record oil company profits. In Baltimore, a local political group called for a protest demonstration. And why not? The form of the demonstration they called at this time when filling your tank was a three-hour chore was a *motorcade*. Of course, nobody came.

Todd Gitlin writing about SDS and the new left of the sixties said at the time that if we failed it would have been a "failure of nerve." Perhaps he was right, then. But today I would say that if we fail it will have been a failure of imagination. Most people have no sense of how to move outside the present — even in their imagination.

Consider this fact: In repeated opinion polls, most people say that they are not satisfied with their jobs. Job dissatisfaction is high, and it has been increasing over the last 25 years. But when sociologists ask "would you continue working at your job even if you didn't have to?" a majority say "yes."

Why is that? Because most people simply can't imagine what else they could do with their time.

Here's a small social experiment. Ask your friends to imagine how they could construct a society in which there was little or no crime. Most people who answer you are going to say one of two things: either that it can't be done or that they can't think of anything. Either way they are denying themselves the use of their own imagination.

Another way that people will answer is by designing a society that is even more repressive and more totalitarian than anything we now have. Why do they do that? Not because they want a more repressive society, but because they can only think in terms of what we have now. They are trapped in the present.

Americans suffer from a failure of imagination. And the American left itself has not shown that it can escape the present. Without imagination, the left is trapped in its own present, a world of demonstrations and of negative protest.

Let me tell you another story. This is a fish story. In Baltimore, a new multimillion-dollar aquarium for the educational and recreational display of fish opened in 1981. While it was in the planning stage, I attended an unusual meeting of Marxists, libertarian socialists, and members of the city planning department. At the meeting, I proposed that at least half the aquarium should be used for the production of food fish. The technology is the same whether one is displaying a Chesapeake Bay Blue Fish (which may die out from Kepone poisoning) or a Hawaiian humuhumunukunukuapua'a. The food fish could be sold at cost to those on food stamps or to nonprofit institutional buyers. I thought people would eat up the idea. And I also proposed that part of the food fish facility be used to teach people about fish and perhaps even hydroponics. The Marxists labeled my program "utopian." (The charge of utopianism, by the way, is another good example of the rhetoric of failure.) The city planners seemed angry, as if my proposal was frivolous. The only direct comment came from one of the chief planners: "It was not the city's job to feed its population."

GETTING FROM HERE TO THERE

HERE IS THE OUTLINE of how we are traveling. First, we will talk of the logic of alternative institutions; second, building collective organizations; third and briefly, the building of economic resources; and fourth, political education. These four aspects of a revolutionary transfer culture entail some degree of civil noncooperation and direct action. However, massive noncooperation and large-scale, militant confrontations with state and corporate power require a prior level of organization and experience. Insofar as we want to think of "stages" in the development of a transfer culture, then we should regard mass civil disobedience within the final stage of the toppling of the old structures of society.

Alternative Institutions. If there are any priorities in my scheme, anything to be called a "first step," I would say it was the building of *alternative institutions*. The reason for this is that I see such institutions as the building blocks of a transfer culture. They are the institutions of the new society as closely as we can approximate them within the old society. Moreover, in the process of building alternative institutions, we will invariably confront almost all of the problems of fashioning a transfer culture.

A political community, like any society, has to meet certain basic requirements. It "has to" if it is to maintain itself and provide a good life for its members. Every political community must have a means of replacing its members and teaching newcomers its culture. These are usually the functions of families, communes, schooling arrangements and the political media. Every political community must have some systematic way of reconfirming membership, of reaffirming its values, and reviving the solidarity of its residents. These are usually the functions of music, theater, the written and visual arts. Every political community must be able to sustain itself through producing goods and distributing them to its members. Every political community must be able to protect itself against repression by the agents of the state. Finally, every political community must have some system of social control that preserves communal order, as well as some means of preserving the autonomy of the individual within the structural arrangements and needs of the community.

Sociologists refer to all of these "musts" as functional prerequisites. These are the problems that must be solved if we are going to build a political community and its transfer culture. And the building block is the alternative institution. It is an organization of people designed to work at, to cope with, to solve some of these basic problems of community. Building a transfer culture means building the institutions that support political community.

An alternative institution is a group of people who have organized themselves into residential or work arrangements. Take that as a start of a definition. As work or living arrangements, the alternative institution doesn't do anything that any established institution doesn't do. What it does, it does differently; and it does so in a politicized context. Its hallmark is how it builds its economic resources, how it structures its internal organization, and what forms of internal education it conducts. Critical to an alternative institution is the content of its internal education program.

Although we will discuss all of these issues in detail in following sections here's a preview. The economic status of an alternative institution is designed to minimize dependency on the money system and financial institutions of the larger society. The membership of alternative institutions operates on principles of collective organization. Decisions are made collectively, work assignments rotated, and knowledge and skills continually shared. In formal programs of internal education, experienced workers teach the inexperienced. And all study together around the issues of political struggle that unite them.

Finally, the alternative institution has to maintain itself as a *counter-institution*. That is, it must always direct some of its resources to direct assaults on the institutional structures it is trying to change.

Collective Organization. The goal of organizing ourselves collectively is to empower each and every member of the collective. That goal has to be the guide for all decisions made about how the organization should operate.

There is an old shaggy dog story about the ship's captain who every morning after breakfast would go to his personal safe, take out a slip of paper, look at it, then return it and lock the safe. He did it, so the story goes, for 35 years until his death. After the Captain's funeral, the ship's officers assembled. Years of curiosity had to be satisfied. They opened the safe and removed the now ragged and smudged piece of paper. On it were written a few simple words of guidance: "Port is left. Starboard is right."

I think we might issue a slip of paper to all collective members. On it I would write "diffuse power" and "empower everyone."

In the context of hierarchical organizations and competitive interpersonal relations, in the context of male chauvinism and the valuing of "strong leadership," collective social arrangements are very fragile. In this society relatively few people can even maintain decent cooperative work or living arrangements. The collective process is far more demanding.

The new society can only be built and sustained through a collective process. The "collective" is the basic unit of anarchist organization.

How do collectives work? Really the same as any organization. The bottom line is different. Virtually all hierarchical organizations measure their "effectiveness" by economic criteria, e.g., the number of units produced at a specific cost for a specific time period. In a collective, effectiveness is generally assessed by worker-defined criteria. And while worker satisfaction is given primacy, it is also weighed against economic and political criteria.

In a collective organization, the process of work is at least as important as the product of work. Responsibility for the organization is shared by all members, and all members have open access to organizational information.

In a collective, there is a built-in process to empower everyone and to inoculate the organization against elitism. It is a dual process. The first task is the rotation of people across all jobs. The goal is not necessarily for everyone to do everything (although that is an ideal). The goal is for everyone to have sufficient knowledge of every job so that no person or elite can monopolize that knowledge. The second task is to distribute the routine maintenance work of the organization (often called the "dirty work") so that it is regularly shared by all persons.

The process of empowering people in an organization requires a formal program of education. Obviously, you can't rotate people to new jobs without their being taught the basic skills necessary for the job. That's one part of collective education. A second part is training in the interpersonal skills of collective work. A standard example is training in the processes of criticism, group evaluation and conflict resolution. These skills are vital, especially for people raised in the destructive cultures of Western Society.

What I have presented is only a sketch. The principles of collective organization, however, are substantially well-known. And the collective work, or living, experience is unforgettable. For most people in the capitalist world, the experience is inaccessible. It is like all other elements of a revolutionary culture. The knowledgeable elites recognize its revolutionary potential and intensify their critique (or repression). And for most people who have succumbed to the self-alienating folkways of the society, the idea of collective living or working is inconceivable.

Economic Resources. In the building of the transfer culture, we need to free ourselves as much as we can from a dependency on the capitalist workplace and the economic institutions of society.

Let's talk first about working in mainstream economic settings. Almost all of us do it sometime or other. If you have to put in 40 hours a week plus travel time to a straight job, there isn't much time left after you subtract sleeping, eating, exercise, personal hygiene — the basic round of necessities. That's the major co-optation of straight jobs. It's not that you sell your labor power to the capitalist, as Marxists would say. It is that you are also selling them that energy you could be directing into building the transfer culture. The fact of the matter is that until we can build our own economic resources, we may have to fund our political work through selling our minds and bodies to those who will pay. It is, after all, an old profession.

There are some guidelines for the anarchist in the employ of the capitalist. Be clear about what you are doing. Making money is not the end, unless of course all of the money you make goes directly for survival. We should enter straight settings as guerrillas — exploiting the workplace for its resources and intelligence. (A good measure of this publication has been made possible by white collar guerrillas.)

We insinuate our politics; we pack up and leave. It is challenging political work.

Reducing our dependency on the capitalist workplace means removing ourselves from the consumer-oriented culture, reducing our economic needs, developing alternative institutions, and building an alternative economic network.

Communal living, the trading of labor and resources, skills exchanges, time and labor banks, land trusts, people's funds, and even an alternative money system are all part of the economic program for a transfer culture. They are all sketched in varying detail in the anarchist literature.

The chains of the middle class are like golden fetters. You are imprisoned by them and yet they are valuable. To break these chains may provide freedom, but it may also mean economic insecurity. To be free to worry about where you are going to sleep tonight is not very liberating.

The revolutionary is declassed or s/he is not a revolutionary. And, while disengaging oneself from one's economic class is difficult and anxiety-producing, to say the least, the matter of survival has to be kept always in view. No guerrilla force extends itself too long beyond its supply lines and network of citizen support. "The revolution is not a dinner party," Mao Zedong reminded his people's liberation army. But he never meant that people didn't eat.

The first step in building economic independence has to start with how you live. (And that, of course, is why that is such a big step.) It is also why I chose not to present the "blueprints" of the various schemes for economic self-reliance. We have many options in building a political lifestyle. The one option we don't have as anarchists is that of staying within the social class structure. And even here, the options for maintaining our marginality are matters of our courage and our imagination.

Political education. Education is so important that no state lets it go unregulated. It is so important that no movement for social change can survive without an educational program.

Education is not propaganda. That is, it is not a manipulative, one-sided attempt to discredit old ideas or declare the value of a political movement. Education is not graffiti. That is, it is not a case of displaying symbols or slogans of a political movement in public places. Propaganda and graffiti can be educational. They often serve a useful function in political work. They are, however, not the means for building a transfer culture.

Political education can be described as education that both motivates people to work for change and prepares them to lead a political life. A complete "program" of political education accomplishes four objectives. First, it provides an analysis and critique of what is under study. Next, it delegitimizes the established authority involved. Third, it presents a sketch of alternatives to existing conditions and authority structures. Finally, in the most difficult component, political education leads people to a new sense of self-awareness. It compels the "student" to re-examine her or his relationship to what is being studied.

Consider these four objectives as the ideal standards of any program of political education. They should all be represented in a program, but programs will vary in the degree to which they emphasize one or another objective. Most left programs are strong on analysis and critique, weak in sketching alternatives, and weakest in coping with self-education.

In general, people are unaware of the politics of self. Self-rejection is commonplace in this society. It serves as a mechanism of social control. First of all it keeps people from directing their own behavior. When your identity is in doubt, your ability to act is paralyzed. Secondly, self-rejection keeps people from establishing close personal relationships. People who reject themselves necessarily reject others.

My own sketches for developing a program of political self-education are incomplete. As educators, and all anarchists are educators, we have to help people accomplish two tasks. People have to learn how to learn. That's our first task, to help them to do so. In most educational contexts, children and adults are given the problems and then either given the solutions or told where to find them. Formulating the problems for oneself and exploring the pathways to solution are the essence of "learning how to learn." The second task necessary is that of helping people expand their repertory of behaviors and experiences. Autonomy is in large part a consequence of successful adventures in a diverse range of experiences.

Teaching yourself skills that embody self-change is like taking direct action with yourself as the target. You don't really need a formal teacher, but you do need a personal support network.

There are two targets of direct action on oneself that are good starting points. One appears to be highly individualistic. I call it, fancifully, the "reintegration of mind and body." I don't mean anything very philosophically complex by my label. I merely mean to point out that most people are alienated from their bodies. When a person can't look at their own naked body in a mirror, they are in a state of profound self-alienation. But people are alienated, rejecting, or abusive of their body in many ways. You can see it most openly in how people eat, how they care for themselves physically, and in how they move. You can see it in their repression of their sexuality. The rejection of one's physical self is an integral part of self-rejection. People lose their autonomy (or never gain it) insofar as they have no control over aspects of their physical being. You can view this reintegration of the physical and mental as highly individualistic. But placed in its social context, it is an act of anarchist self-education.

Another form of political self-education is "criticism/self-criticism." It is necessarily part of the collective process. Usually constructive, critical feedback sessions are reserved for times following group meetings (or performances, or production schedules). These periods are set aside for the collective to evaluate the individual contributions to the collective. It is, properly done, a time for growth, for collective and personal change. As an educational act, constructive feedback is necessary for maintaining personal growth and materially satisfying interpersonal relationships in a collective. And these are requisites for maintaining the political focus of a collective. I have discussed only two of the forms of political education, but that is only because they are the least discussed in current political circles. From an anarchist standpoint, self-education is critical. I have used the term in two finely different ways. One meaning is the "ability to teach yourself new materials." The other meaning refers to the "ability to change oneself," that is, to teach yourself new ways of behaving toward yourself. To be able to educate yourself is a necessary condition for becoming autonomous. And there is no anarchy without autonomy.

Education for equality. There is another dimension of political education that needs highlighting. It flows concurrently with the process of self-education; call it education for equality. I think that we often confuse our commitment to equality as sufficient, as an end in itself. I think this is a serious error. None of us have escaped being socialized into this integrally stratified hierarchical society. This is to say that we have so internalized its meanness that we are often unaware when we act out learned roles of oppressor or oppressed.

Let me give two illustrations from social psychological research. In one study, researchers observed the behavior of women elementary school teachers, most of whom identified themselves as feminists. The observers noted whom the teachers called on and what kinds of praise they gave the students for their work. What they found was that the boys and girls were treated differently and were rewarded differently according to the subjects under discussion. What was significant about the research is that none of the teachers were aware of their sexist behavior. In another study involving black and white applicants for jobs, observers noted subtle differences in the behavior of whites interviewing candidates of different races. The difference involved such dimensions as the physical distance maintained, eye contact, smiling, and length of the interview. Once again, the people being studied had no conception of their differential treatment of others.

We all know how hard it can be to motivate ourselves (or others) to learn something even when we are aware that it is something we don't know and should know. In this case the problem is far more difficult. Education for an egalitarian society is a personal challenge, and it will be the challenge for educators everywhere. The guidebooks are only now being written.

Resistance as a way of life. The potential for resistance — for honest, courageous, stand-up-and-be-counted resistance—is everywhere in everyday life. Power is exercised everywhere, so it is it can be resisted everywhere. The political activist simply has to expect to be "in struggle" almost all of the time. We need also to understand that working to build a revolutionary transfer culture makes us marginal persons in this society. We are "marginal" in part because we are not a part of the mainstream institutions or cultural practices of the society, but also because we live in that borderland between the existing society and a new society. We live our lives and build our alternatives in that borderland. As my favorite anarchist slogan goes, "We are building the new society in the vacant lots of the old." My theory of a revolutionary transfer culture is incomplete—and certainly subject to revision. Our theoretical scenario ends with a visible left, with a high density of revolutionary symbols permeating the larger society, and with hundreds of thousands of collectives loosely organized into networks and federations. The scenario ends as we are about to start the next act, massive economic noncooperation and large-scale resistance to state authority. The act ends with the deflation of state authority.

In moving from here to there, in building our transfer culture, there are some certainties. The more successful and well-developed is our political culture, the more severely will the State move against us. I do not know whether we can withstand the repression. I do not even think that is now knowable. But even if we "fail," and social anarchists are repressed, large numbers of people will have changed from the experience. They will become the seeds for a new crop of revolutionaries. Again, even if we fail, striving to build the new society is the way I prefer to live.

ORGANIZING COMMUNITIES

TOM KNOCHE

Many anarchists probably cringe at the notion of any person or group being "organized" and believe that the very idea is manipulative. They can point to countless community organization leaders who ended up on government payrolls. They can't see how winning traffic lights and playgrounds does any more than help the system appear pluralistic and effective.

Such skepticism makes sense. Community organizing has always been practiced in many different ways to accomplish many different things. In reviewing the history of neighborhood organizing, Robert Fisher summed it up this way:

> While neighborhood organizing is a political act, it is neither inherently reactionary, conservative, liberal or radical, nor is it inherently democratic and inclusive or authoritarian and parochial. It is above all a political method, an approach used by various segments of the population to achieve specific goals, serve certain interests, and advance clear or ill-defined political perspectives. (Fisher, 1984; p.158)

If we just look at some of the progressive strains of community organizing thought, we still face a lot of confusion about what it is and how it is used. Saul Alinsky, a key figure in the development of community organizing as we know it today, wrote:

> We are concerned about how to create mass organizations to seize power and give it to the people; to realize the democratic dream of equality, justice, peace, cooperation, equal

and full opportunities for education, full and useful employment, health and the creation of those circumstances in which man can have the chance to live by the values that give meaning to life. We are talking about a mass power organization that will change the world. (Alinsky 1971; p.3)

The Midwest Academy, a training institute for community organizers founded by some ex-civil rights and SDS leaders, asserts that:

More and more people are finding that what is needed is a permanent, professionally staffed community membership organization which can not only win real improvements for its members, but which can actually alter the relations of power at the city and state level. These groups [citizen groups] are keeping government open to the people and are keeping our democratic rights intact. (Max, 1977; p.2)

A senior member of ACORN (Association of Communities Organized for Reform Now), a national association of mostly urban community organizations, describes the goal of organizing as strengthening people's collective capacities to bring about social change (Staples, 1984; p.1). ACORN organized local communities, then employed its constituency at the national level, attempting to move the Democratic Party to the left.

Finally, a participant in a workshop on community organizing I conducted a number of years ago characterized community organizing as "manipulating people to do trivial things."

In this article, I will focus on how community organizing can be useful in advancing an anarchist vision of social change. Community organizations that build on an anarchist vision of social change are different from other community organizations because of the purposes they have, the criteria they have for success, the issues they work on, the way they operate and the tactics they use.

My experience with community organizing spans a 16-year period including four years in Baltimore, Maryland and 12 in Camden, New Jersey. I have primarily worked with very low-income people on a wide range of issues. I will draw heavily on my personal experience in this article. I use the term "community organizing" to refer to social change efforts which are based in local geographically defined areas where people live. This is the key distinction between community organizing and other forms of organizing for social change which may be based in workplaces or universities, involving people where they work or study instead of where they live. Some issue-oriented organizations are considered community organizations if their constituency is local.

GOALS OF ANARCHIST ORGANIZING

Anarchist community organizing must be dedicated to changing what we can do today and undoing the socialization process that has depoliticized so many of us. We can use it to build the infrastructure that can respond and make greater advances when our political and economic systems are in crisis and are vulnerable to change.

The following purposes illustrate this concept.

1. Helping people experiment with decentralized, collective and cooperative forms of organization.

We have to build our American model of social change out of our own experience; we can't borrow revolutionary theory in total from that developed in another historical and/or cultural context. Community organizations can help people log that experience and analyze it. Because of our culture's grounding in defense of personal liberty and democracy, social change engineered by a vanguard or administered by a strong central state will not work here.

David Bouchier is on the right track when he says, "For citizen radicals evolution is better than revolution because evolution works" (Bouchier, 1987; p. 139). We must learn new values and practice cooperation rather than competition. Community organizations can provide a vehicle for this "retooling." "This means that a cultural revolution, a revolution of ideas and values and understanding, is the essential prelude to any radical change in the power arrangement of modern society. The purpose of radical citizenship is to take the initiative in this process" (Bouchier, p. 148).

Any kind of alternative institution (see Ehrlich, *et. al., Reinventing Anarchy*, p. 346), including cooperatives, worker managed businesses, etc., that offers a chance to learn and practice community control and worker self-management, is important. We must experience together how institutions can be different and better. These alternative institutions should be nonprofit, controlled and staffed by residents of the community they serve, and supported by the people who benefit from their existence. Most charities and social service agencies do not qualify as alternative institutions because they are staffed and controlled by people who usually are not part of the community they serve; they therefore foster dependence.

The recent proliferation of community land trusts in this country is an exciting example of community-based, cooperative and decentralized organizations. Through these organizations, people are taking land and housing off the private market and putting them in their collective control.

I have been a board member of North Camden Land Trust in Camden, New Jersey since its inception in 1984. The land trust now controls about thirty properties. A group of thirty low income homeowners who previously were tenants without much hope of home ownership now collectively make decisions concerning this property. The development of the land trust embodies many of the elements that describe community organizing grounded in a social anarchist vision for society.

2. Increasing the control that people have over actions that affect them, and increasing local self-reliance.

This involves taking some measure of control away from large institutions like government, corporations and social service conglomerates and giving it to the people most affected by their actions. David Bouchier describes this function as attaining "positive freedoms." Positive freedoms are rights of self-government that are not dependent on or limited by higher powers (Bouchier, p. 9).

In the neighborhood where I live and work, residents are starting to demand control over land use decisions. They stopped the state and local governments' plan to build a second state prison on the waterfront in their neighborhood. Instead of stopping there, the residents, through a series of block meetings and a neighborhood coalition, have developed a "Peoples' Plan" for that waterfront site. Control of land use has traditionally rested with local government (and state and federal government to a much more limited extent), guided by professional planners and consultants. Neighborhood residents believe they should control land use in their neighborhood, since they are the ones most directly affected by it.

The concept of self-reliant communities described by David Morris (1987) also helps us understand the shift in power we are talking about. Self-reliant communities organize to assert authority over capital investment, hiring, bank lending, etc. — all areas where decision making traditionally has been in the hands of government or private enterprise.

3. Building a counterculture that uses all forms of communication to resist illegitimate authority, racism, sexism, and capitalism. In low-income neighborhoods, it is also important that this counterculture become an alternative to the dominant culture which has resulted from welfare and drugs.

The Populist movement can teach us a lot about building a counterculture. That movement used the press, person-to-person contact via roving rallies and educational lectures, an extensive network of farm cooperatives and an alternative vision of agricultural economics to do this (Goodwyn, 1976; 1981).

Every movement organization has to use the media to advance its ideas and values. Educational events, film, community-based newspapers, etc., are all important. The local community advocacy organization in North Camden has done a good job of combining fundraising with the development of counterculture. They have sponsored alternative theater which has explored the issues of battered women, homelessness, and sexism. After each play, the theater group conducted an open discussion with the audience about these issues. These were powerful experiences for those who attended.

The question of confronting the dominant culture in very low-income neighborhoods is one of the greatest challenges facing community organizations. Many families have now experienced welfare dependence for *four generations,* a phenomenon which has radically altered many peoples' value systems in a negative way. People must worry about survival constantly, and believe that anything they can get to survive they are entitled to, regardless of the effect on others. It has not fostered a cooperative spirit. The response of low-income people to long-term welfare dependency is not irrational, but it is a serious obstacle to functioning in a system of decentralized, cooperative work and services.

One experience in this regard is relevant. A soup kitchen called Leavenhouse has operated in Camden for 10 years, during nine of which it was open to anyone who came. A year ago, the soup kitchen changed into a feeding cooperative on weekdays. Guests now have to either work a few hours in the kitchen or purchase a ticket for five dollars which is good for the entire month. Daily average attendance has dropped from 200 to about 20. The idea of cooperating to provide some of the resources necessary to sustain the service is outside the value system of many people who previously used the kitchen. Leavenhouse realizes now that it must address the reasons why people have not responded to the co-op, and is planning a community outreach campaign designed to build some understanding, trust and acceptance of the idea of cooperative feeding.

The 20 people who have joined the co-op have responded favorably. They appreciate the more tranquil eating environment and feel good about their role in it. The co-op members now make decisions about the operation of their co-op. Friendships and information sharing (primarily about jobs) have been facilitated. Fewer people are being served, but meaningful political objectives are now being realized.

4. Strengthening the "social fabric" of neighborhood units — that network of informal associations, support services, and contacts that enables people to survive and hold on to their sanity in spite of rather than because of the influence of government and social service bureaucracies in their lives.

John McKnight (1987) has done a good job of exposing the failure of traditional social service agencies and government in meeting people's needs for a support structure. They operate to control people. Informal associations ("community of associations"), on the other hand, operate on the basis of consent. They allow for creative solutions, quick response, interpersonal caring, and foster a broad base of participation.

A good example of fulfilling this purpose is the bartering network that some community organizations have developed. The organization simply prints a listing of people and services they need along with a parallel list of people and services they are willing to offer. This strengthens intraneighborhood communication. In poor neighborhoods, this is especially effective because it allows people to get things done without money, and to get a return on their work which is not taxable.

Concerned Citizens of North Camden (CCNC) has supported the development of a Camden "Center for Independent Living" — an organization that brings handicapped and disabled people in the city together to collectively solve the problems they face. Twelve-step groups are another example of informal, nonprofessional associations that work for people.

CRITERIA FOR SUCCESS

Many community organizations measure success by "winning." The tangible result is all that matters. In fact, many organizations evaluate the issues they take on by whether or not they are "winnable." The real significance of what is won and how it is won are of less concern.

For organizations that embrace an anarchist vision, the process and the intangible results are at least as important as any tangible results. Increasing any one organization's size and influence is not a concern; stimulating many decentralized, politically active groups is a concern. The success of community organizing can be measured by the extent to which the following mandates are realized.

1. People learn skills needed to analyze issues and confront those who exert control over their lives;

2. People learn to interact, make decisions and get things done collectively — rotating tasks, sharing skills, confronting racism, sexism and hierarchy;

3. Community residents realize some direct benefit or some resolution of problems they personally face through the organizing work;

4. Existing institutions change their priorities or way of doing things so that the authority of government, corporations and large institutions is replaced by extensions of decentralized, grassroots authority; and

5. Community residents feel stronger and better about themselves because of their participation in the collective effort.

PICKING ISSUES

Much of the literature about community organizing suggests that issues should be selected which are: 1) winnable; 2) involve advocacy, not service; and 3) build the organization's constituency, power and resources. "Good issue campaigns should have the twin goals of winning a victory and producing organizational mileage while doing so" (Staples, 1984; p.53).

These guidelines have always bothered me, and my experience suggests that they are off the mark. Issues should be picked primarily because the organization's members believe they are important and because they are consistent with one or more of the purposes listed above. Let me offer a few guidelines which are a bit different.

1. Service and advocacy work must go hand in hand, especially in very needy communities.

People get involved with groups because they present an opportunity for them to gain something they want. It may be tangible or intangible, but the motivation to get involved comes with an expectation of relatively short-term gratification. The job of community organizations is to facilitate a process where groups of people with similar needs or problems work together for the benefit of all. Through this process, people learn to work cooperatively and learn that their informal association can usually solve problems more effectively and quickly than established organizations.

I will offer an example to illustrate this point. When Concerned Citizens of North Camden (CCNC) organized a squatter campaign in 1981, the folks who squatted and took all of the risks did so because they wanted a house, and because they believed squatting was the best way to get one. Each one of the original 13 squatter families benefited because they got title to their house. The advocacy purpose was served because a program resulted that allowed 150 other families to get a house and some funds to fix it up over the subsequent five years. Because CCNC has stayed involved with each family and facilitated a support network with them (up to the present), 142 of the houses are still occupied by low-income families.

The government bureaucracy tried to undermine this program on numerous occasions, but without success. Participants willingly rallied in each crisis because they benefited in a way they valued deeply. The squatter movement allowed them to win something that they knew they would never realistically be able to win through any traditional home ownership programs. The squatters were poor, most had no credit histories and most were Hispanic. Official discredit, for whatever reasons, was meaningless because people knew the effort had worked for them.

In my experience, I have never been part of a more exciting and politically meaningful effort than the CCNC squatting effort in 1981. The initial squatting with 13 families was followed by five years of taking over abandoned houses which the City reluctantly sanctioned because of the strength and persistence of the movement.

2. Issues that pit one segment of the community against another — for example, issues which favor homeowners over renters, blacks over Puerto Ricans, etc. — should be avoided.

Most issues can be addressed in ways that unify neighborhood residents rather than divide them.

3. An informal involvement in broad political issues should be maintained on a consistent basis.

While I believe the kind of decentralized associations which form the basis for any anarchist vision of social change are most easily formed and nurtured at the local level (neighborhood or citywide), people must also connect in some way with broader social change issues. Social change cannot just happen in isolated places; we must build a large and diverse movement.

We need to integrate actions against militarism, imperialism, nuclear power, apartheid, etc., with action on local issues. They often can and should be tied together. This requires getting people to regional and national political events from time to time, and supporting local activities which help people to connect with these broader issues.

4. Avoid the pitfalls of electoral politics.

This is a very controversial area of concern for community organizations. The organizations I have worked with in Camden have vacillated in their stance vis-a-vis electoral politics.

The danger of cooptation through involvement in this arena is severe. Whenever a group of people start getting things done and build a credible reputation in the community, politicians will try to use the organization or its members to their advantage.

I have yet to witness any candidate for public office who maintained any kind of issue integrity. Once in the limelight, people bend toward the local interests that have the resources necessary to finance political campaigns. They want to win more than they want to advance any particular platform on the issues. We delude ourselves if we believe any politicians will support the progressive agenda of a minority constituency when their political future depends on them abandoning it.

I have participated in organizing campaigns where politicians were exploited because of vulnerability and where one politician was successfully played off against another. It is much easier for a community organization to use politicians to advance a cause if neither the organization nor its members are loyal to any officeholder. My experience says that any organized and militant community-based organization can successfully confront elected officials — regardless whether they are friends or enemies.

For organizations committed to the long-term process of radical social change, the way they operate is more important than any short-term victories that might be realized. The discipline, habits and values that are developed and nurtured through an organization's day-to-day life are an important part of the revolutionary process. Some guidelines for operation follow.

1. Have a political analysis and provide political education.

Lower-class and working-class neighborhood organizing must develop long-range goals which address imbalances in a class society, an alternative vision of what people are fighting for, and a context for all activity, whether pressuring for a stop sign or an eviction blockage. Otherwise, as has repeatedly happened, victories that win services or rewards will undermine the organization by "proving" that the existing system is responsive to poor and working people and therefore, in no need of fundamental change. (Fisher, 1984; p.162)

Any organization which is serious about social change and committed to democratic control of neighborhoods and workplaces must devote considerable energy to self-development — building individual skills and self-confidence and providing basic political education. The role of the state in maintaining inequality and destroying self-worth must be exposed.

This is particularly necessary in low income and minority neighborhoods where people have been most consistently socialized to believe that they are inferior, that the problems they face are individual ones rather than systemic ones, and where poor education has left people without the basic skills necessary to understand what goes on around them. Self-esteem is low, yet social change work requires people who are self-confident and assertive.

This dilemma is another of the major challenges in community organizing. The socialization process that strips people of their self-esteem is not easily or quickly reversed. This problem mandates that all tasks be performed in groups (for support and skill-sharing), and that training and preparation for all activities be thorough.

2. Be collectively and flexibly organized; decentralize as much as possible.

Radical organizations must always try to set an example of how organizations can be better than the institutions we criticize. All meetings and financial records should be open and leadership responsibilities rotated. Active men and women must work in all aspects of the organization — office work, fundraising, decision making, financial management, outreach, housekeeping, etc.

Teams of people should work on different projects, with coordination provided by an elected council. Pyramidal hierarchy with committees subordinate to and constrained by a strong central board should be avoided. The organization must remain flexible so that it can respond quickly to needs as they arise.

3. Maintain independence.

This is extremely important and extremely difficult. No organization committed to radical social change can allow itself to become financially dependent on the government or corporations. This does not mean that we can't use funds from government or private institutions for needed projects, but we can't get ourselves in a position where we owe any allegiance to the funders.

In 1983, the Farm Labor Organizing Committee was involved in a march from Toledo, Ohio to the Campbell's Soup headquarters in Camden, New Jersey. They were demanding three-party collective bargaining between Campbell's, the farmers it buys from, and the farm laborers who pick for the farmers. A coalition of groups in Camden worked to coordinate the final leg of the march through Camden. Many community-based organizations in Camden, however, refused to participate because they were dependent on donations of food or money from Campbell's Soup.

The bankruptcy of such behavior was driven home last year when Campbell's closed their Camden plant and laid off 1,000 workers. They made no special effort to soften the impact on the workers or the community.

All resources come at a price — even donations. We simply cannot accept funds from individuals or groups who condition their use in ways that constrain our work, or we must ignore the conditions and remain prepared to deal with the consequences later.

Alternative funding sources are providing a badly needed service in this regard. In Philadelphia, the Bread and Roses Community Fund raises money for distribution to social change organizations. In 1983, it spun off the Delaware Valley Community Reinvestment Fund, an alternative lending institution which provides credit for community-based housing and community development projects. Social change organizations in the Philadelphia/Camden area are extremely

Reinventing Anarchy, Again

indebted to these two support organizations. They play a vital role in helping organizations to maintain their independence.

4. Reach out to avoid isolation, but keep the focus local.

Community-based organizations must maintain loose ties with other grassroots groups. Progressive groups should be able to easily coalesce when that makes sense. We can always benefit from ideas and constructive criticism from supportive people who are not wrapped up in the day to day activity of our own organization.

This is another way in which left-wing fundraising/grantmaking groups like the Bread and Roses Community Fund in the Philadelphia area play an important role. They identify and bring together those groups in the region with a similar political agenda. Through Bread and Roses, the community advocacy organization in North Camden (CCNC) has maintained a very loose but productive relationship with the Kensington Joint Action Council (KJAC) in Philadelphia. KJAC squatted first, and helped CCNC plan its squatter campaign. CCNC spun off a land trust first and assisted KJAC in the development of their own land trust, Manos Unidas. Some ideas they developed for their land trust in terms of building comradery among members are now being considered by North Camden Land Trust.

Statewide and national organizations try very hard to pull in active local organizations and get leaders involved in issues at the state level. Be wary of the drain this can place on the local work. Cloward and Piven, in their *Poor Peoples' Movements,* do a wonderful job of illustrating this danger in their discussion of welfare rights organizing. Successes are won via direct action, not via formal organization.

5. Do not foster cross-class ties.

This applies especially to community organizing in low income areas where the local resources are extremely scarce. Many well-to-do "do-gooder" organizations like to have a ghetto project. It makes them feel good. Community organizations do not exist to alleviate ruling class guilt. Dependency on upper-class skills and money is a problem. Poor and working people must wage their own struggle.

An illustration of this is provided by the soup kitchen in North Camden. Suburban church folks, once they heard about Leavenhouse, were more than willing to send in volunteers each day to prepare and serve the meal. Leavenhouse told them not to bother, except perhaps occasionally with two or three people at a time. This allows the soup kitchen to develop local ownership, and for neighborhood residents to feel good about taking care of each other. It avoids the traditional social service model where one group comes into the city and delivers a service to another group of people who lives there and takes it.

Leavenhouse does accept money and food donations from outside the neighborhood, but its basic operating costs are covered with the rent of the community members who actually live at Leavenhouse. The outside income is extra; without it Leavenhouse will not shut down.

6. Have a cultural and social dimension.

Cultural and social events not only help to build a counterculture, but they help people feel good about who they are and where they come from. This is an important dynamic in overcoming powerlessness. Political music and film are especially effective in building class unity and strength, and in providing basic political education.

7. Staff the organization, to the greatest extent possible, with local workers and volunteers.

This seems obvious, but many community organizations draw on outsiders to perform the bulk of their work.

In Camden, nonprofit community organizations which provide affordable housing do it in three different ways. One organization matches suburban church groups with vacant houses. The church groups then purchase materials and provide volunteer labor to do the rehabilitation work. Another group relies on contractors to perform the work, few of which are based in Camden. A third group has hired and trained neighborhood residents to do all rehabilitation work. The workers are paid a decent wage for what they do. The latter approach develops skills in the neighborhood, allows neighborhood residents to feel good about improving their community, and fosters cooperative work habits which the construction crew members will carry into other organizations in the community.

Since the crew employed by the third organization is paid a decent wage, the first organization mentioned above rehabilitates more houses for less money. Again, when the commitment is to social change, the short-term tangible results are not the most important measures of success.

TACTICS

A considerable body of literature has been written about tactics in organizing and political work. I do not want to rehash all of that here, so I'll offer just a few guidelines about tactics that have consistently proven themselves. The discussion here is relevant to advocacy campaigns designed to take some measure of authority from government or private interest and put it in community control, or to force a reallocation of resources (public or private) in the interest of the community.

1. Be disruptive.

The tendency today is for community organizations to be less militant and confrontational, working through established community and political leaders to "engineer" the changes they want. No tendency could be more dangerous to the future of community organizing. The historical record and my experience say the opposite. We must be disruptive. No guideline is more important in the consideration of tactics. We can't move the system by testifying at hearings, negotiating at meetings and lobbying elected officials.

We must defy the rules of the system that fails to meet our needs. We must use guerrilla tactics that harass, confront, embarrass and expose that system and its functionaries.

2. Clear, precise and measurable demands are the cornerstone of any organizing campaign.

A group must know exactly what they want before they begin to confront the opposition.

3. Gradually escalate the militancy of your tactics.

The tactics in a campaign should gradually escalate in militancy, so that people new to political struggle are not intimidated. Let the militancy of the tactics increase at about the same pace as the intensity of their anger.

4. Address different targets simultaneously.

The tactics should be simultaneously directed at different parts of the system that are responsible for the injustice or grievance that needs to be resolved.

In the campaign to stop construction of a second State prison in their neighborhood, North Camden residents directed tactics at the Commissioner of Corrections, the private landowner who was willing to sell the waterfront land to the state for the prison, local politicians, the governor and the two gubernatorial candidates.

5. Avoid legal tactics.

Legal challenges are difficult. They take a lot of energy and money, people who aren't trained in the law have a very difficult time understanding the process, and they are easy to lose. I have never experienced success with a legal challenge.

When North Camden residents opposed construction of the first State prison in their neighborhood, they sued the state on environmental and land use grounds because the state planned to use valuable waterfront land for the prison. After a year of preparations, the case was heard before an Administrative Law judge. He threw the case out on a technicality. Understand that he was appointed by a governor who had made a public commitment to construct 4,000 more prison beds during his term in office.

Our legal system is set up to protect the interests of private property. Using it to dismantle the institutions that thrive on private property is obviously problematic.

6. Use direct action.

Direct actions are those that take the shortest route toward realization of the ends desired, without depending on intermediaries. A simple example might help to clarify. If a group of tenants is having a problem with a landlord refusing to make needed repairs, they can respond in several ways. They could take the landlord to court. They could get the housing and health inspectors to issue violations and pressure the landlord to make repairs. Or they could withhold rent from the landlord themselves, and use the money withheld to pay for the repairs. Along the same vein, they might picket the landlord's nice suburban home and leaflet all of his neighbors with information about how he treats people. The first two options put responsibility for getting something done in the hands of a government agency or law enforcement official. The latter course of actions keeps the tenants in control of what happens.

At a major state-funded construction project in Camden, residents wanted to make sure that city residents and minorities got construction jobs. Following the lead of some militant construction workers in New York City, they organized people who were ready to work, and blocked the gate to the job site at starting time. Their position was simple; they would move when local people were hired. The group got talked into negotiating and supporting an affirmative action program that would force the contractor to hire local people whenever the union hall couldn't provide a minority or city resident to fill an opening. The enforcement of that program was so mired in red tape that only a handful of local workers got hired. The group would have fared much better if they had stuck with their original tactic — the most direct one.

7. Have fun.

The tactics used should be fun for the participants. This isn't always possible, but often is. Street theater can often be used to change a routine action into a fun one. Let me provide a few examples.

When Concerned Citizens of North Camden (CCNC) ran its homeowner program (the program which resulted from the squatting in 1981), the City tried various mechanisms to discredit it. On one occasion when they threatened to cut some of the public fund involved in it, CCNC conducted a funeral march with about 100 people and carried a coffin from North Camden to City Hall where a hearing was being held on the Community Development Block Grant funds. Right in the middle of the hearing, a squatter came out from inside the coffin and told the crowd how the people's movement could not be silenced and made a mockery of the whole hearing. The effect was spectacular, as was the press coverage the next day.

When trying to stop the second prison, residents circulated a special issue of the community newspaper that made fun of the land owner, the mayor and the Commissioner of Corrections. The front page of the paper included photos of the three, captioned with the names of the Three Stooges (the resemblance was striking). The text on the front page made fun of each person's role in the project. We circulated the paper at a big public meeting which all three of these individuals attended. It helped give people courage and set the atmosphere for people to freely speak their minds. When people talk about the prison campaign, they laugh and remember "the three stooges."

Finally, when the homeless problem started to escalate in Camden (1983), we learned that people were being turned away from available shelters because there was not enough space. Leavenhouse, a local soup kitchen, then started to serve its meals on the steps of City

Hall one day each week. This created a party atmosphere; a couple hundred people would gather to eat and hang out every Wednesday at noon. As the weather got colder it became less fun, but the persistence was important. Three months after we started, in December, the City agreed to make a public building available as a shelter and agreed to adopt a policy that no homeless person would be denied shelter in Camden. The good aspect of this action was that homeless people were able to participate and help make it happen. It was a concrete way that they could have fun and feel good about helping to improve their own situation.

CONCLUDING COMMENTS

The kind of community organizing described here is not easy or straightforward. It can be extremely frustrating, with many pitfalls, temptations and diversions pushing it off the track and allowing it to assume a more liberal posture. This article described some of the main challenges: overcoming the welfare/drugs culture; maintaining independence; and working with people with few skills and low self-esteem. One other deserves mention — mobility.

In our society, mobility is expected. People are supposed to move to take a better job, to find a better house, etc. It is acceptable to displace people to build new expressways and universities. The average American moves once every five years. This mobility affects the stability of community organizations. Leaders and workers may get trained, get involved and then leave before they have been able to give much back to the organization. The drug traffic in many low-income neighborhoods exacerbates the stability problem; families face crises on a regular basis which take priority over community involvement.

The revolutionary work of community organizations would be enhanced with more population stability. Why aren't jobs created for people where they are? Why aren't a mix of housing types and sizes available within all communities? Why isn't displacement avoided at all cost? We need to address these questions if our communities are going to be more fertile areas for community organizing.

Community organizing from an anarchist perspective acknowledges that no revolution will be meaningful unless many Americans develop new values and behavior. This will require a history of work in cooperative, decentralized, revolutionary organizations in communities, workplaces and schools. The task before us is to build and nurture these organizations wherever we can. There are no shortcuts.

BIBLIOGRAPHY

Alinsky, Saul D. *Rules for Radicals*. New York: Random House, 1971.

Baldelli, Giovanni. *Social Anarchism*. New York: Aldine-Atherton, 1971.

Bouchier, David. *Radical Citizenship*. New York: Schocken Books, 1987.

Boyte, Harry. *Community is Possible*. New York: Harper & Row, 1984.

Cawley, Kaye, Mayo and Thompson (eds.). *Community or Class Struggle?* London: Stage 1, 1977.

Ehrlich, Howard J., Ehrlich, Carol, DeLeon, David, and Morris, Glenda (eds.). *Reinventing Anarchy*. Boston: Routledge & Kegan Paul, 1979.

Fisher, Robert. *Let the People Decide: Neighborhood Organizing in America*. Boston: Twayne Publishers, 1984.

Fisher, Robert and Romanofsky, Peter (eds.). *Community Organization for Urban Social Change*. Westport: Greenwood Press, 1981.

Foner, Philip S. (ed.). *The Life and Writings of Frederick Douglass*. New York: International Publishers, 1975.

Goodwyn, Lawrence. *The Populist Moment*. New York: Oxford University Press, 1981.

Goodwyn, Lawrence. *Democratic Promise: The Populist Moment in America*. New York: Oxford University Press, 1976.

Piven, Frances Fox and Cloward, Richard A. *Poor People's Movements*. New York: Vintage Books, 1979.

Kahn, Si. *Organizing*. New York: McGraw-Hill, 1982.

Lamb, Curt. *Political Power in Poor Neighborhoods*. New York: John Wiley and Sons, 1975.

Max, Steve, "Why Organize?" Chicago: Steve Max and the Midwest Academy, 1977.

McKnight, John, "Regenerating Community," in *Social Policy*, Winter 1987, pp. 54-58.

Morris, David, "A Globe of Villages: Self-Reliant Community Development," in *Building Economic Alternatives*, Winter, 1987, pp. 7-14.

Robinson, Chris. *Plotting Directions: An Activists' Guide*. Philadelphia: Recon Publications, 1982.

Roussopoulos, Dimitrios (ed.). *The City and Radical Social Change*. Montreal: Black Rose Books, 1982.

Schecter, Stephen. *The Politics of Urban Liberation*. Montreal: Black Rose Books, 1978.

Speeter, Greg. *Power: A Repossession Manual*. Amherst: University of Massachusetts, Citizens Involvement Training Project, 1978.

Staples, Lee. *Roots to Power*. New York: Praeger, 1984.

Ward, Colin. *Anarchy in Action*. New York: Harper & Row, 1973.

CONSENSUS

CAROLINE ESTES

Decision-making by consensus is a very old process about which there is much new interest. Primitive tribes and cultures have used it for thousands of years. Early Jesuits in the 17th century called it Communal Discernment. The Society of Friends (Quakers) has used it for over three hundred years, calling it seeking unity or gathering the sense of the meeting. In the past decade or two it has come into use in settings as diverse as businesses, intentional communities, and social action groups.

In simplest terms, consensus refers to agreement (on some decision) by *all* members of a group. The consensus *process* is the process the group goes through to reach this unity of agreement. Its assumptions, methods and results are different from Robert's *Rules of Order* or parliamentary process.

During the past 25 years, since I was first exposed to the use of consensus in Quaker meetings, I have been involved in some widely different situations in which consensus has been successfully used. In 1965, at the time of the Free Speech Movement in Berkeley, I watched this process being used in both the small council that was the governing body and the large mass meetings of up to 5,000 persons. The council was made up of such diverse representatives as Goldwater Republicans, Marxists, Maoists, Democrats, Republicans, Socialists, "Hippies" and simple activists. Mario Savio, leader of the movement, said that during the entire, tense, dramatic time, the group made only two strategic mistakes in carrying out the sit-ins, marches and confrontations, and these were the two times they came to a place where they weren't able to reach consensus, and so they voted. Both votes led them in the wrong direction. Similarly, in the large mass meetings, there was consistent agreement among those assembled, after much talking and discussion. There is no doubt it was a tense and exciting time — and that the unity in that group was very strong.

Since then I have worked with many groups that use this type of decision-making, whether in community gatherings, neighborhood meetings or Family meetings. I have found that it works as more than just a decision-making technique, for the unity and understanding it fosters serve in many ways to advance the basic purposes of these groups.

THE BASIS

CONSENSUS IS BASED ON THE BELIEF that each person has some part of the truth and no one has all of it, no matter how we would like to believe so, and on a respect for all persons involved in the decision that is being considered.

In our present society the governing idea is that we can trust no one, and therefore we must protect ourselves if we are to have any security in our decisions. The most we will be willing to do is compromise. This leads to a very interesting way of viewing the outcome of working together. It means we are willing to settle for less than the very best — and that we will always have a sense of dissatisfaction with any of our decisions unless we can somehow maneuver others involved in the process. This leads to a skewing of honesty and forthrightness in our relationships.

In the consensus process, we start from a different basis. The assumption is that we are all trustworthy (or at least can become so). The process allows each person complete power over the group. The central idea for the Quakers was the complete elimination of majorities, and minorities. If there were differences of view at a Quaker meeting, as there were likely to be in such a body, the consideration of the question at issue would proceed, with long periods of solemn hush and meditation, until slowly the lines of thought drew together towards a point of unity. Then the clerk would frame a minute of conclusion, expressing the "sense of the meeting."

Built into the consensual process is the belief that all persons have some part of the truth, or what in spiritual terms might be called "some part of God" in them, and that we will reach a better decision by putting all of the pieces of the truth together before proceeding. There are indeed times when it appears that two pieces of the truth are in contradiction to each other, but with clear thinking and attention, the whole may be perceived which includes both pieces or many pieces. The either/or type of argument does not advance this process.

Instead the process is a search for the very best solution to whatever is the problem. That does not mean that there is never room for error — but on the whole, in my experience, it is rare.

This process also makes a direct application of the idea that all persons are equal — an idea that we are not entirely comfortable with, since it seems on the surface that some people are more equal than others. But if we do indeed trust one another and do believe that we all have parts of the truth, then at any time one person may know more or have access to more information but at another time, others may know more or have more access or better understanding. Even when we have all the facts before us, it may be the spirit that is lacking and comes forth from another who sees the whole better than any of the persons who have some of the parts. All of these contributions are important.

Decisions which all have helped shape and in which all can feel united make the carrying out of the necessary action go forward with more efficiency, power and smoothness. This applies to persons, communities and nations. Given the enormous issues and problems before us, we need to use the ways that will best enable us to move forward together. "When people join their energy streams, miracles can happen."

THE PROCESS

HOW DOES THIS PROCESS ACTUALLY WORK? Consensus can be a powerful tool, yet like any tool, it needs to be used rightly. Its misuse can cause great frustration and disruption. To make the most of its possibilities we need to understand its parts and its process.

Consensus needs four ingredients — a group of people willing to work together, a problem or issue that requires a decision by the group, trust that there is a solution, and perseverance to find the truth.

It is important to come to meetings with a clear and unmadeup mind. That is not to say that prior thinking should not have been done, but simply that the thinking must remain open throughout the discussion — or else there is no way to come to the full truth. This means everyone, not just some of the group. Ideas and solutions must be sought from all assembled, and all must be listened to with respect and trusts. It is the practice of oneness for those who are committed to the idea — or the search for the best possible solution, for those who are more pragmatic.

The problems to be considered come in all sizes, from "who does the dishes" to "how to reach accord on de-escalating the arms race." The consensus process begins with a statement of the problem — as clear as possible in language as simple as possible. It is important that the problem not be stated in such a way that an answer is built in, but that there be an openness to looking at all sides of the issue — whatever it may be. It is also necessary to state it in the positive: "We will wash the dishes with detergent and hot water," not "We will not wash the dishes in cold water." Or, "we need to wash the dishes so they are clean and sanitary," not, "The dishes are very dirty, and we are not washing them correctly." Stating the issues in the positive begins the process of looking for positive solutions and not a general discussion on everything that is bad, undesirable or awful.

The meeting needs a facilitator/clerk/convener, a role whose importance cannot be too strongly emphasized. It is this person whose responsibility it is to see that all are heard, that all ideas are incorporated if they seem to be part of the truth, and that the final decision is agreed upon by all assembled.

Traits that help the facilitator are patience, intuition, articulateness, ability to think on his/her feet and a sense of humor. It is important also for a facilitator to look within to see if there is something that is missing — a person who has been wanting to speak but has been too shy, an idea that was badly articulated but has the possibility to help with the solution, anything that seems of importance on the nonverbal level. This essence of intuition can often be of great service to the group by releasing some active but unseen deterrent to the continued development of a solution.

The facilitator must be able to constantly state and restate the position of the meeting and at the same time show that progress is being made. This helps the group to move ahead with some dispatch.

And last but by no means least — a sense of humor. There is nothing like a small turn of phrase at a tense moment to lighten up the discussion and allow a little relaxation. Once you have found a good clerk or facilitator, don't let him/her go.

Often there are those who want to talk more than is necessary and others who don't speak enough. The facilitator needs to be able to keep the discussion from being dominated by a few and to encourage those who have not spoken to share their thoughts. There are a number of techniques for this. One is to suggest that no one speak more than once, until everyone has spoken; another is to have men and women speak alternately. This is particularly helpful for a short time if one gender seems to be dominating the discussion. However, it is not well to have any arbitrary technique used for too long. It is well to use these ways to bring a balance into the group, but these artificial guidelines should be abandoned as soon as possible. For instance, alternating of men and women might be used for one session — but then let whoever wants to speak in the next session. My experience is that a single two- or three-hour session with guidelines usually establishes a new pattern, and there is little need for the artificial guidelines to be continued.

No matter how well the discussion is carried forward, how good the facilitator and how much integrity there is in a group, there sometimes comes a point when all are in agreement but one or two. At that point there are three courses open. One is to see whether the individuals are willing to "step aside." This means that they do not agree with the decision but do not feel it is wrong and are willing to have it go forward, but do not want to be a party to carrying the action forward.

During the gathering of the sense of the meeting, if more than two or three persons start to step aside from a decision, then the facilitator should be alert to the fact that maybe the best decision has not yet been reached. This would depend on the size of the group, naturally. At Alpha, an intentional community, it is okay for one person to step aside, but as soon as another joins that one, the clerk begins to watch and to re-examine the decision. It might be that at that time the facilitator would ask for a few minutes of silence to see if there was another decision or an amendment that should be considered that had been overlooked and would ease the situation.

Another possibility is to lay aside the issue for another time. This alternative always seems to raise serious questions. However, we need to have some perspective on what we are doing. It is likely that the world will continue to revolve around the sun for another day, week, or year, whether we come to a decision at this moment or at another; and the need to make a decision now is often not as important as the need to come to unity around whatever decision is made.

Personal experience has shown me that even the most crucial decisions, seemingly time-bound, can be laid aside for a while — and that the time, whether a few hours or days, is wisely allowed and when again assembled we come to a better decision than was possible in the beginning.

The third possibility is that one or two people may be able to stop the group or meeting from moving forward. At that time there are several key ingredients to be considered. On the part of the meeting, it is important that the meeting see the person who is holding the meeting as doing so out of that person's highest understanding and beliefs. The individual(s) who are holding the group from making a decision must also have examined themselves well to know that they are not doing so out of self-interest, bias, vengeance or any other emotion or idea except the very strong feeling and belief that the decision is wrong — and that they would be doing the group a great disservice by allowing it to go forward.

This is always one of those times when feelings can run high, and it is important for the meeting, or group, not to use pressure on those who differ. It is hard enough to feel that you are stopping the group from going forward, without having additional pressure exerted to go against your examined reasons and deeply felt understandings.

In my personal experience of living with the consensus process full-time for 12 years, I need to say that I have seen the meeting held from going forward on only a handful of occasions, and in each case the person was correct — and the group would have made a mistake by moving forward.

There is another situation which does occur, though rarely, where one person is consistently at odds with everyone else. Depending on the type of group and its membership, it would be well to see if this person is in the right organization or group. If there is a consistent difference, the person cannot feel comfortable continuing, and the group needs to meet and work with that person.

One reason it is important that each decision be well seasoned is that the consensus is a very conservative process. Once a decision has been made, it takes a consensus to change the decision. This means that whatever has been arrived at needs to be able to be relied on for some time, and thus decisions should not be arrived at in haste. One way a decision can be tried, but not necessarily need to be changed, is to put a time limit on it. For instance, if you want to try a new way of handling the cleaning of the house, then you might say: "We will allot one hour a day to housekeeping for the next month. At the end of the month, either we will reconsider the decision or it will no longer be operable." At Alpha Farm we have done this on a number of occasions, usually trying a decision for a year and then either making a final decision or dropping it entirely. This necessitates keeping minutes, which is another aspect of consensus that needs to be heeded.

Minutes on decisions that have been made need to be stated by the clerk or facilitator or minute-taker at the time of the decision, so that all present know they have agreed to the same thing. It is not well for minutes to be taken and then read at the next meeting, unless there is to be a meeting very soon. The reason for this seems obvious: those who make the decision are the ones to carry it out — and if there is a month or more before they are stated, then the same people may not all be present, and the minutes may or may not be correct, but the time for correction is past. This is a particularly important but little-adhered-to part of the process.

Recently, I was privileged to facilitate the first North American Bioregional Congress, held in Missouri. Over 200 persons arrived from all over the continent, and some from abroad, and worked together for five days, making all decisions by consensus. Some of those present had used the process before or were currently using it in the groups they worked with at home; but many had not used it, and there was a high degree of skepticism when we began as to whether such a widely diverse group of people could work in that degree of harmony and unity. On the final day of the Congress, there were a very large number of resolutions, position papers and policies put forward from committees that had been working all week long. All decisions that were made that day were made by consensus — and the level of love and trust among participants was tangible. Much to the surprise of nearly everyone, we came away with a sense of unity and forward motion that was near-miraculous, but believable.

THE HABIT OF DIRECT ACTION

DAVID WIECK

All action, we can see upon reflection, realizes *some* belief. Indirect action is often criticized on the ground that the means employed are unreliable; a strong point, but perhaps applied too sweepingly, and I think less fundamental than another. I want to distinguish (as direct action) that action which, in respect to a situation, *realizes the end desired*, so far as this lies in one's power or the power of one's group; from action (indirect action) which realizes *an irrelevant or even contradictory end*, presumably as a means to the 'good' end. The most significant — but not the only — distinction lies in the kind of fact thereby created for other persons. It is direct action to present a person with the kind of attitude towards 'race' which one advocates; it is indirect action to rely on legal enforcement because in this is realized the concept that these people must obey the law simply because it is the law, and this may hopelessly obscure the aim.

Persons with no patience often make a bad distinction between 'talk' and 'action.' It can be seen that the important distinction is between talk that is mere moral assertion or propositional argument, and talk (in fact: direct action) which conveys a feeling, an attitude, relevant to the desired end.

To take a homely example. If a butcher weighs one's meat with his or her thumb on the scale, one may complain about it and tell him he is a bandit who robs the poor, and if he persists and one does nothing else, this is mere talk; one may call the Department of Weights and Measures, and this is indirect action; or one may, talk failing, insist on weighing one's own meat, bring along a scale to check the butcher's weight, take one's business somewhere else, help open a co-operative store, etc., and these are direct actions.

Proceeding with the belief that in every situation, every individual and group has the possibility of some direct action on some level of generality, we may discover much that has been unrecognized, and the importance of much that has been underrated. So politicalized is our thinking, so focused to the motions of governmental institutions, that the effects of direct efforts to modify one's environment are unexplored.

The habit of direct action is, perhaps, identical with the habit of being a free person, prepared to live responsibly in a free society. Saying this, one recognizes that just this moment, just this issue, is not likely to be the occasion when we all come of age. All true. The question is, when will we begin?

AFTERWORD

[Wherein the editor collects his notes, reiterates some points, makes a few new observations, provides some curmugdeonly advice, figuratively embraces his dear readers, and takes his leave.]

1

As every good teacher knows, it is a valuable technique to tell students what it is you are going to tell them, tell them, and then tell them what it is you have just told them. These afterwords are not that, but I thought it would be important to leave you with a definition of anarchism that both describes these contents and which you can use to tell others what it is you have been reading.

John Clark in *The Anarchist Moment* offers this four-part statement on the nature of anarchist theory:

> (1) a view of an ideal, non-coercive, non-authoritarian society; (2) a criticism of existing society and its institutions, based on this anti-authoritarian idea; (3) a view of human nature that justifies the hope for significant progress toward the ideal; and (4) a strategy for change, involving immediate institution of non-coercive, non-authoritarian, and decentralist alternatives. (Pp. 126-127)

2

I think we need to understand that we live in a revolutionary period. The dominant institutions of capitalism and the state are decomposing. Many of the central ideas of capitalism, Marxism, and state socialism are being challenged. But what really makes it a revolutionary period is that these events are occurring at the same time when so many people are putting forward a vision of a better society and are taking steps to build that society now.

Afterword

3

I subscribe to the big bang theory of revolution. The first stage of the revolutionary process, I believe, requires the deflation of legitimate authority. If people are to think for themselves, to act in their own leadership capacities, to look for models elsewhere, then they have got to break away from the familiar authorities who have been their past guides. This is not easy for most people.

I think that we underestimate the power of legitimate authority. The beliefs people come to accept or reject are intimately related to the panoply of positive and negative authorities they carry in their minds. Positive authorities are sometimes significant others in a person's life. Mostly they are the persons who occupies a particular status: the president or pope, the professor or expert. These authorities not only set the agenda, they tell people what to think. Saddam Hussein is another Hitler, George Bush told the world, and within days millions of people parroted "Saddam Hussein is another Hitler."

These legitimate authorities do something else as well; they *confuse* people. That is, in order to maintain their own positions and persist in their controlling and exploitative activities, they need to prevent people from thinking about and truly understanding what is going on in their world.

Barry Sussman, for 10 years the director of polling for the *Washington Post*, wrote in retrospect in his final column:

> I was struck early and often by how little they [the American public] know about public affairs. . . . I am also struck, as I hear and watch the pronouncements of government and political party leaders, at how much of what they say is geared to keeping the people unaroused and disengaged from public affairs. (*The Washington Post National Weekly Edition*, January 19, 1987, p. 37)

The delegitimation of authority can take many forms and it needs to take many forms. When Dick Lourie can open his poem, "Civics 1: Nothing Fancy," with "The President is a piece of shit. I said the President is a piece of shit," mindless readers become mindful. The anti-authoritarian critiques of many left and radical writers are of obvious value.

Attacks on the symbols of authority are of strategic importance as well. Note the response to flag burning or Andres Serrano's "Piss Christ," an art piece displaying a crucifix floating in a bottle of urine.

In short, in a note that is already too long, we need to understand that a persistent, politically upfront, nonpredictable, multimedia campaign of delegitimation may someday have its return in that big bang — the deflation of political authority.

4

Like most anarchists, I believe that voting only serves to legitimate the electoral system. Brian Martin's superb critique of that system in his "Democracy without Elections," doesn't need to be reiterated here. Yet, there are two cases in which I slink to the polls.

Case one. A candidate as indicated by platform and personality will likely do lasting damage to the social good. Ronald Reagan is a case in point. Much in the same way that I would try to intervene if I observed someone assaulting another person, I would intervene here by casting a vote against the Reagan clone.

Case two. The first self-declared Lesbian runs for city council. Assuming that her politics were at least to the left of innocuous, I would again cast a ballot. I would do so on the grounds that the election would in fact be a poll on sexual orientation. The election of an openly lesbian candidate can not, presumably, do any more harm than the election of a heterosexual candidate. It might, however, serve an educative function for many people and it may be a source of comfort for many others. I would not vote for her re-election, nor would I vote for a second lesbian candidate.

In neither case do I vote as a consenting participant, but out of a sense of personal obligation. As a political person this is just some of the dirty work that needs to be done.

5

Anarchists have not spoken well to the issues of war, nor have they put forward a vision of how we can have a safer world today. It seems to me that we ought to promote openly ideas of nonprovocative defense, nonintervention agreements, and civilian-based defense. None of these ideas are new in world affairs, and they have worked in different contexts where they have been applied.

Civilian-based defense and its concomitant, nonviolent resistance, make invasion far too costly. We have enough working knowledge and models of peaceful alternatives to war and a strictly military defense so that we know that the massive militarization of Western societies has more to do with internal controls and capitalist exploitation than with defense. Imagine if the same amount of resources, money, planning, time, and education went into the organization of nonviolent resistance as goes into the military.

Military planners spend their time training and rehearsing scenarios of war. Peace planners need to do the same with the understanding, as an old saying goes, "There is no way to peace. Peace is the way."

6

Violence has become part of the repertory of everyday behavior. Our language is redundant with metaphors of violence; television revels in it. Parents beat children; children abuse their parents. Homicide and suicide have become two of the leading causes of teen-age deaths in the United States. The chances in this country of being a violent crime victim are now greater than the chances of being hurt in a traffic accident. "Do it to them before they do it to you" became the new golden rule of the 1980s.

Violence keeps people frightened and apart. It is a political instrument, not a disposition of human behavior. Anarchists in these times, perhaps more than ever, need to remind people of the history and triumphs of nonviolence, and to rebut the claims of instinctive aggression and the inevitability of war. We need to be able to model nonviolent alternatives and to study and teach the techniques of conflict resolution.

7

As someone trained in the craft of social research, I have often wondered what it would be like to assemble a room full of anarchist social scientists. Social science knowledge, it should be apparent, is used constantly to justify capitalist, authoritarian and hierarchical social arrangements. We need to mobilize our own resources to be able to counter the establishment reading and conduct of social research. Besides, we have our own agenda.

8

My button which features the peace symbol popularized during the 1960s and the inscription "Back by popular demand," is one which I wore regularly.

I wear buttons as a form of agitprop. More frequently than you can imagine I am able to get into a conversation with people about what the button signifies. This is a story about one such conversation. I had walked into an office, greeting the receptionist, whom I knew. She looked up, spotted my button and began laughing. "Only you would wear a button like that," she giggled. This was not the usual reaction. "What's so funny," I asked.

"Back by popular demand! You're the only one I know who'd say that about himself."

In the conversation that followed we were able to establish that she had no idea that the design on the button was a peace symbol, and she had reacted only to the words. When I told this story to a friend, she countered with her own experience. One day while she was wearing a ring which featured a carved peace symbol, a coworker observing it commented with great surprise, "I didn't know you owned a Mercedes!"

Yet another friend reacted with another story. He was checking out at the supermarket, wearing his "No Nukes" button on his jacket. The cashier looked up at it and asked him out of genuinely sociable curiosity what "noo-kees" meant.

There are two lessons to be learned in these stories. One is that most of us who are political activists tend to live a somewhat ghettoized life. Part of the result of that is that we have developed our own language and symbols. We need to be careful as we move outside our ghettos that we do in fact speak the language of the people we are trying to communicate with. The second lesson for me is that we should not overlook how it is that political symbols and ideas are lost by the establishment chroniclers. Leftist victories and the symbols of political opposition are erased from the cultural memory, and it is up to us to keep alive the remembrance of things past.

There is, perhaps, another lesson that we need to draw from this. We need to increase the density of our symbols of opposition and pride, our symbols of resistance and celebration. Surely the peace symbol should be as well recognized as the swastika or the corporate logo of General Motors.

9

There are other symbols which people don't really understand that evoke a response, sometimes an emotional response. "Anarchism" is one of these. For example, I frequently meet people who will tell me that they too are anarchists. When we talk about it, I find that often what they really mean to say is that they want to claim the right to do whatever they want to do: "Like do my own thing man."

Once, when a production of the Great Atlantic Radio Conspiracy was reviewed in a counterculture newspaper, the reviewer criticized the program for being too polished. Presumably, if the Conspiracy were truly anarchist, it would have been cruder. One critic charged the Conspiracy with being elitist because it didn't hold public meetings and it insisted that collective members be able to do library research and write clearly.

The magazine *Social Anarchism* has its share of stories as well. One is the reaction of a poet whose submission of poetry had been rejected, in part, because it was replete with unintentionally comic, mixed metaphors. He wrote an angry letter to the poetry editor telling her that straight metaphors were a bourgeois conceit, and that if she really were an anarchist she would have recognized his right to construct his metaphors as he chose.

I am not talking about the media stereotypes of anarchism. I am talking about the responses of people who in some way identify themselves as anarchists. Those responses are sometimes quite personal as well. A working-class anarchist friend was disturbed with me for years because I drink wine with my supper. To him, that was a mark of decadence and a betrayal of my politics. An anarchist couple who invited me to their house for the first time, apologized for their owning a color television set. When I observed that it was the same model I had, they were relieved and surprised.

As in all stereotyping, there is a lurking kernel of reality in all of these stories. For me, the lurking message is something else. I am not concerned here with how we grow stereotypes, I am concerned with how we grow anarchists. The answer to that question seems to be, "Not very well, thank you."

The role of anarchists, to paraphrase a comment by Murray Bookchin, is to grow other anarchists. I think we have to take that role seriously, and in the United States, most American anarchists do not. Modeling, mentoring, arguing, caring, nurturing — we all know the techniques. What is needed is the motivated commitment to build affinity groups, study groups, mutual support networks, work collectives, and communes.

10

Anarchists, like other folks, are grown in many varieties. We need to be able to deal with that, and to deal with it intensively. Gender and sexual orientation, class and ethnicity, age and culture are all divisions that keep us apart. While we may habitually act as if they didn't matter, that is, we may act without confronting the differences, invariably some difficulty occurs that forces their acknowledgement.

We do not really know what "multiculturalism" means, although it is the liberal left catchword of the 1990s. And what do gender and racial equality mean when most people have grown up in separate male and female, black and white subcultures? We need, first, to acknowledge that having been socialized in different subcultures, we do not necessarily share the same underlying assumptions. And then we have to acknowledge that we may not discover these differences until we begin the process of working and living in cooperative and collective settings. It is in this context of working and living together that we can begin, by negotiating our differences, and eventually by resocializing ourselves, to build an anarchist community.

11

"If you don't get it from yourself," a Zen proverb asks, "where will you go for it?" It is not so much that we have to change the societal rules of the game as we have to change ourselves. If we can change ourselves, we can redefine the game. We can, and probably do, change ourselves by trying to change the society. And in engaging in the process of social change, we influence change in others. Moreover, we can not change the behavior of others without it causing a change in ourselves. Personal and social change are organically related.

The central problem of modern society may well be the problem of autonomy. To be autonomous is to have power over yourself. Having power over yourself is an inoculation against the power of others. It is the people autonomous who can be united. The people autonomous can never be defeated.

CONTRIBUTORS

Howard J. Ehrlich, the editor, also edits the magazine, *Social Anarchism*. He writes regularly and conducts workshops on prejudice, intergroup relations, and ethnoviolence.

Jay Amrod was a midwestern anarchist organizer.

Freddie Baer is a San Franciscan collage artist and graphic designer. A book of her work, *Ecstatic Incisions: The Collages of Freddie Baer*, is available from AK Press.

George Benello, deceased, was an early antinuclear activist. He was engaged actively in the organization and writing about worker self-managed enterprises.

Bob Black is an iconoclastic wordsmith and lawyer.

Murray Bookchin is arguably the most prolific anarchist writer. His works span four decades and have turned on two generations of American anarchists.

David Bouchier is a British-born writer, radio broadcaster, and sociologist. His works include *The Feminist Challenge* and *Radical Citizenship*.

George Bradford is a founding member and regular contributor to the *Fifth Estate*, the oldest continuing anarchist publication in the U.S.

L. Susan Brown holds a doctorate in educational philosophy and writes regularly from Toronto on anarchist theory and feminism.

Lev Chernyi was the pen name of a well-known midwestern anarchist editor and writer who now goes by the *nom de plume* Jason McQuinn.

John Clark is a professional philosopher who teaches his trade in New Orleans. His works have appeared widely in philosophical and anarchist circles. His books include *The Philosophical Anarchism of William Godwin* and *Renewing the Earth: The Promise of Social Anarchism*.

Terri Clark is a musician and jazz singer.

David DeLeon is a historian of American radical intellectual history who teaches in Washington, DC. He was co-editor of *Reinventing Anarchy*.

Diane de Prima is a poet who works have inspired at least two generations of writers and activists.

Phylis Campbell Dryden is a poet and journalist living in upstate New York.

Carol Ehrlich was a founding member of the Great Atlantic Radio Conspiracy, co-founder of *Social Anarchism* and co-editor of *Reinventing Anarchy*. She works as an editor for a university press.

Robert Graham writes from British Columbia on anarchist history and ideas.

Johann Humyn Being lives and ingeniates collages in San Francisco.

Charles Keil is a musicologist, teacher and anthropologist.

Tom Knoche is a part-time teacher and community organizer who coordinates a soup kitchen in Camden, New Jersey.

Peggy Kornegger works and writes from Boston.

Richard Kostelanetz is a New York City-based writer who has published many books of poetry, fiction, and criticism.

Elaine Leeder is the chair of the sociology and social work department at Ithaca College (New York).

Brian Martin teachers science and technology studies at the University of Wollongong in Australia. He is active in the environmental, peace, and radical science movements. His books includes *Uprooting War*.

Glenda Morris, a resident of York, England, was for many years a member of the Great Atlantic Radio Conspiracy collective. She was co-editor of *Reinventing Anarchy*.

Jim Murray is a poet, historian, and arts activists who works with the Alliance for Cultural Democracy.

Ruthann Robson is a radical anarchist feminist, poverty lawyer, and poet. She was a member of the *Kalliope* collective which published a journal of women's art.

Kirkpatrick Sale is a writer whose books include, *SDS, Dwellers in the Land: The Bioregional Vision*, and *Rebels Against the Future: The Luddites and Their War on the Industrial Revolution*.

Colin Ward has been engaged for almost half a century as an anarchist editor, writer, teacher, architect, and commentator on urban affairs. He was one of the editors of *Freedom* and a founder of *Anarchy*, both distinguished magazines.

Susan White teaches film and literature at the University of Arizona. She has served as the literary editor of *Social Anarchism* and was a member of the Great Atlantic Radio Conspiracy collective.

Kingsley Widmer is author on ten books of literary and cultural criticism, including *The End of Culture: Essays on Sensibility in Contemporary Culture* and *Counterings: Utopian Dialectics in Contemporary Contexts*.

David Thoreau Wieck has been an anarchist writer and activist since the early 1940s.

John Yates is a graphic artist who works and resides in San Francisco. His work has appeared in numerous publications and on t-shirts, record and CD sleeves. A book of his work, *Stealworks: The Graphic Details of John Yates*, is available from AK Press.

CREDITS

1. Jay Amrod and Lev Chernyi, "Beyond Character and Morality: Towards Transparent Communications and Coherent Organization," was first published in *Reinventing Anarchy*.
2. George Benello, "The Challenge of Mondragon," was first published in *Black Rose*, Winter 1986-87.
3. Bob Black, "The Abolition of Work," was the title piece of his book published by Loompanics in 1986.
4. Murray Bookchin, "Anarchism: Past and Present," was originally delivered as a lecture at the Conference on Marxism and Anarchism at the University of California Los Angeles, May 29, 1980. It was revised in August, 1992 for publication here.
5. David Bouchier, "Hard Questions for Social Anarchists," is adapted from his book *Radical Citizenship: The New American Activism* (New York: Schocken Books, 1987).
6. George Bradford, "Media — Capital's Global Village," was originally published in the *Fifth Estate*, Fall 1984.
7. L. Susan Brown, "Beyond Feminism and Human Freedom," is a revised version of an essay originally published in *Our Generation*, Fall, 1990.
8. John Clark, "Anarchism and the Present World Crisis," is reprinted from his book, *The Anarchist Moment* (Montreal: Black Rose Books, 1984).
9. Terri Clark, "Jazz — Circling in Anarchism," was written for an anthology of anarchist-feminist writing that was never published. It was supplied for publication here by Elaine Leeder, senior editor of that anthology.
10. David DeLeon, "For Democracy Where We Work: A Rationale for Social Self-Management," was first published as a pamphlet, *Research Group One Report No. 28* in June, 1977 and reprinted in *Reinventing Anarchy*.
11. Diane di Prima, "Revolutionary letter no. 1," and "Revolutionary letter no. 19," appeared first in *Revolutionary Letters* (San Francisco: City Lights Books, 1971) and were reprinted in *Reinventing Anarchy*.
12. Phylis Campbell Dryden, "Warning label," was first published in *Social Anarchism*, No. 6, 1982.
13. Carol Ehrlich, "Socialism, Anarchism, and Feminism," was first published as a Research Group One pamphlet in 1977 and reprinted in *Reinventing Anarchy*. This version is abridged slightly.
14. Howard J. Ehrlich, "Anarchism and Formal Organizations," is a slightly abridged version of the essay first published in *Reinventing Anarchy*.

15. Howard J. Ehrlich, "How to Get from Here to There — Building a Revolutionary Transfer Culture," first appeared in *Social Anarchism*, No. 4, 1982.

16. Howard J. Ehrlich, Carol Ehrlich, David DeLeon, and Glenda Morris, "Questions and Answers About Anarchism," was written for the original *Reinventing Anarchy*.

17. Caroline Estes, "Consensus," originally appeared in *In Context* magazine and was reprinted in *Social Anarchism*, No. 10, 1985.

18. Robert Graham, "The Anarchist Contract," was written for this anthology.

19. Charles Keil, "Anarchomusicology and Participation," is published here for the first time.

20. Tom Knoche, "Organizing Communities," was written for this anthology and originally published in *Social Anarchism*, No. 18, 1993.

21. Peggy Kornegger, "Anarchism: The Feminist Connection," was published in *Reinventing Anarchy*. It was excerpted from *The Second Wave*, Spring 1975.

22. Richard Kostelanetz, "Anarchist Art: The Example of John Cage," was published originally in *Anarchist Studies*, No. 1, 1993.

23. Elaine Leeder, "Let Out Mothers Show the Way," was originally published in *Social Anarchism*, No. 12, 1986-87.

24. Brian Martin, "Democracy Without Elections," is an abridged version of his essay originally published in *Social Anarchism*, #21, 1995.

25. Glenda Morris, "Poetry," was originally published in *Social Anarchism*, No. 6, 1983.

26. Jim Murray, "Where Did Karl Marx Sit?" was published in *Social Anarchism*, No. 12, 1986.

27. Ruthann Robson, "Living Our Lives," was originally published in *Social Anarchism*, No. 14, 1989.

28. Kirkpatrick Sale, "The Necessity of the State," is reprinted from his book, *Human Scale* (N.Y.: Coward, McCann & Geoghgan, 1980).

29. Colin Ward, "Anarchism and the Informal Economy," was first published in *The Raven*, No. 1, 1988.

30. Susan White, "Anarchist Perspective on Film," was written for this anthology.

31. Kingsley Widmer, "Three Times Around the Track: American Workouts Towards Anarchism," is a revised version of his essay published first in *Reinventing Anarchy*.

32. David Thoreau Wieck, "The Habit of Direct Action," is reprinted from *Reinventing Anarchy* and first appeared in *Anarchy*, No. 13, 1962.

BOOKS BY MURRAY BOOKCHIN FROM AK PRESS

SOCIAL ANARCHISM OR LIFESTYLE ANARCHISM: AN UNBRIDGEABLE CHASM by Murray Bookchin; ISBN 1 873176 83 X; 96pp two color cover, perfect bound 5-1/2 x 8-1/2; £5.95/£7.95.This book asks — and tries to answer — several basic questions that affect all Leftists today. Will anarchism remain a revolutionary social movement or become a chic boutique lifestyle subculture? Will its primary goals be the complete transformation of a hierarchical, class, and irrational society into a libertarian communist one? Or will it become an ideology focused on personnel well-being, spiritual redemption, and self-realization within the existing society?

In an era of privatism, kicks, introversion, and post-modernist nihilism, Murray Bookchin forcefully examines the growing nihilistic trends that threaten to undermine the revolutionary tradition of anarchism and co-opt its fragments into a harmless personalistic, yuppie ideology of social accommodation that presents no threat to the existing powers that be. This small book, tightly reasoned and documented, should be of interest to all radicals in the "postmodern age," socialists as well as anarchists, for whom the Left seems in hopeless disarray. Includes the essay *The Left That Was*.

TO REMEMBER SPAIN: THE ANARCHIST AND SYNDICALIST REVOLUTION OF 1936 by Murray Bookchin; ISBN 1 873176 87 2; 80pp two color cover, perfect bound 5-1/2 x 8-1/2; £4.50/ $6.00. In these essays, Bookchin places the Spanish Anarchist and anarchosyndicalist movements of the 1930s in the context of the revolutionary workers' movements of the pre-World War II era. These articles describe, analyze, and evaluate the last of the great proletarian revolutions of the past two centuries. They form indispensable supplements to Bookchin's larger 1977 history, *The Spanish Anarchists: The Heroic Years, 1868–1936* (to be reprinted by AK Press). Read together, these works constitute a highly informative and

theoretically significant assessment of the anarchist and anarchosyndicalist movements in Spain. They are invaluable for any reader concerned with the place of the Spanish Revolution in history and with the accomplishments, insights, and failings of the anarchosyndicalist movement. Most significant, Bookchin draws lessons for today about left-libertarian forms of organization and much-needed modifications of radical politics in the present period.

 **Friends of AK Press**

In the last 12 months, AK Press has published around 15 new titles. In the next 12 months we should be able to publish roughly the same, including new work by Murray Bookchin, CRASS, Daniel Guerin, Noam Chomsky, Jello Biafra, Stewart Home, new audio work from Noam Chomsky, plus more. However, not only are we financially constrained as to what (and how much) we can publish, we already have a huge backlog of excellent material we would like to publish sooner, rather than later. If we had the money, we could easily publish 30 titles in the coming 12 months.

Projects currently being worked on include previously unpublished early anarchist writings by Victor Serge; more work from Noam Chomsky, Murray Bookchin and Stewart Home; Raoul Vaneigem on the surrealists; a new anthology of computer hacking and hacker culture; a short history of British Fascism; the collected writings of Guy Aldred; a new anthology of cutting edge radical fiction and poetry; new work from Freddie Baer; an updated reprint of *The Floodgates of Anarchy*; the autobiography and political writings of former Black Panther and class war prisoner Lorenzo Kom'boa Ervin, and much, much more. As well as working on the new AK Press Audio series, we are also working to set up a new pamphlet series, both to reprint long neglected classics and to present new material in a cheap, accessible format.

Friends of AK Press is a way in which you can directly help us try to realize many more such projects, much faster. Friends pay a minimum of $15/£10 per month into our AK Press account. All moneys received go directly into our publishing. In return, Friends receive (for the duration of their membership), automatically, as and when they appear, one copy free of every new AK Press title. Secondly, they are also entitled to 10 percent discount on everything featured in the current AK Distribution mail-order catalog (upwards of 3,000 titles), on any and every order. **Friends**, if they wish, can be acknowledged as a **Friend** in all new AK Press titles.

To find out more on how to contribute to Friends of AK Press, and for a Friends order form, please do write to:

AK Press
PO Box 40682
San Francisco, CA
94140-0682

AK Press
P.O. Box 12766
Edinburgh, Scotland
EH8 9YE

Some Recent Titles from AK Press

WHICH WAY FOR THE ECOLOGY MOVEMENT by Murray Bookchin; ISBN 1 873176 26 0; 80pp two color cover, perfect bound 5-1/2 x 8-1/2; £4.50/$6.00. Bookchin calls for a critical social standpoint that transcends both "biocentrism" and "ecocentrism"; for a new politics and ethics of complementarity, in which people, fighting for a free, nonhierarchical, and cooperative society, being to play a creative role in natural evolution. Bookchin attacks the misanthropic notions that the environmental crisis is caused mainly by overpopulation or humanity's genetic makeup. He resolutely points to the social and economic causes as the problem the environmental movement must deal with.

THE REALIZATION AND SUPPRESSION OF THE SITUATIONIST INTERNATIONAL: AN ANNOTATED BIBLIOGRAPHY 1972-1992 by Simon Ford. ISBN 1-873176-82-1; 149pp two color cover, perfect bound; £7.95/$11.95. This annotated bibliography contains over 600 references that chart its rise to fame from obscurity to celebrity. More than a bibliography it is the most substantial reference book yet produced on the group. It also provides a gateway to the related worlds of underground publishing, anarchism, and the contemporary avant-garde. This will be of vital interest to all those researchers, activists, and students fascinated by the S.I. and their aftermath. In addition to listing and describing every significant publication on the S.I., the bibliography is a rich resource of information on related groups such as Gruppe Spur, The Second Situationist International, Cobra, and Lettrisme. There are also two sections solely devoted to documenting the little known British and American "pro-sit" scenes.

IMMEDIATISM by Hakim Bey; ISBN 1 873176 42 2; 64 pp four color cover, perfect bound 5-1/2 x 8-1/2; £4.00/$6.00. A new stunning collection of essays from the author of Temporary Autonomous Zone, beautifully illustrated by Freddie Baer.

PUSSYCAT FEVER by Kathy Acker, illustrated by Diane DiMassa and Freddie Baer; ISBN 1-873176-63-5; 80pp two color cover, perfect bound 5-1/2 x 8-1/2; £4.00/$7.00.

END TIME: NOTES ON THE APOCALYPSE by G.A. Matiasz; ISBN 1873176 96 1; 320 pp four color cover, perfect bound 5-1/2 x 8-1/2; £5.95/$8.00. A first novel by G.A. Matiasz, an original voice of slashing, thought provoking style. "A compulsively readable thriller combined with a very smart meditation on the near-future of anarchism, End Time proves once again that science fiction is our only literature of ideas." — Hakim Bey

STEALWORKS: THE GRAPHIC DETAILS OF JOHN YATES by John Yates; ISBN 1 873176 51 1; 136 pp two color cover, perfect bound 8-1/2 x 11; £7.95/$11.95. A collection to date of work created by a visual mechanic and graphic surgeon. His work is a mixture of bold visuals, minimalist to-the-point social commentary, and involves the manipulation and reinterpretation of culture's media imagery.

AK Press publishes and distributes a wide variety of radical literature. For our latest catalog featuring these and several thousand other titles, please send a large self-addressed, stamped envelope to:

AK Press
PO Box 40682
San Francisco, CA
94140-0682

AK Press
P.O. Box 12766
Edinburgh, Scotland
EH8 9YE